The Social Contract *and* The First and Second Discourses

JEAN-JACQUES ROUSSEAU

Edited and with an Introduction by Susan Dunn

with essays by

Gita May

Robert N. Bellah

David Bromwich

Conor Cruise O'Brien

Yale University Press

New Haven and London

Printed in the United States of America by Vail-Ballou Press, Binghamton, New York.

Library of Congress Cataloging-in-Publication Data

Rousseau, Jean-Jacques, 1712–1778.

[Selections. English. 2002]

The social contract ; and, The first and second discourses / Jean-Jacques Rousseau ; edited and with an introduction by Susan Dunn ; with essays by Gita May . . . [et al.].

p. cm. — (Rethinking the Western tradition)

Includes bibliographical references.

ISBN 0-300-09140-0 (cloth : alk. paper) — ISBN 0-300-09141-9 (pbk. : alk. paper)

1. Political science—Early works to 1800. 2. Social contract—Early works to 1800.
3. Civilization—Early works to 1800. I. Dunn, Susan. II. May, Gita. III. Title. IV. Series.

JC179 .R7 2002

320'.01—dc21 2001046557

A catalogue record for this book is available from the British Library.

The paper in this book meets the guidelines for permanence and durability of the Committee on Production Guidelines for Book Longevity of the Council on Library Resources.

10 9 8 7 6 5 4 3 2 1

10-95

Rethinking
the
Western
Tradition

The volumes in this series
seek to address the present debate
over the Western tradition
by reprinting key works of
that tradition along with essays
that evaluate each text from
different perspectives.

Contributors

Robert N. Bellah is Elliott Professor of Sociology Emeritus at the University of California at Berkeley. He is the author of numerous books, including *Beyond Belief* and *The Broken Covenant,* and is co-author of *Habits of the Heart* and *The Good Society.*

David Bromwich is Housum Professor of English at Yale University. He is the author of several books, including *Politics by Other Means: Higher Education and Group Thinking, Skeptical Music: Essays on Modern Poetry,* and *A Choice of Inheritance: Self and Community from Edmund Burke to Robert Frost.*

Susan Dunn is professor of French literature and the history of ideas at Williams College. She is the author of *The Deaths of Louis XVI: Regicide and the French Political Imagination* and *Sister Revolutions: French Lightning, American Light,* and is co-author with James MacGregor Burns of *The Three Roosevelts.*

Gita May is professor of French literature at Columbia University. She is the author of *De Jean-Jacques Rousseau à Madame Roland: Essai sur la sensibilité préromantique et révolutionnaire, Diderot et Baudelaire, critiques d'art, Madame Roland and the Age of Revolution,* and *Stendhal and the Age of Napoleon.*

Conor Cruise O'Brien is a statesman, diplomat, and political commentator who lives in Dublin, Ireland. He is the author of many books including *God Land: Reflections on Religion and Nationalism, The Great Melody: A Thematic Biography and Commented Anthology of Edmund Burke,* and *The Long Affair: Thomas Jefferson and the French Revolution, 1785–1800.*

Contents

Introduction:
Rousseau's Political Triptych

SUSAN DUNN

Is there any deed more shocking, more hateful, more infamous than the willful burning of a library? Is there any blow more devastating to the core of human civilization? In the mid-eighteenth century, Jean-Jacques Rousseau startled — and excited — his readers by praising Caliph Omar, who in the year 650 ordered the incineration of the glorious library in Alexandria.[1]

In his first important work, *The Discourse on the Sciences and Arts* (1750), also known as the First *Discourse*, Rousseau held that the search for knowledge was so socially and morally destructive that book burning and the subsequent return to ignorance, innocence, and poverty would be a step forward rather than a step backward in the history of civilization. He was convinced that only cultural and material regression could accompany the movement of society toward morality. The entire rational enterprise of the Enlightenment found itself unexpectedly under fierce and principled attack.

When Rousseau burst upon the intellectual scene, the philosophers and writers of eighteenth-century France had for decades been passionately engaged in an audacious, innovative project: the questioning and dismantling of all the traditional underpinnings of their society. Their daring charge entailed exposing to the light of reason all preconceived ideas, supernatural dogmas and superstitious beliefs, all political and social assumptions. Intellectuals were challenging the theological foundation of monarchy, the privileges of the aristocracy, the doctrines of Catholicism. Having wiped their intellectual slate as clean as they could, men of letters in France embarked upon the bold plan of using human reason to address people's needs: how they should live, govern themselves, organize society, and conceive morality. Their goal was a rational society dedicated to equality, freedom, and happiness. Life had become an intellectual adventure, and people were optimistic that they could shape their own destinies.

Rousseau had once participated in this luminous and probing culture. He too had wanted to embrace all knowledge; he too had known the joy of intellectual curiosity, the bliss of creativity. Mingling and collaborating with artists, musicians, philosophers, and writers — the great *philosophe*

Voltaire, the composer Rameau, the versatile man of letters Diderot, the witty playwright Marivaux, the *philosophe* Fontenelle — he had reveled in the aristocratic world of brilliant salons, where luxury, elegance, and genius combined to make life a joy for the mind and the senses.[2] But his fascination with the sophisticated world of the Enlightenment was also colored by bitterness and resentment, the result of his humiliating experience in 1743 working as the secretary for the French Ambassador in Venice; by his disappointments in life, especially his dismay in 1745 at not having received more recognition for his part in a musical collaboration with Voltaire and Rameau; and by his own deep insecurities and demons, his paranoid feeling that he was the target of various cabals conspiring to undermine and discredit him. Suddenly his eyes bore into the heart of this dazzling culture. He judged. He condemned. Behind the splendid façade, he concluded, lay a world that was superficial, corrupt, and cruel.

Astonishingly, Rousseau turned against the entire Enlightenment project. He branded the daring intellectual, scientific, and artistic culture of eighteenth-century France a lie, a vast devolution, a symptom of alarming moral decline. Nothing more than a fake veneer, the century's worldly accomplishments were all the more perfidious because they masked so effectively the deep corruption of a decadent, unequal society. The quest for knowledge and intellectual advancement was a superficial luxury that, instead of serving society, reinforced its self-indulgence and decay. "We have physicists, geometers, chemists, astronomers, poets, musicians, painters," he remarked, adding tellingly that "we no longer have citizens."

People, Rousseau was convinced, had been deceived, seduced, and corrupted by the radiance of the Enlightenment. And what was worse, they cherished their corruption, for it seemed to mark the summit of progress and civilization. Everywhere Rousseau saw educated individuals who resembled "happy slaves," preferring the glitter of high culture to true freedom and happiness.[3] The search for knowledge had merely taken on a life of its own, divorced from the real needs of society and citizens.

Skepticism and vain inquiry attracted people more than a search for a meaningful life. People believed that they knew everything, Rousseau remarked, but they did not know the meaning of the words magnanimity, equity, temperance, humanity, courage, fatherland, and God. Overwhelmed by pretension, affectation, and deceit, the values that create robust citizens and a healthy society — self-sacrifice, sincere friendships, love of country — had disappeared.

The principles of science and philosophy and the decadent values implicit in the arts on the one hand and the requirements of a healthy society on the other, Rousseau insisted, are irremediably at odds with one another. Whereas science searches for the truth by fostering doubt and undermining faith and virtue, a vigorous, patriotic society, Rousseau contended, requires *assent* to the principles of its foundation.

What then is the mission of the intellectual in society? The proper, socially useful role of philosophers and men of letters, according to Rousseau, was not to spread mistrust, not to make piecemeal proposals for incremental reform, not to seek fame and glory for themselves through their intellectual acrobatics, but rather to offer, as he himself would, a radical prescription for the complete social and political overhaul of the nation and for the moral regeneration of its citizens.[4]

In his mind's eye, he saw, in the place of a decadent culture that valued superficial luxury, prosperity, and free though vain inquiry, a muscular, Spartan society that imposed rules and discipline and asked its citizens for sacrifice. In such a polity, virtuous citizens would have no need for futile intellectual pursuits. Indeed, Spartan virtue itself is anti-intellectual. Derived from the Latin word for "man," *vir,* virtue implied not just moral goodness, but rather strength, courage, and, above all, self-sacrifice and self-discipline.

Even so, Rousseau was not suggesting that French men and women rush out and torch the libraries of France — or copies of his own book. On the contrary, in an already unhealthy, decadent society, science and philosophy might, to some extent, be useful. Certain great individuals — such as Bacon, Descartes, Newton — might serve as guides for humanity, and a few others might be permitted to follow in their footsteps and even outdistance them. In an already corrupt society, the arts and sciences, harmful for "average" people, could, in the hands of a few people of genius, perhaps bring some true enlightenment to all.[5]

The Discourse on the Sciences and Arts won first prize in the Dijon Academy's intellectual competition, a contest that had asked writers and philosophers to respond to the question, "Has the revival of sciences and arts contributed to improving morality?" With Rousseau's friend Diderot having arranged for the essay's publication, the *Discourse* took Paris by storm, becoming a best-seller. Were people merely captivated by Rousseau's contrarian viewpoint and fascinated by harsh criticism of their radiant and celebrated culture? Or were they intrigued by his surprising, anachronistic resurrection of Spartan concepts of virtue, self-sacrifice, and duty?

Already in the seventeenth century, the shrewd aristocratic writer of maxims, the duke de La Rochefoucauld, had criticized the high culture of France, noting that "luxury and excessive *politesse* in states are a sure sign of increasing decadence, because as all individuals become attached to their private interests, they turn away from the public good."[6] And in 1748, the great political philosopher Montesquieu had also condemned the "manufactures, commerce, finances, wealth, and luxury" of the modern world for displacing civic and political virtue.[7] But Rousseau's attack on modernity was far more consistent and ambitious — and more psychologically acute — than that of the other *philosophes,* and it is he alone who can be credited with composing the jolting introduction to one of the most original, provocative, and far-reaching challenges to Western society ever undertaken.

The first seeds of a powerful, world-historical Revolution had been planted. The "paradoxes" of the First *Discourse* exploded "like a bombshell," wrote the English economist and philosopher John Stuart Mill.[8] "Rousseau produced more effect with his pen," Lord Acton said, "than Aristotle, or Cicero, or St. Augustine, or St. Thomas Aquinas, or any other man who ever lived."[9] Of all the great *philosophes* of the French Enlightenment — Montesquieu, Diderot, Voltaire — it was Rousseau who would have the most profound and enduring impact on history, not only on the Revolution in France but on almost all modern, democratic movements for political liberation. He was the most radical political theorist of his times, the most utopian. But it was also Rousseau who unwittingly set the stage for the totalitarian states of the twentieth century, for "one-party democracy," and for communitarianism gone haywire.

How can this paradox be explained?

ROUSSEAU'S *DISCOURSE ON INEQUALITY*

Three years after composing his First *Discourse,* Rousseau leaped at the chance to add a further dimension to his political philosophy. The Dijon Academy was proposing another intellectual competition. This time the subject concerned the origins of inequality. Rousseau's entry, his *Discourse on the Origin and Foundation of Inequality Among Mankind* (1753), also known as the Second *Discourse,* occupies a pivotal place in his thought. On the one hand, it looks back to the *Discourse on the Sciences and Arts,* giving a historical and theoretical explanation for the decadence and corruption he diagnosed in eighteenth-century French society. On the other hand, it looks forward to his next great work, *The Social Contract,* by suggesting the necessity of finding an alternate, healthier path along which society and citizens can evolve.

Why had inequality become so rooted in society, Rousseau asked himself. How had such a wide variety of people, poor as well as rich, come to accept or profit from outrageous social and economic disparities? How did we arrive at our present condition?

In order to fathom the different causes of inequality and analyze the successive stages in its development, Rousseau decided to play the role of theoretical anthropologist, hypothesizing about the lives that people might have led in the "state of nature," before social relations and organized society molded and corrupted human behavior. Rousseau admitted that the "state of nature" he imagined might never have existed. Still, such theoretical conjecturing was necessary, he insisted, to "judge properly of our present state."[10]

Rousseau tried to let his imagination go back in time as far as he could to envision human beings stripped of even the most primitive social relations, stripped even of language itself. In an act of impressive intellectual originality, he pared off all accretions, all the wants, needs, habits, skills, beliefs, emotions, and values that one develops in society, revealing the "bare bones" of the human being.

A century earlier, the English political theorist Thomas Hobbes had also hypothesized about the "state of nature." In one of the most famous sentences of his classic text *Leviathan* (1651), Hobbes had maintained that human life in the state of nature was "solitary, poor, nasty, brutish, and short." Though people were free and equal, they were engaged in perpetual warfare with one another.

Now it was Rousseau's turn to sketch a portrait of life in the state of nature, and he would present a very different picture of primitive human beings. He envisioned the state of nature as a kind of dormancy period. People were free and equal, he theorized, but they lived mostly solitary lives, feeling little need for others. Though they had sexual relations with one another, they formed no lasting bonds. There existed among them neither cooperation nor conflict.

They lived entirely in the present, experiencing only spontaneous drives. Still, they felt a harmony with the world because their desires never exceeded their needs and because they were able to satisfy both needs and desires immediately. They were independent and devoid of aggression toward one another. Were they happy? Perhaps. But their moral and rational faculties remained largely asleep. Though they did have an "instinct" for pity for the suffering of others along with a "survival instinct" of their own, they were for the most part untouched by morality. Neither love nor friendship nor family nor thought nor speech impinged upon their primitive solitude. These early humans were all potential and virtuality.

The notion of a state of nature was a useful fiction. It furnished Rousseau with theoretical "evidence" for claiming a radical dichotomy between our present demeaning condition and the Eden we left behind. Here was an original standard against which all future human dislocation could be measured.

This vision of the state of nature, moreover, provided Rousseau with a basis for his belief in human "perfectibility." Now he could argue that if modern individuals appeared corrupt, unequal, and enslaved, it is society — not human nature — that is to blame. Thus a remedy to the situation might be found. Because of people's vast rational and ethical potential, it was possible and reasonable to propose an alternate route for their social, political, and moral development. This was the challenge Rousseau accepted: he was convinced that it was his mission to chart that course, not backward to the state of nature, but forward toward a more rational, social, and moral Eden.

Given our equality and freedom in the state of nature, why did inequality come to define the human condition in most societies? How would Rousseau explain entire civilizations under the spell of servitude and the yoke of despotism?

Very early in human history, according to Rousseau's hypothetical scenario, people began to work and collaborate occasionally with one another. This was the beginning of a long golden age that saw the appearance of family units and patriarchal authority but not yet of private property. Husbands and wives, parents and children dwelled together under one roof, experiencing the "sweetest sentiments" known to human beings, "conjugal and paternal love." Each family resembled a "little society" in which members were united by mutual affection and liberty. There was commerce among the different families; human faculties, social rituals, and a sense of morality evolved somewhat, all contributing to "the happiest and most durable epoch" in human history, an interim period "between the indolence of the primitive state and the petulant activity of egoism."

But then came the fall from tranquillity and the downward spiral into history and corruption. This period began when people realized that, with rational effort and work, they could transform the natural world. A new intellectual energy was unleashed, destroying the simplicity and harmony that had reigned in the state of nature between one's needs and one's desires. The novel concept of the division of labor also took hold, robbing people of their self-sufficiency. Now new technological advances, such as agriculture and metallurgy, were introduced, accompanied by the notion of "private property." People competed for property, increasing their wealth at the expense of others. Production started to surpass people's needs, feeding a new hunger for superfluous, "luxury" goods. Equality was vanquished by ambition and greed.

Exacerbating economic inequality was a new insidious form of psychological inequality. As people started to acquire wealth and property, they began to compare themselves to their neighbors, seeking to distinguish themselves and assert their own superiority. Rousseau perceived that this quest for esteem is, at bottom, a desire for inequality. In 1899 the American economic theorist Thorstein Veblen would label this syndrome "conspicuous consumption."[11] Rousseau incisively remarked that the cost to individuals of these new desires for prestige (*proestigium* in Latin means "illusion") was alienation from themselves. For they viewed their accomplishments, their worth, and themselves through the appraising eyes of their rivals, experiencing their lives through their judgmental gaze, belonging less to themselves than to others. To earn the regard of others, it became more important to *appear* than to *be*. One tried to satisfy one's ego while robbing oneself of authenticity and equality — as well as of the compassion one had felt for others in the state of nature.

The disappearance of equality, social divisions resulting from the division of labor, the unequal distribution of property, the isolation of the rich from the poor, Rousseau contends, were followed by exploitation, violence, and frightening disorder. "The usurpations of the rich, the pillagings of the poor, the unbridled passions of all, by stifling the cries of natural compassion, and the still feeble voice of justice," concluded Rousseau, "rendered men avaricious, wicked and ambitious."[12] At this point, Rousseau and Hobbes merge. Human society has degenerated into a state of war of all against all.

Now a rich and powerful individual, for whom violence and war are as pernicious as they are for the weak members of society, makes the people an offer they cannot refuse. He proposes that they all unite, enter into a "social contract" and form a polity. The people would be assured order, security, peace, and justice in exchange for their freedom. The rich man too desires law and order, so that he may enjoy his possessions in tranquillity, unthreatened by social unrest. Thus the weak assent to inequality and acquire chains as the rich consolidate and institutionalize their power. Economic expropriation has expanded to encompass political expropriation. The basis of this social contract is deception and exploitation. Might makes right. People are fully enslaved — by their promise of obedience to their ruler, by their own ambition and vanity, their inauthentic desires for luxury as well as their need for the admiration of others.

Finally, in a rapidly sketched nightmarish vision of the accelerated collapse of society into chaos, Rousseau envisaged political intrigue, factions, and civil strife leading to the complete disintegration of legitimate government. Chosen leaders become hereditary leaders. The social fabric disintegrates, people's natural pity for the suffering of others is extinguished. The last degree of inequality has been reached. Now despotism raises its hideous head. The political relationship is no longer merely between the powerful and the weak but between master and slave. The vertiginous descent into human degradation and corruption is complete.

Once again, people find themselves solitary and atomized, as they were in the state of nature. Ironically, they are also once again *equal*. The difference, Rousseau noted, is that now they are equal because they are all *nothing*. The only law is the arbitrary will of the master. Life is now indeed nasty and brutish. But whereas Hobbes had located such degradation in the "state of nature," Rousseau discovers it at the end of human social development.

Rousseau has taken us to the edge of the abyss. The Second *Discourse* ends with a sanguinary vision of revolution. "The insurrection, which ends in the death or deposition of a sultan," concludes Rousseau, "is as *juridical* an act as any by which the day before he disposed of the lives and fortunes of his subjects. Force alone upheld him, *force alone overturns him*." Perhaps there is hope for radical change—through revolution.[13]

But change will be meaningless unless there is a profound rethinking of the social contract, society, and social relations. Rousseau always believed in the Enlightenment notion of human perfectibility. Human nature, he suggested, is malleable; our moral and rational faculties can be nurtured, educated, and guided so that our full humanity can blossom. Even if society has made us unequal and unfree, even if it has made us the deluded toys of our own psychological alienation from ourselves, the victims of our limitless desires for superficial pleasures and superfluous knowledge, even if it has reduced us to the abject slaves of powerful rulers, it is possible to reconceive and restructure social relations and political institutions on a radically different basis. Rousseau's next work, *The Social Contract,* leads us away from the catastrophic vision with which he concluded his Second *Discourse* and toward a new utopian future.

In a sense, Rousseau's whole project follows traditional Christian thinking. Like Christian theologians, Rousseau sees human development in terms of three stages: Eden, the Fall, Redemption. For him, the Fall signifies, not a separation from God or an accusation against human beings, but rather a "fall" from the benign state of nature into a long, devastating, and totally negative period of corruption and degradation.[14]

Redemption will occur, not through faith and grace, not through anything supernatural or mystical, but on the contrary through a purely rational and human prescription for political and social happiness: his revolutionary — and troubling — *Social Contract,* his attempt to conceive a moral, consensual polity that assures freedom and equality while nourishing simple Spartan virtue.

A NEW KIND OF SOCIAL CONTRACT

A startling break with all traditional notions of government and society, Rousseau's *Social Contract* (1762) comprised the final part of his political triptych. In this work, he presents a radical political vision, yet one that is perfectly consistent with his attacks on corruption and inequality in his two *Discourses.*

The ideal society he proposes in *The Social Contract* is, more than anything else, a communitarian society in which the responsibilities and duties of citizenship outweigh individual rights and freedoms. Selflessly, citizens bind and commit themselves to the common good of all, willing to make sacrifices for their political community. Their virtue is richly rewarded. Through their devotion to their community, their self-discipline, and patriotism, they thrive as human beings, thus realizing their full rational and moral potential.

The citizens of this cohesive community have entered into a stunningly original social pact, different from all previous notions of a social contract. Other political thinkers, such as Hobbes, had also surmised that at the bases of societies lay founding contracts. But for these theorists, the social pact was always an act of submission. Hobbes, for example, contended that in order to escape from the state of perpetual warfare that existed in the brutish "state of nature," people entered into a pact, a contract, in which they signed away their freedom and all their rights to a sovereign who would rule over them, guaranteeing them life, security, and order. The ruler's power over them was absolute.

Rousseau brands these kinds of contracts null and void. Even though the people may have voluntarily consented to the pact, he considered such consent invalid.[15] If one of the parties to a contract is degraded or harmed in any way, the contract, he judged, is void. People may give up property, he reasoned, but they may not consent to give up life or freedom, the essential elements of their humanity. Consent is not sufficient to create legitimate authority.

More crucial than consent is the *nature* of the contract itself. For a contract to be valid, all parties must profit equally from its terms. Rousseau's idea of a social contract is therefore not a pact between rulers and ruled, powerful and weak, masters and slaves. On the contrary, the only parties to the contract are the people themselves who consent only to rule over themselves. (The opening words of the American constitutional contract, written twenty-five years after Rousseau's *Social Contract,* are "We the People," words more Rousseauian in spirit than Jefferson's mention of the "consent of the governed" in the Declaration of Independence.)

This kind of pact could hardly be more revolutionary. The only legitimate social contract, according to Rousseau, is one in which the people themselves are sovereign. Their sovereignty, like their freedom, is unalienable, and they may not transfer their sovereignty to anyone else or submit to the will of any others.[16] The originality of Rousseau's social contract is that the people bind themselves to a contract but do not subject themselves to any authority except that of their own *collective will*—their "General Will." Indeed, towering above them, revered by all, looms the strange concept of the people's "General Will."

The General Will. This unusual notion is the key to Rousseau's communitarian vision. What did he mean by the General Will?

Rousseau held that a democratic society possesses a General Will. This "will" reflects what enlightened people would want if they were able to make decisions solely as social beings and citizens and not as private individuals. *Individuals* may possess private wills that express their particular interests, but *citizens* must recognize and concur with the General Will that mirrors the good of all. The General Will is not tantamount to the will of all citizens. Nor is it the sum of all individual wills or the expression of a compromise or consensus among them. Nor is it the equivalent of the will of the majority, for even the majority can be corrupt or misguided. In other words, it is a theoretical construct. The General Will is *general,* not because a broad number of people subscribe to it but because its object is always the common good of all.

Thus, hovering strangely above and beyond the wills of all, the General Will is "always constant, unalterable, and pure,"[17] always mirroring perfectly the common good of all members of the community. The ultimate authority—and ultimate sovereignty—thus reside not really in the people, who may err in their estimation of the General Will, unable to transcend their private wills, but rather in the infallible General Will itself—the power of Reason, the enlightened collective moral conscience.[18]

True freedom, Rousseau maintains, consists in *choosing* to *obey* the General Will. But how can freedom be equated with obedience?

Rousseau recognized two different types of freedom. The first, enjoyed by people in the state of nature, denoted their freedom to act as they wished, in a variety of diverse ways. This was a *negative* form of freedom, freedom from constraints. But there is another, higher form of freedom, according to Rousseau, a *positive* freedom. This is not freedom *from* constraint, but rather freedom *for* some higher good, for the enjoyment of the good, moral life.[19] This kind of freedom, more heroic and ambitious than negative freedom, can belong to the citizen who is able to suppress his private will and consciously choose the common good over his own desires and personal benefit. This individual has mastered himself, becoming a moral and hence a truly free being. The originality of Rousseau's vision resides in his concept of freedom, not as the province of the autonomous individual but rather as that of the self-sacrificing citizen.

Indeed, the more that people identify with the community, the "freer" they are. Whereas primitive individuals in the state of nature were thoroughly indifferent and unattached to one another, in Rousseau's utopia, citizens are unreservedly involved with one another. The solitary independence that people may have enjoyed in the state of nature is not something that Rousseau aspired to recover. On the contrary, he wishes to see it transformed into its opposite—voluntary dependence and interdependence, happy obedience to the General Will.

We cannot recapture our original autonomy, but we can instead secure a higher freedom, the freedom to govern ourselves as we collectively wish.[20] Still, the primitive being and the socialized citizen have something in common, for both are innocent, genuine, unaffected—both are the polar opposite of the corrupt, decadent inhabitants of eighteenth-century Enlightenment France.

Rousseau has taken us on a fantastic voyage—from radical independence in the state of nature, to abject servitude in society, to complete social involvement in his utopia. We have journeyed from animal freedom to moral freedom.[21]

Does personal "happiness" fit into Rousseau's plan? In truth, he does not promise happiness. People may have been happier, he admits, in their solitary lives in the state of nature, knowing neither good nor evil, their existences revolving around the immediate satisfaction of their physical needs. But Rousseau was convinced that individuals, through their identification with the community, could attain something higher than private happiness: *meaningful* lives. No longer drowning in infernal rat-races, competing and striving to impress others, pursuing elusive, inauthentic goals that never lead to real satisfaction, people by choosing to live as parts of a whole and to share in the common happiness of all have a chance at real fulfillment and peace of mind.

Here is Rousseau's vision of a good society. Citizens are free and equal, not because they own equal property or possess equal talents, but rather because they share an equal measure of civic rights and responsibilities. By renouncing their autonomy and participating in and obeying the General Will, they assure that they will all be treated fairly and with equal consideration and respect. The political community represents the *one and only* channel through which human beings can live and act as fully aware moral agents, accepting and carrying out the duties assigned to them by their own human dignity.

Still, Rousseau's utopian vision is oddly apolitical. He displayed no interest in political struggles for power; he devoted no time to conceiving political or parliamentary institutions. Nor was he concerned with economic justice, advising only that the rich exercise moderation and that the poor restrain their envy.[22] Rather than reflect on parliamentary rules or an economic bill of rights, he imagined instead a relatively small community of citizens, living in "peace, union, and equality" without complex laws. He rejected the idea of a representative democracy, for representatives would rob citizens not only of their sovereignty but also of their civic responsibilities.

Periodically all citizens simply and harmoniously come together to ratify, not to debate, the General Will and the laws that emanate from it. In these periodic acts of "direct democracy," citizens attempt to discover the General Will. They must deliberate alone and by themselves, never in concert with others — for any kind of associations would lead them to identify with the "partial" interests of a faction, not the general interest of all.[23] When citizens vote, their act of voting is conceived, not as a way for them to express their individual wills or to forge a compromise among opposing factions, but purely as a mechanism for "discovering" the General Will.

These assemblies, while engaging citizens in a referendum on the General Will, do not engage them in a participatory democracy. These are not "town-meetings," for citizens neither govern nor make policies. Nor are citizens free to assemble en masse when they wish; only assemblies convoked by the magistrates are lawful and valid.[24] Rousseau's goal was cohesion, harmony, and peace, not self-government.

Politics, Rousseau taught, was a simple affair; the General Will was obvious; collective deliberation was not necessary; and decisions required nothing more than common sense.[25] The people obey only their own General Will which never imposes arbitrary or unnecessary obligations on them. The laws that citizens ratify reflect their collective sense of the General Will. When they obey their society's laws, they "obey no one, but simply their own will."[26] While people must agree unanimously to the original social contract, all other legislative decisions are made by a simple majority.[27] Though these laws are supposed to affect all subjects collectively, Rousseau, in a strange and disappointing retreat, oddly contradicts himself by opening up the possibility that certain citizens may be denied rights or privileges that are accorded to others.[28] The law, Rousseau allows, "may indeed decree that there shall be privileges, but cannot confer them on any person by name."[29]

The people possess the body of laws handed down to them by their Founder, Rousseau's mythical "Legislator," a clairvoyant wise man who, like Lycurgus in Sparta, Numa in Rome, and Moses for the Jewish nation, has formulated laws tailored to his particular people, laws that give a "soul" to the nation and that conciliate pure justice and the particular circumstances of the polity. After having established the legal code, which is endowed with "divine authority" and the "prestige of the gods," the Legislator can withdraw, his task accomplished.[30] A small group of men, or still better, one man, a monarch, constitutes the people's "executive," existing only as the servant of the people's will, but nevertheless constituting the polity's active government.

Rousseau has conceived a radically original society, geared not to individuals obsessed with maximizing their own private interests,[31] but instead to citizens who possess a strong moral sense of their responsibilities and duties toward one another and toward the community. The polity fosters their equality and enhances their freedom to lead meaningful lives and realize their most profound human aspirations. The blossoming of their humanity is inseparable from their citizenship and their conformity to the State's prescription for the "good life." Rousseau has restored to us, one scholar wrote, the "fundamental sweetness of life."[32]

DEMOCRACY WITHOUT PLURALISM

Do you hear the piercing wail of sirens, warning of danger?

The General Will — arbitrary, coercive, and ultimately illusory — has come to dominate all of society and its laws. Every citizen must submit to its infallible, unlimited authority. What king ever ruled so absolutely?

It must now be clear that Rousseau has conceived a utopian, ethical, democratic polity that includes no channels for the expression of dissent or opposition. Having defined the General Will as infallible and sovereign, Rousseau could not logically imagine any legitimate opposition to it. Political "freedom" in such a solidary, unified society requires submission and obedience to the General Will.

And yet, at the dawn of the twenty-first century, we know that the determining features of democracy are the legitimacy of opposition and political parties. How can there be political freedom without the right to oppose those who govern?[33]

But in Rousseau's utopia, those who disagree with the General Will are simply in error, expressing selfish, "particular" interests that perversely thwart the common good of all. Even the majority of citizens can be in error, for Rousseau explicitly wrote that often there can be a great difference between the will of all and the General Will[34] (though, wanting it both ways, he also stated that "all the characteristics of the General Will" are found in the will of the plurality).[35] In any case, there can be no role for minority opinion. Neither dissenting individuals nor groups, political parties, or factions can be tolerated by the cohesive whole. To persist in questioning or opposing the General Will is to abdicate one's membership in the polity, to give up one's political rights, and ultimately to be executed, "less as a citizen than as an enemy."[36] But before putting "rebels" and "traitors" to death, the sovereign people must attempt to make those who have difficulty recognizing the General Will see the light. "Whoever refuses to obey the general will," Rousseau decreed, "shall be constrained to do so by the whole body: which means nothing else than that he shall be *forced* to be free."[37]

Forced to be free? These paradoxical words shock us, and rightly so, for they cast their dark shadow on some of the grimmest periods of the twentieth century. Yet Rousseau's goal was freedom, community, and morality, not mass repression. Rousseau would contend that if society constrains people to be free, socializes them to suppress their animal instincts and selfish desires, and educates them to choose the General Will over their private wills, it is in the name of their own human dignity.

Socialization and education or mind-control? The health of the society and the willingness of citizens to obey the General Will, Rousseau acknowledges, depend on citizens' belief in a civil religion that binds their hearts to the State and makes them delight in their civic duties.[38]

So essential is this religion to the well-being of the polity that nonbelievers must be banished — not because they are impious, Rousseau explains, but rather because they are "unsociable." And if heretics must be put to death, it is in the name of the sanctity of the law. "If any one, after publicly acknowledging these dogmas [of the civil religion]," Rousseau wrote, "behaves like an unbeliever in them, he should be punished with *death;* he has committed the greatest of crimes, he has lied before the laws."[39]

Buttressing the civil religion, a "board of censors" guides and molds people's judgment and then "declares" the nature of public opinion.[40] Though Rousseau asserts that this censorial tribunal merely preserves morality by preventing the corruption of public opinion, he admits that this board will "fix" opinions when they are not yet determined. This seems to mean that instead of a continuous and open national debate on the common good, the government would control the equivalent of editorial and op-ed pages and shape public attitudes. One of Rousseau's critics contends that the "Censorship" would inevitably come to supervise not only the press but also art, theater, and all other means of communication.[41]

Individual wills shattered by the power of the General Will. Self-interest supplanted by sacrifice and sharing. Conflict and opposition banned in the name of unity and consensus. Public opinion shaped by a censorial Big Brother. Rousseau's ideal political community, through the sheer force of its coercive and unitary communitarian spirit, comes to dominate every aspect of human life — intellectual life, social life, moral life. This is the very definition of modern totalitarianism — as well as of the militaristic Spartan society that Rousseau first lauded in his *Discourse on the Sciences and Arts,* a society in which man's entire being is absorbed by his role as citizen.[42]

Ironically though not surprisingly, Rousseau admitted toward the end of his life that he himself would never have chosen or been able to be part of such a solidary community. "I was never really suited to civil society, with all its burdens, obligations and duties," he confessed. His "independent nature" refused the submissions and compromises necessary in communal life. "As soon as I sense a yoke, . . . I become rebellious . . . . When I am supposed to do the opposite of what I want to do, I refuse to do it, no matter what happens."[43]

What then motivated Rousseau to conceive a society in which dissent and conflict are outlawed and submission to the General Will the only legitimate form of political behavior? Why was the notion of a dynamic, competitive political arena, one that tolerates conflict and rewards self-confident individuals and vociferous interest groups, alien to his imagination? Was it his own anti-social personality and need for solitude, his fear that others were always trying to injure him, his long pattern of living under the paternalistic or maternalistic protection of wealthy patrons?

In Rousseau's ideal society, every person, he wrote, is "perfectly independent of all the rest, and in absolute dependence on the State."[44] This, in fact, corresponds perfectly to the penetrating definition of "democratic despotism" that the great political sociologist Alexis de Tocqueville offered in 1856. Tocqueville described a society in which isolated, atomized individuals—though equal—are barred from group action and cooperation as well as from meaningful political participation on a variety of levels—local, county, state, national—spread throughout society. Instead of participating in self-government and receiving this kind of hands-on education in citizenship, they are ruled over by a central government, the sole locus of political power.[45] But for his part, Rousseau was more disposed to the notion of obedience to the General Will than to the notion of a participatory government; he was more comfortable with the idea of the atomization of citizens than with the idea of citizens joining and working together to make demands and claims upon the state.

Did Rousseau articulate the principles of a revolutionary democratic, moral community, tapping deep human yearnings for belonging, solidarity, and sharing? Or did he unwittingly create the enduring blueprint for horrific totalitarian regimes that repress their people in the name of "one-party democracy"? Does his *Social Contract* offer redemption and salvation after the Fall—or a disguised inferno?

Is his legacy the kibbutz or the Gulag?

ROUSSEAU IN THE AGE OF REVOLUTION

Rousseau admired Niccolò Machiavelli. He called the early sixteenth-century political theorist a "profound politician" and lover of liberty.[46] Machiavelli would not have returned the compliment.

Machiavelli's most gleaming political insight was that a republic is energized by conflict: without conflict there are no politics and no freedom. Tumult, he wrote in 1513, was "the guardian of Roman liberties" and "deserved the highest praise." When tumult is absent, when everyone in a state is tranquil, he noted, "we can be sure that it is not a republic." The Florentine perceived that conflict is the foundation of freedom and politics. When the Roman people demonstrated and clamored for their rights, he remarked, their demands, far from being harmful, eventually produced "all laws favorable to liberty." Machiavelli understood that the very nature of politics is *conflictual* and that only tolerance for opposition and conflict can guarantee the survival of political freedom.[47]

Nearly three hundred years later, James Madison not only revived Machiavelli's ideas but acted upon them, making the people's right to form factions and engage in non-violent political conflict the foundation of his plan for republican government. Thomas Jefferson went even further, establishing the crucial principle of the legitimacy of opposition by fostering and exploiting a system of political parties that enabled Americans to organize and oppose the politicians in power.

The American Revolution had proceeded from stage to stage, accomplishing its goals: the war of the 1770s had brought independence. The Philadelphia Convention of 1787 created stable democratic institutions and a venerated Constitution, to which the founders added a Bill of Rights in 1791, and the watershed election of 1800 established the precedent of a defeated incumbent party peacefully turning over power to the opposition.

But while Madison and Jefferson emphasized *tumult,* factions, and parties, on the other side of the Atlantic the leaders of the French Revolution — Sieyès, Robespierre, Saint-Just, and others — were mesmerized by Rousseau's dream of harmony and unanimity. Their Revolution that began with the storming of the Bastille and the idealistic "Declaration of the Rights of Man and Citizen" plunged into a downward spiral, descending into Terror and the hideous reign of the guillotine, devouring its adversaries and its followers as well as its leaders. Finally, ten years later, in a plebiscite in 1799, an exhausted people voted for the Constitution that guaranteed the autocracy of Napoleon. The vote was 3,011,007 to 1,562. In the nineteenth century, the word "republic" had become a smear-word; France would not know republican government until 1871. "He was a madman, your Rousseau," commented Napoleon. "It was he who led us into our present predicament."[48]

THE FRENCH REVOLUTION

When Rousseau's remains were installed in the Pantheon in Paris in 1794, Joseph Lakanal, who had been one of the members of the revolutionary legislative Convention, remarked, "It is not the *Social Contract* that brought about the Revolution. Rather, it is the Revolution that explained to us the *Social Contract.*"[49]

Indeed, revolutionaries in France had not always heeded Rousseau's advice as they designed their blueprint for the new institutions of France.

They created, for example, a representative democracy — not the "direct democracy" that Rousseau had advocated. But if the Revolution's institutions were not inspired by his work, if they were, on the contrary, influenced in some respects more by centuries of monarchical absolutism, the Revolution's spirit certainly belonged to Rousseau.[50] Or, as one scholar recently observed, Rousseau may not have "caused" the French Revolution, but "he provided the terms in which the logic of events could be interpreted."[51]

A harmonious, communitarian society à la Rousseau would be the Revolution's antidote to centuries of injustice and class stratification. Just as Rousseau saw his utopian society as a form of redemption after the degradation of the fall, the leaders of 1789 similarly believed, as the historian François Furet notes, that a unitary, unanimous polity, committed to the General Will, would "regenerate" humanity after the degradation of the ancien régime.[52]

On the eve of the French Revolution, one of Rousseau's most influential disciples, Emmanuel Sieyès, authored the incendiary political pamphlet, "What Is the Third Estate?"[53] During that winter of 1788–1789, as France stood at the brink of financial collapse, King Louis XVI decided to convene the Estates General, hoping that they could resolve the crisis. Following the centuries-old formula, representatives of the three orders — the nobility, the clergy, and the Third Estate — would meet, each order deliberating separately. The nobility and the clergy together consisted of about 200,000 members; the Third Estate, that is, the rest of the population, 25 million. Even before the meeting took place, spokesmen for the Third Estate were objecting to this antiquated structure and demanding that the Third Estate be accorded representation equal to the two other orders combined.

But in his pamphlet Sieyès went even further, making a far more radical demand. Bitterly denouncing the entire anachronistic institution of the Estates General, he declared that there should be a single National Assembly comprised solely of representatives of the Third Estate. The nation and the Third Estate, he argued, were one and the same.[54]

"What is the Third Estate?" Sieyès demanded in his lapidary style. "Everything. What has it been in the political order up to now? Nothing. What is it asking for? To become something." Instantaneously Sieyès excluded the two privileged orders from membership in the nation. Without them, France would be more, not less. Separate, privileged orders were like malignant fluids attacking a sick body and had to be "neutralized."[55] "There cannot be one will as long as we permit three orders," he patiently explained, as if echoing Rousseau. "At best, the three orders might agree.

But they will never constitute *one* nation, *one* representation and *one* common will."[56]

When the Estates General convened in the spring of 1789, Sieyès audaciously proposed that the Third Estate declare itself the National Assembly. His profoundly revolutionary motion passed by an overwhelming majority. The "Declaration of the Rights of Man and Citizen," composed in August 1789, decreed that the nation — the Third Estate — was sovereign. Just eight months after the publication of his ideas, Sieyès's theoretical blueprint for France had become the new reality.

The key to Sieyès's vision of a new France — and the concept that shaped the Revolution's politics and became its mantra — was *unity*. The salvation of France and the success of the Revolution appeared to hinge on the unanimity and indivisibility of the nation. Sieyès conceived the Third Estate *not* as a diverse population of heterogeneous individuals each acting in his own self-interest, but rather as a homogeneous mass. Following Rousseau, he envisioned members of the nation not only as equal but also as like-minded, sharing the same opinions, ideals, and revolutionary goals.

Individuals might differ from one another in their private lives, Sieyès allowed, but those differences occur "beyond the sphere of citizenship."[57] Citizens' rights and freedoms derived from their status as equal and concurring members of society, from their submission to the General Will. Any individual who "exits from the common quality of citizen" cannot "participate in political rights."[58]

For Sieyès, as for Rousseau before him, there could be no legitimate role for dissenting individuals or minority factions to play in self-government.[59] Sieyès contended that all citizens, by virtue of having accepted and entered into their society's social contract, agree to be bound by the will of the majority. A citizen is obliged to "view the common will as his own." Should he refuse to yield to the majority, his only alternative is to leave the polity. Thus the sole solution envisaged by Sieyès to the problem of possible political conflict between an individual and the group was expatriation. Similarly, a minority faction has no right to oppose the majority, since the majority could be assumed to speak for the General Will.[60]

Freedom meant the Rousseauian "freedom" to obey the General Will, not the freedom to pursue one's own private interests and happiness. "Everyone must forget his own interest and pride," instructed the twenty-six year old Louis-Antoine de Saint-Just, the Revolution's most radical ideologue. "Private happiness and interest are a violence against the social order. . . . Your interest demands that you forget your interest; the only salvation is through the public good."[61]

Factions and parties were anathema. What justification could there be for bodies that represent "partial" and private interests in a nation of equal and self-sacrificing citizens, all committed to the "common good"? Danton expressed the party line: "You must absorb this truth: factions cannot exist in a republic."[62] Making no attempt to disguise the Jacobins' refusal to tolerate opposition, Saint-Just proclaimed in February 1794 that "what constitutes a republic is the total destruction of everything that stands in opposition to it."[63]

And yet the radical Jacobins, who would ultimately control the Revolution and govern France during the reign of Terror, were themselves a distinct minority. They prevailed in their quest to dominate the Convention by successfully presenting their radical party ideology as the General Will. The people, the Jacobins announced, wanted what the Jacobins wanted, and the Jacobins knew and expressed the General Will, capitalizing on this most falsifiable of concepts. Their strategy was to denounce and remove duly elected representatives for nothing more than their minority views and to eliminate all dissent in the name of unanimity and unity.

But unity divides. Unity excludes. Unity polarizes. The corollary of the nation's unity is the elimination of any individuals or groups that disrupt that unity. People who do not concur with the nation's interests and goals, who persist in voicing their own private interests, who threaten the nation's unanimity are considered *enemies* to be banished or punished. Thus, the Rousseauian yearning for cohesion, solidarity, and oneness imposes the psychology of the purge.[64]

Indeed, during the Terror of 1793–1794, the revolutionary Convention in France would mandate the death penalty for any attempt to threaten the unity of the Republic. A revolutionary Tribunal was established in March 1793 to ferret out domestic enemies, all the "traitors" and "conspirators" who threatened the nation's unity. Just as Rousseau had recommended, if citizens could not be "forced to be free," those who persisted in betraying the civil religion of harmony and sociability could be put to death.

Of course, unity never reigned in France. During the tumultuous years of the French Revolution, the mesmerizing cult of unity was a veil behind which seethed dissension and discord. Politicians, journalists, philosophers, and economists disagreed on all the major issues of the day, as rational people in any country would.

Numerous factions — monarchiens, Brissotins, Feuillantistes, Montagnards, Girondins, Jacobins, sansculottes, chouans, enragés, Dantonistes, Hébertistes, Robespierristes, Thermidoreans — dotted the political landscape, not only making the study of the French Revolution extremely complicated but also making the simple schism in America between Federalists and Republicans seem, in comparison, downright unimaginative. But so enchanted were the French with the rhetoric of unity and so cynical were political leaders who used the Rousseauian myth of unity to isolate and defeat their adversaries and consolidate their own power, that even when people disagreed passionately with one another, they continued to condemn factions and parties as well as the very idea of organized opposition. Even when it was apparent that nothing existed *but* dissension and conflict, revolutionary leaders in France were self-destructively blind and intellectually opposed to the idea of an inclusive polity in which a variety of political visions could be tolerated.

Ironically, the revolutionary cult of unity that rejected dissent, factions, and non-violent political conflict led the French Revolution to the most extreme form of conflict: violence and murder. And this catastrophic failure of democracy can be traced directly to Rousseau's dream of harmony and consensus, to his vision of a fraternal people bound together in political unity, all happily acknowledging and obeying the truth of the sovereign, infallible General Will, and to his exclusion of dissent and opposition. "The contradiction inherent in the abstract attempt to constrain modern man to subordinate everything to the public good," judges the historian Furet categorically, "led to the Terror."[65]

Before it all began, in 1778, Maximilien Robespierre, who would become the mastermind of the Terror, met the legendary philosopher Jean-Jacques Rousseau. "I saw you in your last days," he recalled, "and this memory is a source of proud joy for me." According to Robespierre, Rousseau commented that he had prepared the field and sowed the seeds for the immense change that was about to take place in France, but, like Moses, he would not live to see the promised land. The young lawyer pledged to his master that he would be "constantly faithful to the inspiration" that he had drawn from Rousseau's writings.[66]

Decades later, Alexis de Tocqueville, shortly before his death, was working on a sequel to his study of the French Revolution, *The Old Regime and the Revolution*. In his notes he prophetically discussed the violence that can be produced by abstract ideas such as the General Will. The leaders of the French Revolution, Tocqueville contended, formed a new international "turbulent and destructive race, always ready to strike down and incapable of setting up, that stipulates that there are no individual rights, indeed that there are *no individuals,* but only *a mass* which may stop at nothing to attain its ends." Their revolutionary religion was "one of the most singular, the most active and the most contagious diseases of the human mind."[67]

THE MADISONIAN VISION

Just twenty-five years after Rousseau wrote his *Social Contract*—and two years before revolutionary leaders in France decided on their plan for the new government of France—James Madison composed *Federalist* No. 10. His brilliant political formula for constitutional government turns Rousseau's vision of a political community upside down.[68]

Underlying Madison's political thought is his modest, commonsensical conviction that citizens are all individuals and that as individuals, they are all different. People simply will never agree unanimously on anything. A vast variety of "unavoidable" factors—wealth and property, social class, religion, geography, political ideas, etc.—would always divide people into different interest groups and factions. Indeed, the principle of diversity seemed embedded in human nature, that is, in human rationality. Madison argued that rational people view issues in different ways because reason is essentially imperfect. "As long as the reason of man continues *fallible*," he maintained, "and he is at liberty to exercise it, different opinions will be formed."[69]

Could differences and factions be removed from society, Madison asked. Could conflict be eliminated so that the kind of consensus Rousseau had emphasized could be achieved? Well, unity and unanimity could certainly be achieved by summarily outlawing factions, Madison allowed, but such an option was completely unsatisfactory and unacceptable, because its cost would be freedom itself, that is, people's freedom to act without constraint and express their own interests. People would be forced to sacrifice the very liberty that was "essential to political life." Thus the remedy would be worse than the disease. "Liberty is to faction," Madison wrote in a superb simile, "what air is to fire. . . . But it could not be less folly to abolish liberty, which is essential to political life, because it nourishes faction, than it would be to wish the annihilation of air."

Was there any other way to achieve unity? No. The dream of unity, he noted with disdain, was a theoretical fantasy. In the "civilized communities" of real life, no such "perfect homogeneousness of interests, opinions & feelings" would ever be found.[70] Whereas Rousseau was convinced that human beings could be guided and enlightened if not forced to prefer the common good to their own private interests, Madison believed that self-interest would always dominate human affairs. Significantly, he had already criticized in 1787 the leap that Sieyès—following Rousseau—made in 1789, that is, the leap from the idea of citizens' equality before the law to the idea of citizens' similarity in everything else. "Theoretic politicians," he wrote in *Federalist* No. 10, "have erroneously supposed that by reducing mankind to a perfect equality in their political rights, they would at the same time be perfectly equalized and assimilated in their possessions, their opinions, and their passions."[71] And he was thoroughly uninterested in "regenerating" human beings to suit utopian political blueprints. "What is government itself," he wrote, "but the greatest of all reflections on human nature. If men were angels, no government would be necessary."[72]

Did Madison believe in such a thing as the public or common good? Though he does refer in passing to "the permanent and aggregate interests of the community,"[73] he nevertheless does not posit the existence of a single common good or General Will in society (that is, other than "life, liberty, and the pursuit of happiness"). Although Alexander Hamilton always stressed his belief in the existence of "the public interest" and has even been called the "Rousseau of the Right"[74] by some American historians, Madison's concept of government recognizes the multiple interests and wills of diverse citizens and factions, all competing for influence and power.

Indeed, the Virginian explicitly rejected the idea that there could be a "neutral" agency in government that voiced the public good. Madison was convinced that every participant in government represented some interest or faction. "What are the different classes of legislators," he asked, "but advocates and parties to the causes which they determine?"[75] He confessed that it would be highly desirable to have some kind of "dispassionate umpire in disputes between different passions & interests in the State," but he knew that hopes for such a neutral referee were vain.[76] "Enlightened statesmen," who subordinate clashing interests to the public good, could not be expected to "be at the helm."[77] Factions did not exist in opposition to government: they *constitute* government. Conflict among different factions was not merely tolerated *by* government: conflict *was* government.

Madison's vision of the "good society" could hardly have been more different from Rousseau's. In contrast to Rousseau's vision of a harmonious community, Madison sought to balance conflicting private interest groups, all feverishly pursuing a host of competing notions of the private and public good.

Ultimately, Madison counted on factions to perform a task of paramount importance: resistance to any concentration of power. More than anything else Madison feared the power of an "overbearing" majority. Therefore, the more diverse the society, the more it was broken down into "so many parts, interests and classes," the more likely it would be that any majority would become broad and hence moderate in its goals. And the less likely it would be that the rights of individuals would be threatened by "the combinations of the majority."[78]

This notion of division also underlay Madison's plan for checks and balances. The government would be divided against itself, institutionally split "between different bodies of men, who might watch and check each other."[79] Madison purposefully designed the government so that people and interest groups would collide rather than concur. Adding to institutional division and collision, moreover, were the ideological divisions of the political parties — Federalists and Republicans — that crystallized in the 1790s. Henceforth two rival parties would compete for power and alternately govern, strengthening the young nation by according legitimacy to opposition.

If there was "oneness" in America, it was the fundamental constitutional consensus: a commitment to a government dedicated to the values of life, liberty, and the pursuit of happiness and, as for everything else, an agreement to disagree.

But in France, Rousseau's revolutionary disciples were insisting that the republic be "one and indivisible," that it possess one roaring voice and one indomitable will. Although in retrospect one can imagine that revolutionaries in France, scarred if not traumatized by centuries of monarchical absolutism, might also have sought to divide and fragment power, in fact the opposite was the case. The French were demanding, above all, change, impact, action — they clamored for energetic, majoritarian government, not the stability, inertia, or deadlock that results from the fragmentation of power.

Is there a political model that can wed the potent, populist leadership and majoritarian government that French revolutionaries craved with an adversarial two-party system, while also protecting individual rights and avoiding governmental gridlock?

Yes. The wedding has already taken place. In Great Britain.

MAJORITY RULE WITHOUT CHECKS AND BALANCES

"Whether we speak of differences in opinion or differences in interest," remarked Daniel Defoe, the author of *Robinson Crusoe,* in 1701, "we must own we are the most divided, quarrelsome nation under the sun."[80] Great Britain's affinity for political quarrels has produced the longest-lasting and arguably most vital democracy on the planet.[81]

While Rousseau was theorizing about political unity and harmony, the British were engaged in developing a theory of political parties. Edmund

Burke, a leader of the opposition Whig party, found it inconceivable that representative government could exist without political parties. Why, he wondered in 1770, would like-minded politicians, who want to see their ideas and principles translated into practice, not associate and cooperate with one another? The thought that men would choose *not* to act in concert with others struck Burke as "utterly incomprehensible." "Of what sort of materials must that man be made," he mused in disbelief, "who can sit whole years in Parliament, with five hundred and fifty of his fellow-citizens, . . . in the agitation of such mighty questions . . . without seeing any one sort of men, whose character, conduct, or disposition, would lead him to associate himself with them?"[82]

The dominant features of the modern British model of parliamentary democracy are, as Burke had advocated, two distinct, competitive parties that alternate in power, a strong elected executive, and — as far as the executive and legislature are concerned — no marked constitutional separation of powers. After a political party in Great Britain wins a national election, the party leader becomes the country's Prime Minister. There are no formal limits to the power of the Prime Minister's government, as long as it retains its parliamentary majority. The party is free to enact all of its policies and programs, thus assuring clear majoritarian rule.

Still, the losing party does not disappear from the scene, for the opposition constitutes an integral, essential part of the constitutional system. "Her Majesty's Opposition" has the duty to criticize the party in power and is as much a part of the polity as the administration itself. Its prime responsibility is not to fell the government in power but rather to offer an alternative government and to present positive — not just oppositional — policies. In addition to these responsibilities, the opposition has rights too — for example, it selects topics of parliamentary debate. A forceful and effective opposition constantly reminds leaders and citizens of a clear alternative to the majority government's policies, yet the majority may continue to enact its policies unimpeded.[83] Together "Her Majesty's Government" and "Her Majesty's Opposition" make up the two halves of the constitutional system.

Paradoxically, adversarial party politics requires consensus — sometimes a high level of consensus, sometimes a minimal level. First of all, there must exist a fundamental consensus in the nation as to the constitutional system itself as well as to citizens' rights and freedoms. Second, though the system depends on ideological conflict, there must not be too much conflict — or too little. If criticism of government is too severe, if the different parties are too polarized, and if conflict is so intense as to eliminate the "mediating center," the social fabric of the society may suffer.[84] Still, too little conflict means that the government is immune from healthy criticism and that significant alternative policies are not being offered. A delicate balancing act is required to produce, in the words of political scientist Robert Dahl, "a society where dissent is low enough to encourage a relatively calm and objective appraisal of alternatives, and yet sufficient to make sure that radical alternatives will not be ignored or suppressed."[85]

For the past two centuries, British and American democracies have accepted the principle of conflict and learned to exploit it. They have integrated conflict into their institutions; they have normalized it and ritualized it and thus tamed it; and they have created rules and procedures for defanging and resolving it. And not only have both political systems thrived on conflict, they have also been remarkably able to weather a variety of other storms — from horrific world wars to violent social upheaval.

Indeed, the United States and England (and her Canadian and Australian offspring) are virtually alone among nations in having been able to withstand all the catastrophes of the twentieth century — two world wars, fascism, Stalinism, a devastating economic depression. Those governments remained stable and intact throughout the century, persevering in their careful, orderly ways while the rest of the world reeled. Is that resilience due — at least in part — to their ability to tolerate, defang, and absorb conflict?

CONFLICT AND COMMUNITY

Yet, at the beginning of the twenty-first century, some American sociologists, political scientists, and philosophers, troubled by a society they see as ever more fractured and disunited, voice a longing for a greater sense of social cohesion. Not content with a rational commitment to pluralism and diversity, feeling an emotional yearning for solidarity and belonging, they accuse James Madison of having effectively thwarted the dream of oneness. They feel that Madison's undeviating emphasis on factions, conflict, and individual rights forever undermines a sense of national community. One historian describes Madison's view of society as an "agglomeration of hostile individuals coming together for their mutual benefit."[86]

But are conflict and community really irreconcilable? This question is a crucial one. For if the American (and British) models of government do indeed preclude the possibility of community, then it would be understandable that revolutionary leaders in France dismissed the American experience and attempted to follow Rousseau's formula for fraternity and community.

In defense of Madisonian government, one can argue, first of all, that there exists in America an unusually rich, diversified, and inclusive political community. Especially since the vote was extended to non-property holders, to African-Americans, and to women, the political arena has been able to encompass new interest groups and accommodate a vast number of voluntary associations, assuring most citizens and most emerging groups membership and representation in the national community.[87]

Second, in the 1950s, the brilliant political theorist Louis Hartz argued that in America there indeed exists "a *peculiar sense of community,*"[88] something more than atomized and self-interested individuals. What holds people together, Hartz maintained, is not the sense that they were different parts of a corporate whole, but rather "the knowledge that they were similar participants in a uniform way of life." At the core of American society stands a glacier resting on "miles of submerged conviction." This shared conviction is the American creed of individualism and freedom — so powerful and self-evident that people do not even realize that they are conforming to an ideology at all. This powerful "common standard," Hartz believed, produces a very real kind of social cohesion among citizens committed to the same common good: life, liberty, and the pursuit of happiness. That fundamental democratic consensus, in England and America, is the glue that binds people together.

When Alexis de Tocqueville visited the United States in 1831, he encountered an active, kinetic society. Coming from lethargic Restoration France, he was astonished by the frenetic activity taking place at all levels of society. "As soon as you step onto American soil," he wrote, "you find yourself in the middle of a kind of *tumult.*" Wherever he looked, people were attending meetings! One group was debating whether to build a new church; another wondering whom to elect as representative; still another considering what kinds of improvements to make in their township.[89] Involvement in the nation's public life had become people's entertainment and pleasure. Meetings seemed to have taken the place of theater!

When citizens join with others to promote their private interests, Tocqueville noted, they discover that their own interests are inseparable from those of other citizens. Through their involvement in civic associations, self-government, and the jury system, these Americans rise above their own narrow self-interest and identify more deeply with the community. Tocqueville termed this "self-interest rightly understood" or enlightened self-interest.

Though such people would be puzzled if one congratulated them on their commitment to a life of "virtue," they nevertheless find fulfillment in helping others and in making sacrifices of their time and wealth for the community. These Americans, Tocqueville observed, tolerate no constraints on their self-interest or their autonomy and would dismiss any lofty moral interpretations of their conduct, yet they seemed to have mastered themselves, to have chosen to lead disciplined, moderate, and considerate lives.

Virtue, if not their calling or their goal, nevertheless colors the habits of their everyday lives. Few Americans, Tocqueville noted, will attain the heady sphere of absolute virtue, but the vast majority of citizens will have made reasonable progress in living decent lives. The key to the vital democratic and moral community they have created? Not a commitment to *obey* the General Will. But rather a commitment to *exercise* freedom and *participate* in self-government and act out of an expansive, enlightened notion of self-interest.

As if nodding simultaneously to both Madison and Rousseau, Tocqueville suggested a modern marriage of self-interest and devotion to the common good, a synthesis of individual freedom and community, an awareness of self as well as a moral and spiritual desire to transcend the self.

Madisonian individualism or Rousseauian community? Maximization of self-interest or sacrifice for the common good? Political conflict or a quest for consensus? Rights conceived as protection for individuals and minorities or rights conceived for the community as a whole? Education as individual self-enhancement or education as the inculcation of civic responsibility and public spirit? These are not just abstract choices — on the contrary, they color our everyday lives as well as the front pages of our newspapers.

When we decry "politics as usual" and wish that Democrats and Republicans would sit down and work out their differences and act only for the "common good" of the country, we are echoing Rousseau; and like him, we believe that we are uttering noble, selfless, "holistic" ideas. When we wish that politics was based not on the struggle among competing interest groups but rather on a shared moral vision of all citizens' interdependence, or when we assert that the rights of the community should precede the rights of a few "selfish" individuals, we are voicing themes that Rousseau articulated more profoundly than any other thinker.

At key moments in American history, the mantra of "rugged individualism" and free competition was interrupted by powerful, welcome reminders of Rousseau's moral, communitarian vision. When the reform-minded President Theodore Roosevelt settled the great anthracite coal strike in 1902, announcing that the interests of both the coal operators and the workers must be "subordinated to the fundamental permanent interests of the whole community,"[90] and a few years later, when, advocating a steeply graduated tax on estates, he declared, "If ever our people become so sordid as to feel that all that counts is moneyed prosperity, ignoble well-being, effortless ease and comfort, then this nation shall perish, as it will deserve to perish, from the earth,"[91] he was enunciating key Rousseauian themes. And when John F. Kennedy electrified a generation by declaring in his inaugural address in 1961, "Ask not what your country can do for you, ask what you can do for your country," Rousseau was speaking to us again — with a Boston accent.

Though some of Rousseau's ideas — about the General Will, unanimity, and dissent — have proven disruptive and counterproductive in established democracies and disastrous in developing democracies, his other ideas — his concept of positive freedom, "freedom *for,*" and his notion of a community dedicated to the common good of all — still inspire and galvanize people who seek a deeper, richer, shared communal life in which self-interest is exchanged for interdependence and in which full participation permits an ethical life as well as personal happiness.[92]

As we continue our ongoing experiments in democracy, Rousseau's writings, along with those of Niccolò Machiavelli, James Madison, Thomas Jefferson, Edmund Burke, Alexis de Tocqueville, and others, inspire, puzzle, and energize us, nourishing our imaginations, sharpening our critical faculties, helping to strengthen our commitment to self-government, pluralism, community, and freedom.

NOTES

1. See Rousseau's last footnote in his *Discourse on the Sciences and Arts.* I wish to thank James MacGregor Burns, Francis C. Oakley, and Richard Miller for reviewing this essay and generously giving me their constructive suggestions.

2. See Jean Guéhenno, *Jean-Jacques Rousseau,* trans. John and Doreen Weightman, 2 vols. (New York: Columbia University Press, 1966), 1:128ff.

3. On the subject of glittering high culture, Thomas Jefferson might have agreed with Rousseau. "I view great cities as pestilential to the morals, the health and the liberties of man," Jefferson wrote in 1800. "True, they nourish some of the elegant arts, but the useful ones can thrive elsewhere, and less perfection in the others, with more health, virtue & free-

dom, would be my choice." Jefferson to Benjamin Rush, 23 September 1800, in *The Writings of Thomas Jefferson,* ed. Paul Leicester Ford (New York: G. P. Putnam's Sons, 1896), 7:459.

4. At the end of Rousseau's *Discourse on the Sciences and Arts,* he specifically counsels the marriage of philosophy and political power, advising kings to welcome into their courts *philosophes* who might help make policies that contribute to human happiness.

5. See Leo Strauss, "On the Intention of Rousseau, in *Hobbes and Rousseau: A Collection of Critical Essays,* ed. Maurice Cranston and Richard Peters (Garden City, N.Y.: Anchor Books, 1972), 261–265 and 281–282.

6. François Duc de La Rochefoucauld, *Maximes, suivies des Réflexions diverses* (Paris: Garnier, 1967), Maxim 629, my translation.

7. Montesquieu, *De l'Esprit des lois,* Bk. 11, ch. 11 in *Oeuvres complètes,* ed. Roger Caillois (Paris: Gallimard, 1951), my translation.

8. John Stuart Mill, *On Liberty* [1859], ed. Currin V. Shields (New York: Macmillan, 1985), 57.

9. Lord Acton, *Letters to Mary Gladstone* (New York: Macmillan, 1904), quotation spoken to Herbert Paul, quoted in Henri Peyre, "The Influence of Eighteenth-Century Ideas on the French Revolution," in *The Making of Modern Europe,* ed. Herman Ausubel, 2 vols. (New York: Dryden Press, 1951), vol. 1.

10. Rousseau, *Discourse on Inequality,* Preface.

11. See Thorstein Veblen, *The Theory of the Leisure Class* (New York: Modern Library, 1934).

12. Rousseau, *Discourse on Inequality,* Second Part.

13. Rousseau's feelings about violent revolution are ambivalent, for he also writes, in the Dedication to the *Discourse on Inequality:* "A people once accustomed to masters are not able to live without them. If they attempt at any time to shake off their yoke, they lose still more freedom . . . they generally become greater slaves to some impostor, who loads them with fresh chains."

14. Paul Bénichou, "L'idée de nature chez Rousseau," in *Pensée de Rousseau,* ed. P. Bénichou, E. Cassirer, et al. (Paris: Seuil, 1984), 128–129.

15. See Rousseau, *The Social Contract,* Bk. 1, ch. 4.

16. See Rousseau, *The Social Contract,* Bk. 1, ch. 6.

17. Rousseau, *The Social Contract,* Bk. 4, ch. 1.

18. See *The Social Contract,* Bk. 2, ch. 1–4.

19. See Isaiah Berlin, *Four Essays on Liberty* (Oxford: Oxford University Press, 1969).

20. See Bénichou, "L'Idée de nature chez Rousseau," 133.

21. See Rousseau, *The Social Contract,* Bk 1, ch. 8.

22. *The Social Contract,* Bk. 2, ch. 11.

23. *The Social Contract,* Bk. 2, ch. 3. Although "associations" may not share in the making of the General Will, Rousseau does not totally exclude them from society, admitting that "if there are partial associations, it is necessary to multiply their number and prevent inequality, as Solon, Numa, and Servius did." See *The Social Contract,* Bk. 2, ch. 3. Still, political philosophers such as Edmund Burke, who recognize the inevitability of ideological conflict and struggles for political power, take a far more positive view of political parties. Burke, a leader of the opposition Whig party, found it inconceivable that representative government could exist without political parties. Why would like-minded politicians, who want to see their ideas and principles translated into practice, not associate and cooperate with one another? He was convinced that "no men could act with effect, who did not act in concert . . . who were not bound together by common opinions, common affections and common interests." See Burke, "Thoughts on the Cause of the Present Discontents" in *The Writings and Speeches of the Right Honourable Edmund Burke* (Boston: Little Brown, Beaconsfield Edition, 1901), 1:529.

24. The Social Contract, Bk. 3, ch. 13.

25. See Bernard Manin, "La délibération politique," *Le Débat,* January 1985, 80.

26. *The Social Contract,* Bk. 2, ch. 4.

27. *The Social Contract,* Bk. 4, ch. 2.

28. Charles Eisenmann, "La Cité de Rousseau," in Bénichou et al., eds., *La Pensée de Rousseau,* 106.

29. Rousseau, *The Social Contract,* Bk. 2, ch. 6.

30. Rousseau, *The Social Contract,* Bk. 2, ch. 7.

31. François Furet, "Rousseau and the French Revolution," in *The Legacy of Rousseau,* ed. Clifford Orwin and Nathan Tarcov (Chicago: University of Chicago Press, 1997), 181.

32. Allan Bloom, "Rousseau's Critique of Liberal Constitutionalism," in *The Legacy of Rousseau,* ed. Orwin and Tarcov, 166.

33. See Robert A. Dahl, ed., "Preface," *Political Oppositions in Western Democracies* (New Haven: Yale University Press, 1966), xviii.

34. Rousseau, *The Social Contract,* Bk. 2, ch. 3.

35. Rousseau, *The Social Contract,* Bk. 4. ch. 2. In 1794, John Adams attacked Rousseau's notion of the General Will writing, "If the majority is 51 and the minority is 49, is it certainly the voice of God? If tomorrow one

should change to 50 vs. 50, where is the voice of God? If two and the minority should become the majority, is the voice of God changed?" See Zoltan Hasaszti, *John Adams and the Prophets of Progress* (Cambridge: Harvard University Press, 1952), 93.

36. Rousseau, *The Social Contract,* Bk. 2, ch. 5.

37. Rousseau, *The Social Contract,* Bk. 1, ch. 7, emphasis added.

38. Rousseau, *The Social Contract,* Bk. 4, ch. 8.

39. Rousseau, *The Social Contract,* Bk. 4, ch. 8, emphasis added.

40. Rousseau, *The Social Contract,* Bk. 4, ch. 7.

41. Lester Crocker, Introduction, in Rousseau, *The Social Contract and Discourse on Inequality,* ed. and trans. Lester Crocker (New York: Washington Square Press, 1967), xxi.

42. See Judith N. Shklar, *Men and Citizens: A Study of Rousseau's Social Theory* (Cambridge: Cambridge University Press, 1969), 12ff.

43. Rousseau, *Les Rêveries du promeneur solitaire* (Paris: Garnier, 1960), 6th Promenade, my translation.

44. Rousseau, *The Social Contract,* Bk. 2, ch. 12.

45. See Alexis de Tocqueville, *L'Ancien Régime et la Révolution,* ed. J.-P. Mayer (Paris: Gallimard, 1952) Book 3, chapter 8, my translation.

46. Rousseau, *The Social Contract,* Bk. 3, ch. 6, text and note. Also, in Bk. 3, ch. 9 of *The Social Contract,* in Rousseau's second note to that chapter, he paraphrases Machiavelli, writing that "a little agitation gives energy to men's minds, and what makes the race truly prosperous is not so much peace as liberty."

47. See Niccolò Machiavelli, *Discorsi sopra la prima deca di Tito Livio,* ed. Piero Gallardo (Milano: Club del Libro, 1966), Bk. I, ch. 4, 5, 6, my translation.

48. Quotation of Napoleon, 1800, in Bernard Manin, "Rousseau," in *A Critical Dictionary of the French Revolution,* ed. François Furet and Mona Ozouf, transl. Arthur Goldhammer (Cambridge: Belknap Press of Harvard University Press, 1989), 830.

49. François Furet, "Rousseau and the French Revolution," in *The Legacy of Rousseau,* ed. Orwin and Tarcov, 181.

50. Furet, "Rousseau and the French Revolution," 178.

51. James Swenson, *On Jean-Jacques Rousseau: Considered as One of the First Authors of the Revolution* (Stanford: Stanford University Press, 2000), x.

52. Furet, "Rousseau and the French Revolution," 179.

53. On Sieyès, see Susan Dunn, *Sister Revolutions: French Lightning, American Light* (New York: Faber & Faber, 1999), 58ff.

54. Sieyès, speech of 20–21 July 1789 in *Orateurs de la Révolution française,* ed. François Furet and Ran Halévi (Paris: Gallimard, 1989), 1:1015.

55. Emmanuel Sieyès, *Qu'est-ce que le tiers état?,* ed. Roberto Zapperi (Geneva: Droz, 1950), ch. 6, 194; ch. 1, 124; ch. 6, 217–218.

56. Sieyès, *Qu'est-ce que le tiers état?,* ed. Zapperi, ch. 6, 198–199, my translation.

57. Sieyès, *Qu'est-ce que le tiers état?,* ed. Zapperi, ch. 6, 208.

58. Sieyès, *Qu'est-ce que le tiers état?,* ed. Zapperi, ch. 6, 211.

59. Sieyès, *Vues sur les moyens d'exécution dont les représentans de la France pourront disposer,* quoted in *Qu'est-ce que le tiers état?,* ed. Zapperi, 76.

60. See Introduction, in *Qu'est-ce que le tiers état?,* ed. Zapperi, 75.

61. Saint-Just, Speech of 28 January 1793, in *Oeuvres complètes,* ed. Michèle Duval (Paris: Lebovici, 1984), 408.

62. Danton, Speech of 29 October 1792 in H. Morse Stephens, *Orators of the French Revolution,* 2 vols. (Oxford: Clarendon Press, 1892), 2:180.

63. Saint-Just, Rapport du comité de salut public, 8 ventôse Year II, in Saint-Just, *Oeuvres complètes,* ed. Michèle Duval (Paris: Lebovici, 1984), 700.

64. R. R. Palmer, *Twelve Who Ruled* (Princeton: Princeton University Press, 1973), 324.

65. Furet, "Rousseau and the French Revolution," 181.

66. Maximilien de Robespierre, *Mémoires,* 2 vols. (Paris: Moreau-Rosier, 1830), 1:166–167 and 209–210. One recent French historian objects strongly to American critics, such as Jacob Talmon, Lester Crocker, and Carol Blum, who trace the totalitarian mentality back to Rousseau. He argues that the subordination of one's private interests to the General Will is simply a patriotic mode of behavior. See Jean-Louis Lecercle, "Jean-Jacques terroriste," in *Rousseau and the Eighteenth Century: Essays in Memory of R. A. Leigh,* ed. Marian Hobson, J. T. A. Leigh, and Robert Wokler (Oxford: The Voltaire Foundation, 1992), 429.

67. Tocqueville, *L'Ancien Régime et la Révolution, Fragments et Notes inédites sur la Revolution,* ed. André Jardin, vol. 2, pt. 2, of Tocqueville, *Oeuvres complètes,* ed. J.-P. Mayer (Paris: Gallimard, 1953), 2:255, 337, 228.

68. On Madison and *Federalist* No. 10, see Susan Dunn, *Sister Revolutions: French Lightning, American Light,* 55ff.

69. Madison, *Federalist* No. 10 (New York: Modern Library, n.d.), 55, emphasis added.

70. Madison, 1833, draft of a letter on majority governments, in *The Mind of the Founder: Sources of the Political Thought of James Madison,* ed. Marvin Meyers (Hanover: University Press of New England, 1981), 415.

71. Madison, *Federalist* No. 10, 58–59.

72. Madison, *Federalist* No. 51, 337.

73. Madison, *Federalist* No. 10, 54.

74. Cecelia Kenyon, "Alexander Hamilton: Rousseau of the Right," *Political Science Quarterly,* June 1958, vol. 72. Although Hamilton believed in the "public good," he felt that it would best be defined by the Federalist ruling elite and not by the people at large. Like Rousseau, Hamilton believed that unity in government and society should prevail. Although he allowed for differences of opinion in the legislature, ultimately all representatives would have to agree. "When a resolution is once taken, the opposition must be at an end," he wrote in *Federalist* 70, adding with a Rousseauian flourish, "that resolution is a law, and resistance to it punishable."

75. Madison, *Federalist* No. 10, 56.

76. Madison, Letter of 16 April 1787, in Robert A. Rutland et al., eds., *The Papers of James Madison* (Charlottesville: University Press of Virginia, 1983), 9:384.

77. Madison, *Federalist* No. 10, 57.

78. Madison, *Federalist* No. 51, 339.

79. Jonathan Elliot, ed., *The Debates in the Several State Conventions on the Adoption of the Federalist Constitution* (Philadelphia: Lippincott, 1937), 5:242.

80. Daniel Defoe, quoted by Lawrence Stone, "The Results of the English Revolutions of the Seventeenth Century," in J. G. A. Pocock, ed., *Three British Revolutions: 1641, 1688, 1776* (Princeton: Princeton University Press, 1980), 75.

81. On English parliamentary democracy, see Susan Dunn, *Sister Revolutions: French Lightning, American Light,* 203ff.

82. Edmund Burke, *Thoughts on the Cause of the Present Discontents* [1770] in *The Writings and Speeches of the Right Honourable Edmund Burke* (Boston: Little Brown, Beaconsfield Edition, 1901), 1:529 and 533–34.

83. On English parliamentary democracy, see Allen Potter, "Great Britain: Opposition with a Capital 'O'," in Dahl, ed., *Political Oppositions in Western Democracies,* 6–8.

84. Robert Alan Dahl, "The American Oppositions," in Dahl, ed., *Political Oppositions in Western Democracies,* 65.

85. Dahl, "Epilogue," in Dahl, ed., *Political Oppositions in Western Democracies,* 392.

86. Gordon Wood, *The Creation of the American Republic* (Chapel Hill: University of North Carolina Press for the Institute of Early American History and Culture, 1969), 607.

87. James MacGregor Burns, *The Deadlock of Democracy* (Englewood Cliffs: Prentice-Hall, 1963), 22.

88. Louis Hartz, *The Liberal Tradition in America: An Interpretation of American Political Thought Since the Revolution* (New York: Harcourt, Brace & World, 1955), 55.

89. Alexis de Tocqueville, *De la démocratie en Amérique,* ed. J.-P. Mayer (Paris: Gallimard, 1951), Vol. 1, Part 2, ch. 6, my translation.

90. Theodore Roosevelt, *An Autobiography* (New York: Macmillan, 1913), 513.

91. Theodore Roosevelt, Speech of 21 October 1907, in *The Roosevelt Policy: Speeches, Letters and State Papers,* ed. William Griffith (New York: Current Literature Publishing Company, 1919), 2: 634.

92. See Robert N. Bellah et al., *The Good Society* (New York: Knopf, 1991).

Chronology of Rousseau's Life

1712	Rousseau is born in Geneva in a Protestant family of French origin. His mother dies in childbirth. As a child, Rousseau loves to read serious books.
1722	Rousseau's father is forced to leave Geneva, and the young Jean-Jacques is raised by a Protestant minister, Lambercier. He spends two happy years with Lambercier.
1727	Rousseau begins work as an apprentice to an engraver.
1728	Rousseau flees Geneva. In Annecy, France, he meets twenty-nine-year old Madame de Warens, a new convert to Catholicism. She takes in the sixteen-year old young man. Years later he credits her with changing his life. With her encouragement, he converts from Protestantism to Catholicism. He works as a servant for Madame de Vercellis and for the Count de Gouvon. Guilty of a petty theft, Rousseau accuses an innocent maid of the crime, an experience that will haunt him with shame.
1729	He returns to Madame de Warens, whom he calls from then on his "Mommy." He spends several months at a Catholic seminary in Annecy but discovers in himself no vocation for religion.
1730–1732	He spends a year hiking from place to place in Switzerland; during the winter months, he lives in Neufchatel, where he gives music lessons and composes. He goes to Paris for the first time. Though he wants to find work as a tutor, the only position he is offered is that of a servant. In Lyon in 1731, he earns money by transcribing musical scores, work he will perform and enjoy for the rest of his life.
1732	Rousseau returns to Madame de Warens, first in Chambéry, then at her estate outside of Chambéry, Les Charmettes.

1732–1736   These are happy years for Rousseau; he writes, composes, gives music lessons, and studies. In 1734, he and Madame de Warens become lovers.

1737   Rousseau goes to Geneva to claim his maternal inheritance, then travels to Montpellier. When he returns to Madame de Warens, he finds himself displaced by another young man, Wintzenried. Rousseau remains at Les Charmettes.

1740   He finds work in Lyon as the tutor for the children of Monsieur de Mably. Unhappy, he returns a final time to Madame de Warens at Les Charmettes.

1742   Up to this point, Rousseau's life has been relatively carefree and haphazard. The next part of his life will be marked by ambition to succeed in a competitive, elite society and by the prodigious output of masterpieces in a variety of different fields, from opera to political theory. Rousseau goes to Paris. He presents a proposal for a new method of musical notation, for which he receives encouragement rather than the financial success he had hoped for. He becomes acquainted with many of the famous men of letters of Paris, such as Marivaux, Fontenelle, Diderot, and others; he frequents fashionable, aristocratic salons.

1743   Looking for other upper-class women to protect and help him, he finds work as tutor in the family of Madame Dupin. He tries his hand at writing plays and an opera. Another woman, Madame de Broglie, finds him a position in Venice.

1743–44   Rousseau works in Venice as secretary to Monsieur de Montaigu, the French Ambassador. He is treated more as a servant than as a gentleman. He insults Monsieur de Montaigu, who forces him to leave Venice. From his experience in Italy he gains a love of Italian music and a bitter loathing for social inequality.

1744–1745   Rousseau returns to Paris; he moves among some of the fashionable salons of the day, but feels ill at ease and insecure. He begins his lifelong relationship with Thérèse Lavasseur, an indigent, uneducated servant. In 1745 he sends their first child off to a foundling home. He and Thérèse will send their next four children too to the Foundling Home. His excuse: his poverty, the customs of the times, the ability of the State to teach the children a trade. Also in 1745, Rousseau is asked to work on revising Voltaire's and Rameau's comedy-ballet, "Les Fêtes de Ramire"; the opera is a success but Rousseau receives no credit for his work. He feels persecuted. Once again he works for Madame Dupin as her secretary. A friend of Diderot since 1742, Rousseau contributes essays on music to Diderot's great project of the *Encyclopedia*.

1746–1748   Rousseau accompanies the Dupin family, as their secretary, to their château of Chenonceaux in the Loire Valley, where he enjoys the aristocratic life. He composes music and writes poems and plays. Dupin writes a book about Montesquieu's *De l'Esprit des lois,* which had just been published. Rousseau thus becomes steeped in political theory. He is asked to be mentor to the Dupins' nineteen-year-old son, an experience that will resonate in his work on education, *Emile*.

1749   One day, while meditating on the question of a new intellectual competition, "Has the revival of the sciences and the arts contributed to improving morality?" Rousseau decides to answer the question by attacking the Enlightenment. The course of his life and his ideas is forever changed.

1750   Rousseau wins the competition for his *Discourse on the Sciences and Arts* and becomes a celebrity in Paris. He ends his work for the Dupin family and earns his living by copying music and other material.

1751   The first volume of the *Encyclopedia* is published.

1752   Rousseau composes *Le Devin du village (The Village Soothsayer)*, a comic opera. The opera is very well received, and Rousseau is informed that the king, Louis XV, would like to meet him and might even offer him a pension. But paralyzed by insecurity and fear, he declines.

1753   The success of *Le Devin du village* provides Rousseau with an income and with fame. He publishes "Letter on French Music" in which he praises Italian music and disparages French music.

1754   Rousseau writes his *Discourse on the Origins of Inequality*. He then returns to Geneva, converts back to Calvinism and reclaims the status of "Citizen of the free state of Geneva."

1755   Rousseau publishes his Second Discourse, *The Discourse on the Origins of Inequality,* which Voltaire attacks in a letter to Rousseau. Rousseau's article, *Discourse on Political Economy,* is published in the *Encyclopedia.* He returns to France. His moody temperament propels him to break up with most of his friends.

1756–1757   At the invitation of Madame d'Epinay, Rousseau moves to her estate, the Hermitage, north of Paris, where he delights in the beautiful surroundings. This is a very creative period for him, during which he works on his *Dictionary of Music.* In response to Voltaire's pessimistic "Poem about the Disaster in Lisbon" (an earthquake that killed thousands) Rousseau writes his *Letter to Voltaire on Providence* (1756), expressing his belief in benevolent Providence. He works on *Emile,* his reflections on an ideal education. Rousseau also begins writing *The Social Contract.* The other Encyclopedists attack him for his withdrawal from society.

1757   Rousseau falls in love with a countess, Madame d'Houdetot, the sister-in-law of Madame d'Epinay, though boasting of their chasteness. She becomes a model for the heroine of his epistolary novel, *Julie, or the New Héloïse.* Rousseau breaks off with Madame d'Epinay. He moves to the estate of the Maréchal of Luxembourg in Montmorency. He breaks ties with his friends Grimm and Diderot. He quarrels also with the *philosophe* and Encyclopedist d'Alembert.

1758–1762   This is a relatively calm period in Rousseau's life, during which he lives in Montmorency. In 1758 he publishes his "Letter to d'Alembert on the Theatre" ("Lettre sur les spectacles") in which he condemns the "immorality" of theater. The "Lettre" provokes a huge outcry. In 1760, Rousseau breaks off definitively with Voltaire, writing to him, "I hate you."

1759   Voltaire publishes *Candide, or Optimism,* a darkly pessimistic work, contradicting Rousseau's faith in a beneficent Providence.

1761   Rousseau publishes his "pre-Romantic" novel about sublimated passion, *Julie, or The New Héloïse.* The novel also depicts Rousseau's ideal society, a small, self-sufficient community.

1762	Rousseau publishes *The Social Contract* and *Emile: or, On Education*. He publishes his *Profession of Faith of a Savoyard Vicar,* in which he discusses Deism. This book, as well as *Emile,* disturb both the Parliament and the Church in France, an order for his arrest is issued, and he flees to Switzerland.
1762–1770	Rousseau travels from place to place, hoping to find asylum, still preoccupied with grievances against his friends. The city of Geneva refuses him asylum because of his political and religious ideas. In 1762 he moves to Môtiers near Neufchatel, territory of the King of Prussia. For a year and a half his life is relatively calm. The order for his arrest is almost rescinded when Voltaire intervenes against him.
1764	He publishes *Letters Written from the Mountain,* attacking Voltaire.
1765	Voltaire calls for Rousseau's death. Rousseau's house in Môtiers is stoned, and he flees. He spends a few happy weeks on the island of Saint-Pierre in the Bienne Lake. He goes to Strasbourg, then to Paris. He suffers from a variety of psychological ailments. Rousseau writes his *Project for a Constitution for Corsica.*
1766	Rousseau accepts the invitation of the English political philosopher David Hume to stay in England. Voltaire continues to denounce Rousseau in the English press. Rousseau breaks off with Hume. He moves to the estate of Richard Davenport in Derbyshire where he spends a year. He enjoys studying botany while completing the first part of his *Confessions.*
1767–1769	Rousseau returns to France; he wanders clandestinely from place to place, finally spending a year in the village of Monquin. He publishes his *Musical Dictionary;* he works on his *Confessions,* and he studies botany.
1770–1771	After eight years of wandering, Rousseau moves to Paris, where he lives in poverty. He finishes writing his groundbreaking *Confessions.* He composes his *Letters on Botany* and writes his *Considerations on Government in Poland.*
1772	Dissatisfied with his *Confessions* and preoccupied with justifying and explaining himself, he begins writing

Dialogues: Rousseau Judge of Jean-Jacques. He devotes himself to music and botany. Rousseau is saddened in 1774 by news of the death of Louis XV. The hatred of mankind, he explains, had been divided between Louis XV and himself; now he would have to bear the entire burden himself.

1776–1778   He works on his *Reveries of the Solitary Walker* (*Rêveries du promeneur solitaire*), a poignant, introspective work. In 1777 Rousseau tends the ill Thérèse. He makes a public plea for financial help.

1778   At the invitation of the Marquis de Girardin, Rousseau moves to Ermenonville, outside of Paris. He is shaken by news of the death of Voltaire. "My existence was bound up with his," he says. He dies on 2 July 1778, five days after his sixty-sixth birthday.

1794   Rousseau's ashes are moved to the Pantheon in Paris.

A Note on the Translations

The translation of *The Discourse on the Sciences and Arts* is a new translation by Susan Dunn. The translation of *The Discourse on the Origin and Foundations of Inequality Among Mankind* is Lester Crocker's reworking of an anonymous translation from 1761. The translation of *The Social Contract* is Susan Dunn's reworking of an 1895 translation by Henry J. Tozer.

The First Discourse: Discourse on the Sciences and Arts

A DISCOURSE

That won First Prize
at the Academy of Dijon.
In the Year 1750.

On the following question proposed by the Academy:
Has the revival of the Sciences and Arts
contributed to improving morality?

By a Citizen of Geneva

Barbarus hic ego sum qui non intelligor illis.
(People consider me a barbarian because they do not
understand me.) — Ovid.

Preface

Here is one of the greatest and grandest questions ever debated. This Discourse is not concerned with those metaphysical subtleties that have come to dominate all aspects of literature and from which the Announcements of Academic Competitions are not always exempt; rather it is concerned with those truths that pertain to human happiness.

I foresee that I shall not readily be forgiven for the position I have dared to take. Setting myself up against all that is most admired today, I expect no less than a universal outcry against me; nor is the approval of a few wise men enough to let me count on that of the public. But I have taken my stand, and I do not care about pleasing cultured or fashionable people. There will always be people enslaved by the opinions of their times, their country, their society. A man who today plays the freethinker and the philosopher would, for the same reason, have been only a fanatic during the time of the League.[1] No author, who wishes to live on beyond his own epoch, should write for such readers.

One more word, and I am done. Not expecting the honor conferred on me, I have, since submitting my Discourse, so altered and expanded it as to make it almost a new work; but today I felt bound to publish it just as it was when it received the prize. I have only added a few notes and left two easily recognizable additions, of which the Academy might not have approved. Equity, respect, and gratitude seemed to me to demand this acknowledgment.

Discourse

Decipimur specie recti.
We are deceived by the appearance of good.
—Horace.

"Has the revival of the sciences and the arts contributed to improving or corrupting morality?" This is the issue to be examined. Which side should I take in this question? The one, Gentlemen, that becomes a respectable man, who knows nothing and thinks himself none the worse for it.

I sense that it will be difficult to adapt what I have to say for this Tribunal. How can I presume to criticize the sciences before one of the most learned assemblies in Europe, to praise ignorance before a famous Academy and reconcile my contempt for study with the respect due to truly learned scholars? I was aware of these inconsistencies, but not discouraged by them. It is not science, I said to myself, that I am attacking; it is virtue that I am defending before virtuous men. Integrity is even more precious to good people than erudition is to scholars. What then do I have to fear? The enlightenment of the assembly that listens to me? That, I acknowledge, is to be feared, but in relation to the construction of the discourse, not to the views I hold. Equitable sovereigns have never hesitated to decide against themselves in doubtful cases; and indeed the most advantageous situation in which a just claim can be made is that of being defended before a fair and enlightened arbitrator, who is judge in his own case.

This reasoning, which reassures me, merges with another inducement that helped me make up my mind: that is, after championing the cause of truth, as I intuitively see it, whatever success I have, there is one reward that cannot fail me; I shall find it within my own heart.

PART ONE

It is a great and beautiful spectacle to see man emerge from nothingness through his own efforts, dissipating, by the light of his reason, the darkness in which nature had enveloped him; rising above himself, soaring intellectually to celestial heights, striding like the sun across the vastness of the universe, and, what is grander still and more difficult, retreating back into himself, there to study man and come to know his nature, his duties, and his destiny. All these marvels we have seen revived within the past few generations.

Europe had relapsed into the barbarism of the earliest ages. The inhabitants of this part of the world, which is at present so enlightened, were living, a few centuries ago, in a state worse than ignorance. A kind of scientific jargon, more contemptible than mere ignorance, had usurped the name of knowledge, setting up an almost invincible obstacle to its return. A revolution was needed to bring people back to common sense; it came at last from the place from which it was least expected. It was the stupid Moslem, the eternal scourge of Letters, who was responsible for their rebirth. The fall of the throne of Constantine[2] brought to Italy the debris of ancient Greece. With these precious spoils, France in turn was enriched. The sciences soon followed literature; the art of writing was joined by the art of thinking, an order that might seem strange, but is perhaps only too natural. People began to perceive the principal advantage of communication with the Muses, that of making people more sociable by inspiring them with the desire to please one another with works worthy of their mutual regard.

The mind has its needs, as does the body. The needs of the body constitute the foundation of society, those of the mind its ornamentation. While government and law provide for the security and well-being of people in their collective life, the sciences, letters, and arts — less despotic though perhaps more powerful — wrap garlands of flowers around the chains that weigh people down. They stifle the sense of freedom that people once had and for which they sensed that they were born, making them love their own servitude, and turning them into what is called a civilized people. Need erected thrones; the sciences and arts consolidated them. Let the Powers that rule the earth cherish all talents and protect those who practice them!*

*Princes always like to see among their subjects the proliferation of an appreciation for enjoyable arts and luxury that do not result in the exporting of wealth. For they very well know that, in addition to nourishing the pettiness of soul that lends itself to servitude,

Civilized peoples, cultivate your talents! Happy slaves, you are indebted to them for the delicate, exquisite tastes you are so proud of, that sweetness of disposition and urbanity of manners that make social relations so easy and pleasant — in short, the appearance of all the virtues without the possession of a single one.

Through this kind of civility, all the more captivating because so unassuming, Athens and Rome once distinguished themselves during the celebrated days of their splendor and magnificence: through the same kind of civility our own century and our nation will undoubtedly surpass all other epochs and peoples. The tone of philosophy without pedantry, manners that are natural yet courteous, as distant from Teutonic rusticity as from Italian pantomime: these are the fruits of the taste acquired through liberal studies and perfected through social relations.

How delightful it would be for those who live among us if our external appearance were always a true mirror of our hearts, if good manners were also virtue, if the maxims we spout were truly the rules of our conduct, if true philosophy were inseparable from the title of a philosopher! But so many good qualities seldom go together, and virtue rarely walks amidst such pomp and state. Richness of attire may herald a man of wealth, and elegance a man of taste; but the healthy, robust man is recognized by other signs. It is beneath the rustic clothes of the farmer, and not beneath the gilt of the courtier, that we should look for strength and vigor of body. External apparel is no less foreign to virtue than strength and vigor are to the soul. A good man is an athlete who likes to wrestle in the nude. He scorns all those vile trappings that inhibit his strength and that, for the most part, were invented only to conceal some deformity.

Before Art had molded our manners and taught our passions to speak an artificial language, our morals were rough-hewn but natural, and differences in behavior immediately announced differences in character. In truth, human nature was no better than now, but people found security in the ease with which they could see through one another, and this advantage, of which we no longer appreciate the value, saved them from many vices.

---

the artificial wants that a people imposes on itself only enslaves them more. Alexander, wishing to keep the Ichthyophagi in a state of dependence, compelled them to give up fishing and subsist on the same food as that of other peoples. The primitive people of America, who go naked and live off what they hunt, have never been conquered. Indeed, what kind of yoke could be imposed on people who are in need of nothing?

Today, as more subtle study and more refined taste have reduced the art of pleasing to a system, there prevails in our manners a loathsome and deceptive conformity: all minds seem to have been cast in the same mold. Incessantly politeness makes demands, decorum issues orders. Incessantly we obey rituals, never our own intuition. We no longer dare to appear as we really are, and under this perpetual restraint, people who form the herd known as society, finding themselves in these same circumstances, will all behave in exactly the same ways, unless more powerful motives prevent them from doing so. We never know therefore with whom we are dealing: in order to know one's friend, one must wait for some critical occasion, that is, wait until it is too late, for it is precisely on those occasions that knowledge of that friend would have been essential.

What a parade of ills accompany this uncertainty! No more sincere friendships, no more real regard for another, no more deep trust. Suspicions, resentments, fears, coldness, reserve, hatred, and betrayal habitually hide under that uniform and perfidious veil of politeness, under that lauded sophistication which we owe to the enlightenment of our century. Instead of profaning the name of the Master of the Universe by swearing, we will insult Him with blasphemies, though our scrupulous ears will take no offense. We might not brag about our own worth, but we will disparage that of others. We might not outrageously insult our enemy, but we will slander him with finesse. Our hatred of other nations may diminish, but our own patriotism will die along with it. Lamentable ignorance will be superseded by dangerous skepticism. Certain excesses will be condemned, certain vices abhorred, but others will be honored in the name of virtue, and people will be obliged either to have them or to pretend to have them. Whoever wishes to praise the sobriety of our wise men may do so, but as for me, I see nothing there but a refinement of intemperance as unworthy of my praise as their duplicitous simplicity.*

This is the kind of purity that our morals have acquired. This is how we have become worthy people. Let literature, the sciences, and the arts claim their fair share of this salutary work. I shall add but one thought: suppose that someone who lives in a faraway land should want to understand our European morals on the basis of the present state of the sciences in our society, on the basis of the perfection of the arts, the propriety of our public

---

*"I love," said Montaigne, "to debate and discuss, but only with very few people, and that for my own gratification. For to serve as a spectacle for the Great and show off one's wit and talents is, in my opinion, a trade very ill-becoming a man of honor." It is the trade of all our intellectuals, save one.

entertainments, the politeness of our manners, the affability of our conversation, our constant protestations of goodwill, and those tumultuous gatherings of people of all ages and ranks, who seem, from dawn to dusk, eager only to please one another; this foreigner, I maintain, would guess that our morals are exactly the opposite of what they are.

Where there is no effect, it is pointless to look for a cause: but here the effect is certain and the depravity real, and our souls have been corrupted to the extent that our sciences and our arts have advanced toward perfection. Will it be said that this is a misfortune peculiar to the present age? No, Gentlemen; the evils caused by our vain curiosity are as old as the world. The daily ebb and flow of the tides are not more regularly influenced by the moon that lights the nighttime sky than the fate of our morality and integrity by the advancement of the sciences and the arts. We have seen virtue gradually flee as their light dawned above the horizon, and the same phenomenon has been observed in all times and in all places.

Behold Egypt, that first school of the Universe, that fertile climate under an imperturbable sky, that famous land from which Sesostris once set out to conquer the world. Egypt became the mother of philosophy and the fine arts, and soon afterward she became the conquest of Cambyses[3] and then that of the Greeks, the Romans, the Arabs, and finally the Turks.

Behold Greece, once peopled by heroes, who twice vanquished Asia, once in Troy and once on their own soil. Nascent literature had not yet brought corruption into the hearts of its inhabitants; but progress in the arts, the dissipation of morals, and the Macedonian yoke[4] followed one upon the other. And Greece, always learned, always sensual, always a slave, no longer derived anything from its cycles other than a change of masters. All the eloquence of Demosthenes[5] could not breathe life back into a body depleted by luxury and the arts.

It is in the time of Ennius and Terence[6] that Rome, founded by a shepherd and made famous by farmers, begins to degenerate. But after the appearance of an Ovid, a Catullus, a Martial, and that gang of obscene authors, whose names alone make decency blush, Rome, once the Temple of Virtue, becomes the Theater of Crime, the shame of nations, and the plaything of barbarians. This capital of the world ultimately falls under the same yoke it had imposed on so many other nations, and the day of her fall was the eve of the day when one of her citizens was awarded the title of Arbiter of Good Taste.[7]

What shall I say about that Metropolis of the Eastern Empire, which, by its position, seemed destined to be the capital of the entire world, about that refuge for the sciences and arts at a time when they were banned from the rest of Europe, though perhaps more out of wisdom than barbarity? The most shameful debauchery and corruption, treason, blackhearted assassinations and poisonings, the most atrocious crimes all put together, this is what constitutes the fabric of the history of Constantinople. Here we have the mouth of the river from which the Enlightenment of our century has flowed, the Enlightenment in which we bask.

But why bother to seek in ancient times proof of a fact for which we have sufficient evidence before our very eyes? There is in Asia an immense land where rewards for learning lead to the highest offices of the State. If the sciences improved morality, if they taught men how to shed their blood for their country, if they inspired them with courage, then perhaps the Chinese would be wise, free, and invincible. But if there is no vice that does not reign over them, no crime with which they are not familiar, if neither the enlightenment of government officials nor the supposed wisdom of the law, nor the huge population of this vast Empire could not save them from the yoke of the illiterate and brutish Tartar, then what good were all their scholars? What benefit came from the honors bestowed upon them? Perhaps a population of slaves and felons?

Contrast these portraits with a picture of the morals of that small number of peoples that, safe from the contagion of vain knowledge, have by dint of their virtue created their own happiness, making themselves an example for other nations. Such were the first inhabitants of Persia — an unusual nation where people learned virtue just as we learn science; with ease they conquered Asia and earned the glory of having the history of their political institutions pass for a philosophical novel.[8] Such were the Scythians, about whom magnificent songs of praise have come down to us. Such were the Germans, whose simplicity, innocence, and virtue gave respite to a writer[9] weary of detailing the crimes and heinous deeds of an enlightened, wealthy, and lewd nation. Such indeed had been Rome in the days of its poverty and unenlightenment. And such even today is that rough-hewn nation celebrated for its courage, that not even adversity could vanquish and whose fidelity not even bad examples could corrupt.*

It is hardly because of stupidity that virtuous nations have preferred

---

*I dare not speak about those happy nations who did not even know the name of the vices we struggle to suppress, about the primitive people of America, whose simple and natural mode of government Montaigne ["Of Cannibals," in *Essays*] instinctively preferred not only to the laws of Plato, but even to the most idealistic visions of government that philosophy can conjure. He cites innumerable examples that are impressive for those who can appreciate them. But my word! he says, they don't even wear knickers!

other activities to those of the mind. They realized that in other lands idle men whiled away their time debating the ultimate good, vice and virtue, and that presumptuous logicians, extolling none other but themselves, contemptuously branded all other nations barbarians. But these virtuous nations evaluated their morals and learned to dismiss their ideas.*

How could I forget that, in the very heart of Greece, there arose a city as famous for the happy unenlightenment of its inhabitants as for the wisdom of its laws, that republic of demigods rather than of men, so superior did their virtues seem to those of mere humanity? O Sparta! you outshine forever a vain doctrine! While the fine arts ushered vice into Athens, while a tyrant was carefully collecting the works of the prince of poets,[10] you drove from your walls the arts and artists, the sciences and scholars!

The difference was clear in the outcome. Athens became the home of civility and good taste, the land of orators and philosophers. The elegance of her buildings equaled that of her language; wherever one looked one saw marble and canvas brought to life by the hands of the most skilled masters. It is Athens that gave us those astonishing works that will serve as models for every corrupt epoch. The picture of Lacedaemon is less dazzling. *There, the neighboring nations used to say, men are born virtuous, the very air they breathe seems to inspire them with virtue.* But nothing remains of them except the memory of their heroic deeds. But should we value such monuments less than the curious statues that Athens passed down to us?

Certain wise men, one must admit, were able to withstand the sweeping torrent and preserved their integrity as they dwelt with the Muses. But listen to the opinion expressed by the foremost and most unhappy among them,[11] concerning the scholars and artists of his day.

"I have considered the poets," he says, "and I view them as people who dupe themselves as much as others, who act like wise men and are taken for such, but who are not that at all.

"From poets," continues Socrates, "I turned to artists. No one knew less about the arts than I; no one was more convinced that artists possessed great secrets. Yet I realized that they were really no better off than the poets;

*I would truly like someone to tell me what the Athenians themselves thought about eloquence, when they were so very careful to banish declamation from that upright tribunal, against whose judgments even the Gods did not appeal. What did the Romans think of medicine when they banished it from their Republic? And when a shred of human feeling induced the Spanish to prevent their lawyers from entering America, what must they have thought of their own jurisprudence? Could one say that they hoped, by this deed, to make up for all suffering they had caused those unfortunate Indians?

indeed both artists and poets suffer from the same misapprehension. Because the most skillful among them perform well in their specialty, they take themselves for the wisest of men. Their presumption irremediably diminished their knowledge in my eyes. Indeed, putting myself in the place of the Oracle and asking myself who I would rather be, what I am or what they are, and asking myself what I would like to know, what they have learned or the knowledge that I know nothing, I was able to respond truthfully to myself and to God: I want to remain what I am.

"None of us — neither the sophists, poets, orators, artists, nor I — know what is truth, goodness, and beauty. But the difference between us is this: though these people know nothing, they all believe that they know something; whereas for my part, if I know nothing, I have no doubt about my ignorance. So that all this superiority of wisdom conferred on me by the Oracle contracts into my clear understanding that I am ignorant of what I do not know."

Here we have the wisest of men, in the opinion of the gods, the most learned of Athenians in the opinion of all of Greece, Socrates extolling ignorance! If he came back to life today, would he be persuaded by our learned men and artists to change his mind? No, Gentlemen, this fair-minded man would still hold our vain sciences in contempt. He would not help enlarge that pile of books that engulfs us from all sides; and the only rule he would bequeath, as he did before, to his disciples and to our children would be the example and the memory of his virtue. This is a noble education.

What Socrates had begun at Athens, Cato the Elder continued in Rome, inveighing against those artful and deceptive Greeks who corrupted the virtue and undermined the courage of his fellow citizens. But the sciences, arts, and dialectic reasoning prevailed once more: Rome overflowed with philosophers and orators, military discipline was neglected, agriculture was scorned, people embraced new cults and forgot their Fatherland. The sacred names of freedom, disinterestedness, and obedience to the law were displaced by those of Epicurus, Zeno, and Arcesilaus. *Since scholars have begun to appear among us,* their own philosophers used to say, *good people have been eclipsed.* Until then, the Romans had been happy to cultivate virtue; all was lost when they began to study it.

O Fabricius![12] What would your noble soul have thought if, unhappily for you, called back to life, you had seen the pompous visage of Rome, the city saved by your valor and on which your name bestowed more glory than all her conquests? "My Gods!" you would have said, "what has become of those thatched roofs and rustic hearths where moderation and virtue once dwelled? What fatal splendor has displaced Roman simplicity? What is this strange tongue? What are these effeminate manners? What is the meaning of all these statues, paintings, and buildings? Madmen, what have you done? Have you, the Masters of all Nations, become the slaves of the shallow men you conquered? Are these rhetoricians who govern you? Was it only to enrich architects, painters, sculptors, and actors that you shed your blood in Greece and Asia? Are the spoils of Carthage the prize of a flute player? Romans! lose no time! demolish those amphitheaters, smash those statues, burn those paintings, drive out those slaves who subjugate you and whose fatal arts corrupt you. Let other hands win fame with such vain talents; the only talent worthy of Rome is that of conquering the world and making virtue its ruler. When Cyneas took our Senate for an Assembly of Kings, he was blind to vain pomp and affected elegance. He was deaf to that superficial eloquence, the occupation and the delight of futile men. What then was the majesty that Cyneas beheld? O Citizens, the sight he saw could never be produced by all your wealth and culture; the most noble sight ever glimpsed beneath the heavens, the Assembly of two hundred virtuous men, worthy of ruling Rome and governing the earth."

But let us sail through time and space and see what has been happening in our own lands and beneath our very eyes. Or better still, let us cast aside the loathsome tableaus that offend our feelings, thus sparing ourselves the task of repeating the same things with different words. It was not in vain that I invoked the specter of Fabricius. Indeed, what words did I put in the mouth of that great man that I could not have put in the mouth of a Louis XII or a Henry IV? Among us, in truth, Socrates would not have drunk the hemlock, but he would have drunk from an even more bitter chalice the insults of mockery and scorn a hundred times worse than death.

Now we see how luxury, licentiousness, and slavery have always been the punishment for the presumptuous efforts man has made to escape from blissful ignorance in which eternal Wisdom had placed us. That opaque veil with which Wisdom cloaked her actions should have warned us that we were not destined for a vain quest for knowledge. Is there a single one of her lessons from which we have profited or which we have neglected with impunity? Let all nations once and for all realize that nature wanted to protect us from knowledge, just as a mother snatches a dangerous weapon from the hands of her child. Let them know that all the secrets she hides from us are so many ills from which she protects us and that the very difficulty they encounter in searching for knowledge is not the least of her kindnesses. Men are perverse; but they would be far worse if they had had the misfortune to be born learned.

How humiliating these reflections are for humanity! How mortified by them our pride must be! What! Could probity be the daughter of ignorance? Could knowledge and virtue be incompatible? Is virtue inconsistent with learning? What conclusions might not be drawn from such suppositions? But to reconcile these apparent contradictions, we need only examine in detail the vanity and vacuity of those pretentious titles that dazzle us and that we bestow so liberally on human learning. Let us, therefore, consider the sciences and the arts in themselves. Let us see just what comes out of their progress, and let us not hesitate to recognize the truth of those points where our own reasoning confirms historical inductions.

PART TWO

There was an ancient tradition that spread from Egypt to Greece that a God hostile to human tranquillity was the inventor of the sciences.* What must the Egyptians, in whose country the sciences were born, have thought of them? Indeed, they were able to behold the fountainhead from which they sprang. In fact, whether we leaf through the annals of the world or supplement uncertain chronicles with philosophical research, we will not find a wellspring of human knowledge that corresponds to our idealized vision. Astronomy was born from superstition; eloquence from ambition, hatred, flattery, and falsehood; geometry from avarice; physics from vain curiosity; all of them, even moral philosophy, stem from human pride. Thus the sciences and arts owe their birth to our vices; we would be less in doubt as to their benefits, if they owed their birth to our virtues.

The defect of their origin is all too clear in the objects of their pursuit. What would we do with the arts, without the luxury that nourishes them? Without human injustice, what use would we have of jurisprudence? What would become of History, if there were neither tyrants, wars, nor conspira-

---

*It is easy to understand the meaning in the Prometheus fable: it does not seem that the Greeks, who chained Prometheus to the Caucasus, were any better disposed to him than the Egyptians to their god Theutus. "The satyr, according to an ancient fable, wanted to kiss and embrace fire, the first time he saw it; but Prometheus cried out to him, Satyr, you will mourn the beard on your chin, for it burns when you touch it." This is the subject of the frontispiece. [Rousseau does not provide the rest of the quotation from Plutarch about Prometheus. Prometheus adds: "It burns when one touches it, but it gives light and warmth, and is an implement serving all crafts providing one knows how to use it well." See Havens, 209.]

tors? In short, who would want to spend a life in barren speculations, if each person, sensitive only to the duties of man and the needs of nature, had time only for his country, his friends, and the suffering of others? Were we created so that we would die staring into the well from which truth has fled? This thought alone should be sufficient to repel immediately any person who would seriously endeavor to find enlightenment in philosophy.

So many dangers surround us! so many false paths in scientific research! How many errors, a thousand times more dangerous than the truth is useful, must one overcome to arrive at the truth? The hurdles are clear, for human error is liable to an infinite number of combinations, whereas truth has only one manner of being. Besides, who seeks it sincerely? By what signs can even the most committed person be sure to recognize it? In the throng of diverse opinions, what criterion will we use to judge the truth correctly?* And what is the most problematic: if we are so lucky as to finally discover it, who among us will know how to use it wisely?

If our sciences are vain in the objects they pursue, they are even more dangerous in the effects they produce. Born in idleness, they nourish it in turn, and an irreparable waste of time is the first harm they inevitably inflict on society. In the political world as well as in the moral world, it is bad not to do good, and every useless citizen can be regarded as a pernicious man. Explain to me, then, you celebrated philosophers, who taught us what are the ratios in which bodies attract one another in a vacuum, what are, in the revolutions of the planets, the relations of spaces traversed at equal intervals; what curves have conjugate points, points of inflection, and cusps; how man sees everything in God; how the soul and body correspond like two clocks, without communicating; what stars may be inhabited; and which insects reproduce in extraordinary ways. Explain to me, then, I say, you who have given us so much sublime knowledge. If you had never taught us anything, would there be fewer of us, would we be less well governed, less fearsome, less flourishing or more perverse? Think again about the importance of your accomplishments; if the works of the most enlightened of our scholars and our best citizens procure for us so little of use, tell us what we should think of that crowd of obscure writers and idle men of letters who pointlessly devour the very substance of the State.

*The less we know, the more we think we know. Did the Peripatetics harbor any doubts? Did not Descartes construct the universe with cubes and vortices? And in Europe today is there a single lightweight physicist who does not purport to explain boldly the profound mystery of electricity, which will perhaps be forever the despair of true philosophers?

Did I say idle? How I wish they only were! Our morals would be healthier and society more peaceful. But these vain and futile declaimers go forth on all sides, armed with their lethal paradoxes, subverting the foundations of our faith, and annihilating virtue. They scornfully snicker at old-fashioned words like Patriotism and Religion, devoting their talents and philosophy to the destruction and defamation of all that people hold sacred. Not that they in truth despise virtue or our dogmas; they are the enemies of public opinion; to bring them back to church it might suffice to exile them to live among atheists. O passion for prestige, do you stop at nothing?

The misuse of time is a great evil. Even greater evils accompany literature and the arts. One is luxury, produced like them by indolence and men's vanity. Luxury rarely appears without the sciences and arts, and they never appear without it. I realize that our philosophy, always rich in bizarre maxims, maintains, contrary to the lessons of history, that luxury creates the splendor of States; but after denying the importance of luxury taxes, will Philosophy also deny that good morals are essential for the survival of Empires and that luxury is diametrically opposed to good morals? Let us admit that luxury is an accurate sign of wealth; let us even admit, if you like, that it serves to increase wealth. What conclusion should we draw from this paradox so worthy of our epoch, and what will become of virtue when no price is too high to pay for wealth? The political philosophers of the ancient world talked incessantly about morality and virtue; today they speak only about business and money. One will inform you that in a given country a man is worth the price he will sell for in Algiers; another, thinking along similar lines, will point to some countries where people are worth nothing and to others where they are worth less than nothing. They gauge the value of human beings in terms of livestock. According to them, a man is worth no more to the State than the value of his consumption. Thus one Sybarite would have been worth at least thirty Lacedaemonians. Guess, then, which one of the two republics, Sparta or Sybaris, was conquered by a handful of peasants and which one made Asia tremble.

The monarchy of Cyrus was conquered by thirty thousand men, led by a prince poorer than the lowest Persian Satrap, and the Scythians, the most destitute of all nations, were able to resist the most powerful monarchs of the universe. Two renowned republics competed for world empire; one was very rich, the other had nothing, and it was the latter that destroyed the former. The Roman Empire in its turn, after having engulfed all the wealth of the universe, fell prey to people who did not even know what wealth was. The Franks conquered the Gauls, and the Saxons England, their only treasures their bravery and their poverty. A bunch of poor mountain people, whose greed focused only on a few sheepskins, after breaking Austrian pride, crushed the opulent and mighty House of Burgundy, feared by all the potentates of Europe. Lastly, all the power and all the wisdom of the heir of Charles V, buttressed by all the treasures of the Indies, were decimated by a handful of herring fishermen. Let our political philosophers deign to suspend their calculations and reflect on these examples, and let them learn once and for all that with money we have everything, except morality and citizens.

What is really at stake in this question of luxury? To know which is more crucial for Empires, to be brilliant and fleeting or virtuous and enduring. I say brilliant, but with what kind of radiance? A taste for luxury and a taste for probity do not cohabit in the same souls. No, it is not possible that minds degraded by a multiplicity of trivial concerns could ever rise to any greatness, and even if they had the might, they would not have the courage.

Every artist loves applause. The praise of his contemporaries is the most precious part of his reward. What will he do to obtain praise, if he has the misfortune of being born in a nation and at a time when fashionable scholars let superficial youth set the tone, where people sacrifice their taste to the tyrants of their freedom,* where masterpieces of dramatic poetry and marvels of harmony are abandoned because one sex dares approve only what befits the pusillanimity of the other? What will he do, Gentlemen? He will lower his genius to the level of his times and will prefer to compose ordinary works that will be appreciated during his lifetime, instead of marvels that would be valued only long after his death. Tell us, exalted Voltaire, how many virile and strong works of beauty you gave up for our false delicacy, and how much of what is great and noble did that mentality of gallantry, which delights in what is shallow and petty, cost you?

Thus the dissolution of morality, the necessary consequence of luxury, results in turn in the corruption of taste. If by chance there can be found among extraordinarily talented men a single one who has strength of character and who refuses to bow to the mentality of his century and disgrace

---

*I am far from thinking that this ascendancy of women is an evil in itself. It is a gift nature gave them for the good of humankind. Better guided, it could produce as much good as today it does harm. We do not sufficiently realize what benefits society would gain from giving a better education to the half of the human race that rules the other. Men will always be what is pleasing to women. So if you wish them to be great and virtuous, teach women what nobility and virtue are. Meditations on this subject, which long ago attracted Plato, deserve to be expanded upon by a pen worthy of following in the wake of such a master and defending such a noble cause.

himself with puerile works, woe unto him! He will die in indigence and oblivion. I wish that this were only a prediction and not a fact confirmed by experience! Carle, Pierre,[13] the time has come when your brushes, destined to embellish the majesty of our temples with sublime and sacred images, will drop from your hands or else be prostituted to adorn the panels of a coach with lewd paintings. And you, inimitable Pigalle,[14] rival of Praxiteles and Phidias, you whose chisel the ancients would have employed to carve them gods worthy of idolatry, at least in our own eyes; Pigalle, even your hand must stoop to scraping the belly of a pasha or else remain idle.

We cannot reflect on morality without fondly looking back on that picture of simplicity of long ago. A lovely shore, adorned only by the hands of nature, toward which our eyes are constantly turned and from which we turn away only with regret. When innocent and virtuous people were happy to have the gods witness their deeds, they dwelt together with them in the same huts; but soon they became wicked and wearied of such inconvenient intruders, relegating them to magnificent Temples. But then they drove their deities out of the Temples and moved into them themselves; in any case, the Temples of the gods were no longer very different from the houses of the citizens. This was the zenith of depravity, and immorality never reached greater heights than when it was seen supported, as it were, at the entryways of the palaces of the mighty by marble columns, sculpted on Corinthian capitals.

As the comforts of life increase, as arts are brought to perfection and as luxury spreads, true courage flags, military virtues fade, and this too is the work of the sciences and all those arts that are practiced in the privacy of one's home. When the Goths sacked Greece, all the libraries were saved from burning only by an idea suggested by one of them, that it would be wise to leave for their enemies a few things standing so as to distract them from military training and keep them diverted with indolent and sedentary hobbies. Charles VIII found himself master of Tuscany and the kingdom of Naples, virtually without having drawn his sword, and all the members of his court attributed this stunning ease to the fact that the defeated princes and nobles of Italy took far greater enjoyment in pursuing the subtleties of knowledge than in practicing the martial arts. Thus, says the sensible man who relates these two points, a multiplicity of examples teaches us that in military matters and in everything related to them, the pursuit of science, instead of strengthening and invigorating virile courage, tends to undermine and feminize it.

The Romans admitted that military virtue died in their land when they began to appreciate paintings, engravings, jeweled and enameled objects and to cultivate the fine arts. And as if that nation were destined to serve unceasingly as an example for others, the rise of the Medicis and the revival of Letters once more destroyed, perhaps for ever, the military reputation that Italy seemed to have recovered a few centuries earlier.

The ancient republics of Greece, with that wisdom that radiated from most of their institutions, forbade their citizens to pursue all those tranquil and sedentary occupations, which while enervating and corrupting the body soon also undermine the vigor of the soul. How can men cope with hunger, thirst, fatigue, danger, and death, if they are overwhelmed by the smallest need and discouraged by the slightest difficulty? With how much courage will soldiers tolerate overwork when they are entirely unaccustomed to it? With how much enthusiasm will they go on forced marches under officers who do not even have the strength to journey on horseback? Will someone now insist on defending the renowned merit of these scientifically trained modern warriors? We hear much praise of their valor during a battle that lasts but a day, but we do not hear about how they bear overwork, how they stand the rigor of the seasons and the inclemency of the weather. Nothing but a little sun or snow or the absence of a few superfluities is enough to dissolve and destroy one of our best armies in a few days. Intrepid warriors! Listen for once to the truth you so seldom hear. You are good soldiers, I know. You would have triumphed along with Hannibal at Cannae and at Trasimene: with you Caesar would have crossed the Rubicon and enslaved his country; but it is not with you that the former would have crossed the Alps and not with you that the latter would have conquered your ancestors.

Fighting does not always determine the successful outcome of a war; as far as Generals are concerned, there is an art that is superior to that of winning battles. A man who runs bravely into the line of fire might nevertheless be a very poor officer. Even in the common soldier, a little more strength and vigor might be more necessary than a lot of bravery, which is no protection from death. And what does it matter to the State whether its troops perish by sickness or frozen winter or the enemy's sword?

If studying the sciences is harmful to military qualities, it is even more harmful to moral qualities. From early childhood an absurd system of education enhances our mind and corrupts our judgment. I see everywhere immense institutions, where at great cost our youth are educated, learning everything except their duties. Your children will not know their own language, but they will speak others that are useful nowhere; they will be able to write poetry that they can barely understand; unable to tell truth from error, they will know the art of making both of them unrecognizable to others with specious arguments; but the meaning of the words magnanimity, equity, temperance, humanity, and courage they will not know. The dear name of the Fatherland will never ring in their ears, and if they are taught about God, they will learn fear instead of awe.* I would have preferred, a wise man said,[15] that my pupil had spent his time on the tennis court instead; at least then he would have a healthy body. I know that children must be kept occupied, and that idleness is for them the danger most to be feared. What, then, should they learn? A fine question! Let them learn what they ought to do to behave as men,† not what they ought to forget.

Our gardens are decorated with statues and our galleries with paintings. What would you imagine these masterpieces of art, exhibited for public

---

Pensées philosophiques, Diderot.

†This was the kind of education the Spartans received, according to the greatest of their kings. It is something worthy of great consideration, says Montaigne, that the excellent rules of Lycurgus — in truth monstrously perfect and yet so solicitous of the raising of children, as if that were their principal purview — in the very home of the Muses make little mention of scholarly learning: as if these noble youths, disdaining every other yoke, required, instead of teachers of the sciences, only instructors in valor, prudence, and justice.

Let us see now how the same author speaks about the ancient Persians. Plato, he says, relates that the heir to the throne was brought up in the following way: At his birth he was given, not to women, but to eunuchs who, because of their virtue, had great standing with the king. The eunuchs were responsible for giving him a beautiful and healthy physique and for teaching him, at the age of seven, to ride and to hunt. When he reached fourteen, he was placed in the hands of four men, the wisest, the most just, the most moderate, and the most courageous persons in the kingdom. The first taught him religion, the second taught him to be always truthful, the third to master his own cupidity, the fourth to have no fear. All of them, let me add, taught him to be good; none taught him to be learned.

Astyages, in Xenophon, asks Cyrus to give him an account of his last lesson. It was this, he said: In our school an older boy with a small tunic gave it to one of his schoolmates who was small in size, snatching that boy's tunic for himself. Having been asked by our master to settle their feud, I decided that things should be left as they were at that point and that both seemed better off. But the master scolded me, for I had bothered to take into account appropriateness, when instead I should have taken into account only justice, which holds that there should be no interference with one's property. And he says that he was punished for it, just as we are punished in our villages when we forget the first aorist tense of τύπτω. My schoolmaster would have to give me quite a speech, *in genere demonstrativo,* to convince me that his school is as good as this one.

admiration, represent? The defenders of our nation? or even greater men who enriched it with their virtue? No. There are images of every folly of the heart and mind, carefully extracted from ancient mythology and offered early on to the curiosity of our children — without a doubt so that they may have before their eyes models for bad deeds, even before they can read.

What else could produce these abuses if not the deplorable inequality introduced among us by the prestige accorded to talent and the abasement of virtue? This indeed is the most obvious result of all our studying and the most dangerous of all its consequences. We no longer ask if a man has integrity but rather if he has talent; we do not ask if a book is useful but merely if it is well written. Rewards are showered on clever minds, but virtue receives no honors. A thousand prizes are offered for fine essays, none for fine deeds. But can someone tell me if the glory of having written the best of the discourses crowned by the Academy is comparable to the merit of having established the prize?

A wise man does not run after success, but he is not indifferent to glory, and when he sees it so poorly distributed, his virtue, which a little emulation might have energized and thus made beneficial to society, languishes and dies away in destitution and obscurity. This is what ultimately happens when pleasing talents eclipse useful ones, something that has been only too well confirmed since the revival of the sciences and arts. We have physicists, geometers, chemists, astronomers, poets, musicians, painters; we no longer have citizens; or if a few remain, scattered over our abandoned countryside, they are left to perish there, indigent and shunned. This is the condition to which those who give bread to us and milk to our children have been reduced, and this is the respect they wrest from us.

Still I must confess that the harm is not as great as it might have become. Eternal Providence, by placing curative herbs alongside of noxious plants and by making maleficent animals contain the antidote to their lesions, has taught the Sovereigns of the earth, who are its ministers, to imitate its wisdom. By following this example, that great Monarch,[16] on whose glory every age will bestow new radiance, drew from the very bosom of the arts and sciences, that source of a thousand moral lapses, those renowned societies which are responsible for both the dangerous trust of human knowledge and the sacred trust of morals — and responsible as well for maintaining the purity of those trusts and for demanding the purity of the members they admit.

These wise institutions, solidified by his august successor and imitated by all the kings of Europe, will at least serve as a brake on intellectuals, men of letters, who, all aspiring to the honor of being admitted into these Academies, will keep watch over themselves and endeavor to make themselves worthy of such honor by useful works and irreproachable morals. Those Academies, which, in their competitions for prizes bestowed on literary merit, will propose subjects aimed at reviving the love of virtue in citizens' hearts, will show that such love reigns among them and will give to all nations that rare, sweet pleasure of seeing learned societies devote themselves to showering the human race not only with pleasurable enlightenment but also with salutary edification.

I am not interested in hearing an objection that only confirms my argument. So many precautions show all too well the necessity for taking them, and people do not seek remedies for ills that do not exist. Why should these, by their very insufficiency, share the traits of ordinary remedies? The numerous establishments created for the benefit of scholars are only too able to deceive them concerning the objects of the sciences and to turn minds toward their cultivation. It would seem, from the kinds of precautions people take, that we have a surplus of farmers and fear a shortage of philosophers. I do not wish to attempt a comparison between agriculture and philosophy, which people would reject. I shall only ask: What is philosophy? What do the writings of the most famous philosophers contain? What are the lessons of these friends of wisdom? To listen to them, would one not take them for a gang of charlatans each calling out from a different corner on a public square: Come to me, I alone do not deceive? One claims that there are no bodies and that all is mere reflection. Another, that there is no other substance than matter, and no other God than the world. One asserts that neither virtues nor vices exist and that goodness and moral evil are illusions. Another that men are wolves and can devour one another in good conscience. O great philosophers! Why not keep these profitable lessons for your own friends and children? You would soon reap your rewards, and we would not need to fear finding among our own friends and children your disciples.

These indeed are the marvelous men who were showered with the esteem of their contemporaries during their lifetimes and for whom immortality was reserved after their deaths! These are the wise maxims we have received from them, and which we will pass on, from generation to generation, to our descendants. Did paganism, though susceptible to all the derangements of human reason, leave posterity anything comparable to the shameful monuments prepared for posterity by Printing, during the reign of the gospel? The impious writings of a Leucippus and a Diagoras died with them.[17] The art of immortalizing the extravagances of the human mind had not yet been invented. But thanks to the characters of typography* and the use we make of them, the pernicious reveries of a Hobbes and a Spinoza will endure forever. Go, famous writings, of which the ignorance and na-iveté of our forefathers would have been incapable, go along to our descendants with those even more dangerous works that reek of the moral corruption of our century, and together convey to the centuries to come a faithful history of the progress and benefits of our sciences and our arts. If they read what you have to say, you will permit them no doubt as to the question we debate today. And unless they are even more irrational than we, they will raise their hands to Heaven and say, with bitter hearts, "Almighty God, you who hold all souls in your hands, deliver us from the enlightenment and deadly arts of our forefathers, give us back ignorance, innocence and poverty, the only treasures that can make us happy and that are precious in your sight."

But if the advancement of the sciences and the arts has contributed nothing to our true happiness, if it has corrupted morality, and if the corruption of morality has adulterated purity of taste, what shall we think of that throng of facile authors who removed from the entrance to the Temple of the Muses the obstacles that nature had placed there as a test of strength for those who might be tempted to seek knowledge? What shall we think of those collators of works who mindlessly battered down the portal of the sciences, letting into their sanctuary rabble unworthy of approaching it? How much better it would have been if all those who could not go far in a career in letters had been turned away at the entrance and steered toward arts useful to society. A person who will never be more than a bad poet or a

---

*If we consider the horrible disorders that printing has already produced in Europe, and if we judge the future in light of the progress this evil makes every day, we can easily predict that sovereigns will not delay in making as much effort to banish this awful art from their states as they made to establish it. The Sultan Achmet, yielding to the insistent demands of certain supposed people of taste, had agreed to establish a printing press in Constantinople. But the press had barely begun to function when people felt obliged to destroy it and throw its machinery into a well. It is said that Caliph Omar, when asked what should be done with the library in Alexandria, answered in the following words: If the books in this library contain anything opposed to the Koran, they are bad and they must be burned. If they contain only the doctrine of the Koran, burn them anyway: they are superfluous. Our scholars have cited this reasoning as the height of absurdity. Imagine, however, Gregory the Great instead of Omar and the Bible instead of the Koran, the Library would still have been burned, and this might perhaps be the most noble deed in the life of that illustrious Pontiff.

third-rate geometer might have become an excellent cloth maker. Those who were destined by nature to become her disciples hardly needed teachers. A Bacon, a Descartes, and a Newton, those tutors of humanity, had none themselves, and, moreover, what guides could have led them as far as their vast genius took them? Ordinary teachers would only have shrunk their intelligence by squeezing it into the narrow confines of their own. The first obstacles they encountered taught them to how to apply themselves and how to work at leaping over the vast space they had mapped out. If a few men should be permitted to devote themselves to the study of the sciences and the arts, it should be only those who feel strong enough to walk alone in their footsteps and to outdistance them. It is for these few to erect monuments to the glory of the human mind. But if we want nothing to be beyond their genius, nothing must be beyond their hopes. That is the only encouragement they need. Little by little, the soul assumes the size of the subjects that preoccupy it, and thus it is great events that make great men. The Prince of Eloquence was Consul of Rome, and perhaps the greatest of philosophers Lord Chancellor of England.[18] Can it be believed that if one had been a professor at some university and the other a modest fellow in some Academy, can it be believed, I say, that their works would not have reflected their conditions? May kings, therefore, never disdain welcoming into their councils people who are most able to give them good advice; may they renounce that old prejudice, invented by the pride of the great, that the art of governing nations is more difficult than that of enlightening them, as if it was easier to engage people to do good voluntarily than to compel them to do so by force. May learned people of the first rank find honorable asylum in their courts; may they receive there the only recompense worthy of them, that of contributing by their influence to the happiness of the nations that they will have taught to be wise. Only then will we see what virtue, science, and authority can do when energized by noble emulation and working together for the felicity of humanity. But as long as power remains alone on one side and enlightenment and wisdom alone on the other, the learned will rarely focus on great things, Princes will even more rarely perform great ones, and nations will continue to be wretched, corrupt, and unhappy.

As for us, ordinary people on whom Heaven bestowed no great talents nor destined for so much glory, let us remain in our obscurity. Let us not run after a reputation that would only elude us and which, in the present state of things, would never pay us back what it had cost us, even if we possessed all the qualifications to obtain it. What good is it to seek our happiness in the opinions of others if we can find it within ourselves? Let us leave to others the responsibility for instructing nations in their duties and confine ourselves to fulfilling our own. We have no need of other knowledge.

O virtue, sublime science of simple souls! Are so much effort and so much preparation really necessary to know you? Are your principles not engraved in all our hearts? Does it not suffice to learn your laws, to meditate and listen to the voice of our conscience in the silence of our passions? That is the true philosophy; let us be content with that; and without envying the glory of those famous men who find immortality in the Republic of Letters, let us try to put between them and us that glorious distinction observed long ago between two great peoples,[19] that one knew how to speak well, and the other knew how to behave.

NOTES

Note to readers: Footnotes in the First Discourse *are Rousseau's own notes that appeared in the original version.*

1. The "Holy League" refers to French Catholics who tried to outlaw Protestantism in the sixteenth century.

2. Constantinople was captured by the Crusaders in 1203 and was conquered by Turkey in 1453. (See Rousseau, *Discours sur les sciences et les arts,* ed. George R. Havens [New York: Modern Language Association of America, 1946], 180.)

3. Cambyses II, King of Persia, conquered Egypt in 525 B.C. (Havens, 190).

4. King Philip of Macedonia conquered the principal Greek city-states in 338 B.C. (Havens, 191).

5. Demosthenes, the great Athenian orator, opposed Macedonian power in Greece.

6. Ennius, an early Latin poet (239 B.C. to 170 B.C.). Terence, a Latin author of comedies (194 B.C. to 159 B.C.).

7. Petronius.

8. Xenophon's *Cyropaedia* (Havens, 196).

9. Tacitus (c. A.D. 55 to c. A.D. 117), see his *De moribus Germanorum* (Havens, 197).

10. Pisistratus, tyrant in Athens (554 B.C.–527 B.C.) was said to have collected the writings of Homer (Havens, 200–201).

11. Plato, Rousseau's free translation of *Apologia for Socrates.*

12. Fabricius, mentioned in Seneca and Plutarch, is the image of the great virtuous man.

13. Charles-André ("Carle") Van Loo (1705–1765) and Jean-Baptiste-Marie Pierre (1713–1789) were celebrated artists. (See Havens, 226–227).

14. Jean-Baptiste Pigalle (1714–1785), French sculptor. (Havens, 228)

15. Montaigne.

16. Louis XIV founded five such honorific "academies."

17. Leucippus, the teacher of Democritus. Diagoras, Democritus's disciple.

18. Cicero and Francis Bacon.

19. Athens and Sparta.

The Second Discourse:
Discourse
on the
Origin and Foundations
of
Inequality Among Mankind

*Non in depravatis, sed in his quae bene secundum
naturam se habent, considerandum est quid sit naturale.* *
ARISTOTLE, *Politics, 1, 2.*

* "We should consider what is natural not in things which are depraved, but in those
which are rightly ordered according to nature."

Notice Regarding the Notes

I have appended a few notes to this work, following my indolent custom of working by fits and starts. These notes sometimes digress too far from the subject to be read with the text. Therefore I have placed them at the end of the Discourse, *in which I have tried my best to follow a straight path. Those who have the courage to continue may enjoy beating the bushes a second time and try to go through the notes. As to the others, it is no great matter if they do not read them at all.*

J.-J. Rousseau

Dedication
to the
Republic of Geneva

Convinced that it belongs only to a virtuous citizen to present his country those acknowledgments it may become her to receive, I have been for thirty years past, endeavoring to render myself worthy to offer you some public homage. In the meantime, this fortunate occasion replacing in some degree the insufficiency of my efforts, I have presumed rather to follow the dictates of zeal, than to wait till I should be authorized by merit. Having had the good fortune to be born a subject of Geneva, how could I reflect on the natural equality of mankind, and that inequality which they have introduced, without admiring the profound wisdom by which both the one and the other are happily combined in this State, and contribute, in a manner the most conformable to the law of nature, and the most favorable to community, to the security of public order and the happiness of individuals? In my researches after the best and most sensible maxims, which might be laid down for the constitution of government, I was surprised to find them all united in yours; so that had I not been a fellow-citizen, I should have thought it indispensable in me to present such a picture of human society to that people, who of all others, seem to be possessed of its greatest advantages, and to have best guarded against its abuses.

If I had had to choose the place of my birth, I should have preferred a community proportioned in its extent to the limits of the human faculties; that is to the possibility of being well governed: in which every person being capable of his employment, no one should be obliged to commit to others the trust he ought to discharge himself: a State in which its individuals might be so well known to each other, that neither the secret machinations of vice, nor the modesty of virtue should be able to escape the notice and judgment of the public; and in which the agreeable custom of seeing and knowing each other, should occasion the love of their country to be rather an affection for its inhabitants than for its soil.

I should have chosen for my birthplace a country in which the interest of the sovereign could not be separated from that of the subject; to the end that all the motions of the machine of government might ever tend to the general happiness. And as this could not be the case, unless where the sovereignty is lodged in the people, it follows that I should have preferred a prudently tempered democracy.

I should have been desirous to live and die free: that is, so far subject to the laws that neither I, nor any other body else, should have it in our power to cast off their honorable yoke: that agreeable and salutary yoke to which the haughtiest necks bend with the greater docility, as they are formed to bear no other.

I should have desired, therefore, that no person within the State should be able to say he was above the laws; nor that any person without, should be able to dictate such as the State should be obliged to obey. For, whatever the constitution of a government, if there be a single member of it who is not subject to the laws, all the rest are necessarily at his discretion. And if there be a national chief within, and a foreign chief without, however they may divide their authority, it is impossible that both should be duly obeyed and the State well governed.

I should not have chosen to live in a republic of recent institution, however excellent its laws, for fear the government being otherwise framed than circumstances might require, it might either disagree with the new subjects, or the subjects disagree with the new government; in which case the State might be shaken to pieces and destroyed almost as soon as founded.

For it is with liberty as it is with solid and succulent foods, or with rich wines, proper to nourish and fortify robust constitutions accustomed to them, but pernicious, destructive and intoxicating to weak and delicate temperaments, to which they are not adapted. A people once accustomed to masters are not able to live without them. If they attempt at any time to shake off their yoke, they lose still more freedom; for, by mistaking licentiousness for liberty, to which it is diametrically opposed, they generally become greater slaves to some impostor, who loads them with fresh chains. The Romans themselves, an example for every succeeding free people, were incapable of governing themselves on their expulsion of the Tarquins. Debased by slavery, and the ignominious tasks imposed on them, they were at first no better than a stupid mob, which it was requisite to manage and govern with the greatest wisdom; so that, being accustomed by degrees to breathe the salutary air of liberty, their minds which had been enervated or rather brutalized under the burden of slavery, might gradually acquire that severity of manners and spirit of fortitude which rendered them at length the most respectable nation upon earth.

I should have searched out for my country, therefore, some peaceful and happy republic, whose antiquity lost itself, as it were, in the obscurity of time: one that had experienced only such salutary shocks as served to display and confirm the courage and patriotism of its subjects; and whose citizens, long accustomed to a prudent independence, were not only free, but worthy of their freedom.

I should have made choice of a country, diverted, by a fortunate impotence, from the brutal love of conquest; and secured, by a still more fortunate situation, from becoming itself the conquest of other states: a free city situated between several nations, none of which should find it their interest to attack it, yet all think themselves interested in preventing its being attacked by others: a republic, in short, which should present nothing to tempt the ambition of its neighbors; but might reasonably depend on their assitance in case of need. It would follow that a republican State so happily situated as I have supposed, could have nothing to fear but from itself; and that, if its members accustomed themselves to the exercise of arms, it must be to keep alive that military ardor and courage, which is so suitable to free men, and tends to keep up their taste for liberty, rather than through the necessity of providing for their own defense.

I should have sought a country, in which the legislative power should be vested in all its citizens: for who can better judge than themselves of the propriety of the terms, on which they mutually agree to live together in the same community? Not that I should have approved of plebiscites, like those among the Romans, in which the leaders of the State, and those most interested in its preservation, were excluded from those deliberations on which its security frequently depended; and in which, by the most absurd inconsistency, the magistrates were deprived of privileges enjoyed by the lowest citizens.

On the contrary, I should have desired that, in order to prevent self-interested and ill-designed projects, with any of those dangerous innovations which at length ruined the Athenians, no person should be at liberty to propose new laws at pleasure: but that this should be the exclusive privilege of the magistrates; and that even these should use it with so much caution, that the people on their part should be so reserved in giving their consent to such laws; and that the promulgation of theirs should be attended with so much solemnity, that before the constitution could be affected by them, there might be time enough given for all to be convinced, that it is the great antiquity of the laws which principally contributes to render them sacred and venerable, that the people soon learn to despise those which they see daily altered, and that States, by accustoming themselves to neglect their ancient customs under pretense of improvement, frequently introduce greater evils than those they endeavor to remove.

I should have particularly avoided a republic, as one that must of course be ill-governed, in which the people, imagining themselves capable of subsisting without magistrates, or at least without investing them with any-thing more than a precarious authority, should imprudently reserve to them-selves the administration of civil affairs and the execution of their own laws. Such must have been the rude constitution of the primitive govern-ments, directly emerging from the state of nature; and this was another of the vices that contributed to the dissolution of the republic of Athens.

But I should have chosen a republic, the individuals of which, contented with the privileges of giving sanction to their laws, and of deciding in a body, according to the recommendations of the leaders, the most important public affairs, should have established respectable tribunals; carefully dis-tinguished their several departments; and electing annually some of their fellow-citizens, of the greatest capacity and integrity, to administer justice and govern the State; a community, in short, in which the virtue of the magistrates thus bearing testimony to the wisdom of the people, they would mutually honor each other. So that if ever any fatal misunderstandings should arise to disturb the public peace, even these intervals of confusion and error should bear the marks of moderation, reciprocal esteem, and of a mutual respect for the laws; certain signs and pledges of a reconciliation as lasting as sincere. Such are the advantages, most honorable, magnificent and sovereign Lords, which I should have sought in the country I had chosen.

And if providence had added to all these, a delightful situation, a temper-ate clime, a fertile soil, and the most charming views that present them-selves under heaven, I should desire only, to complete my felicity, the peaceful enjoyment of all these blessings, in the bosom of this happy coun-try; living in agreeable society with my fellow-citizens, and exercising towards them from their own example, the duties of friendship, humanity, and every other virtue, that I might leave behind me the honorable memory of a worthy man, and an incorruptible and virtuous patriot.

But, if less fortunate or too late grown wise, I saw myself reduced to end an infirm and languishing life in other climates, vainly regretting that peaceful repose which I forfeited in the imprudence of my youth, I would at least have entertained the same sentiments within myself, though denied the opportunity of avowing and indulging them in my native country. Af-fected with a tender and disinterested love for my distant fellow-citizens, I should have addressed them from my heart, in about the following terms.

"My dear countrymen, or rather my brethren, since the ties of blood unite most of us, as well as the laws, it gives me pleasure that I cannot think of you, without thinking, at the same time, of all the blessings you enjoy, the value of which none of you, perhaps, are so aware as I to whom they are lost. The more I reflect on your situation, both civil and political, the less can I conceive that the present state of human nature will admit of a better. In all other governments, even when it is a question of securing the greatest welfare of the State, they are always confined to ideal projects, or at least to bare possibilities. But as for you, your happiness is complete. You have nothing to do but enjoy it; you require nothing more to be made perfectly happy, than to know how to be satisfied with being so. Your sovereignty, acquired or recovered by the sword, and maintained for two centuries past by your valor and wisdom, is at length fully and universally acknowledged. Your boundaries are fixed, your rights confirmed and your repose secured by honorable treaties. Your constitution is excellent, dictated by the profoundest wisdom, and guaranteed by friendly and respectable powers. Your State enjoys perfect tranquillity; you have nothing to fear either from wars or conquerors: you have no other master than the wise laws you have yourselves made; and which are administered by upright magistrates of your own choosing. You are neither so wealthy as to be enervated by softness, and so to lose, in the pursuit of frivolous pleasures, a taste for real happiness and solid virtue; nor yet are you so poor as to require more assistance from strangers than your own industry is sufficient to procure you. In the meantime that precious liberty, which is maintained in great States only by exorbitant taxation, costs you hardly anything for its preservation.

"May a republic, so wisely and happily constituted, last forever, as well for an example to other nations, as for the felicity of its own subjects! This is the only wish you have left to make; the only subject of your solicitude. It depends, for the future, on yourselves alone, not to make you happy, your ancestors have saved you that trouble, but to render that happiness lasting, by your prudence in its enjoyment. It is on your constant unanimity, your obedience to the laws, and your respect for the magistrates, that your preservation depends. If there remain among you the smallest seeds of enmity or distrust, hasten to root them up, as an accursed leaven from which sooner or later will result your misfortunes and the destruction of the State. I conjure you all to examine the bottom of your hearts, and to hearken to the secret voice of your own consciences. Is there any among you who can find, throughout the universe, a more upright, more enlightened and more respectable body than that of your own magistracy? Do not all its members set you an example of moderation, of simplicity of manners, of respect for the laws, and of the most sincere reconciliation? Place, therefore, without reservations that salutary confidence in such wise leaders, which reason ever owes to virtue. Consider they are the objects of your own choice; that they justify that choice; and that the honors, due to those whom you have exalted to dignity, are necessarily reflected back on yourselves. Is there any among you so ignorant, as not to know that, when the laws lose their force, and the magistrates their authority, neither the persons nor properties of individuals are any longer secure? Why, therefore, should you hesitate to do that cheerfully and confidently, which your true interest, your duty and even common prudence will ever require?

"Let not a culpable and fatal indifference to the support of the constitution, ever induce you to neglect, in case of need, the prudent advice of the most enlightened and zealous of your fellow-citizens: but let equity, moderation and firmness of resolution continue to regulate all your proceedings; exhibiting you to the whole universe as an example of a valiant and modest people, equally jealous of their honor and their liberty. Beware particularly, this is the last advice I shall give you, of sinister interpretations and calumniating reports, the secret motives of which are often more dangerous than the actions at which they are leveled. The whole house will be awake and take the first alarm, given by a trusty and watchful mastiff, who barks only at the approach of thieves; but we ever abominate the impertinent yelping of those noisy curs, who are perpetually disturbing the public repose, and whose continual and ill-timed warnings prevent our attending to them when they may be needed."

And you, most honorable and magnificent Lords, you, the worthy and respectable magistrates of a free people, permit me to offer you in particular my duty and homage. If there be in the world a station capable of conferring honor on the persons who fill it, it is undoubtedly that which virtue and talents combine to bestow; that of which you have rendered yourselves worthy, and to which you have been promoted by your fellow-citizens. Their worth adds a new luster to yours; since men who are capable of governing others have chosen you to govern them, I cannot help esteeming you as superior to all other magistrates, as a free people, and particularly that over which you have the honor to preside, is by its wisdom and knowledge superior to the populace of other States.

May I be permitted to cite an example of which ought to have survived a better remnant; an example which will be ever near and dear to my heart. I cannot recall to mind, without the most agreeable emotions, the person and manners of that virtuous citizen, to whom I owe my being, and by whom I was instructed, in my infancy, in the respect which is due to you. I see him still, subsisting on his manual labor, and improving his mind by the study of the sublimest truths. I see, lying before him, the works of Tacitus, Plutarch, and Grotius, intermixed with the tools of his trade. At his side stands his darling son, receiving, alas with too little profit, the tender instructions of the best of fathers. But, though the follies of a wild youth caused me a while to forget his prudent lessons, I have at length the happiness to experience that, whatever propensity one may have to vice, it is not easy for an education, thus affectionately bestowed, to be ever entirely thrown away.

Such, my most honorable and magnificent lords, are the citizens, and even the common inhabitants of the country under your government; such are those intelligent and sensible men, of which, under the name of mechanics and tradespeople, it is usual, in other nations to entertain a false and contemptible idea. My father, I own it with pleasure, was not a distinguished man among his fellow citizens. He was only such as they are all: and yet, such as he was, there is no country in which his acquaintance would not have been coveted, and cultivated even with advantage by men of the first distinction. It would not become me, nor is it, thank heaven, at all necessary for me to remind you of the regard which such men have a right to expect of their magistrates, to whom they are equal both by birth and education, and inferior only by that preference which they voluntarily pay to your merit, and in so doing lay claim on their part to some sort of gratitude.

It is with a lively satisfaction I learn with how much gentleness and condescendence you temper that gravity which becomes the ministers of the law; and that you so well repay them, by your esteem and attentions, that respect and obedience which they justly pay to you. This conduct is not only just but prudent, as it wisely tends to obliterate many unhappy events, which ought to be buried in eternal oblivion;* it is also by so much the more prudential, as this generous and equitable people find a pleasure in their duty; as they are naturally inclined to doing you honor, as those who are the most zealous to maintain their own rights and privileges are at the same time the best disposed to respect yours.

It ought not to be thought surprising that the leaders of a civil society should have its welfare and glory at heart: but it is uncommonly fortunate for them, when those persons who look upon themselves as the magistrates, or rather the masters of a more holy and sublime country, demonstrate their affection for the earthly spot which maintains them. I am happy in having it

---

* Rousseau is referring to uprisings by a large part of the population which was oppressed by the ruling oligarchy. The description of the government of Geneva is largely false, and an example of Rousseau's frequent tactics of duplicity. He is trying to win the favor of the Genevan authorities. — translator

in my power to make so singular an exception in favor of my own country; and to rank, in the number of its best citizens, those zealous depositaries of the sacred articles of our established faith; those venerable pastors whose powerful and captivating eloquence is so much the better calculated to enforce the maxims of the gospel, as they are themselves the first to put them in practice.

The whole world is informed of the great success with which the oratory of the pulpit is cultivated at Geneva; but, being too much used to hear divines preach one thing, and see them practice another, few people have an opportunity to know how far the true spirit of Christianity, holiness of manners, severity with regard to themselves and indulgence to their neighbors, prevail throughout the whole body of our ministers. It is, perhaps, in the power of the city of Geneva alone to produce an edifying example of so perfect a union subsisting between its clergy and men of letters. And it is in great degree, on their wisdom, their known moderation, and on their zeal for the prosperity of the State that I build my hopes of its constant and perpetual tranquillity.

At the same time, I remark, with a pleasure mixed with surprise and veneration, how much they detest the horrid maxims of those holy and barbarous men, of whom history furnishes us with more than one example; who, in order to support the pretended prerogative of the deity, that is to say their own interest, have been so much the less sparing of human blood, as they were more assured that their own should be always respected.

I must not here forget that precious half of the republic, which makes the happiness of the other; and whose tenderness and prudence preserve its tranquillity and virtue. Amiable and virtuous daughters of Geneva, it will be always the lot of your sex to govern ours. Happy, so long as your chaste influence, solely exercised within the limits of conjugal union, is exerted only for the glory of the State and the happiness of the public. It is thus the female sex commanded at Sparta; and thus that you deserve to command at Geneva.

What man can be such a barbarian as to resist the voice of honor and reason, breathing from the lips of an affectionate wife? Who would not despise the tawdry charms of luxury, on beholding the simplicity and modesty of an attire, which, from the luster it derives from you, seems to be the most favorable to beauty? It is your task to perpetuate, by the insinuating spirit of your manners, by your innocent and amiable influence, a respect for the laws of the State, and harmony among individuals. It is yours to reunite divided families by happy marriages; and, above all things, to correct, by the persuasive mildness of your lessons and the modest graces of your discourse, those extravagances which our young people pick up in other countries; from whence, instead of many useful things that come within the reach of their observation and practice, they bring home hardly anything but a puerile air and ridiculous manner, acquired among loose women, and the admiration of I know not what pretended grandeur, a paltry indemnification for slavery and unworthy of the real greatness of true liberty.

Continue, therefore, always to be what you are, the chaste guardians of our manners, and the gentle links of our peace; exerting on every occasion the privileges of the heart and of nature to the advantage of moral obligation and the interests of virtue.

I flatter myself no sinister event will ever prove me to have been mistaken, in building on such a foundation my hopes of the felicity of my fellow-citizens and the glory of the republic. It must be confessed, however, that with all these advantages, it will not shine with that exterior luster, by which the eyes of the generality of mankind are affected, a puerile and fatal taste for which is the most mortal enemy to the happiness and liberty of a State.

Let dissolute youth seek elsewhere those transient pleasures which are followed by long repentance. Let pretenders to taste elsewhere admire the grandeur of palaces, the beauty of equipages, the sumptuousness of furniture, the pomp of public entertainments, with all the refinements of luxury and effeminacy. Geneva boasts nothing but men; such a sight has nevertheless its value, and those who have a taste for it are at least as good as the admirers of the other things.

Deign, most honorable, magnificent and sovereign lords, all and each, to receive, and with equal goodness, this respectful testimony of the interest I take in your common prosperity. And, if I have been so unhappy as to be guilty of any indiscreet transport, in this glowing effusion of my heart, I beseech you to pardon, and impute it to the tender affection of a real patriot, and to the ardent and lawful zeal of a man, who places his own greatest felicity in the prospect of seeing you happy.

I am, with the most profound respect, most honorable, magnificent and sovereign lords,

Your most humble,
and most obedient servant
and fellow-citizen.
JEAN-JACQUES ROUSSEAU

Chambéry,
June 12, 1754

Preface

The most useful and least perfected of all human studies is, in my opinion, that of man, and I dare say that the inscription on the Temple of Delphi did alone contain a more important and difficult precept than all the huge volumes of the moralists.* I therefore consider the subject of this discourse as one of the most interesting questions philosophy can propose, and, unhappily for us, one of the most knotty philosophers can labor to solve: For how is it possible to know the source of the inequality among men, without knowing men themselves? And how shall man be able to see himself, such as nature formed him, in spite of all the alterations which a long succession of years and events must have produced in his original constitution, and how shall he be able to distinguish what is of his own essence, from what the circumstances he has been in and the progress he has made have added to, or changed in, his primitive condition? The human soul, like the statue of Glaucus which time, the sea and storms had so much disfigured that it resembled a wild beast more than a god, the human soul, I say, altered in society by the perpetual succession of a thousand causes, by the acquisition of numberless discoveries and errors, by the changes that have happened in the constitution of the body, by the perpetual jarring of the passions, has in a manner so changed in appearance as to be scarcely distinguishable; and by now we perceive in it, instead of a being always acting from certain and invariable principles, instead of that heavenly and majestic simplicity which its author had impressed upon it, nothing but the shocking contrast of passion that thinks it reasons, and an understanding grown delirious.

But what is still more cruel, as every advance made by the human species serves only to remove it still further from its primitive condition, the more we accumulate new knowledge, the more we deprive ourselves of the means of acquiring the most important of all; and it is, in a manner, by the mere dint of studying man that we have lost the power of knowing him.

It is easy to perceive that it is in these successive alterations of the

* The inscription read, "Know thyself," and "Nothing in excess."

human constitution that we must look for the first origin of those differences that distinguish men, who, it is universally allowed, are naturally as equal among themselves as were the animals of every species before various physical causes had introduced those varieties we now observe among some of them. In fact, it is not possible to conceive how these first changes, whatever causes may have produced them, could have altered, all at once and in the same manner, all the individuals of the species. It seems obvious that while some improved or impaired their condition, or acquired divers good or bad qualities not inherent in their nature, the rest continued a longer time in their primitive state; and such was among men the first source of inequality, which it is much easier thus to point out in general, than to trace back with precision to its true causes.

Let not then my readers imagine that I dare flatter myself with having seen what I think is so difficult to discover. I have opened some arguments; I have risked some conjectures; but not so much from any hopes of being able to solve the question, as with a view of throwing upon it some light, and giving a true statement of it. Others may with great facility penetrate further on the same road, but none will find it an easy matter to get to the end of it. For it is no such easy task to distinguish between what is natural and what is artificial in the present constitution of man, and to make oneself well acquainted with a state which, if ever it did, does not now, and in all probability never will exist, and of which, notwithstanding, it is absolutely necessary to have just notions to judge properly of our present state. A man must be even more a philosopher than most people think, to take upon himself to determine exactly what precautions are requisite to make solid observations upon this subject; and, in my opinion, a good solution of the following problem would not be unworthy of the Aristotles and Plinys of our age: What experiments are requisite to know man as constituted by nature, and which are the best methods of making these experiments in the midst of society? For my own part, I am so far from pretending to solve this problem, that I think I have sufficiently reflected on the subject of it to dare answer beforehand, that the wisest philosophers would not be too wise to direct such experiments, nor the most powerful sovereigns too powerful to make them; a concurrence of circumstances which there is hardly any reason to expect, and especially with that perseverance, or rather that succession of knowledge, penetration, and good will requisite on both sides to insure success.

These investigations, so difficult to make and which hitherto have been so little thought of, are however the only means left us to remove a thousand difficulties which prevent our seeing the true foundations of human society.

It is this ignorance of the nature of man that casts so much uncertainty and obscurity on the genuine definition of natural right: for the idea of right, as Monsieur Burlamaqui* says, and still more that of natural right, are ideas evidently relative to the nature of man. It is therefore from this very nature of man, he continues, from his constitution and his state, that we are to deduce the principles of this science.

It is impossible to observe, without both surprise and scandal, the little agreement there is to be found on this important subject between the different authors that have treated it. Among the gravest writers, you will scarce find two of the same opinion. Not to speak of the ancient philosophers, who, one would imagine, had set out to contradict each other in regard to the most fundamental principles, the Roman jurisconsults make man and all other animals, without distinction, subject to the same natural law, because they consider under this name, rather that law which nature imposes upon herself than that which she prescribes; or, more probably, on account of the particular acceptation of the word, law, among these jurisconsults, who, on this occasion, seem to have understood nothing more by it than the general relations established by nature between all animated beings for the sake of their common preservation. The moderns, by not admitting anything under the word law but a rule prescribed to a moral being, that is to say, a being intelligent, free, and considered with a view to his relations to other beings, must of course confine to the only animal endowed with reason, that is, to man, the competency of the natural law; but then, by defining this law, every one of them his own way, they establish it on such metaphysical principles, that so far from being able to find out these principles by themselves, there are very few persons among us capable of so much as understanding them. Thus, therefore, all the definitions of these learned men, definitions in everything else so constantly at variance, agree only in this, that it is impossible to understand the law of nature, and consequently to obey it, without being a very subtle reasoner and a very profound metaphysician. This is no more nor less than saying that men must have employed for the establishment of society a fund of knowledge, which it is a very difficult matter, nay absolutely impossible, for most persons to develop, even in a state of society.

As men, therefore, are so little acquainted with nature, and agree so ill about the meaning of the word *law,* it would be very difficult for them to agree on a good definition of natural law. Accordingly, all those we meet with in books, besides lacking uniformity, err by being derived from several

* Author of *Principes du droit naturel* (Geneva, 1747).

kinds of knowledge which men do not naturally enjoy, and from advantages they can have no notion of, as long as they remain in a state of nature. The writers of these books set out by examining what rules it would be proper for men to agree to among themselves for their common interest; and then they proceed to give the name of natural law to a collection of these rules, without any other proof than the advantage they find would result from a universal compliance with it. This is, no doubt, a very easy method of striking out definitions, and of explaining the nature of things by an almost arbitrary fitness.

But as long as we remain unacquainted with the constitution of natural man, it will be in vain for us to attempt to determine what law he received, or what law suits him best. All we can plainly distinguish in regard to that law is that for it to be law, not only the will of him whom it obliges must be able to submit to it knowingly, but also that, for it to be natural, it must speak immediately by the voice of nature.

Laying aside therefore all the scientific treatises, which teach us merely to consider men such as they have made themselves, and confining myself to the first and most simple operations of the human soul, I think I can distinguish in it two principles prior to reason; one of them interests us deeply in our own preservation and welfare, the other inspires us with a natural aversion to seeing any other being, but especially any being like ourselves, suffer or perish. It is from the concurrence and the combination our mind is capable of forming between these two principles, without there being the least necessity for adding to them that of sociability, that, in my opinion, flow all the rules of natural right; rules, which reason is afterwards obliged to reestablish upon other foundations, when by its successive developments, it has at last stifled nature itself.

By proceeding in this manner, we shall not be obliged to make man a philosopher before he is a man. His obligations are not dictated to him merely by the slow voice of wisdom; and as long as he does not resist the internal impulses of compassion, he never will do any harm to another man, nor even to any sentient being, except in those lawful cases where his own preservation happens to come in question, and it is of course his duty to give himself the preference. By this means too we may put an end to the ancient disputes concerning the participation of other animals in the law of nature; for it is plain that, as they want both reason and free will, they cannot be acquainted with that law; however, as they partake in some measure of our nature in virtue of that sensibility with which they are endowed, we may well imagine they ought likewise to partake of the benefit of the natural law, and that man owes them a certain kind of duty.* In fact, it seems that, if I am obliged not to injure any being like myself, it is not so much because he is a reasonable being, as because he is a sensible being; and this quality, by being common to men and beasts, ought to exempt the latter from any unnecessary injuries the former might be able to do them.

This same study of original man, of his real needs, and of the fundamental principles of his duties, is likewise the only good method we can take, to surmount an infinite number of difficulties concerning the origin of moral inequality, the true foundations of political bodies, the reciprocal rights of their members, and a thousand other similar questions that are as important as they are ill-understood.

If we consider human society with a calm and disinterested eye, it seems at first sight to show us nothing but the violence of the powerful and the oppression of the weak; the mind is shocked at the cruelty of the one, and equally grieved at the blindness of the other; and as nothing is less stable in human life than those exterior relations, which chance produces oftener than wisdom, and which are called weakness or power, poverty or riches, human establishments appear at the first glance like so many castles built upon quicksand; it is only by taking a nearer survey of them, and by removing the dust and the sand which surround and disguise the edifice, that we can perceive the unshakable basis upon which it stands, and learn to respect its foundations. Now, without a serious study of man, his natural faculties and their successive developments, we shall never succeed in making these distinctions, and in separating, in the present constitution of things, what comes from the divine will from what human contrivance has aspired to do. The political and moral reflections, to which the important question I examine gives rise, are therefore useful in many ways; and the hypothetical history of governments is, in regard to man, an instructive lesson in every respect. By considering what we should have become, had we been left to ourselves, we ought to learn to bless him, whose gracious hand, correcting our institutions, and giving them an unshakable foundation, has thereby prevented the disorders which they otherwise must have produced, and made our happiness flow from means, which seemed bound to complete our misery.

> *Quem te Deus esse*
> *Jussit, et humana qua parte locatus es in re, Disce.*†

* Descartes had maintained that animals are merely machines, without conscious feeling.

† "Learn whom God has ordered you to be and in what part in human affairs you have been placed." (Persius, *Satires*, III, 71).

QUESTION
Posed by the Academy of Dijon

What is the origin of inequality
among mankind and does
natural law decree inequality?

Discourse
on the Origin and the Foundations
of Inequality Among Mankind

It is of man I am to speak; and the question into which I am inquiring informs me that it is to men that I am going to speak; for to those alone, who are not afraid of honoring truth, it belongs to propose discussions of this kind. I shall therefore defend with confidence the cause of mankind before the sages, who invite me to stand up in its defense; and I shall think myself happy, if I can but behave in a manner not unworthy of my subject and of my judges.

I conceive two species of inequality among men; one which I call natural, or physical inequality, because it is established by nature, and consists in the difference of age, health, bodily strength, and the qualities of the mind, or of the soul; the other which may be termed moral, or political inequality, because it depends on a kind of convention, and is established, or at least authorized by the common consent of mankind. This species of inequality consists in the different privileges, which some men enjoy, to the prejudice of others, such as that of being richer, more honored, more powerful, and even that of exacting obedience from them.

It were absurd to ask, what is the cause of natural inequality, seeing the bare definition of natural inequality answers the question: it would be more absurd still to inquire, if there might not be some essential connection between the two species of inequality, as it would be asking, in other words, if those who command are necessarily better men than those who obey; and if strength of body or of mind, wisdom or virtue are always to be found in individuals, in the same proportion with power, or riches: a question, fit perhaps to be discussed by slaves in the hearing of their masters, but unbecoming free and reasonable beings in quest of truth.

What therefore is precisely the subject of this discourse? It is to point out, in the progress of things, that moment, when, Right taking place of violence, nature became subject to law; to unfold that chain of amazing events, in consequence of which the strong submitted to serve the weak, and the people to purchase imaginary ease, at the expense of real happiness.

The philosophers, who have examined the foundations of society, have all perceived the necessity of tracing it back to a state of nature, but not one of them has ever got there. Some of them have not scrupled to attribute to men in that state the ideas of justice and injustice, without troubling themselves to prove that he really must have had such ideas, or even that such ideas were useful to him: others have spoken of the natural right of every man to keep what belongs to him, without letting us know what they meant by the word *belong*; others, without further ceremony ascribing to the strongest an authority over the weakest, have immediately brought government into being, without thinking of the time requisite for men to form any notion of the things signified by the words authority and government. All of them, in fine, constantly harping on wants, avidity, oppression, desires, and pride, have transferred to the state of nature ideas picked up in the bosom of society. In speaking of savages they described citizens. Nay, few of our own writers seem to have so much as doubted, that a state of nature did once actually exist; though it plainly appears by sacred history, that even the first man, immediately furnished as he was by God himself with both instructions and precepts, never lived in that state, and that, if we give to the Books of Moses that credit which every Christian philosopher ought to give to them, we must deny that, even before the Deluge, such a state ever existed among men, unless they fell into it by some extraordinary event: a paradox very difficult to maintain, and altogether impossible to prove.

Let us begin, therefore, by laying aside facts, for they do not affect the question. The researches, in which we may engage on this occasion, are not to be taken for historical truths, but merely as hypothetical and conditional reasonings, fitter to illustrate the nature of things, than to show their true origin, like those systems, which our naturalists daily make of the formation of the world. Religion commands us to believe that men, having been drawn by God himself out of a state of nature, are unequal, because it is His pleasure they should be so; but religion does not forbid us to draw conjectures solely from the nature of man, considered in itself, and from that of the beings which surround him, concerning the fate of mankind, had they been left to themselves. This is then the question I am to answer, the question I propose to examine in the present discourse. As mankind in general has an interest in my subject, I shall endeavor to use a language suitable to all nations; or rather, forgetting the circumstances of time and place in order to think of nothing but the men I speak to, I shall suppose myself in the Lyceum of Athens, repeating the lessons of my masters before the Platos and the Xenocrates of that famous seat of philosophy as my judges, and in presence of the whole human species as my audience.

O man, of whatever country you are, whatever your opinions may be, attend to my words; here is your history such as I think I have read it, not in books composed by your fellowmen, for they are liars, but in the book of nature which never lies. All that comes from her will be true, nor will there be anything false, but where I may happen, without intending it, to introduce something of my own. The times I am going to speak of are very remote. How much are you changed from what you once were! It is in a manner the life of your species that I am going to write, from the qualities which you have received, and which your education and your habits have succeeded in depraving, but could not destroy. There is, I feel, an age at which every individual would choose to stop; and you will look for the age at which, had you your wish, your species had stopped. Discontented with your present condition for reasons which threaten your unhappy posterity with still greater vexations, you will perhaps wish it were in your power to go back; and this sentiment ought to be considered a panegyric of your first ancestors, a criticism of your contemporaries, and a source of terror to those who may have the misfortune of coming after you.

First Part

However important it may be, in order to form a proper judgment of the natural state of man, to consider him from his origin, and to examine him, as it were, in the first embryo of the species, I shall not attempt to trace his organization through its successive developments: I shall not stop to examine in the animal system what he may have been in the beginning, in order to have become at last what he actually is. I shall not inquire, whether, as Aristotle thinks, his extended nails were no better at first than crooked talons; whether his whole body was not, bear-like, thickly covered with hair; and whether, walking upon all fours, his looks directed to the earth, and confined to a horizon of a few paces extent, did not at once point out the nature and limits of his ideas. I could only form vague, and almost imaginary, conjectures on this subject. Comparative anatomy has not as yet made sufficient progress; and the observations of natural philosophy are too uncertain, to establish upon such foundations the basis of any solid reasoning. For this reason, without having recourse to the supernatural information with which we have been favored on this head, or paying any attention to the changes, that must have happened in the internal, as well as external conformation of man, in proportion as he applied his limbs to new purposes, and took to new foods, I shall suppose his conformation to have always been, what we now behold it; that he always walked on two feet, made the same use of his hands that we do of ours, extended his looks over the whole face of nature, and measured with his eyes the vast extent of the heavens.*

If I strip this being, thus constituted, of all the supernatural gifts which he may have received, and of all the artificial faculties, which he could not have acquired but by slow degrees; if I consider him, in a word, such as he must have issued from the hands of nature; I see an animal less strong than some, and less agile than others, but, upon the whole, the most advantageously organized of any: I see him satisfying his hunger under an oak, and his thirst at the first brook; I see him laying himself down to sleep at the foot of the same tree that afforded him his meal; and there are all his wants completely supplied.

The earth, left to its own natural fertility, and covered with immense woods that no hatchet ever disfigured, offers at every step food and shelter to every species of animals. Men, dispersed among them, observe and imitate their industry, and thus rise as high as the instinct of beasts; with this advantage, that, whereas every species of beasts is confined to one peculiar instinct, man, who perhaps has not any that particularly belongs to him, appropriates to himself those of all other animals, and lives equally upon most of the different foods, which they only divide among themselves; a circumstance which qualifies him to find his subsistence more easily than any of them.

Accustomed from their infancy to the inclemency of the weather, and to the rigor of the different seasons; inured to fatigue, and obliged to defend, naked and without arms, their life and their prey against the other wild inhabitants of the forest, or at least to avoid their fury by flight, men acquire a robust and almost unalterable constitution. The children, bringing with them into the world the excellent constitution of their parents, and strengthening it by the same exercises that first produced it, attain by this means all the vigor that the human frame is capable of. Nature treats them exactly in the same manner that Sparta treated the children of her citizens; those who come well formed into the world she renders strong and robust, and destroys all the rest; differing in this respect from our societies, in which the State, by permitting children to become burdensome to their parents, murders them without distinction in the wombs of their mothers.

The body being the only instrument that savage man is acquainted with, he employs it to different uses, of which ours, for want of practice, are incapable; and we may thank our industry for the loss of that strength and

---

* Rousseau was well acquainted with the theory of evolution that had been sketched by his friend, Diderot, in his *Pensées sur l'interprétation de la nature* (1753).

agility, which necessity obliges him to acquire. Had he a hatchet, would his hand so easily snap off from an oak so stout a branch? Had he a sling, would it hurl a stone to so great a distance? Had he a ladder, would he climb so nimbly up a tree? Had he a horse, would he run with such swiftness? Give civilized man but time to gather about him all his machines, and no doubt he will outmatch the savage: but if you have a mind to see a contest still more unequal, place them naked and unarmed one opposite to the other; and you will soon discover the advantage there is in perpetually having all our forces constantly at our disposal, in being constantly prepared against all events, and in always carrying ourselves, as it were, whole and entire about us.

Hobbes would have it that man is naturally void of fear, and intent only upon attacking and fighting. An illustrious philosopher* thinks on the contrary, and Cumberland and Pufendorf likewise affirm it, that nothing is more timid than man in a state of nature, that he is always in a tremble, and ready to fly at the first motion he perceives, at the first noise that strikes his ears. This, indeed, may be very true in regard to objects with which he is not acquainted; and I make no doubt of his being terrified at every new sight that presents itself, whenever he cannot distinguish the physical good and evil which he may expect from it, nor compare his strength with the dangers he has to encounter; circumstances that seldom occur in a state of nature, where all things proceed in so uniform a manner, and the face of the earth is not liable to those sudden and continual changes occasioned in it by the passions and inconstancies of men living in bodies. But savage man living dispersed among other animals and finding himself early under a necessity of measuring his strength with theirs, soon makes a comparison between both, and finding that he surpasses them more in address, than they surpass him in strength, he learns not to be any longer in dread of them. Turn out a bear or a wolf against a sturdy, active, resolute savage (and this they all are), provided with stones and a good stick, and you will soon find that the danger is at least equal on both sides, and that after several trials of this kind, wild beasts, who are not fond of attacking each other, will not be very disposed to attack man, whom they have found every whit as wild as themselves. As to animals who have really more strength than man has address, he is, in regard to them, what other weaker species are, who find means to subsist notwithstanding; he has even this great advantage over such weaker species, that being equally fleet with them, and finding on every tree an almost inviolable asylum, he is always at liberty to accept or to

* Montesquieu, in the *Esprit des lois,* I, ii.

refuse the encounter, to fight or to fly. Let us add that it appears that no animal naturally makes war on man, except in the case of self-defense or extreme hunger; nor ever expresses against him any of these violent antipathies, which seem to indicate that one species is intended by nature for the food of another.

But there are other more formidable enemies, and against which man is not provided with the same means of defense; I mean natural infirmities, infancy, old age, and sickness of every kind; melancholy proofs of our weakness, whereof the two first are common to all animals, and the last chiefly attends man living in a state of society. It is even observable in regard to infancy, that the mother being able to carry her child about with her, wherever she goes, can perform the duty of a nurse with a great deal less trouble than the females of many other animals, who are obliged to be constantly going and coming with no small labor and fatigue, one way to look out for their own subsistence, and another to suckle and feed their young ones. True it is that, if the woman happens to perish, her child is exposed to the greatest danger of perishing with her; but this danger is common to a hundred other species, whose young ones require a great deal of time to be able to provide for themselves; and if our infancy is longer than theirs, our life is longer likewise; so that, in this respect too, all things are in a manner equal; not but that there are other rules concerning the duration of the first age of life, and the number of the young of man and other animals, but they do not belong to my subject. With old men, who stir and perspire but little, the demand for food diminishes with their abilities to provide it; and as a savage life would exempt them from the gout and the rheumatism, and old age is of all ills that which human assistance is least capable of alleviating, they would at last go off, without its being perceived by others that they ceased to exist, and almost without perceiving it themselves.

In regard to sickness, I shall not repeat the vain and false declamations made use of to discredit medicine by most men, while they enjoy their health; I shall only ask if there are any solid observations from which we may conclude that in those countries, where the healing art is most neglected, the mean duration of man's life is shorter than in those where it is most cultivated. And how is it possible this should be the case, if we inflict more diseases upon ourselves than medicine can supply us with remedies? The extreme inequalities in the manner of living of the several classes of mankind, the excess of idleness in some, and of labor in others, the facility of irritating and satisfying our sensuality and our appetites, the too exquisite and out of the way foods of the rich, which fill them with fiery juices, and bring on indigestions, the unwholesome food of the poor, of which even, bad as it is, they very often fall short, and the want of which tempts them, every opportunity that offers, to eat greedily and overload their stomachs; late nights, excesses of every kind, immoderate transports of all the passions, fatigues, mental exhaustion, in a word, the numberless pains and anxieties annexed to every condition, and which the mind of man is constantly a prey to; these are the fatal proofs that most of our ills are of our own making, and that we might have avoided them all by adhering to the simple, uniform and solitary way of life prescribed to us by nature. Allowing that nature intended we should always enjoy good health, I dare almost affirm that a state of reflection is a state against nature, and that the man who meditates is a degenerate animal. We need only call to mind the good constitution of savages, of those at least whom we have not destroyed by our strong liquors; we need only reflect, that they are strangers to almost every disease, except those occasioned by wounds and old age, to be in a manner convinced that the history of human diseases might be easily written by pursuing that of civil societies. Such at least was the opinion of Plato, who concluded from certain remedies made use of or approved by Podalirius and Machaon at the Siege of Troy, that several disorders, which these remedies were found to bring on in his days, were not known among men at that remote period; and Celsus relates that dieting, so necessary nowadays, was first invented by Hippocrates.

Man therefore, in a state of nature where there are so few sources of sickness, can have no great occasion for physic, and still less for physicians; neither is the human species more to be pitied in this respect, than any other species of animals. Ask those who make hunting their recreation or business, if in their excursions they meet with many sick or feeble animals. They meet with many carrying the marks of considerable wounds, that have been perfectly well healed and closed up; with many, whose bones formerly broken, and whose limbs almost torn off, have completely knit and united, without any other surgeon but time, any other regimen but their usual way of living, and whose cures were not the less perfect for their not having been tortured with incisions, poisoned with drugs, or worn out by fasting. In a word, however useful medicine well administered may be to us who live in a state of society, it is still past doubt, that if, on the one hand, the sick savage, destitute of help, has nothing to hope for except from nature, on the other, he has nothing to fear but from its ills; a circumstance which often renders his situation preferable to ours.

Let us therefore beware of confusing savage man with the men with whom we associate. Nature behaves towards all animals left to her care

with a predilection that seems to prove how jealous she is of that prerogative. The horse, the cat, the bull, nay the ass itself, have generally a higher
stature, and always a more robust constitution, more vigor, more strength
and courage in their forests than in our houses; they lose half these advantages by becoming domestic animals; it looks as if all our attention to treat
them kindly, and to feed them well, served only to bastardize them. It is thus
with man himself. In proportion as he becomes sociable and a slave to
others, he becomes weak, fearful, mean-spirited, and his soft and effeminate way of living at once completes the enervation of his strength and of
his courage. We may add, that there must be still a wider difference between
man and man in a savage and domestic condition, than between beast and
beast; for as men and beasts have been treated alike by nature, all the
comforts with which men indulge themselves, still more than they do the
beasts tamed by them, are so many particular causes which make them
degenerate more markedly.

Nakedness, therefore, the want of houses, and of all these superfluities,
which we consider as so very necessary, are not such mighty evils in respect
to these primitive men, and much less still any obstacle to their preservation. Their skin, it is true, is destitute of hair; but then they have no occasion
for any such covering in warm climates; and in cold climates they soon
learn to apply to that use those of the animals they have conquered; they
have only two feet to run with, but they have two hands to defend themselves with, and provide for all their wants; their children, perhaps, learn to
walk later and with difficulty, but their mothers carry them with ease; an
advantage not granted to other species of animals, with whom the mother,
when pursued, is obliged to abandon her young ones, or regulate her step by
theirs. In short, unless we admit those singular and fortuitous concurrences
of circumstances, which I shall speak of hereafter, and which, it is very
possible, may never have existed, it is evident, in any case, that the man
who first made himself clothes and built himself a cabin supplied himself
with things which he did not much need, since he had lived without them till
then; and why should he not have been able to support, in his riper years, the
same kind of life, which he had supported from his infancy?

Alone, idle, and always surrounded with danger, savage man must be
fond of sleep, and sleep lightly like other animals, who think but little, and
may, in a manner, be said to sleep all the time they do not think: self-
preservation being almost his only concern, he must exercise those faculties
most which are most serviceable in attacking and in defending, whether to
subdue his prey, or to prevent his becoming that of other animals: those
organs, on the contrary, which softness and sensuality can alone improve,

must remain in a state of rudeness, utterly incompatible with all manner of delicacy; and as his senses are divided on this point, his touch and his taste must be extremely coarse and blunt; his sight, his hearing, and his smelling equally subtle: such is the animal state in general, and accordingly, if we may believe travelers, it is that of most savage nations. We must not therefore be surprised, that the Hottentots of the Cape of Good Hope distinguish with their naked eyes ships on the ocean, at as great a distance as the Dutch can discern them with their glasses; nor that the savages of America should have tracked the Spaniards with their smell, to as great a degree of exactness, as the best dogs could have done; nor that all these barbarous nations support nakedness without pain, use such large quantities of pimento to give their food a relish, and drink like water the strongest liquors of Europe.

As yet I have considered man merely in his physical capacity; let us now endeavor to examine him in a metaphysical and moral light.

I can discover nothing in any animal but an ingenious machine, to which nature has given senses to wind itself up, and guard, to a certain degree, against everything that might destroy or disorder it. I perceive the very same things in the human machine, with this difference, that nature alone operates in all the operations of the beast, whereas man, as a free agent, has a share in his. One chooses by instinct; the other by an act of liberty; for which reason the beast cannot deviate from the rules that have been prescribed to it, even in cases where such deviation might be useful, and man often deviates from the rules laid down for him to his prejudice. Thus a pigeon would starve near a dish of the best meat, and a cat on a heap of fruit or corn, though both might very well support life with the food which they thus disdain, did they but bethink themselves to make a trial of it. It is in this manner that dissolute men run into excesses, which bring on fevers and death itself; because the mind depraves the senses, and when nature ceases to speak, the will still continues to dictate.

All animals have ideas, since all animals have senses; they even combine their ideas to a certain degree, and, in this respect, it is only the difference of such degree that constitutes the difference between man and beast: some philosophers have even advanced, that there is a greater difference between some men and some others, than between some men and some beasts; it is not therefore so much the understanding that constitutes, among animals, the specific distinction of man, as his quality of a free agent. Nature speaks to all animals, and beasts obey her voice. Man feels the same impulse, but he at the same time perceives that he is free to resist or to acquiesce; and it is in the consciousness of this liberty, that the spirituality of his soul chiefly appears: for natural philosophy explains, in some measure, the mechanism of the senses and the formation of ideas; but in the power of willing, or rather of choosing, and in the consciousness of this power, nothing can be discovered but acts, that are purely spiritual, and cannot be accounted for by the laws of mechanics.

But even if the difficulties, in which all these questions are involved, should leave some room to dispute on this difference between man and beast, there is another very specific quality that distinguishes them, and a quality which will admit of no dispute; this is the faculty of improvement;* a faculty which, as circumstances offer, successively unfolds all the other faculties, and resides among us not only in the species, but in the individuals that compose it; whereas a beast is, at the end of some months, all he ever will be during the rest of his life; and his species, at the end of a thousand years, precisely what it was the first year of that thousand. Why is man alone subject to dotage? Is it not, because he thus returns to his primitive condition? And because, while the beast, which has acquired nothing and has likewise nothing to lose, continues always in possession of his instinct, man, losing by old age, or by accidents, all the acquisitions he had made in consequence of his *perfectibility,* thus falls back even lower than beasts themselves? It would be a melancholy necessity for us to be obliged to allow that this distinctive and almost unlimited faculty is the source of all man's misfortunes; that it is this faculty, which, though by slow degrees, draws him out of his original condition, in which his days would slide away insensibly in peace and innocence; that it is this faculty, which, in a succession of ages, produces his discoveries and mistakes, his virtues and his vices, and, in the long run, renders him both his own and nature's tyrant. (i) It would be shocking to be obliged to commend, as a beneficent being, whoever he was that first suggested to the Orinoco Indians the use of those boards which they bind on the temples of their children, and which secure to them the enjoyment of some part at least of their natural imbecility and happiness.

Savage man, abandoned by nature to pure instinct, or rather indemnified for the instinct which has perhaps been denied to him by faculties capable of immediately supplying its place, and of raising him afterwards a great deal higher, would therefore begin with purely animal functions: to see and to feel would be his first condition, which he would enjoy in common with other animals. To will and not to will, to wish and to fear, would be the first, and in a manner, the only operations of his soul, until new circumstances occasioned new developments.

* Rousseau uses the word *perfectibilité*, which means the capacity to make progress.

Let moralists say what they will, the human understanding is greatly indebted to the passions, which, on their side, are likewise universally allowed to be greatly indebted to the human understanding. It is by the activity of our passions, that our reason improves; we covet knowledge merely because we covet enjoyment, and it is impossible to conceive, why a man exempt from fears and desires should take the trouble to reason. The passions, in their turn, owe their origin to our needs, and their increase to our progress in science; for we cannot desire or fear anything, but in consequence of the ideas we have of it, or of the simple impulses of nature; and savage man, destitute of every species of knowledge, experiences no passions but those of this last kind; his desires never extend beyond his physical wants; (k) He knows no goods but food, a female, and rest; he fears no evils but pain, and hunger; I say pain, and not death; for no animal, merely as such, will ever know what it is to die, and the knowledge of death, and of its terrors, is one of the first acquisitions made by man, in consequence of his deviating from the animal state.

I could easily, were it necessary, cite facts in support of this opinion, and show that the progress of the mind has everywhere kept pace exactly with the wants to which nature had left the inhabitants exposed, or to which circumstances had subjected them, and consequently to the passions, which inclined them to provide for these wants. I could exhibit in Egypt the arts starting up, and extending themselves with the inundations of the Nile; I could pursue them in their progress among the Greeks, where they were seen to bud, grow, and rise to the heavens, in the midst of the sands and rocks of Attica, without being able to take root on the fertile banks of the Europus; I would observe, that, in general, the inhabitants of the north are more industrious than those of the south, because they can less do without industry; as if nature thus meant to make all things equal, by giving to the mind that fertility she has denied to the soil.

But leaving aside the uncertain testimony of history, who does not perceive that everything seems to remove from savage man the temptation and the means of altering his condition? His imagination paints nothing to him; his heart asks nothing from him. His moderate wants are so easily supplied with what he everywhere finds ready to his hand, and he stands at such a distance from the degree of knowledge requisite to covet more, that he can neither have foresight nor curiosity. The spectacle of nature, by growing quite familiar to him, becomes at last equally indifferent. It is constantly the same order, constantly the same revolutions; he has not sense enough to feel surprise at the sight of the greatest wonders; and it is not in his mind we must look for that philosophy, which man must have to know how to observe once, what he has every day seen. His soul, which nothing disturbs, gives itself up entirely to the consciousness of its present existence, without any thought of even the nearest futurity; and his projects, equally confined with his views, scarce extend to the end of the day. Such is, even at present, the degree of foresight in the Caribbean: he sells his cotton bed in the morning, and comes in the evening, with tears in his eyes, to buy it back, not having foreseen that he should want it again the next night.

The more we meditate on this subject, the wider does the distance between mere sensation and the most simple knowledge become in our eyes; and it is impossible to conceive how man, by his own powers alone, without the assistance of communication, and the spur of necessity, could have got over so great an interval. How many ages perhaps revolved, before man beheld any other fire but that of the heavens? How many different accidents must have concurred to make them acquainted with the most common uses of this element? How often have they let it go out, before they knew the art of reproducing it? And how often perhaps has not every one of these secrets perished with the discoverer? What shall we say of agriculture, an art which requires so much labor and foresight; which depends upon other arts; which, it is very evident, can be practiced only in a society which had at least begun, and which does not so much serve to draw from the earth food which it would yield them without all that trouble, as to oblige her to produce those things which are preferable to our taste? But let us suppose that men had multiplied to such a degree, that the natural products of the earth no longer sufficed for their support; a supposition which, by the way, would prove that this kind of life would be very advantageous to the human species; let us suppose that, without forge or workshops, the instruments of husbandry had dropped from the heavens into the hands of savages, that these men had overcome that mortal aversion they all have for constant labor; that they had learned to foretell their wants at so great a distance of time; that they had guessed exactly how they were to break the earth, sow the grain and plant trees; that they had found out the art of grinding their corn, and improving by fermentation the juice of their grapes; all operations which must have been taught them by the gods, since we cannot conceive how they should make such discoveries of themselves; after all these fine presents, what man would be mad enough to cultivate a field, that may be robbed by the first comer, man or beast, who takes a fancy to the produce of it. And would any man consent to spend his days in labor and fatigue, when the rewards of his labor and fatigue became more and more precarious in proportion of his want of them? In a word, how could this situation engage men to cultivate the earth, as long as it was not parceled out among them, that is, as long as a state of nature subsisted.

Though we should suppose savage man as well-versed in the art of thinking, as philosophers make him; though we were, following them, to make him a philosopher himself, discovering by himself the sublimest truths, forming to himself, by the most abstract arguments, maxims of justice and reason drawn from the love of order in general, or from the known will of his Creator: in a word, though we were to suppose his mind as intelligent and enlightened as it would have had to be, and is in fact found to have been dull and stupid; what benefit would the species receive from all these metaphysical discoveries, which could not be communicated, but must perish with the individual who had made them? What progress could mankind make in the forests, scattered up and down among the other animals? And to what degree could men mutually improve and enlighten each other, when they had no fixed habitation, nor any need of each other's assistance; when the same persons scarcely met twice in their whole lives, and on meeting neither spoke to, or so much as knew each other.

Let us consider how many ideas we owe to the use of speech; how much grammar exercises and facilitates the operations of the mind; let us, besides, reflect on the immense pains and time that the first invention of languages must have required: let us add these reflections to the preceding; and then we may judge how many thousand ages must have been requisite to develop successively the operations, which the human mind is capable of producing.

I must now beg leave to stop one moment to consider the perplexities attending the origin of languages. I might here barely cite or repeat the researches made, in relation to this question, by the Abbé de Condillac,* which all fully confirm my system, and perhaps even suggested to me the first idea of it. But, as the matter in which this philosopher resolves the difficulties he himself raises concerning the origin of arbitrary signs shows that he supposes, what I doubt, namely a kind of society already established among the inventors of languages; I think it my duty, at the same time that I refer to his reflections, to give my own, in order to expose the same difficulties in a light suitable to my subject. The first that offers itself is how languages could become necessary; for as there was no correspondence between men, nor the least necessity for any, there is no conceiving the necessity of this invention, nor the possibility of it, if it was not

---

* In the *Essai sur l'origine des connaissances humaines* (1746).

indispensable. I might say, with many others, that languages are the fruit of the domestic intercourse between fathers, mothers, and children: but this, besides its not answering the difficulties, would be committing the same error as those, who reasoning on the state of nature, transfer to it ideas gathered in society, always consider families as living together under one roof, and their members as observing among themselves a union, equally intimate and permanent as that which exists among us, where so many common interests unite them; whereas in this primitive state, as there were neither houses nor cabins, nor any kind of property, everyone took up his lodging at random, and seldom continued above one night in the same place; males and females united without any premeditated design, as chance, occasion, or desire brought them together, nor had they any great occasion for language to make known what they had to say to each other. They parted with the same ease. (l) The mother suckled her children, when just born, for her own sake; but afterwards when habit had made them dear to her, for theirs; but they no sooner gained strength enough to run about in quest of food than they separated even from her, and as they scarcely had any other method of not losing each other, than that of remaining constantly in each other's sight, they soon came to a point of not even recognizing each other when they happened to meet again. I must further observe, that the child having all his wants to explain, and consequently more things to say to his mother, than the mother can have to say to him, it is he that must be at the chief expense of invention, and the language he makes use of must be in a great measure his own work; this makes the number of languages equal to that of the individuals who are to speak them; and this multiplicity of languages is further increased by their roving and vagabond kind of life, which allows no idiom time enough to acquire any consistency; for to say that the mother would have dictated to the child the words he must employ to ask her this thing and that, may well enough explain in what manner languages, already formed, are taught, but it does not show us in what manner they are first formed.

Let us suppose this first difficulty conquered: Let us for a moment consider ourselves on this side of the immense space, which must have separated the pure state of nature from that in which languages became necessary, and let us, after allowing their necessity, examine how languages could begin to be established: a new difficulty this, still more stubborn than the preceding; for if men stood in need of speech to learn to think, they must have stood in still greater need of the art of thinking to invent that of speaking; and though we could conceive how the sounds of the voice came to be taken for the conventional interpreters of our ideas we should not be the nearer knowing who could have been the interpreters of this convention for such ideas, which, in consequence of their not corresponding to any sensible objects, could not be indicated by gesture or voice; so that we can scarcely form any tolerable conjectures concerning the birth of this art of communicating our thoughts, and establishing a correspondence between minds: a sublime art which, though so remote from its origin, philosophers still behold at such a prodigious distance from its perfection, that I never met with one of them bold enough to affirm it would ever arrive there, even though the revolutions necessarily produced by time were suspended in its favor; though prejudice could be banished from, or would at least consent to sit silent in the presence of our academies; and though these societies should consecrate themselves, entirely and during whole ages, to the study of this thorny matter.

The first language of man, the most universal and most energetic of all languages, in short, the only language he needed, before there was a necessity of persuading assembled multitudes, was the cry of nature. As this cry was never extorted but by a kind of instinct in the most urgent cases, to implore assistance in great danger, or relief in great sufferings, it was of little use in the common occurrences of life, where more moderate sentiments generally prevail. When the ideas of men began to extend and multiply, and a closer communication began to take place among them, they labored to devise more numerous signs, and a more extensive language: they multiplied the inflections of the voice, and added to them gestures, which are, in their own nature, more expressive, and whose meaning depends less on any prior determination. They therefore expressed visible and movable objects by gestures, and those which strike the ear by imitative sounds: but as gestures scarcely indicate anything except objects that are actually present or can be easily described, and visible actions; as they are not of general use, since darkness or the interposition of a material object renders them useless; and as besides they require attention rather than excite it; men at length bethought themselves of substituting for them the articulations of voice, which, without having the same relation to any determinate object, are, in quality of conventional signs, fitter to represent all our ideas; a substitution, which could only have been made by common consent, and in a manner pretty difficult to practice by men, whose rude organs were unimproved by exercise; a substitution, which is in itself still more difficult to be conceived, since such a common agreement would have required a motive, and speech therefore appears to have been exceedingly requisite to establish the use of speech.

We must suppose, that the words, first made use of by men, had in their minds a much more extensive signification, than those employed in languages of some standing, and that, considering how ignorant they were of the division of speech into its constituent parts, they at first gave every word the meaning of an entire proposition. When afterwards they began to perceive the difference between the subject and attribute, and between verb and noun, a distinction which required no mean effort of genius, the substantives for a time were only so many proper names, the infinitive was the only tense, and as to adjectives, great difficulties must have attended the development of the idea that represents them, since every adjective is an abstract word, and abstraction is an unnatural and very painful operation.

At first they gave every object a peculiar name, without any regard to its genus or species, things which these first originators of language were in no condition to distinguish; and every individual presented itself in isolation of their minds, as they are in the picture of nature. If they called one oak A, they called another oak B: so that their dictionary must have been more extensive in proposition as their knowledge of things was more confined. It could not but be a very difficult task to get rid of so diffuse and embarrassing a nomenclature; as in order to marshal the several beings under common and generic denominations, it was necessary to be first acquainted with their properties, and their differences; to be stocked with observations and definitions, that is to say, to understand natural history and metaphysics, advantages which the men of these times could not have enjoyed.

Besides, general ideas cannot be conveyed to the mind without the assistance of words, nor can the understanding seize them except by means of propositions. This is one of the reasons why mere animals cannot form such ideas, nor ever acquire the perfectibility, which depends on such an operation. When a monkey leaves without the least hesitation one nut for another, are we to think he has any general idea of that kind of fruit, and that he compares its archetype with these two individual bodies? No certainly; but the sight of one of these nuts calls back to his memory the sensations which he has received from the other; and his eyes, modified after some certain manner, give notice to his palate of the modification it is in its turn going to receive. Every general idea is purely intellectual; let the imagination tamper ever so little with it, it immediately becomes a particular idea. Endeavor to represent to yourself the image of a tree in general, you never will be able to do it; in spite of all your efforts it will appear big or little, with thin or thick foliage, light or dark; and were you able to see nothing in it, but what can be seen in every tree, such a picture would no longer resemble any tree. Beings perfectly abstract are perceivable in the same manner, or are only conceivable by the assistance of speech. The definition of a triangle can alone give you a just idea of that figure: the moment you form a triangle in your mind, it is this or that particular triangle and no other, and you cannot avoid giving breadth to its lines and color to its area. We must therefore make use of propositions; we must therefore speak to have general ideas; for the moment the imagination stops, the mind can continue to function only with the aid of discourse. If therefore the first inventors could give no names to any ideas but those they had already, it follows that the first substantives could never have been anything more than proper names.

But when by means, which I cannot conceive, our new grammarians began to extend their ideas, and generalize their words, the ignorance of the inventors must have confined this method to very narrow bounds; and as they had at first too much multiplied the names of individuals for want of being acquainted with the distinctions called genus and species, they afterwards made too few genera and species for want of having considered beings in all their differences: to push the divisions far enough, they must have had more knowledge and experience than we can allow them, and have made more researches and taken more pains, than we can suppose them willing to submit to. Now if, even at this present time, we every day discover new species, which had before escaped all our observations, how many species must have escaped the notice of men, who judged of things merely from their first appearances! As to the primitive classes and the most general notions, it were superfluous to add that these they must have likewise overlooked: how, for example, could they have thought of or understood the words, matter, spirit, substance, mode, figure, motion, since even our philosophers, who for so long a time have been constantly employing these terms, can themselves scarcely understand them, and since the ideas annexed to these words being purely metaphysical, they could find no models of them in nature?

I stop at these first advances, and beseech my judges to suspend their reading a little, in order to consider, what a great way language has still to go, in regard to the invention of physical substantives alone (though the easiest part of language to invent), to be able to express all the sentiments of man, to assume an invariable form, to bear being spoken in public, and to influence society. I earnestly entreat them to consider how much time and knowledge must have been requisite to find out numbers, abstract words, the aorists, and all the other tenses of verbs, the particles, and syntax, the method of connecting propositions and arguments, of forming all the logic of discourse. For my own part, I am so frightened by the difficulties that multiply at every step, and so convinced of the almost demonstrated impossibility of languages owing their birth and establishment to means that were merely human, that I must leave to whoever may please to take it up, the task of discussing this difficult problem, "Which was the more necessary, society already formed to invent languages, or languages already invented to form society?"

Whatever these origins may have been, we may at least infer from the little care which nature has taken to bring men together by mutual wants, and make the use of speech easy to them, how little she has done towards making them sociable, and how little she has contributed to anything which they themselves have done to become so. In fact, it is impossible to conceive, why, in this primitive state, one man should have more occasion for the assistance of another, than one monkey, or one wolf for that of another animal of the same species; or supposing that he had, what motive could induce another to assist him; or even, if he did so, how he, who wanted assistance, and he from whom it was wanted, could agree upon the conditions. I know we are continually told that in this state man would have been the most wretched of all creatures; and if it is true, as I fancy I have proved it, that he must have continued many ages without either the desire or the opportunity of emerging from such a state, their assertion could only serve to justify a charge against nature, and not any against the being which nature had thus constituted. But, if I thoroughly understand this term *wretched*, it is a word that either has no meaning, or signifies nothing but a privation attended with pain, and a suffering state of body or soul: now I would fain know what kind of misery can be that of a free being, whose heart enjoys perfect peace, and body perfect health? and which is most likely to become insupportable to those who enjoy it, a civil or a natural life? In civil life we can scarcely meet a single person who does not complain of his existence; many even throw away as much of it as they can, and the united force of divine and human laws can hardly put a stop to this disorder. Was ever any free savage known to have been so much tempted to complain of life, and do away with himself? Let us therefore judge with less pride on which side real misery is to be placed. Nothing, on the contrary, would have been so unhappy as savage man, dazzled by flashes of knowledge, racked by passions, and reasoning about a state different from that in which he saw himself placed. It was in consequence of a very wise providence, that the faculties, which he potentially enjoyed, were not to develop themselves, except in proportion as there offered occasions to exercise them, lest they should be superfluous or troublesome to him when he did not yet want them, or tardy and useless when he did. He had in his instinct alone everything requisite to live in a state of nature; in his cultivated reason he has barely what is necessary to live in a state of society.

It appears at first sight that, as there was no kind of moral relations between men in this state, nor any known duties, they could not be either good or bad, and had neither vices nor virtues, unless we take these words in a physical sense, and call vices, in the individual, the qualities which may prove detrimental to his own preservation, and virtues those which may contribute to it; in which case we should be obliged to consider him as most virtuous, who made least resistance against the simple impulses of nature. But without deviating from the usual meaning of these terms, it is proper to suspend the judgment we might form of such a situation, and be on our guard against prejudice, until, balance in hand, we have examined whether there are more virtues or vices among civilized men; or whether their virtues do them more good than their vices do them harm; or whether the improvement of their understanding is sufficient compensation for the mischief they do to each other, in proportion as they become better informed of the good they ought to do; or whether, on the whole, they would not be much happier in a condition, where they had nothing to fear or to hope from each other, than to have submitted to universal dependence, and to have obliged themselves to depend for everything upon those, who do not think themselves obliged to give them anything.

But above all things let us beware of concluding with Hobbes, that man, as having no idea of goodness, must be naturally bad; that he is vicious because he does not know what virtue is; that he always refuses to do any service to those of his own species, because he believes that none is due to them; that, in virtue of that right which he justly claims to everything he wants, he foolishly looks upon himself as proprietor of the whole universe. Hobbes very plainly saw the flaws in all the modern definitions of natural right: but the consequences, which he draws from his own definition, show that the sense in which he understands it is equally false. This author, to argue from his own principles, should say that the state of nature, being that in which the care of our own preservation interferes least with the preservation of others, was consequently the most favorable to peace, and the most suitable to mankind; whereas he advances the very reverse in consequence of his having injudiciously included in that care which savage man takes of his preservation, the satisfaction of numberless passions which are the work of society, and have made laws necessary. A bad man, says he, is a robust child. But this is not proving that savage man is a robust child; and though we were to grant that he was, what could this philosopher infer from such a concession? That if this man, when robust, depended on others as much as when feeble, there is no excess that he would not be guilty of. He would make nothing of striking his mother when she delayed ever so little to give him the breast; he would claw, and bite, and strangle without remorse the first of his younger brothers, that ever so accidentally jostled or otherwise disturbed him. But these are two contradictory suppositions in the state of nature, to be robust and dependent. Man is weak when dependent, and his own master before he grows robust. Hobbes did not consider that the same cause, which hinders savages from making use of their reason, as our jurisconsults pretend, hinders them at the same time from making an ill use of their faculties, as he himself pretends; so that we may say that savages are not bad, precisely because they don't know what it is to be good; for it is neither the development of the understanding, nor the curb of the law, but the calmness of their passions and their ignorance of vice that hinder them from doing ill: *tanto plus in illis proficit vitiorum ignoratio, quam in his cognitio virtutis.** There is besides another principle that has escaped Hobbes, and which, having been given to man to moderate, on certain occasions, the ferocity of self-love, or the desire of self-preservation previous to the appearance of that love (o) tempers the ardor, with which he naturally pursues his private welfare, by an innate abhorrence to see beings suffer that resemble him. I shall not surely be contradicted, in granting to man the only natural virtue, which the most passionate detractor of human virtues could not deny him, I mean that of pity, a disposition suitable to creatures weak as we are, and liable to so many evils; a virtue so much the more universal, and withal useful to man, as it takes place in him before all manner of reflection; and so natural, that the beasts themselves sometimes give evident signs of it. Not to speak of the tenderness of mothers for their young; and of the dangers they face to screen them from danger; with what reluctance are horses known to trample upon living bodies; one animal never passes unmoved by the dead carcass of another animal of the same species: there are even some who bestow a kind of sepulture upon their dead fellows; and the mournful lowings of cattle, on their entering the slaughterhouse, publish the impression made upon them by the horrible spectacle they are there struck with. It is with pleasure we see the author of the Fable of the Bees,[†] forced to acknowledge man a compassionate and sensitive being; and lay aside, in the example he offers to confirm it, his cold and subtle style, to place before us the pathetic picture of a man, who, with his hands tied up, is obliged to behold a beast of prey tear a child from the arms of his mother, and then with his teeth grind the tender limbs, and with

---

* "So much more does ignorance of vice profit these than knowledge of virtue the others." (Justin, *Histories*, II, 2.)

† Mandeville.

his claws rend the throbbing entrails of the innocent victim. What horrible emotions must not such a spectator experience at the sight of an event which does not personally concern him? What anguish must he not suffer at his not being able to assist the fainting mother or the expiring infant?

Such is the pure impulse of nature, anterior to all manner of reflection; such is the force of natural pity, which the most dissolute manners have as yet found it so difficult to extinguish, since we every day see, in our theatrical representations, those men sympathize with the unfortunate and weep at their sufferings, who, if in the tyrant's place, would aggravate the torments of their enemies. Mandeville was aware that men, in spite of all their morality, would never have been better than monsters, if nature had not given them pity to assist reason: but he did not perceive that from this quality alone flow all the social virtues which he would dispute mankind the possession of. In fact, what is generosity, what clemency, what humanity, but pity applied to the weak, to the guilty, or to the human species in general? Even benevolence and friendship, if we judge right, will appear the effects of a constant pity, fixed upon a particular object: for to wish that a person may not suffer, what is it but to wish that he may be happy? Though it were true that commiseration is no more than a sentiment, which puts us in the place of him who suffers, a sentiment obscure but active in the savage, developed but dormant in civilized man, how could this notion affect the truth of what I advance, but to make it more evident? In fact, commiseration must be so much the more energetic, the more intimately the animal, that beholds any kind of distress, identifies himself with the animal that labors under it. Now it is evident that this identification must have been infinitely more perfect in the state of nature, than in the state of reason. It is reason that engenders self-love, and reflection that strengthens it; it is reason that makes man shrink into himself; it is reason that makes him keep aloof from everything that can trouble or afflict him; it is philosophy that destroys his connections with other men; it is in consequence of her dictates that he mutters to himself at the sight of another in distress, You may perish for aught I care, I am safe. Nothing less than those evils, which threaten the whole community, can disturb the calm sleep of the philosopher, and force him from his bed. One man may with impunity murder another under his windows; he has nothing to do but clap his hands to his ears, argue a little with himself to hinder nature, that startles within him, from identifying him with the unhappy sufferer. Savage man lacks this admirable talent; and for want of wisdom and reason, is always ready foolishly to obey the first whispers of humanity. In riots and street brawls the populace flock together, the prudent man sneaks off. It is the dregs of the people, the market women, that part the combatants, and hinder gentlefolks from cutting one another's throats.

It is therefore certain that pity is a natural sentiment, which, by moderating in every individual the activity of self-love, contributes to the mutual preservation of the whole species. It is this pity which hurries us without reflection to the assistance of those we see in distress; it is this pity which, in a state of nature, takes the place of laws, manners, virtue, with this advantage, that no one is tempted to disobey her gentle voice: it is this pity which will always hinder a robust savage from plundering a feeble child, or infirm old man, of the subsistence they have acquired with pain and difficulty, if he has but the least prospect of providing for himself by any other means: it is this pity which, instead of that sublime maxim of rational justice, *Do to others as you would have others do to you,* inspires all men with that other maxim of natural goodness a great deal less perfect, but perhaps more useful, *Do good to yourself with as little prejudice as you can to others.* It is in a word, in this natural sentiment, rather than in finespun arguments, that we must look for the cause of that reluctance which every man would experience to do evil, even independently of the maxims of education. Though it may be the peculiar happiness of Socrates and other geniuses of his stamp to reason themselves into virtue, the human species would long ago have ceased to exist, had it depended entirely for its preservation on the reasonings of the individuals that compose it.

With passions so tame, and so salutary a curb, men, rather wild than wicked, and more attentive to guard against harm than to do any to other animals, were not exposed to any dangerous dissensions: as they kept up no manner of intercourse with each other, and were of course strangers to vanity, to respect, to esteem, to contempt; as they had no notion of what we call thine and mine, nor any true idea of justice; as they considered any violence they were liable to as an evil that could be easily repaired, and not as an injury that deserved punishment; and as they never so much as dreamed of revenge, unless perhaps mechanically and unpremeditatedly, as a dog who bites the stone that has been thrown at him; their disputes could seldom be attended with bloodshed, were they never occasioned by a more considerable stake than that of subsistence: but there is a more dangerous subject of contention, which I must not leave unnoticed.

Among the passions which ruffle the heart of man, there is one of a hot and impetuous nature, which renders the sexes necessary to each other; a terrible passion which despises all dangers, bears down all obstacles, and which in its transports seems proper to destroy the human species which it is destined to preserve. What must become of men abandoned to this lawless and brutal rage, without modesty, without shame, and every day disputing the objects of their passion at the expense of their blood?

We must in the first place allow that the more violent the passions, the more necessary are laws to restrain them: but besides that the disorders and the crimes, to which these passions daily give rise among us, sufficiently prove the insufficiency of laws for that purpose, we would do well to look back a little further and examine, if these evils did not spring up with the laws themselves; for at this rate, even if the laws were capable of repressing these evils, it is the least that might be expected from them, that they should check a mischief which would not exist without them.

Let us begin by distinguishing between what is moral and what is physical in the passion called love. The physical part of it is that general desire which prompts the sexes to unite with each other; the moral part is that which determines this desire, and fixes it upon a particular object to the exclusion of all others, or at least gives it a greater degree of energy for this preferred object. Now it is easy to perceive that the moral part of love is a factitious sentiment, engendered by society, and cried up by the women with great care and address in order to establish their empire, and secure command to that sex which ought to obey. This sentiment, being founded on certain notions of beauty and merit which a savage is not capable of having, and upon comparisons which he is not capable of making, can scarcely exist in him: for as his mind was never in a condition to form abstract ideas of regularity and proportion, neither is his heart susceptible of sentiments of admiration and love, which, even without our perceiving it, are produced by our application of these ideas; he listens solely to the dispositions implanted in him by nature, and not the taste which he never could have acquired; and any woman answers his purpose.

Confined entirely to what is physical in love, and happy enough not to know these preferences which sharpen the appetite for it, at the same time that they increase the difficulty of satisfying such appetite, men, in a state of nature, must be subject to fewer and less violent fits of that passion, and of course there must be fewer and less violent disputes among them in consequence of it. The imagination, which causes so many ravages among us, never speaks to the heart of savages, who peaceably wait for the impulses of nature, yield to these impulses without choice and with more pleasure than fury; and the need once satisfied, all desire is lost.

Nothing therefore can be more evident, than that it is society alone, which has added even to love itself as well as to all the other passions, that impetuous ardor, which so often renders it fatal to mankind; and it is so much the more ridiculous to represent savages constantly murdering each other to glut their brutality, as this opinion is diametrically opposite to experience, and the Caribbeans, the people in the world who have as yet deviated least from the state of nature, are to all intents and purposes the most peaceable in their amours, and the least subject to jealousy, though they live in a burning climate which seems always to add considerably to the activity of these passions.

As to the inductions which may be drawn, in respect to several species of animals, from the battles of the males, who in all seasons cover our poultry yards with blood, and in spring particularly cause our forests to ring again with the noise they make in disputing their females, we must begin by excluding all those species where nature has evidently established, in the relative power of the sexes, relations different from those which exist among us: thus from the battles of cocks we can form no induction that will affect the human species. In the species, where the proportion is better observed, these battles must be owing entirely to the fewness of the females compared with the males, or what amounts to the same, to the intervals of refusal, during which the female constantly refuses the advances of the males; for if the female admits the male but two months in the year, it is all the same as if the number of females were five-sixths less: now neither of these cases is applicable to the human species, where the number of females generally surpasses that of males, and where it has never been observed that, even among savages, the females had, like those of other animals, their stated times of heat and indifference. Besides, among several of these animals the whole species takes fire all at once, and for some days nothing is to be seen among them but confusion, tumult, disorder and bloodshed; a state unknown to the human species, where love is never periodical. We cannot therefore conclude from the battles of certain animals for the possession of their females, that the same would be the case of man in a state of nature; and even if we did, since these contests do not destroy the other species, there is at least equal room to think they would not be fatal to ours; and it is very probable that they would cause fewer ravages than they do in society, especially in those countries where, morality being as yet held in some esteem, the jealousy of lovers and the vengeance of husbands every day produce duels, murders, and even worse crimes; where the duty of an eternal fidelity serves only to propagate adultery; and the very laws of continence and honor necessarily increase dissoluteness, and multiply abortions.

Let us conclude that savage man, wandering about in the forests, without industry, without speech, without any fixed residence, an equal stranger to war and every social tie, without any need of his fellows, as well as without any desire of hurting them, and perhaps even without ever distinguishing them individually one from the other, subject to few passions, and finding in himself all he wants, let us, I say, conclude that savage man had no knowledge or feelings but such as were proper to that situation; that he felt only his real necessities, took notice of nothing but what it was his interest to see, and that his understanding made as little progress as his vanity. If he happened to make any discovery, he could the less communicate it as he did not even know his children. The art perished with the inventor; there was neither education nor improvement; generations succeeded generations to no benefit; and as all constantly set out from the same point, whole centuries rolled on in the rudeness and barbarity of the first age; the race was grown old, and man still remained a child.

If I have enlarged so much upon the supposition of this primitive condition, it is because I thought it my duty, considering what ancient errors and inveterate prejudices I have to extirpate, to dig to the very roots, and show in a true picture of the state of nature, how much even natural inequality falls short in this state of that reality and influence which our writers ascribe to it.

In fact, we may easily perceive that among the differences, which distinguish men, several pass for natural, which are merely the work of habit and the different kinds of life adopted by men living in a social way. Thus a robust or delicate constitution, and the strength and weakness which depend on it, are oftener produced by the hardy or effeminate manner in which a man has been brought up, than by the primitive constitution of his body. It is the same thus in regard to the forces of the mind; and education not only produces a difference between those minds which are cultivated and those which are not, but even increases the difference which is found among the former in proportion to their culture; for let a giant and a dwarf set out in the same road, the giant at every step will acquire a new advantage over the dwarf. Now, if we compare the prodigious variety in the education and way of living of the various orders of men in a civil state, with the simplicity and uniformity that prevail in the animal and savage life, where all the individuals feed on the same food, live in the same manner, and do exactly the same things, we shall easily conceive how much the difference between man and man in the state of nature must be less than in the state of society, and how greatly every social inequality must increase the natural inequalities of mankind.

But even if nature in the distribution of her gifts should really affect all the preferences that are imputed to her, what advantage could the most favored derive from her partiality, to the prejudice of others in a state of things which admits hardly any kind of relation between them? Of what service can beauty be, where there is no love? What will wit avail people who don't speak, or cunning those who have no business? Authors are constantly crying out, that the strongest would oppress the weakest; but let them explain what they mean by the word oppression. One man will rule with violence, another will groan under a constant subjection to all his caprices: this is indeed precisely what I observe among us, but I don't see how it can be said of savage men, into whose heads it would be a hard matter to drive even the meaning of the words domination and servitude. One man might indeed seize the fruits which another had gathered, the game which another had killed, the cavern which another had occupied for shelter; but how is it possible he should ever exact obedience from him, and what chains of dependence can there be among men who possess nothing? If I am driven from one tree, I have nothing to do but look out for another; if one place is made uneasy to me, what can hinder me from taking up my quarters elsewhere? But suppose I should meet a man so much superior to me in strength, and withal so depraved, so lazy and so barbarous as to oblige me to provide for his subsistence while he remains idle; he must resolve not to take his eyes from me a single moment, to bind me fast before he can take the least nap, lest I should kill him or give him the slip during his sleep: that is to say, he must expose himself voluntarily to much greater troubles than what he seeks to avoid, than any he gives me. And after all this, let him abate ever so little of his vigilance; let him at some sudden noise but turn his head another way; I am already buried in the forest, my fetters are broken, and he never sees me again.

But without insisting any longer upon these details, everyone must see that, as the bonds of servitude are formed merely by the mutual dependence of men one upon another and the reciprocal necessities which unite them, it is impossible for one man to enslave another, without having first reduced him to a condition which, as it does not exist in a state of nature, must leave every man his own master, and render the law of the strongest altogether vain and useless.

Having proved that inequality in the state of nature is scarcely felt, and that it has very little influence, I must now proceed to show its origin and trace its progress, in the successive developments of the human mind. After having showed that *perfectibility*, the social virtues, and the other faculties, which natural man had received as potentialities, could never be developed of themselves, that they needed the fortuitous concurrence of several foreign causes, which might never arise, and without which he must have eternally remained in his primitive condition, I must proceed to consider and bring together the different accidents which may have perfected the human understanding while debasing the species, and made man wicked by making him sociable, and from so remote a time bring man at last and the world to the point at which we now see them.

I must own that, as the events I am about to describe might have happened many different ways, I can determine my choice only by mere conjecture; but aside from the fact that these conjectures become reasons, when they are the most probable that can be drawn from the nature of things and the only means we can have of discovering truth, the consequences I mean to deduce from mine will not be merely conjectural, since, on the principles I have just established, it is impossible to form any other system, that would not supply me with the same results, and from which I might not draw the same conclusions.

This will make it unnecessary for me to dwell on the manner in which the lapse of time compensates for the slight probability of events; on the surpising power of very trivial causes, when their action is constant; on the impossibility, on the one hand, of destroying certain hypotheses, while on the other we cannot give them the degrees of certainty of facts; on its being the business of history, when two facts are proposed, as real, and connected by a chain of intermediate facts which are either unknown or considered as such, to furnish such facts as may actually connect them; and the business of philosophy, when history is silent, to point out similar facts which may answer the same purpose; finally, on the power of similarity, in regard to events, to reduce facts to a much smaller number of different classes than is generally imagined. It suffices me to offer these matters to the consideration of my judges; it suffices me to have conducted my inquiry in such a manner as to save the general reader the trouble of considering them at all.

Second Part

The first man, who after enclosing a piece of ground, took it into his head to say, *this is mine*, and found people simple enough to believe him, was the real founder of civil society. How many crimes, how many wars, how many murders, how many misfortunes and horrors, would that man have saved the human species, who pulling up the stakes or filling up the ditches should have cried to his fellows: Beware of listening to this impostor; you are lost, if you forget that the fruits of the earth belong equally to us all, and the earth itself to nobody! But it is highly probable that things had by then already come to such a pass, that they could not continue much longer as they were;

for as this idea of property depends on several prior ideas which could only spring up gradually one after another, it was not formed all at once in the human mind: men must have made considerable progress; they must have acquired a great stock of industry and knowledge, and transmitted and increased it from age to age before they could arrive at this last point of the state of nature. Let us therefore take up things at an earlier stage, and collect into one point of view, and in their most natural order, the slow succession of events and discoveries.

Man's first feeling was that of his existence, his first care that of preserving it. The productions of the earth yielded him all the assistance he required, instinct prompted him to make use of them. Hunger and other appetites made him at different times experience different modes of existence; one of these excited him to perpetuate his species; and this blind propensity, quite void of anything like pure love or affection, produced nothing but an act that was merely animal. Their need once gratified, the sexes took no further notice of each other, and even the child was nothing to his mother, the moment he could do without her.

Such was the condition of infant man; such was the life of an animal confined at first to pure sensations, and so far from harboring any thought of forcing her gifts from nature, that he scarcely availed himself of those which she offered to him of her own accord. But difficulties soon arose, and there was a necessity for learning how to surmount them: the height of some trees, which prevented his reaching their fruits; the competition of other animals equally fond of the same fruits; the fierceness of many that even aimed at his life; these were so many circumstances, which obliged him to apply to bodily exercise. There was a necessity for becoming active, swift-footed, and sturdy in battle. The natural arms, which are stones and the branches of trees, soon offered themselves to his reach. He learned to surmount the obstacles of nature, to fight when necessary with other animals, to fight for his subsistence even with other men, or indemnify himself for the loss of whatever he found himself obliged to yield to a stronger.

In proportion as the human species grew more numerous, and extended itself, its difficulties likewise multiplied and increased. The difference of soils, climates and seasons succeeded in forcing them to introduce some difference in their way of living. Bad harvests, long and severe winters, and scorching summers which parched up all the fruits of the earth, required a new resourcefulness and activity.* On the seashore, and the banks of rivers, they invented the line and the hook, and became fishermen and fish-eaters.

* The French word *industrie* combines both meanings.

In the forests they made themselves bows and arrows, and became hunts-men and warriors. In the cold countries they covered themselves with the skins of the beasts they had killed; thunder, a volcano, or some happy accident made them acquainted with fire, a new resource against the rigors of winter: they discovered the method of preserving this element, then that of reproducing it, and lastly the way of preparing with it the flesh of ani-mals, which heretofore they had devoured raw.

This reiterated applying of various things to himself, and to one another, must have naturally engendered in the mind of man the idea of certain relations. These relations, which we express by the words, great, little, strong, weak, swift, slow, fearful, bold, and the like, compared occasionally, and almost without thinking of it, produced in him some kind of reflection, or rather a mechanical prudence, which pointed out to him the precautions most essential to his safety.

The new knowledge resulting from this development increased his supe-riority over other animals, by making him aware of it. He applied himself to learning how to ensnare them; he played them a thousand tricks; and though several surpassed him in strength or in swiftness, he in time became the master of those that could serve him, and a sore enemy to those that could do him mischief. Thus it was that the first look he gave into himself pro-duced the first emotion of pride in him; thus it was that at a time he scarcely knew how to distinguish between the different orders of beings, in consider-ing himself the highest by virtue of his species he prepared the way for his much later claim to preeminence as an individual.

Though other men were not to him what they are to us, and he had scarcely more intercourse with them than with other animals, they were not overlooked in his observations. The conformities, which in time he was able to perceive between them, and between himself and his female, made him presume of those he did not perceive; and seeing that they all behaved as he himself would have done in similar circumstances, he concluded that their manner of thinking and feeling was quite conformable to his own; and this important truth, when once engraved deeply on his mind, made him follow, by an intuition as sure and swift as any reasoning, the best rules of conduct, which for the sake of his own safety and advantage it was proper he should observe toward them.

Instructed by experience that the love of well-being is the sole spring of all human actions, he found himself in a condition to distinguish the few cases, in which common interest might authorize him to count on the assis-tance of his fellows, and those still fewer, in which a competition of inter-ests should make him distrust them. In the first case he united with them in the same herd, or at most by some kind of free association which obliged none of its members, and lasted no longer than the transitory necessity that had given birth to it. In the second case every one aimed at his own private advantage, either by open force if he found himself strong enough, or by ruse and cunning if he felt himself the weaker.

Such was the manner in which men were gradually able to acquire some gross idea of mutual engagements and the advantage of fulfilling them, but this only as far as their present and obvious interest required; for they were strangers to foresight, and far from troubling their heads about a distant futurity, they gave no thought even to the morrow. Was a deer to be taken? Every one saw that to succeed he must faithfully stand to his post; but suppose a hare to have slipped by within reach of any one of them, it is not to be doubted that he pursued it without scruple, and when he had seized his prey never reproached himself with having made his companions miss theirs.

We may easily conceive that such an intercourse scarcely required a more refined language than that of crows and monkeys, which flock together almost in the same manner. Inarticulate exclamations, a great many gestures, and some imitative sounds, must have been for a long time the universal language of mankind, and by joining to these in every country some articulate and conventional sounds, of which, as I have already said, it is not very easy to explain the first institution, there arose particular languages, but rude, imperfect, and such nearly as are to be found at this day among several savage nations. Hurried on by the rapidity of time, the abundance of things I have to say, and the almost imperceptible progress of the first improvements, my pen flies like an arrow over numberless ages; for the slower the succession of events, the more quickly are they told.

At length, these first advances enabled man to make others at a greater rate. He became more industrious in proportion as his mind became more enlightened. Men, soon ceasing to fall asleep under the first tree, or take shelter in the first cave, hit upon several kinds of hatchets of hard and sharp stones, and employed them to dig the ground, cut down trees, and with the branches build huts, which they afterwards bethought themselves of plastering over with clay or mud. This was the epoch of a first revolution, which produced the establishment and distinction of families, and which introduced a species of property, and already along with it perhaps a thousand quarrels and battles. As the strongest however were probably the first to make themselves cabins, which they knew they were able to defend, we may conclude that the weak found it much shorter and safer to imitate, than to attempt to dislodge them: and as to those, who were already provided with cabins, no one could have any great temptation to seize upon that of his neighbor, not so much because it did not belong to him, as because he did not need it; and as he could not make himself master of it without exposing himself to a very sharp fight with the family that was occupying it.

The first developments of the heart were the effects of a new situation, which united husbands and wives, parents and children, under one roof; the habit of living together gave birth to the sweetest sentiments the human species is acquainted with, conjugal and paternal love. Every family became a little society, so much the more firmly united, as mutual attachment and liberty were its only bonds; and it was now that the sexes, whose way of life had been hitherto the same, began to adopt different ways. The women became more sedentary, and accustomed themselves to stay at home and look after the children, while the men rambled abroad in quest of subsistence for the whole family. The two sexes likewise by living a little more at their ease began to lose somewhat of their usual ferocity and sturdiness: but if on the one hand individuals became less able to engage separately with wild beasts, they on the other were more easily got together to make a common resistance against them.

In this new state of things, the simplicity and solitariness of man's life, the paucity of his wants, and the instruments which he had invented to satisfy them leaving him a great deal of leisure, he employed it to supply himself with several conveniences unknown to his ancestors; and this was the first yoke he inadvertently imposed upon himself, and the first source of evils which he prepared for his descendants; for besides continuing in this manner to soften both body and mind, these conveniences having through use lost almost all their ability to please, and having at the same time degenerated into real needs, the privation of them became far more intolerable than the possession of them had been agreeable; to lose them was a misfortune, to possess them no happiness.

Here we may a little better discover how the use of speech was gradually established or improved in the bosom of every family, and we may likewise form conjectures concerning the manner in which divers particular causes may have propagated language, and accelerated its progress by rendering it every day more and more necessary. Great inundations or earthquakes surrounded inhabited districts with water or precipices. Portions of the continent were by revolutions of the globe torn off and split into islands. It is obvious that among men thus collected, and forced to live together, a common idiom must have started up much sooner, than among those who freely wandered through the forests of the mainland. Thus it is very possible that the inhabitants of the islands, after their first essays in navigation, brought among us the use of speech; and it is very probable at least that society and languages commenced in islands, and even were highly developed there, before the inhabitants of the continent knew anything of either.

Everything now begins to wear a new aspect. Those who heretofore wandered through the woods, by taking to a more settled way of life, gradually flock together, coalesce into several separate bodies, and at length form in every country a distinct nation, united in character and manners, not by any laws or regulations, but by the same way of life, and alimentation, and the common influence of the climate. Living permanently near each other could not fail eventually to create some connection between different families. The transient commerce required by nature soon produced, among the youth of both sexes living in neighboring huts, another kind of commerce, which besides being not less agreeable is rendered more durable by mutual association. Men begin to consider different objects, and to make comparisons; they imperceptibly acquire ideas of merit and beauty, and these soon give rise to feelings of preference. By seeing each other often they contract a habit, which makes it painful not to see each other always. Tender and agreeable sentiments steal into the soul, and are by the smallest opposition wound up into the most impetuous fury: jealousy kindles with love; discord triumphs; and the gentlest of passions requires sacrifices of human blood to appease it.

In proportion as ideas and feelings succeed each other, and the head and the heart become active, men continue to shake off their original wildness, and their connections become more intimate and extensive. They now began to assemble round a great tree: singing and dancing, the genuine offspring of love and leisure, became the amusement or rather the occupation of the men and women, free from care, thus gathered together. Everyone began to notice the rest, and wished to be noticed himself; and public esteem acquired a value. He who sang or danced best; the handsomest, the strongest, the most dexterous, or the most eloquent, came to be the most respected: this was the first step towards inequality, and at the same time towards vice. From these first distinctions there arose on one side vanity and contempt, on the other envy and shame; and the fermentation raised by these new leavens at length produced combinations fatal to happiness and innocence.

Men no sooner began to set a value upon each other, and know what esteem was, than each laid claim to it, and it was no longer safe for any man to refuse it to another. Hence the first duties of politeness, even among savages; and hence every voluntary injury became an affront, as besides the hurt which resulted from it as an injury, the offended party was sure to find in it a contempt for his person often more intolerable than the hurt itself. It is thus that every man, punishing the contempt expressed for him by others in proportion to the value he set upon himself, the effects of revenge became terrible, and men learned to be sanguinary and cruel. Such precisely was the degree attained by most of the savage nations with whom we are acquainted. And it is for want of sufficiently distinguishing ideas, and observing at how great a distance these people were from the first state of nature, that so many authors have hastily concluded that man is naturally cruel, and requires a civil government to make him more gentle; whereas nothing is more gentle than he in his primitive state, when placed by nature at an equal distance from the stupidity of brutes, and the pernicious enlightenment of civilized man; and confined equally by instinct and reason to providing against the harm which threatens him, he is withheld by natural compassion from doing any injury to others, so far from being led even to return that which he has received. For according to the axiom of the wise Locke, *Where there is no property, there can be no injury.*

But we must take notice, that the society now formed and the relations now established among men required in them qualities different from those which they derived from their primitive constitution; that as a sense of morality began to insinuate itself into human actions, and every man, before the enacting of laws, was the only judge and avenger of the injuries he had received, that goodness of heart suitable to the pure state of nature by no means was suitable for the new society; that it was necessary punishments should become severer in the same proportion that the opportunities of offending became more frequent, and the dread of vengeance add strength to the too weak curb of the law. Thus, though men had become less patient, and natural compassion had already suffered some alteration, this period of the development of the human faculties, holding a just mean between the indolence of the primitive state and the petulant activity of egoism, must have been the happiest and most durable epoch. The more we reflect on this state, the more convinced we shall be, that it was the least subject of any to revolutions, the best for man, (p) and that nothing could have drawn him out of it but some fatal accident, which, for the common good, should never have happened. The example of savages, most of whom have been found in this condition, seems to confirm that mankind was formed ever to remain in it, that this condition is the real youth of the world, and that all ulterior improvements have been so many steps, in appearance towards the perfection of individuals, but in fact towards the decrepitude of the species.

As long as men remained satisfied with their rustic huts; as long as they were content with clothes made of the skins of animals, sewn with thorns and fish bones; as long as they continued to consider feathers and shells as sufficient ornaments, and to paint their bodies different colors, to improve or ornament their bows and arrows, to fashion with sharp-edged stones some little fishing boats, or clumsy instruments of music; in a word, as long as they undertook such works only as a single person could finish, and stuck to such arts as did not require the joint endeavors of several hands, they lived free, healthy, honest and happy, as much as their nature would admit, and continued to enjoy with each other all the pleasures of an independent intercourse; but from the moment one man began to stand in need of another's assistance; from the moment it appeared an advantage for one man to possess enough provisions for two, equality vanished; property was introduced; labor became necessary; and boundless forests became smiling fields, which had to be watered with human sweat, and in which slavery and misery were soon seen to sprout out and grow with the harvests.

Metallurgy and agriculture were the two arts whose invention produced this great revolution. With the poet, it is gold and silver, but with the philosopher, it is iron and corn, which have civilized men, and ruined mankind. Accordingly both one and the other were unknown to the savages of America, who for that very reason have still remained savages; nay other nations seem to have continued in a state of barbarism, as long as they continued to exercise one only of these arts without the other; and perhaps one of the best reasons that can be assigned, why Europe has been, if not earlier, at least more constantly and highly civilized than the other quarters of the world, is that it both abounds most in iron and is most fertile in corn.

It is very difficult to conjecture how men came to know anything of iron, and the art of employing it: for we are not to suppose that they should of themselves think of digging the ore out of the mine, and preparing it for smelting, before they knew what could be the result of such a process. On the other hand, there is the less reason to attribute this discovery to any accidental fire, as mines are formed nowhere but in barren places, bare of trees and plants, so that it looks as if nature had taken pains to keep from us so mischievous a secret. Nothing therefore remains but the extraordinary chance of some volcano, which belching forth metallic substances already fused might have given the spectators the idea of imitating that operation of nature. And we must further suppose in them great courage and foresight to undertake so laborious a work, and have, at so great a distance, an eye to the advantages they might derive from it; qualities scarcely suitable but to minds more advanced than those can be supposed to have been.

As to agriculture, the principles of it were known a long time before the practice of it took place, and it is hardly possible that men, constantly employed in drawing their subsistence from trees and plants, should not have early hit on the means employed by nature for the generation of vegetables; but in all probability it was very late before their industry took a turn that way, either because trees which with hunting and fishing supplied them with food, did not require their attention; or because they did not know the use of grain; or because they had no instruments to cultivate it; or because they were destitute of foresight in regard to future necessities; or lastly, because they lacked means to hinder others from running away with the fruit of their labors. We may believe that on their becoming more industrious they began their agriculture by cultivating with sharp stones and pointed sticks a few vegetables or roots about their cabins; and that it was a long time before they knew the method of preparing wheat, and were provided with instruments necessary to raise it in large quantities; not to mention the necessity there is, in order to follow this occupation and sow lands, to consent to lose something now to gain a great deal later on; a precaution very foreign to the turn of man's mind in a savage state, in which, as I have already remarked, he can hardly foresee in the morning what he will need at night.

For this reason the invention of other arts must have been necessary to oblige mankind to apply themselves to that of agriculture. As soon as some men were needed to smelt and forge iron, others were wanted to maintain them. The more hands were employed in manufactures, the fewer hands were left to provide subsistence for all, though the number of mouths to be supplied with food continued the same; and as some required commodities in exchange for their iron, the rest at last found out the method of making iron serve for the multiplication of commodities. Thus were established on the one hand husbandry and agriculture, and on the other the art of working metals and of multiplying the uses of them.

The tilling of the land was necessarily followed by its distribution; and property once acknowledged, the first rules of justice ensued: for to secure every man his own, every man had to be able to own something. Moreover, as men began to extend their views toward the future, and all found themselves in possession of goods capable of being lost, there was none without fear of reprisals for any injury he might do to others. This origin is so much the more natural, as it is impossible to conceive how property can flow from any other source but work; for what can a man add but his labor to things which he has not made, in order to acquire a property in them? It is the labor of the hands alone, which giving the husbandman a title to the produce of the land he has tilled gives him a title to the land itself, at least until he has gathered in the fruits of it, and so on from year to year; and this enjoyment forming a continued possession is easily transformed into property. The ancients, says Grotius, by giving to Ceres the epithet of legislatrix, and to a festival celebrated in her honor the name of Thesmophoria, insinuated that the distribution of lands produced a new kind of right; that is the right of property different from that which results from the law of nature.

Things thus circumstanced might have remained equal, if men's talents had been equal, and if, for instance, the use of iron and the consumption of commodities had always held an exact proportion to each other; but as nothing preserved this balance, it was soon broken. The man that had most strength performed most labor; the most dexterous turned his labor to best account; the most ingenious found out methods of lessening his labor; the husbandman required more iron, or the smith more grain, and while both worked equally, one earned a great deal by his labor, while the other could scarcely live by his. Thus natural inequality insensibly unfolds itself with that arising from men's combining, and the differences among men, developed by the differences of their circumstances, become more noticeable, more permanent in their effects, and begin to influence in the same proportion the condition of individuals.

Matters once having reached this point, it is easy to imagine the rest. I shall not stop to describe the successive inventions of other arts, the progress of language, the trial and employment of talents, the inequality of fortunes, the use or abuse of riches, nor all the details which follow these, and which every one may easily supply. I shall just give a glance at mankind placed in this new order of things.

Behold then all our faculties developed; our memory and imagination at work; egoism involved; reason rendered active; and the mind almost arrived at the utmost bounds of that perfection it is capable of. Behold all our natural qualities put in motion; the rank and lot of every man established, not only as to the amount of property and the power of serving or hurting others, but likewise as to genius, beauty, strength or skill, merits or talents; and as these were the only qualities which could command respect, it was found necessary to have or at least to affect them. It became to the interest of men to appear what they really were not. To be and to seem became two very different things, and from this distinction sprang haughty pomp and deceitful knavery, and all the vices which form their train. On the other hand, man, heretofore free and independent, was now, in consequence of a multitude of new needs, brought into subjection, as it were, to all nature, and especially to his fellows, whose slave in some sense he became, even by becoming their master; if rich, he stood in need of their services, if poor, of their assistance; even mediocrity itself could not enable him to do without them. He must therefore have been continually at work to interest them in his happiness, and make them, if not really, at least apparently find their advantage in laboring for his: this rendered him sly and artful in his dealings with some, imperious and cruel in his dealings with others, and laid him under the necessity of using ill all those whom he stood in need of, as often as he could not awe them into compliance and did not find it his interest to be useful to them. In fine, an insatiable ambition, the rage of raising their relative fortunes, not so much through real necessity as to overtop others, inspires all men with a wicked inclination to injure each other, and with a secret jealousy so much the more dangerous, as to carry its point with the greater security it often puts on the mask of benevolence. In a word, competition and rivalry on the one hand, and an opposition of interests on the other, and always a secret desire of profiting at the expense of others. Such were the first effects of property, and the inseparable attendants of nascent inequality.

Riches, before the invention of signs to represent them, could scarcely consist in anything but lands and cattle, the only real goods which men can possess. So, when estates increased so much in number and in extent as to take in whole countries and touch each other, it became impossible for one man to aggrandize himself but at the expense of some other; at the same time, the supernumerary inhabitants, who were too weak or too indolent to make such acquisitions in their turn, impoverished without having lost anything, because while everything about them changed they alone remained the same, were obliged to receive or force their subsistence from the hands of the rich. And from that began to arise, according to their different characters, domination and slavery, or violence and rapine. The rich on their side scarcely began to taste the pleasure of commanding, when they preferred it to every other; and making use of their old slaves to acquire new ones, they no longer thought of anything but subduing and enslaving their neighbors; like those ravenous wolves, who having once tasted human flesh, despise every other food, and thereafter want only men to devour.

It is thus that the most powerful or the most wretched, respectively considering their power and wretchedness as a kind of right to the possessions of others, equivalent in their minds to that of property, the equality once broken was followed by the most terrible disorders. It is thus that the usurpations of the rich, the pillagings of the poor, and the unbridled passions of all, by stifling the cries of natural compassion, and the still feeble voice of justice, rendered men avaricious, wicked, and ambitious. There arose between the title of the strongest and that of the first occupier a perpetual conflict, which always ended in battle and bloodshed. The new state of society became the most horrible state of war: Mankind thus debased and harassed, and no longer able to retrace its steps, or renounce the fatal acquisitions it had made; laboring, in short, merely to its confusion by the abuse of those faculties, which in themselves do it so much honor, brought itself to the very brink of ruin.

> *Attonitus novitate mali, divesque miserque,*
> *Effugere optat opes; et quae modo voverat, odit.* *

But it is impossible that men should not sooner or later have made reflections on so wretched a situation, and upon the calamities with which they were overwhelmed. The rich in particular must have soon perceived how much they suffered by a perpetual war, of which they alone supported all the expense, and in which, though all risked life, they alone risked any property. Besides, whatever color they might pretend to give their usurpations, they sufficiently saw that these usurpations were in the main founded upon false and precarious titles, and that what they had acquired by mere force, others could again by mere force wrest out of their hands, without leaving them the least room to complain of such a proceeding. Even those, who owed all their riches to their own industry, could scarce ground their acquisitions upon a better title. It availed them nothing to say, It was I built this wall; I acquired this spot by my labor. Who traced it out for you, another might object, and what right have you to expect payment at our expense for doing that we did not oblige you to do? Don't you know that numbers of your brethren perish, or suffer grievously for want of what you have too much of, and that you should have had the express and unanimous consent of mankind to appropriate to yourself more of the common subsistence, more than you needed for yours? Destitute of valid reasons to justify, and sufficient forces to defend himself; crushing individuals with ease, but with equal ease crushed by banditti; one against all, and unable, on account of mutual jealousies, to unite with his equals against enemies united by the common hopes of pillage; the rich man, thus pressed by necessity, at last conceived the deepest project that ever entered the human mind: this was to employ in his favor the very forces that attacked him, to make allies of his enemies, to inspire them with other maxims, and make them adopt other institutions as favorable to his pretensions, as the law of nature was unfavorable to them.

With this view, after laying before his neighbors all the horrors of a

---

* Both rich and poor, shocked at their newfound ills, would fly from wealth, and hate what they had sought. (Ovid, *Metamorphoses*, XI, 127.)

situation, which armed them all one against another, which rendered their possessions as burdensome as their wants, and in which no one could expect any safety either in poverty or riches, he easily invented specious arguments to bring them over to his purpose. "Let us unite," said he, "to secure the weak from oppression, restrain the ambitious, and secure to every man the possession of what belongs to him: Let us form rules of justice and of peace, to which all may be obliged to conform, which shall give no preference to anyone, but may in some sort make amends for the caprice of fortune, by submitting alike the powerful and the weak to the observance of mutual duties. In a word, instead of turning our forces against ourselves, let us collect them into a sovereign power, which may govern us by wise laws, may protect and defend all the members of the association, repel common enemies, and maintain a perpetual concord and harmony among us."

Many fewer words of this kind would have sufficed to persuade men so uncultured and easily seduced, who had besides too many quarrels among themselves to live without arbiters, and too much avarice and ambition to live long without masters. All gladly offered their necks to the yoke, thinking they were securing their liberty; for though they had sense enough to perceive the advantages of a political constitution, they had not experience enough to see beforehand the dangers of it. Those among them who were best qualified to foresee abuses were precisely those who expected to benefit by them; even the soberest judged it requisite to sacrifice one part of their liberty to insure the rest, as a wounded man has his arm cut off to save the rest of his body.

Such was, or must have been the origin of society and of law, which gave new fetters to the weak and new power to the rich; irretrievably destroyed natural liberty, fixed forever the laws of property and inequality; changed an artful usurpation into an irrevocable right; and for the benefit of a few ambitious individuals subjected the rest of mankind to perpetual labor, servitude, and misery. We may easily conceive how the establishment of a single society rendered that of all the rest absolutely necessary, and how, to withstand united forces, it became necessary for the rest of mankind to unite in their turn. Societies once formed in this manner, soon multiplied or spread to such a degree, as to cover the face of the earth; and not to leave a corner in the whole universe, where a man could throw off the yoke, and withdraw his head from under the often ill-conducted sword which he saw perpetually hanging over it. The civil law being thus become the common rule of citizens, the law of nature no longer obtained except between the different societies, where under the name of the law of nations, it was modified by some tacit conventions to render commerce possible, and supply the place of natural compassion, which, losing by degrees all that influence over societies which it originally had over individuals, no longer exists but in some great souls, who consider themselves as citizens of the world, force the imaginary barriers that separate people from people, after the example of the sovereign being from whom we all derive our existence, and include the whole human race in their benevolence.

Political bodies, thus remaining in a state of nature among themselves, soon experienced the inconveniencies that had obliged individuals to quit it; and this state became much more fatal to these great bodies, than it had been before to the individuals who now composed them. Hence those national wars, those battles, those murders, those reprisals, which make nature shudder and shock reason; hence all those horrible prejudices, which make it a virtue and an honor to shed human blood. The worthiest men learned to consider cutting the throats of their fellows as a duty; at length men began to butcher each other by thousands without knowing for what; and more murders were committed in a single action, and more horrible disorders at the taking of a single town, than had been committed in the state of nature during ages together upon the whole face of the earth. Such are the first effects we may conceive to have arisen from the division of mankind into different societies. Let us return to their institution.

I know that several writers have assigned other origins to political society; as for instance, the conquests of the powerful, or the union of the weak; and it is no matter which of these causes we adopt in regard to what I am going to establish. That which I have just laid down, however, seems to me the most natural, for the following reasons. First, because, in the first case, the right of conquest being in fact no right at all, it could not serve as a foundation for any other right, the conqueror and the conquered ever remaining with respect to each other in a state of war, unless the conquered, restored to the full possession of their liberty, should freely choose their conqueror for their chief. Until then, whatever capitulations might have been made between them being founded upon violence, and thus *ipso facto* null and void, there could not have existed in this hypothesis either a true society, or a political body, or any other law but that of the strongest. Secondly, because these words *strong* and *weak,* are, in the second case, ambiguous; for during the interval between the establishment of the right of property or prior occupancy, and that of political government, the meaning of these terms is better expressed by the words *poor* and *rich,* as before the establishment of laws men in reality had no other means of subjecting their equals, but by invading their property, or by parting with some of their own property to them. Thirdly, because the poor having nothing but their liberty to lose, it would have been the height of madness in them to give up willingly the only blessing they had left without obtaining some consideration for it; whereas the rich being sensitive if I may say so, in every part of their possessions, it was much easier to do them mischief, and therefore more incumbent upon them to guard against it; and because, in fine, it is but reasonable to suppose that a thing has been invented by him to whom it could be of service, rather than by him to whom it must prove detrimental.

Government in its infancy had no regular and permanent form. For want of a sufficient fund of philosophy and experience, men could see no further than the present inconveniencies, and never thought of providing for future ones except as they arose. In spite of all the labors of the wisest legislators, the political state still continued imperfect, because it was in a manner the work of chance; and, as the foundations of it were ill laid, time, though sufficient to reveal its defects and suggest the remedies for them, could never mend its original faults. It was always being mended; whereas they should have begun as Lycurgus did at Sparta, by clearing the ground and removing all the old materials, so that they could then put up a good edifice. Society at first consisted merely of some general conventions which all the members bound themselves to observe, and the performance of which the whole body guaranteed to every individual. Experience was necessary to show the great weakness of such a constitution, and how easy it was for those who infringed it to escape the conviction or chastisement of faults, of which the public alone was to be both the witness and the judge; the laws could not fail of being eluded a thousand ways; inconveniencies and disorders could not but multiply continually, until it was at last found necessary to think of committing to private persons the dangerous trust of public authority, and to magistrates the care of enforcing obedience to the decisions of the people. For to say that chiefs were elected before the confederacy was formed, and that the ministers of the laws existed before the laws themselves, is a supposition too ridiculous to deserve serious refutation.

It would be equally unreasonable to imagine that men at first threw themselves into the arms of an absolute master, without any conditions or consideration on his side; and that the first means contrived by jealous and unconquered men for their common safety was to run headlong into slavery. In fact, why did they give themselves superiors, if it was not to be defended by them against oppression, and protected in their lives, liberties, and properties, which are in a manner the elements of their being? Now in the relations between man and man, the worst that can happen to one man being to see himself at the mercy of another, would it not have been contrary to the dictates of good sense to begin by making over to a chief the only things they needed his assistance to preserve? What equivalent could he have offered them for so great a right? And had he presumed to exact it on pretense of defending them, would he not have immediately received the answer in the fable: What worse will an enemy do to us? It is therefore past dispute, and indeed a fundamental maxim of all political law, that people gave themselves chiefs to defend their liberty and not to be enslaved by them. *If we have a Prince,* said Pliny to Trajan, *it is in order that he may keep us from having a master.*

Politicians argue in regard to the love of liberty with the same sophistry that philosophers do in regard to the state of nature; by the things they see they judge of things very different which they have never seen, and they attribute to men a natural inclination to slavery, on account of the patience with which the slaves within their notice bear the yoke; not reflecting that it is with liberty as with innocence and virtue, the value of which is not known but by those who possess them, and the taste for which is lost when they are lost. I know the charms of your country, said Brasidas to a satrap who was comparing the life of the Spartans with that of the Persepolites; but you cannot know the pleasures of mine.

As an unbroken courser erects his mane, paws the ground, and rages at the bare sight of the bit, while a trained horse patiently suffers both whip and spur, just so the barbarian will never reach his neck to the yoke that civilized man carries without murmuring, but prefers the most stormy liberty to a peaceful slavery. It is not therefore by the servile disposition of enslaved nations that we might judge of the natural dispositions of man for or against slavery, but by the prodigies done by every free people to secure themselves from oppression. I know that the former are constantly crying up that peace and tranquillity they enjoy in their irons, and that *miserrimam servitutem pacem appellant:** But when I see the latter sacrifice pleasures, peace, riches, power, and even life itself to the preservation of that one treasure so disdained by those who have lost it; when I see freeborn animals through a natural abhorrence of captivity dash their brains out against the bars of their prison; when I see multitudes of naked savages despise European pleasures, and brave hunger, fire and sword, and death itself to preserve their independence, I feel that it is not for slaves to argue about liberty.

As to paternal authority, from which several have derived absolute government and every other mode of society, it is sufficient, without having recourse to Locke and Sidney, to observe that nothing in the world differs

---

* "They call the most wretched slavery peace." (Tacitus, *Histories*, IV, 17.)

more from the cruel spirit of despotism than the gentleness of that authority, which looks more to the advantage of him who obeys than to the utility of him who commands; that by the law of nature the father continues master of his child no longer than the child stands in need of his assistance; that after that term they become equal, and that then the son, entirely independent of the father, owes him no obedience, but only respect. Gratitude is indeed a duty which we are bound to pay, but which benefactors cannot exact. Instead of saying that civil society is derived from paternal authority, we should rather say that it is to the former that the latter owes its principal force. No one individual was acknowledged as the father of several other individuals, until they settled about him. The father's goods, which he can indeed dispose of as he pleases, are the ties which hold his children to their dependence upon him, and he may divide his substance among them in proportion as they shall have deserved by a continual deference to his commands. Now the subjects of a despotic chief, far from having any such favor to expect from him, as both themselves and all they have are his property, or at least are considered by him as such, are obliged to receive as a favor what he relinquishes to them of their own property. He does them justice when he strips them; he treats them with mercy when he suffers them to live.

By continuing in this manner to test facts by right, we should discover as little solidity as truth in the voluntary establishment of tyranny; and it would be a hard matter to prove the validity of a contract which was binding only on one side, in which one of the parties should stake everything and the other nothing, and which could only turn out to the prejudice of him who had bound himself. This odious system is even today far from being that of wise and good monarchs, and especially of the kings of France, as may be seen by divers passages in their edicts, and particularly by that of a celebrated piece published in 1667 in the name and by the orders of Louis XIV. "Let it therefore not be said that the Sovereign is not subject to the laws of his Realm, since the contrary is a maxim of the law of nations which flattery has sometimes attacked, but which good princes have always defended as the tutelary divinity of their Realms. How much more reasonable is it to say with the sage Plato, that the perfect happiness of a State consists in the subjects obeying their prince, the prince obeying the laws, and the laws being equitable and always directed to the good of the public?" I shall not stop to consider whether, liberty being the noblest faculty of man, it is not degrading our nature, lowering ourselves to the level of brutes, who are the slaves of instinct, and even offending the author of our being, to renounce without reserve the most precious of his gifts, and to submit to committing all the crimes he has forbidden us, merely to gratify a mad or a cruel master;

and whether that sublime craftsman must be more irritated at seeing his work dishonored than at seeing it destroyed. I shall only ask what right those, who were not afraid thus to degrade themselves, could have to subject their posterity to the same ignominy, and renounce for them, blessings which come not from their liberality, and without which life itself must appear a burden to all those who are worthy to live.

Pufendorf says that, as we can transfer our property from one to another by contracts and conventions, we may likewise divest ourselves of our liberty in favor of other men. This, in my opinion, is a very poor way of arguing; for, in the first place, the property I cede to another becomes a thing quite foreign to me, and the abuse of which can no way affect me; but it concerns me greatly that my liberty is not abused, and I cannot, without incurring the guilt of the crimes I may be forced to commit, expose myself to become the instrument of any. Besides, the right of property being of mere human convention and institution, every man may dispose as he pleases of what he possesses: but the case is otherwise with regard to the essential gifts of nature, such as life and liberty, which every man is permitted to enjoy, and of which it is doubtful at least whether any man has a right to divest himself: by giving up the one, we degrade our being; by giving up the other we annihilate it as much as it is our power to do so; and as no temporal enjoyments can indemnify us for the loss of either, it would be an offense against both nature and reason to renounce them for any consideration. But though we could transfer our liberty as we do our property, it would be quite different with regard to our children, who enjoy the father's property only by the transmission of his right; whereas liberty being a blessing, which as men they hold from nature, their parents have no right to strip them of it; so that, just as to establish slavery it was necessary to do violence to nature, so it was necessary to alter nature to perpetuate such a right; and the jurisconsults, who have gravely pronounced that the child of a slave is born a slave, have in other words decided that a man will not be born a man.

It therefore appears to me incontestibly true, that not only governments did not begin by arbitrary power, which is but the corruption and extreme term of government, and at length brings it back to the law of the strongest against which governments were at first the remedy; but even that, supposing they had begun in this manner, such power being illegal in itself could never have served as a foundation for social law, nor of course for the inequality it instituted.

Without embarking now upon the inquiries which still remain to be made into the nature of the fundamental pact underlying every kind of government, I shall accept the common opinion, and confine myself here to holding the establishment of the political body to be a real contract between the multitude and the chiefs elected by it. A contract by which both parties oblige themselves to the observance of the laws that are therein stipulated, and form the ties of their union. The multitude having, in regard to their social relations, concentrated all their wills in one, all the articles, in regard to which this will expresses itself, become so many fundamental laws, which oblige without exception all the members of the State, and one of which regulates the choice and power of the magistrates appointed to look to the execution of the rest. This power extends to everything that can maintain the constitution, but extends to nothing that can alter it. To this power are added honors, that may render the laws and their ministers respectable; and the ministers are distinguished by certain prerogatives, which may recompense them for the heavy burdens inseparable from a good administration. The magistrate, on his side, obliges himself not to use the power with which he is entrusted except in conformity to the intention of his constituents, to maintain every one of them in a peaceable possession of his property, and upon all occasions prefer the public good to his own private interest.

Before experience had shown, or knowledge of the human heart had made the abuses inseparable from such a constitution foreseeable, it must have appeared so much the more perfect, as those appointed to look to its preservation had themselves had most interest in it; for magistracy and its rights being built solely on the fundamental laws, as soon as these ceased to exist, the magistrates would cease to be legitimate, the people would no longer be bound to obey them, and, as the essence of the State did not consist in the magistrates but in the laws, each one would rightfully regain his natural liberty.

A little reflection would afford us new arguments in confirmation of this truth, and the nature of the contract might alone convince us that it cannot be irrevocable: for if there were no superior power capable of guaranteeing the fidelity of the contracting parties and of obliging them to fulfill their mutual engagements, they would remain sole judges in their own cause, and each of them would always have a right to renounce the contract, as soon as he discovered that the other had broke the conditions of it, or that these conditions ceased to suit his private convenience. Upon this principle, the right of abdication may probably be founded. Now, to consider, as we do, only what is human in this institution, if the magistrate, who has all the power in his own hands, and who appropriates to himself all the advantages of the contract, has nonetheless a right to renounce his authority; how much better a right should the people, who pay for all the faults of its chief, have to renounce their dependence upon him. But the shocking dissensions and disorders without number, which would be the necessary consequence of so dangerous a privilege, show more than anything else how much human governments stood in need of a more solid basis than that of mere reason, and how necessary it was for the public tranquillity, that the will of the Almighty should interpose to give to sovereign authority a sacred and inviolable character, which should deprive subjects of the fatal right to dispose of it. If mankind had received no other advantages from religion, this alone would be sufficient to make them adopt and cherish it, since it is the means of saving more blood than fanaticism has been the cause of spilling. But let us resume the thread of our hypothesis.

The various forms of government owe their origin to the various degrees of inequality that existed between individuals at the time of their institution. Where a man happened to be preeminent in power, virtue, riches, or credit, he became sole magistrate, and the State assumed a monarchical form. If several of pretty equal eminence stood out over all the rest, they were jointly elected, and this election produced an aristocracy. Those whose fortune or talents were less unequal, and who had deviated less from the state of nature, retained in common the supreme administration, and formed a democracy. Time demonstrated which of these forms suited mankind best. Some remained altogether subject to the laws; others soon bowed their necks to masters. The former labored to preserve their liberty; the latter thought of nothing but invading that of their neighbors, jealous at seeing others enjoy a blessing that they themselves had lost. In a word, riches and conquest fell to the share of the one, and virtue and happiness to that of the other.

In these various modes of government the offices at first were all elective; and when riches did not decide, the preference was given to merit, which gives a natural ascendancy, and to age, which is the parent of deliberateness in council, and experience in execution. The ancients among the Hebrews, and Gerontes of Sparta, the Senate of Rome, nay, the very etymology of our word *Seigneur*, show how much gray hairs were formerly respected. The oftener the choice fell upon old men, the oftener it became necessary to repeat it, and the more the trouble of such repetitions became sensible; intrigues took place; factions arose, the parties grew bitter; civil wars blazed forth; the lives of the citizens were sacrificed to the pretended happiness of the State; and things at last came to such a pass, as to be ready to relapse into their primitive confusion. The ambition of the principal men induced them to take advantage of these circumstances to perpetuate the hitherto temporary offices in their families; the people already inured to dependence, accustomed to ease and the conveniences of life, and too much enervated to break their fetters, consented to the increase of their slavery for the sake of securing their tranquillity; and it is thus that chiefs, become hereditary, contracted the habit of considering their offices as a family estate, and themselves as proprietors of those communities, of which at first they were but mere officers; of calling their fellow-citizens their slaves; of numbering them, like cattle, among their belongings; and of calling themselves the peers of gods, and kings of kings.

By pursuing the progress of inequality in these different revolutions, we shall discover that the establishment of laws and of the right of property was the first term of it; the institution of magistrates the second; and the third and last the changing of legal into arbitrary power; so that the different states of the rich and poor were authorized by the first epoch; those of the powerful and weak by the second; and by the third those of master and slave, which formed the last degree of inequality, and the term in which all the rest at last end, until new revolutions entirely dissolve the government, or bring it back nearer to its legal constitution.

To conceive the necessity of this progress, we are not so much to consider the motives for the establishment of the body politic, as the forms it assumes in its realization; and the faults with which it is necessarily attended: for those vices, which render social institutions necessary, are the same which render the abuse of such institutions unavoidable. And as laws (Sparta alone excepted, whose laws chiefly regarded the education of children, and where Lycurgus established such manners and customs, as made laws almost needless) are in general less strong than the passions, and restrain men without changing them, it would be no hard matter to prove that every government, which carefully guarding against all alteration and corruption should scrupulously comply with the purpose of its establishment, was set up unnecessarily; and that a country, where no one either eluded the laws, or made an ill use of magistracy, required neither laws nor magistrates.

Political distinctions necessarily lead to civil distinctions. The inequality between the people and the chiefs increases so fast as to be soon felt by individuals, and appears among them in a thousand shapes according to their passions, their talents, and circumstances. The magistrate cannot usurp any illegal power without making for himself creatures with whom he must share it. Besides, citizens only allow themselves to be oppressed in proportion as hurried on by a blind ambition, and looking rather below than above them, they come to love authority more than independence. When they submit to fetters, it is only to be the better able to fetter others in their turn. It is no easy matter to reduce to obedience a man who does not wish to command; and the most astute politician would find it impossible to subdue those men who only desire to be independent. But inequality easily gains ground among base and ambitious souls, ever ready to run the risks of fortune, and almost indifferent whether they command or obey, as she proves either favorable or adverse to them. Thus then there must have been a time, when the eyes of the people were bewitched to such a degree, that their rulers needed only to have said to the lowest of men, "Be great you and all your posterity," to make him immediately appear great in the eyes of everyone as well as in his own; and his descendants took still more upon them, in proportion to their distance from him: the more distant and uncertain the cause, the greater the effect; the longer line of drones a family produced, the more illustrious it was reckoned.

Were this a proper place to enter into details, I could easily explain in what manner inequalities of credit and authority become unavoidable among private persons (s) the moment that, united into one body, they are obliged to compare themselves one with another, and to note the differences which they find in the continual intercourse every man must have with his neighbor. These differences are of several kinds; but riches, nobility or rank, power, and personal merit, being in general the principal distinctions, by which men in society measure each other, I could prove that the harmony or conflict between these different forces is the surest indication of the good or bad original constitution of any State: I could show that among these four kinds of inequality, personal qualities being the source of all the rest, riches is that in which they ultimately terminate, because, being the most immediately useful to the prosperity of individuals, and the most easy to communicate, they are made use of to purchase every other distinction. By this observation we are enabled to judge with tolerable exactness, how much any people has deviated from its primitive institution, and what steps it has still to make to the extreme term of corruption. I could show how much this universal desire of reputation, of honors, of preference, with which we are all devoured, exercises, and compares our talents and our forces; how much it excites and multiplies our passions; and, by creating a universal competition, rivalry, or rather enmity among men, how many disappointments, successes, and catastrophes of every kind it daily causes among the innumerable aspirants whom it engages in the same competition. I could show that it is to this itch of being spoken of, to this fury of distinguishing ourselves which seldom or never gives us a moment's respite, that we owe both the best and the worst things among us, our virtues and our vices, our sciences and our errors, our conquerors and our philosophers; that is to say, a great many bad things and a very few good ones. I could prove, in short, that if we behold a handful of rich and powerful men seated on the pinnacle of fortune and greatness, while the crowd grovel in darkness and misery, it is merely because the former value what they enjoy only because others are deprived of it; and that, without changing their condition, they would cease to be happy the minute the people ceased to be miserable.

But these details would alone furnish sufficient matter for a more considerable work, in which we might weigh the advantages and disadvantages of every species of government, relatively to the rights of man in a state of nature, and might likewise unveil all the different faces under which inequality has appeared to this day, and may hereafter appear to the end of time, according to the nature of these several governments, and the revolutions which time must unavoidably occasion in them. We should then see the multitude oppressed by domestic tyrants in consequence of those very precautions taken by them to guard against foreign masters. We should see oppression increase continually without its being ever possible for the oppressed to know where it would stop, nor what lawful means they had left to check its progress. We should see the rights of citizens, and the liberties of nations extinguished by slow degrees, and the groans and protestations and appeals of the weak treated as seditious murmurings. We should see policy confine to a mercenary portion of the people the honor of defending the common cause. We should see taxes made necessary, the disheartened husbandman desert his field even in time of peace, and quit the plough to gird on the sword. We should see fatal and whimsical rules laid down for the code of honor. We should see the champions of their country sooner or later become her enemies, and perpetually holding their daggers to the breasts of their fellow-citizens. Nay the time would come when they might be heard to say to the oppressor of their country:

Pectore si fratris gladium juguloque parentis
Condere me jubeas, gravidaeque in viscera partu
Conjugis, invita peragam tamen omnia dextra. *

From the vast inequality of conditions and fortunes, from the great variety of passions and of talents, of useless arts, of pernicious arts, of

---

* "If you order me to plunge my sword into my brother's breast and into my father's throat and into the vitals of my wife heavy with child, I shall do, nevertheless, all these things even though my hand is unwilling." (Lucan, *Pharsalia,* I, 376–8.)

frivolous sciences, would issue clouds of prejudices equally contrary to reason, to happiness, to virtue. We should see the chiefs foment everything that tends to weaken men united in societies by dividing them; everything that, while it gives society an air of apparent harmony, sows in it the seeds of real dissension; everything that can inspire the different classes with mutual distrust and hatred by an opposition of their rights and interests, and so strengthen that power which controls them all.

It is from the midst of this disorder and these revolutions, that despotism, gradually rearing up her hideous head, and devouring in every part of the State all that still remained sound and untainted, would at last succeed in trampling upon the laws and the people, and establish itself upon the ruins of the republic. The times immediately preceding this last alteration would be times of calamity and trouble; but at last everything would be swallowed up by the monster; and the people would no longer have chiefs or laws, but only tyrants. From this fatal moment all regard to virtue and manners would likewise disppear; for despotism, *cui ex honesto nulla est spes,* * tolerates no other master, wherever it reigns; the moment it speaks, probity and duty lose all their influence, and the blindest obedience is the only virtue to slaves.

This is the last term of inequality, the extreme point which closes the circle and meets that from which we set out. It is here that all private men return to their primitive equality, because they are nothing; and that, subjects having no longer any law but the will of their master, nor the master any other law but his passions, all notions of good and principles of justice again disappear. This is when everything returns to the sole law of the strongest, and of course to a new state of nature different from that with which we began, inasmuch as the first was the state of nature in its purity, and this one the consequence of excessive corruption. There is, in other respects, so little difference between these two states, and the contract of government is so much dissolved by despotism, that the despot is master only so long as he continues the strongest, and that, as soon as they can expel him, they may do it without his having the least right to complain of their violence. The insurrection, which ends in the death or deposition of a sultan, is as juridical an act as any by which the day before he disposed of the lives and fortunes of his subjects. Force alone upheld him, force alone overturns him. Thus all things take place and succeed in their natural order; and whatever may be the upshot of these hasty and frequent revolutions, no one man has reason to complain of another's injustice, but only of his own indiscretion or bad fortune.

* "in which there is no hope afforded by honesty."

By thus discovering and following the lost and forgotten road, which man must have followed in going from the state of nature to the social state, by restoring, together with the intermediate positions which I have been just indicating, those which want of time obliges me to omit, or which my imagination has failed to suggest, every attentive reader must unavoidably be struck at the immense space which separates these two states. In this slow succession of things he may meet with the solution of an infinite number of problems in morality and politics, which philosophers are puzzled to solve. He will perceive that, the mankind of one age not being the mankind of another, the reason why Diogenes could not find a man was, that he sought among his contemporaries the man of a bygone period: Cato, he will then see, fell with Rome and with liberty, because he did not suit the age in which he lived; and the greatest of men served only to astonish that world, which would have cheerfully obeyed him, had he come into it five hundred years earlier. In a word, he will find himself in a condition to understand how the soul and the passions of men by insensible alterations change as it were their very nature; how it comes to pass, that in the long run our wants and our pleasures seek new objects; that, original man vanishing by degrees, society no longer offers to the eyes of the sage anything but an assemblage of artificial men and factitious passions, which are the work of all these new relations, and have no foundation in nature. What reflection teaches us on that score, observation entirely confirms. Savage man and civilized man differ so much at the bottom of their hearts and in their inclinations, that what constitutes the supreme happiness of the one would reduce the other to despair. The first sighs for nothing but repose and liberty; he desires only to live, and to be exempt from labor; nay, the ataraxy of the most confirmed Stoic falls short of his profound indifference to every other object. Civilized man, on the other hand, is always in motion, perpetually sweating and toiling, and racking his brains to find out occupations still more laborious: he continues a drudge to his last minute; nay, he courts death to be able to live, or renounces life to acquire immortality. He pays court to men in power whom he hates, and to rich men whom he despises; he sticks at nothing to have the honor of serving them; he boasts proudly of his baseness and their protection; and proud of his slavery, he speaks with disdain of those who have not the honor of sharing it. What a spectacle must the painful and envied labors of a European minister of state form in the eyes of a Caribbean! How many cruel deaths would not this indolent savage prefer to such a horrid life, which very often is not even sweetened by the pleasure of doing good? But to see the purpose of so many cares, his mind would first have to affix some meaning to these words *power* and *reputation*; he should be apprized that there are men who set value on the way they are looked on by the rest of mankind, who know how to be happy and satisfied with themselves on the testimony of others rather than upon their own. In fact, the real source of all those differences is that the savage lives within himself, whereas social man, constantly outside himself, knows only how to live in the opinion of others; and it is, if I may say so, merely from their judgment of him that he derives the consciousness of his own existence. It is foreign to my subject to show how this disposition engenders so much indifference toward good and evil, notwithstanding such fine discourses on morality; how everything, being reduced to appearances, becomes mere art and mummery; honor, friendship, virtue, and often vice itself, of which we at last learn the secret of boasting; how, in short, ever asking others what we are, and never daring to ask ourselves, in the midst of so much philosophy, humanity and politeness, and such sublime moral codes, we have nothing but a deceitful and frivolous exterior, honor without virtue, reason without wisdom, and pleasure without happiness. It is sufficient that I have proved that this is certainly not the original state of man, and that it is merely the spirit of society, and the inequality which society engenders, that thus change and transform all our natural inclinations.

I have endeavored to reveal the origin and progress of inequality, the institution and abuse of political societies, as far as these things are capable of being deduced from the nature of man by the mere light of reason, and independently of those sacred maxims which give the sanction of divine right to sovereign authority. It follows from this survey that inequality, almost non-existent among men in the state of nature, derives its force and its growth from the development of our faculties and the progress of the human mind, and at last becomes permanent and lawful by the establishment of property and of laws. It likewise follows that moral* inequality, authorized, solely by positive right,† clashes with natural right, whenever it is not in proportion to physical‡ inequality; a distinction which sufficiently determines what we are to think of that kind of inequality which obtains in all civilized nations, since it is evidently against the law of nature that children should command old men, and fools lead the wise, and that a handful should gorge themselves with superfluities, while the starving masses lack the barest necessities of life.

---

* "Moral" should here be interpreted as meaning "social," or "artificial."

† i.e., established laws.

‡ i.e., "natural."

NOTES

(i) A celebrated author,* by calculating the goods and the evils of human life and comparing the two sums, found that the last greatly exceeded the first, and that everything considered life to man was no such valuable present. I am not surprised at his conclusions; he drew all his arguments from the constitution of man in a civilized state. Had he looked back to man in a state of nature, it is obvious that the result of his inquiries would have been very different; that man would have appeared to him subject to very few evils but those of his own making, and that he would have acquitted nature. It has cost us much trouble to make ourselves so miserable. When on the one hand we consider the immense labors of mankind, so many sciences brought to perfection, so many arts invented, so many powers employed, so many abysses filled up, so many mountains leveled, so many rocks rent to pieces, so many rivers made navigable, so many tracts of land cleared, lakes emptied, marshes drained, enormous buildings raised upon the earth, and the sea covered with ships and sailors; and on the other weigh with ever so little attention the real advantages that have resulted from all these works to mankind; we cannot help being amazed at the vast disproportion observable between these things, and deplore the blindness of man, which, to feed his foolish pride and I don't know what vain self-admiration, makes him eagerly court and pursue all the miseries he is capable of feeling, and which beneficent nature had taken care to keep at a distance from him.

That men are wicked, a sad and constant experience renders the proof of it unnecessary; man, however, is naturally good; I think I have demonstrated it; what then could have depraved him to such a degree, unless the changes that have happened in his constitution, the advantages he has made, and the knowledge he has acquired. Let us admire human society as much as we please, it will not be the less true that it necessarily leads men to hate each in proportion as their interests clash; to do each other apparent services, and in fact heap upon each other every imaginable mischief. What are we to think of a commerce, in which the interest of every individual dictates to him maxims diametrically opposite to those which the interest of the community recommends to the body of society; a commerce, in which every man finds his profit in the misfortunes of his neighbor? There is not,

* This author was Maupertuis, whose theory appeared in the *Essai de philosophie morale* (1749).

perhaps, a single man in easy circumstances, whose death his greedy heirs, nay and too often his own children, do not secretly wish for; not a ship at sea, the loss of which would not be an agreeable piece of news for some merchant or another; not a house which a debtor would not be glad to see reduced to ashes with all the papers in it; not a nation, which does not rejoice at the misfortunes of its neighbors. It is thus we find our advantages in the ill fortune of our fellows, and that the loss of one man almost always constitutes the prosperity of another. But, what is still more dangerous, public calamities are ever the objects of the hopes and expectations of innumerable individuals. Some desire sickness, others mortality; some war, some famine. I have seen monsters of men weep for grief at the appearance of a plentiful season; and the great and fatal conflagration of London, which cost so many wretches their lives or their fortunes, may have made the fortune of more than ten thousand persons. I know that Montaigne finds fault with Demades the Athenian for having caused to be punished a workman who, selling his coffins very dear, was a great gainer by the deaths of his fellow-citizens. But Montaigne's reason being, that by the same rule every man should be punished, it is plain that it confirms my argument. Let us therefore look through our frivolous displays of benevolence at what passes in the inmost recesses of the heart, and reflect on what must be that state of things, in which men are forced with the same breath to caress and to destroy each other, and in which they are born enemies by duty, and knaves by interest. Perhaps somebody will object that society is so formed that every man gains by serving the rest. That would be fine, if he did not gain still more by injuring them. There is no legitimate profit that is not exceeded by what may be made illegitimately, and we always gain more by hurting our neighbors than by doing them good. It is only a matter of finding a way to do it with impunity; and this is the end to which the powerful employ all their strength, and the weak all their cunning.

Savage man, when he has dined, is at peace with all nature, and the friend of all his fellows. Does a dispute sometimes happen about a meal? He seldom comes to blows without having first compared the difficulty of conquering with that of finding his subsistence elsewhere; and, as pride has no share in the squabble, it ends in a few cuffs; the victor eats, the vanquished retires to seek his fortune, and all is quiet again. But with man in society it's quite another story; in the first place, necessaries are to be provided, and then superfluities; delicacies follow, and then immense riches, and then subjects, and then slaves. He does not enjoy a moment's relaxation; what is most extraordinary, the less natural and pressing are his wants, the more headstrong his passions become, and what is still worse, the greater is his power of satisfying them; so that after a long run of prosperity, after having swallowed up many treasures and ruined many men, our hero will end up by cutting every throat, until he at last finds himself the sole master of the universe. Such is in miniature the moral picture, if not of human life, at least of the secret ambitions in the heart of every civilized man.

Compare without prejudice the state of social man with that of the savage, and find out, if you can, how many inlets, besides his wickedness, his wants, his miseries, the former has opened to pain and death. If you consider the afflictions of the mind which prey upon us, the violent passions which waste and exhaust us, the excessive labors with which the poor are overburdened, the still more dangerous indolence, to which the rich give themselves up and which kill the one through want, and the other through excess. If you reflect a moment on the monstrous mixture, and pernicious manner of seasoning so many dishes; on the putrefied food; on the adulterated medicines, the tricks of those who sell them, the mistakes of those who administer them, the poisonous qualities of the vessels in which they are prepared; if you but think of epidemics bred by bad air among great numbers of men crowded together, or those occasioned by our delicate way of living, by our passing back and forth from the inside of our houses into the open air, the putting on and taking off our clothes with too little precaution, and by all those conveniences which our boundless sensuality has changed into necessary habits, and the neglect or loss of which afterwards costs us our life or our health; if you set down the conflagrations and earthquakes, which devouring or overturning whole cities destroy the miserable inhabitants by thousands; in a word, if you sum up the dangers with which all these causes are constantly menacing us, you will see how dearly nature makes us pay for the contempt we have showed for her lessons.

I shall not here repeat what I have elsewhere said of the calamities of war; I only wish that sufficiently informed persons are willing or bold enough to make public the detail of the villainies committed in armies by the contractors for food and for hospitals; we should then plainly discover that their monstrous frauds, scarcely concealed, destroy more soldiers than actually fall by the sword of the enemy, so as to make the most gallant armies melt away. The number of those who every year perish at sea, by famine, by the scurvy, by pirates, by shipwrecks, would furnish matter for another very shocking calculation. Besides it is plain, that we are to place to the account of the establishment of property and therefore to that of society, the assassinations, poisonings, highway robberies, and even the punishments for these crimes; punishments, it is true, requisite to prevent greater evils, but which, by making the murder of one man prove the death of two, double in fact the loss to the human species. How many are the shameful methods to prevent the birth of men, and cheat nature? Either by those brutal and depraved appetites which insult her most charming work, appetites which neither savages nor mere animals ever knew, and which could only spring in civilized countries from a corrupt imagination; or by those secret abortions, the worthy fruits of debauch and vicious notions of honor; or by the exposure or murder of multitudes of infants, victims of the poverty of their parents, or the barbarous shame of their mothers; or finally by the mutilation of those wretches, part of whose existence, with that of their whole posterity, is sacrificed to vain singsong, or, which is still worse, the brutal jealousy of some other men: a mutilation, which, in the last case, is doubly outrageous to nature, both by the treatment of those who suffer it, and by the service to which they are condemned.* But what if I undertook to show the human species attacked in its very source, and even in the holiest of all ties, in forming which nature is never listened to until fortune has been consulted, and social disorder confusing all virtue and vice, continence becomes a criminal precaution, and a refusal to give life to beings like oneself, an act of humanity? But without tearing open the veil that hides so many horrors, it is enough to point out the disease for which others will have to find a remedy.

Let us add to this the great number of unwholesome trades which shorten life, or destroy health; such as the digging and preparing of metals and minerals, especially lead, copper, mercury, cobalt, arsenic, realgar;† those other dangerous trades, which every day kill so many men, for example, tilers, carpenters, masons, and quarrymen; let us, I say, unite all these things, and then we shall discover in the establishment and perfecting of societies the reasons for that diminution of the species, which so many philosophers have taken notice of.

Luxury, which nothing can prevent among men who are avid for their own comforts and the deference of others, soon puts the finishing hand to the evils which society had begun; and on pretense of giving bread to the poor, whom it should never have made such, impoverishes all the rest, and sooner or later depopulates the State.

Luxury is a remedy much worse than the disease which it pretends to cure; or rather is in itself the worst of all diseases; both in great and small States. To maintain those crowds of servants and wretches which it creates,

---

* A passage on arranged marriages, which first appeared in the posthumous edition of 1782, is here omitted.

† Arsenic monosulphide; found in the dust of certain caves.

it crushes and ruins the farmer and the townsman; not unlike those scorching south winds, which covering both plants and foliage with devouring insects rob the useful animals of subsistence, and carry famine and death with them wherever they blow.

From society and the luxury engendered by it, spring the liberal and mechanical arts, commerce, letters, and all those superfluities which make industry flourish, and enrich and ruin nations. The reason for such ruin is very simple. It is plain that agriculture, by its very nature, must be the least lucrative of all arts, because its products being of the most indispensable necessity for all men, their price must be proportionate to the abilities of the poorest. From the same principle it may be gathered, that in general arts are lucrative in the inverse ratio of their usefulness, and that in the end of the most necessary must come to be the most neglected. From this we may form a judgment of the true advantages of industry, and of the real effects of its progress.

Such are the evident causes of all the miseries into which opulence at length precipitates the most celebrated nations. In proportion as industry and arts spread and flourish, the despised husbandman, loaded with taxes necessary for the support of luxury, and condemned to spend his life between labor and hunger, leaves his fields to seek in town the bread he should take to it. The more our capital cities strike with wonder the stupid eye of the common people, the greater reason is there to weep, the countryside abandoned, fields lie uncultivated, and the high roads crowded with unfortunate citizens turned beggars or robbers, and doomed, sooner or later to lay down their wretched lives on the wheel or the dunghill. It is thus, that while States grow rich on one hand, they grow weak, and are depopulated on the other; and the most powerful monarchies, after innumerable labors to enrich and depopulate themselves, fall at last a prey to some poor nation, which has yielded to the fatal temptation of invading them, and then grows opulent and weak in its turn, until it is itself invaded and destroyed by some other.

I wish somebody would condescend to inform us what could have produced those swarms of barbarians, which during so many ages overran Europe, Asia, and Africa? Was it to the activity of their arts, the wisdom of their laws, the excellence of their State they owed so prodigious an increase? I wish our learned men would be so kind as to tell us, why instead of multiplying to such a degree, these fierce and brutal men, without sense or science, without restraint, without education, did not murder each other every minute in quarreling for the spontaneous productions of their fields and woods? Let them tell us how these wretches could have the assurance to look in the face such skillful men as we were, with so fine a military discipline, such excellent codes, and such wise laws. Why, in short, since society has been perfected in the northern climates, and so much pains have been taken to instruct the inhabitants in their duties to one another, and the art of living happily and peaceably together, do we no longer see them produce anything like those numberless hosts, which they formerly used to send forth? I am afraid that somebody may at last take it into his head to answer me by saying, that truly all these great things, namely arts, sciences, and laws, were very wisely invented by men, as a salutary plague, to prevent the too great multiplication of mankind, lest this world, which was given us should at length become too small for its inhabitants.

What then? Must societies be abolished? Must *meum* and *tuum* be annihilated, and must man go back to living in forests with the bears? This would be a deduction in the manner of my adversaries, which I choose to anticipate rather than permit them the shame of drawing it. O you, by whom the voice of heaven has not been heard, and who think your species destined only to finishing in peace this short life; you, who can lay down in the midst of cities your fatal acquisitions, your restless spirits, your corrupted hearts and unbridled desires, take up again, since it is in your power, your ancient and primitive innocence; retire to the woods, there to lose the sight and remembrance of the crimes committed by your contemporaries; nor be afraid of debasing your species, by renouncing its enlightenment in order to renounce its vices. As for men like me, whose passions have irretrievably destroyed their original simplicity, who can no longer live upon grass and acorns, or without laws and magistrates; all those who were honored in the person of their first parent with supernatural lessons; those, who discover, in the intention to give immediately to human actions a morality which otherwise they must have been so long in acquiring, the reason of a precept indifferent in itself, and utterly inexplicable in every other system; those, in a word, who are convinced that the divine voice has called all men to the enlightenment and happiness of the celestial intelligences; all such will endeavor to deserve the eternal reward promised their obedience, by practicing those virtues to the practice of which they oblige themselves in learning to know them. They will respect the sacred bonds of those societies to which they belong; they will love their fellows, and will serve them to the utmost of their power; they will religiously obey the laws, and all those who make or administer them; they will above all things honor those good and wise princes who find means to prevent, cure, or palliate the crowd of evils and abuses always ready to overwhelm us; they will animate the zeal of those worthy chiefs, by showing them without fear of flattery the importance of their talk, and the rigor of their duties. But they will not for that reason have any less contempt for a social organization which cannot subsist without the assistance of so many men of worth, who are oftener wanted than found; and from which, in spite of all their cares, there always spring more real calamities than even apparent advantages.

(k) This appears to me as clear as daylight, and I cannot conceive whence our philosophers can derive all the passions they attribute to natural man. Except the bare physical necessities, which nature herself requires, all our other needs are merely the effects of habit, before which they were not needs, or of our cravings; and we don't crave that which we are not in a condition to know. Hence it follows that as savage man longs for nothing but what he knows, and knows nothing but what he actually possesses or can easily acquire, nothing can be so calm as his soul, or so confined as his understanding.

(l)* Mr. Locke, in fine, proves at most that there may be in man a motive to live with the woman when she has a child; but he by no means proves that there was any necessity for his living with her before her delivery and during the nine months of her pregnancy; if a pregnant woman comes to be indifferent to the man by whom she is pregnant during these nine months, if she even comes to be entirely forgotten by him, why should he assist her after her delivery? Why should he help her to rear a child, which he does not know to be his, and whose birth he neither foresaw nor planned? It is evident that Mr. Locke supposes the very thing in question: for we are not inquiring why man should continue to live with the woman after her delivery, but why he should continue to attach himself to her after conception. The appetite satisfied, man no longer stands in need of any particular woman, nor the woman of any particular man. The man does not have the slightest concern, nor perhaps the slightest notion of what must follow his act. One goes this way, the other that, and there is little reason to think that at the end of nine months they should remember ever to have known each other: for this kind of remembrance, by which one individual gives the preference to another for the act of generation, requires, as I have proved in the text, a greater degree of progress or corruption in the human understanding, than man can be supposed to have attained in the state of animality we

* Only the last part of this note is given here. Rousseau is replying to Locke's contention that men and women naturally stayed together in families because of the dependency of their young.

here speak of. Another woman therefore may serve to satisfy the new desires of the man fully as conveniently as the one he has already known; and another man in like manner satisfy the woman's, supposing her subject to the same appetite during her pregnancy, a thing which may be reasonably doubted. But if in the state of nature, the woman, when she has conceived, no longer feels the passion of love, the obstacle to her associating with men becomes still greater, since she no longer has any occasion for the man by whom she is pregnant, or for any other. There is therefore no reason on the man's side for his coveting the same woman, nor on the woman's for her coveting the same man. Locke's argument therefore falls to the ground, and all the logic of this philosopher has not secured him from the mistake committed by Hobbes and others. They had to explain a fact in the state of nature; that is, in a state in which every man lived by himself without any connection with other men, and no one man had any motives to associate with any other, nor perhaps, which is still more serious, men in general to herd together; and it never came into their heads to look back beyond the times of society, that is to say, those times in which men have always had motives for herding together, and in which one man has often motives for associating with a particular man, or a particular woman.

(o) We must not confuse selfishness with self-love; they are two very distinct passions both in their nature and in their effects. Self-love is a natural sentiment, which inclines every animal to look to his own preservation, and which, guided in man by reason and qualified by pity, is productive of humanity and virtue. Selfishness is but a relative and factitious sentiment, engendered in society, which inclines every individual to set a greater value upon himself than upon any other man, which inspires men with all the mischief they do to each other, and is the true source of what we call honor.

This position well understood, I say that selfishness does not exist in our primitive state, in the true state of nature; for every man in particular considering himself as the only spectator who observes him, as the only being in the universe which takes any interest in him, as the only judge of his own merit, it is impossible that a sentiment arising from comparisons, which he is not in a condition to make, should spring up in his mind. For the same reason, such a man must be a stranger to hatred and spite, passions which only the opinion of our having received some affront can excite; and as it is contempt or an intention to injure, and not the injury itself that constitutes an affront, men who don't know how to set a value upon themselves, or compare themselves one with another, may do each other a great deal of mischief, as often as they can expect any advantage by doing it, without ever offending each other. In a word, man seldom considering his fellows in any other light than he would animals of another species, may plunder another man weaker than himself, or be plundered by another that is stronger, without considering these acts of violence otherwise than as natural events, without the least emotion of insolence or spite, and without any other passion than grief at his failure, or joy at his good success.

(p) It is very remarkable, that for so many years past that the Europeans have been toiling to make the savages of different parts of the world conform to their manner of living, they have not as yet been able to win over one of them, not even with the assistance of the Christian religion; for though our missionaries sometimes make Christians, they never make civilized men of them. There is no getting the better of their invincible reluctance to adopt our manners and customs. If these poor savages are as unhappy as some people would have them, by what inconceivable depravity of judgment is it that they so constantly refuse to be governed as we are, or to live happy among us; whereas we read in a thousand places that Frenchmen and other Europeans have voluntarily taken refuge, nay, spent their whole lives among them, without ever being able to quit so strange a kind of life; and that even very sensible missionaries have been known to regret with tears the calm and innocent days they had spent among those men we so much despise. Should it be observed that they are not enlightened enough to judge soundly of their condition and ours, I must answer, that the valuation of happiness is not so much the business of the understanding as of feeling. Besides, this objection may still more forcibly be turned against ourselves; for our ideas are more remote from that disposition of mind requisite for us to conceive the relish, which the savages find in their way of living, than the ideas of the savages are from those by which they may conceive the relish we find in ours. In fact, very few observations are enough to show them that all our labors are confined to two objects, namely the conveniences of life and the esteem of others. But how shall we be able to imagine that kind of pleasure, which a savage takes in spending his days alone in the heart of a forest, or in fishing, or in blowing into a wretched flute without ever being able to fetch a single note from it, or ever giving himself any trouble to learn how to make a better use of it?*

(s) Nay, this rigorous equality of the state of nature, even if it were practicable in civil society, would clash with distributive justice; and as all the

---

* The remainder of this note is not given here.

members of the State owe it services in proportion to their talents and abilities, they should be distinguished in proportion to their services. It is in this sense we must understand a passage of Isocrates, in which he extols the primitive Athenians for having distinguished which of the two following kinds of equality was the more useful, that which consists in sharing the same advantages indifferently among all the citizens, or that which consists in distributing them to each according to his merit. These able politicians, adds the orator, banishing that unjust inequality which makes no difference between the good and the bad, inviolably adhered to that which rewards and punishes every man according to his merit. But in the first place there never existed a society so corrupt as to make no difference between the good and the bad; and in those points concerning morals, where the law can prescribe no measure exact enough to serve as a rule to magistrates, it is with the greatest wisdom that in order not to leave the fate or the rank of citizens at their discretion, it forbids them to judge of persons, and leaves actions alone to their discretion. There are no *mores,* except those as pure as those of the old Romans, that can bear censors, and such a tribunal among us would soon throw everything into confusion. It belongs to public esteem to mark a difference between good and bad men; the magistrate is judge only as to strict law; whereas the multitude is the true judge of manners; an upright and even an intelligent judge in that respect; a judge which may indeed sometimes be imposed upon, but can never be corrupted. The rank therefore of citizens ought to be regulated, not according to their personal merit, for this would be putting it in the power of magistrates to make almost an arbitrary application of the law, but according to the real services they render to the State, since these will admit of a more exact estimation.

The Social Contract

BY J.-J. ROUSSEAU

CITIZEN OF GENEVA

—foederis aequas
Dicamus leges.
(Let us make fair terms for
the compact.)
— The Aeneid, Bk. XI

Prefatory Note

This little treatise is taken from a longer work undertaken at an earlier time without considering my strength, and long since abandoned. Of the various fragments that might be taken from what was done, the following is the most substantial, and appears to me the least unworthy of being offered to the public.

The rest of the work no longer exists.

Contents

BOOK III

BOOK IV

Book I

Introductory Note

I want to inquire whether, taking men as they are and laws as they can be made to be, it is possible to establish some just and reliable rule of administration in civil affairs. In this investigation I shall always strive to reconcile what right permits with what interest prescribes, so that justice and utility may not be at variance.

I enter this inquiry without demonstrating the importance of my subject. I shall be asked whether I am a prince or a legislator that I write on politics. I reply that I am neither; and that it is for this very reason that I write about politics. If I were a prince or a legislator, I would not waste my time saying what ought to be done; I would do it or remain silent.

Born a citizen of a free State, and a member of that sovereign body, however feeble an influence my voice may have in public affairs, the right to vote on them is sufficient to impose on me the duty of informing myself about them; and I feel happy, whenever I meditate on governments, always to discover in my research new reasons for loving that of my own country.

Chapter I

SUBJECT OF THE FIRST BOOK

Man was born free, and everywhere he is in chains. Many a one believes himself the master of others, and yet he is a greater slave than they. How has this change come about? I do not know. What can make it legitimate? I believe I can settle this question.

If I looked only at force and the results that stem from it, I would say that as long as a people is compelled to obey and does obey, it does well; but that, as soon as it can shake off the yoke and does shake it off, it does even better; for, if men recover their freedom by virtue of the same right by which it was taken away, either they are justified in taking it back, or there was no justification for depriving them of it. But the social order is a sacred right that serves as a foundation for all others. This right, however, does not come from nature. It is therefore based on conventions. The question is to know what these conventions are. Before coming to that, I must establish what I have just stated.

Chapter II

PRIMITIVE SOCIETIES

The earliest of all societies, and the only natural one, is the family; yet children remain attached to their father only so long as they need him for their own survival. As soon as this need ceases, the natural bond is dissolved. The children being freed from the obedience which they owed to their father, and the father from the concern he owed his children, become equally independent. If they remain united, it is not because of nature but of choice; and the family itself is kept together only by convention.

This common liberty is a consequence of man's nature. His first law is to attend to his own survival, his first concerns are those he owes to himself; and as soon as he reaches the age of rationality, being sole judge of how to survive, he becomes his own master.

The family is, then, if you will, the first model of political societies; the leader is the analogue of the father, while the people are like the children; and all, being born free and equal, give up their freedom only for their own advantage. The whole difference is that, in the family, the father's love for his children repays him for the concern that he bestows upon them; while, in the State, the pleasure of ruling makes up for the leader's lack of love for his people.

Grotius denies that all human authority is established for the benefit of the governed, and he cites slavery as an example. His steady line of reasoning is to establish right by fact.* A more consistent method might be used, but none more favorable to tyrants.

It is doubtful, then, according to Grotius, whether the human race belongs to a hundred men, or whether these hundred men belong to the human race; and he appears throughout his book to incline to the former opinion, which is also that of Hobbes. In this way we have mankind divided like herds of cattle, each of which has a master, who looks after it in order to devour it.

Just as a herdsman is superior in nature to his herd, so leaders, who are the herdsmen of men, are superior in nature to their people. Such was, according to Philo's account, the reasoning of the Emperor Caligula, inferring truly enough from this analogy that kings are gods, or that men are animals.

The reasoning of Caligula is similar to that of Hobbes and Grotius. Aristotle, before them all, had also said that men are not naturally equal, but that some are born to be slaves and others to rule.

Aristotle was right, but he mistook the effect for the cause. Every man born in slavery is born for slavery; nothing is more certain. Slaves lose everything in their chains, even the desire to escape from them; they love their servitude as the companions of Ulysses loved their brutishness.† If, then, there are slaves by nature, it is because there have been slaves contrary to nature. The first slaves were made by force; their cowardice kept them in bondage.

I have said nothing about King Adam nor about Emperor Noah, the father of three great monarchs who split the universe among them, like the children of Saturn with whom they are likened. I hope that people will give me credit for my moderation; for, as I am a direct descendant of one of these princes, and perhaps of the eldest branch, how do I know whether, by examination of titles, I might not find myself the legitimate king of the human race? Be that as it may, it cannot be denied that Adam was sovereign of the world, as Robinson was of his island, so long as he was its sole inhabitant; and it was a convenient feature of that empire that the monarch, secure on his throne, had nothing to fear from rebellions, or wars, or conspirators.

* "Learned researches in public law are often nothing but the history of ancient abuses; and to devote much labor to studying them is misplaced pertinacity" (*Treatise on the Interests of France in Relation to Her Neighbours,* by the Marquis d'Argenson). That is exactly what Grotius did.

† See a small treatise by Plutarch, entitled *That Brutes Employ Reason.*

Chapter III

THE RIGHT OF THE STRONGEST

The strongest man is never strong enough to be always master, unless he transforms his power into right, and obedience into duty. Hence the right of the strongest — a right in appearance assumed in irony, and in reality established in principle. But will this term ever be explained to us? Force is a physical power; I do not see what morality can result from its effects. To yield to force is an act of necessity, not of will; it is at most an act of prudence. In what sense can it be a duty?

Let us assume for a moment this so-called right. I say that nothing results from it but inexplicable nonsense; for if might makes right, the effect changes with the cause, and any force that can overcome the first can claim its rights. As soon as men can disobey with impunity, they can do so legitimately; and since the strongest is always in the right, it makes sense to act in such a way as to be the strongest. But what kind of right perishes when might disappears? If one is compelled to obey by force, there is no need to obey from duty; and if one is no longer forced to obey, obligation is at an end. We see, then, that this word *right* adds nothing to force; here it means nothing at all.

Obey the powers that be. If that means, Yield to force, the precept is good but superfluous; I reply that it will never be violated. All power comes from God, I admit; but every disease comes from Him too; does it follow that we are prohibited from calling in a physician? If a robber should catch me deep in a forest, am I bound not only to give up my money when forced, but am I also morally bound to do so when I might hide it? For, after all, the gun he holds is a superior force.

Let us agree, then, that might does not make right, and that we are bound to obey none but lawful authorities. Thus we return to my original question.

Chapter IV

SLAVERY

Since no man has any natural authority over his fellow men, and since might is not the source of right, conventions remain as the basis of all lawful authority among men.

If an individual, says Grotius, can alienate his freedom and become the slave of a master, why should a whole people not be able to alienate theirs, and become subject to a king? In this there are many equivocal terms requiring explanation; but let us confine ourselves to the word *alienate*. To alienate is to give or sell. Now, a man who becomes another's slave does not give himself; he sells himself at the very least for his subsistence. But why does a nation sell itself? So far from a king providing his subjects with their subsistence, he draws his from them; and, according to Rabelais, a king does not live on a little. Do subjects, then, give up their persons on condition that their property also shall be taken? I do not see what is left for them to keep.

It will be said that the despot secures for his subjects civil peace. Be it so; but what do they gain by that, if the wars which his ambition brings upon them, together with his insatiable greed and the vexations of his administration, harass them more than their own dissensions would? What do they gain by it if this tranquillity is itself one of their miseries? Men live tranquilly also in dungeons; is that enough to make them contented there? The Greeks confined in the cave of the Cyclops lived peacefully until their turn came to be devoured.

To say that a man gives himself for nothing is to say something absurd and inconceivable; such an act is illegitimate and invalid, for the simple reason that he who performs it is not in his right mind. To say the same thing of a whole nation is to suppose a nation of fools; and madness does not confer rights.

Even if each person could alienate himself, he could not alienate his children; they are born free men; their liberty belongs to them, and no one has a right to dispose of it except them themselves. Before they have reached the age of rationality, the father can, in their name, stipulate conditions for their preservation and welfare, but not surrender them irrevocably and unconditionally; for such a gift is contrary to the ends of nature, and exceeds the rights of paternity. In order, then, that an arbitrary government might be legitimate, it would be necessary for the people in each generation to have the option of accepting or rejecting it; but in that case such a government would no longer be arbitrary.

To renounce one's liberty is to renounce one's essence as a human being, the rights and also the duties of humanity. For the person who renounces everything there is no possible compensation. Such a renunciation is incompatible with human nature, for to take away all freedom from one's will is to take away all morality from one's actions. In short, a convention which stipulates absolute authority on the one side and unlimited obedience on the other is meaningless and contradictory. Is it not clear that we are under no obligations whatsoever toward a man from whom we have a right to demand everything? And does not this single condition, without equivalent, without exchange, presuppose the nullity of the act? For what rights would my slave have against me, since all that he has belongs to me? His rights being mine, this right of me against myself is a meaningless term.

Grotius and others derive from war another origin for the supposed right of slavery. The victor having, according to them, the right of slaying the vanquished, the latter may purchase his life at the cost of his freedom; an agreement so much the more legitimate that it turns to the advantage of both.

But it is clear that this supposed right of slaying the vanquished in no way results from the state of war. Men are not naturally enemies, if only for the reason that, living in their primitive independence, they have no mutual relations sufficiently durable to constitute a state of peace or a state of war. It is the relation of things and not of men that constitutes war; and since the state of war cannot arise from simple personal relations, but only from real relations, private war — war between man and man — cannot exist either in the state of nature, where there is no settled ownership, or in the social state, where everything is under the authority of the laws.

Private combats, duels, and encounters are acts that do not constitute a state of war; and with regard to the private wars authorized by the Establishments of Louis IX, king of France, and suspended by the peace of God, they were abuses of the feudal government, an absurd system if ever there was one, contrary both to the principles of natural right and to all sound government.

War, then, is not a relation between man and man, but a relation between State and State, in which individuals are enemies only by accident, not as men, nor even as citizens,* but as soldiers; not as members of the fatherland, but as its defenders. In short, each State can have as enemies only

---

* The Romans, who understood and respected the rights of war better than any nation in the world, carried their scruples so far in this respect that no citizen was allowed to serve as a volunteer without enlisting expressly against the enemy, and by name against a certain enemy. A legion in which Cato the younger made his first campaign under Popilius having been re-formed, Cato the elder wrote to Popilius that, if he consented to his son's continuing to serve under him, it was necessary that he should take a new military oath, because, the first being annulled, he could no longer bear arms against the enemy (Cicero, *De Officiis* I, II). And Cato also wrote to his son to abstain from appearing in battle until he had taken his new oath. I know that it will be possible to urge against me the siege of Clusium and other particular cases; but I cite laws and customs (Livy, V. 35–37). No nation has transgressed its laws less frequently than the Romans, and no nation has had laws so admirable.

other States and not individual men, inasmuch as it is impossible to claim any true relation between things of different kinds.

This principle also conforms to the established maxims of all ages and to the accepted practices of all civilized nations. Declarations of war are not so much warnings to the powers as to their subjects. The foreigner, whether king, or nation, or private person, that robs, slays, or detains subjects without declaring war against the government, is not an enemy, but a pirate. Even in open war, a just prince, while he rightly takes possession of all that belongs to the State in an enemy's country, respects the person and property of individuals; he respects the rights on which his own are based. The aim of war being the destruction of the hostile State, we have a right to slay its defenders so long as they have arms in their hands; but as soon as they lay them down and surrender, ceasing to be enemies or instruments of the enemy, they become again simply men, and no one has any further right over their lives. Sometimes it is possible to destroy the State without killing a single one of its members; but war confers no right except what is necessary to its end. These are not the principles of Grotius; they are not based on the authority of poets, but are derived from the nature of things, and are founded on reason.

With regard to the right of conquest, it has no other foundation than the law of the strongest. If war does not confer on the victor the right of slaying the vanquished, this right, which he does not possess, cannot be the foundation of a right to enslave them. If we have a right to slay an enemy only when it is impossible to enslave him, the right to enslave him is not derived from the right to kill him; it is, therefore, an iniquitous transaction to make him purchase his life, over which the victor has no right, at the cost of his liberty. In establishing the right of life and death upon the right of slavery, and the right of slavery upon the right of life and death, is it not manifest that one falls into a vicious cycle?

Even if we grant this terrible right of killing everybody, I say that a slave taken in war, or a conquered nation, is under no obligation at all to a master, except to obey him so far as compelled. In taking an equivalent for his life the victor has conferred no favor on the slave; instead of killing him unprofitably, he has destroyed him for his own profit. Far, then, from having acquired over him any authority in addition to that of force, the state of war subsists between them as before, their relationship itself is the effect of it; and the exercise of the rights of war supposes that there is no treaty of peace. They have made a convention. Be it so; but this convention, far from terminating the state of war, supposes its continuance.

Thus, however we might view things, the right of slavery is null and void, not only because it is illegitimate, but because it is absurd and meaningless. These words, *slavery* and *right*, are contradictory and mutually exclusive. Whether spoken by a man to a man, or by a man to a nation, such speech as this will always be equally aberrant: "I make an agreement with you wholly at your expense and wholly for my benefit, and I shall observe it as long as I please, while you also shall observe it as long as I please."

Chapter V

THAT IT IS ALWAYS NECESSARY TO GO BACK TO A FIRST CONVENTION

Even if I conceded all that I have so far refuted, those who favor despotism would be no farther advanced. There will always be a great difference between subduing a multitude and governing a society. When isolated men, however numerous they may be, are subjected one after another to a single person, this seems to me only a case of master and slaves, not of a nation and its leader; they form, if you will, an aggregation, but not an association, for they have neither public property nor a body politic. Such a man, even if he enslaved half the world, is never anything but an individual; his interest, separated from that of the rest, is never anything but a private interest. If he dies, his empire after him is left disconnected and disunited, as an oak disintegrates and becomes a heap of ashes after fire has consumed it.

A people, says Grotius, can give itself to a king. According to Grotius, then, a people is a people before it gives itself to a king. This gift itself is a civil act, and presupposes public deliberation. Consequently, before examining the act by which a people elects a king, it would be well to examine the act by which a people becomes a people; for this act, being necessarily anterior to the other, is the real foundation of the society.

In fact, if there were no anterior convention, where, unless the election were unanimous, would be the obligation upon the minority to submit to the decision of the majority? And from where do the hundred who desire a master derive the right to vote on behalf of ten who do not desire one? The law of the plurality of votes is itself established by convention, and presupposes unanimity at least at one point in time.

Chapter VI

THE SOCIAL PACT

I imagine men reaching a point when the impediments that endangered their survival in the state of nature prevailed by their resistance over the forces that each individual could use to survive in that state. At that point this primitive condition can no longer subsist, and the human race would perish unless it changed its mode of existence.

Now, as men cannot create any new forces, but only combine and control those that do exist, they have no other means of self-preservation than to form by aggregation a sum of forces which may prevail over the resistance, to put them in action by a single motive power, and to make them work in concert.

This sum of forces can be produced only by the combination of many; but the strength and freedom of each man being the chief instruments of his survival, how can he pledge them without doing harm to himself, and without neglecting the concern he owes to himself? This difficulty, applied to my subject, may be expressed in these terms: —

"To find a form of association that may defend and protect with the whole force of the community the person and property of every associate, and by means of which each, joining together with all, may nevertheless obey only himself, and remain as free as before." Such is the fundamental problem of which the social contract provides the solution.

The clauses of this contract are so determined by the nature of the act that the slightest modification would render them pointless and ineffectual; so that, although they have never perhaps been formally enunciated, they are everywhere the same, everywhere tacitly accepted and recognized, until, the social pact being violated, each man returns to his original rights and takes back his natural liberty, while losing the conventional liberty for which he renounced it.

These clauses, rightly understood, can be reduced to a single one, namely, the total alienation to the whole community of each associate with all his rights; for, in the first place, since each gives himself up entirely, the situation is equal for all; and, the conditions being equal for all, no one has any interest in making them burdensome to others.

Further, the alienation being made without reserve, the union is as perfect as it can be, and no individual associate need claim anything more; for, if any rights were left to individuals, since there would be no common superior who could adjudicate between them and the public, each, being on some issue his own judge, would soon claim to be so on all; the state of nature would still exist, and the association would necessarily become tyrannical or pointless.

In short, each giving himself to all, gives himself to no one; and since there is no associate over whom we do not acquire the same rights which we concede to him over ourselves, we gain the equivalent of all that we lose, and more power to preserve what we have.

If, then, we set aside whatever does not belong to the essence of the social contract, we shall find that we can reduce it to the following terms: "Each of us puts in common his person and all his power under the supreme direction of the general will; and in return each member becomes an indivisible part of the whole."

Right away, in place of the particular individuality of each contracting party, this act of association produces a moral and collective body, composed of as many members as the assembly has voices, and which receives from this same act its unity, its common self (*moi*), its life, and its will. This public person, which is thus formed by the union of all the individual members, used to be called a *city*,* and now is called *republic* or *body politic*. When it is passive, it is called by its members *State*, and *sovereign* when it is active, *power* when it is compared to similar bodies. With regard to the associates, they take collectively the name of *people*, and are called individually *citizens*, inasmuch as they participate in the sovereign power, and *subjects*, inasmuch as they are subjected to the laws of the State. But these terms are often confused and are mistaken for one another; it is sufficient to be able to distinguish them when they are used with precision.

* The real meaning of this word has been almost completely erased among the moderns; most people take a town for a city, and a burgess for a citizen. They do not know that houses make the town, and that citizens make the city. This very mistake cost the Carthaginians dear. I have never read of the title citizens (*cives*) being given to the subjects of a prince, not even in ancient times to the Macedonians, nor, in our days, to the English, although nearer liberty than all the rest. The French alone employ familiarly this name *citizen*, because they have no true idea of it, as we can see from their dictionaries; but for this fact, they would, by assuming it, commit the crime of high treason. The name, among them, expresses a virtue, not a right. When Bodin wanted to give an account of our citizens and burgesses he made a gross blunder, mistaking the one for the other. M. d'Alembert has not erred in this, and, in his article *Geneva*, has clearly distinguished the four orders of men (even five, counting mere foreigners) which exist in our town, and of which two only compose the republic. No other French author that I know of has understood the real meaning of the word *citizen*.

Chapter VII

THE SOVEREIGN

We see from this formula that the act of association comprises a reciprocal engagement between the public and individuals, and that every individual, contracting so to speak with himself, is engaged in a double relation, that is, as a member of the sovereign toward individuals, and as a member of the State toward the sovereign. But we cannot apply here the maxim of civil law that no one is bound by engagements made with himself; for there is a great difference between being bound to oneself and to a whole of which one forms part.

We must further observe that public deliberations which bind all subjects to the sovereign in consequence of the two different relations under which each of them is regarded cannot, for a contrary reason, bind the sovereign to itself; and that accordingly it is contrary to the nature of the body politic for the sovereign to impose on itself a law which it cannot transgress. Since it can only be considered under one and the same relation, it is in the position of an individual contracting with himself; from which we see that there is not, nor can there be, any kind of fundamental law that is binding upon the body of the people, not even the social contract. This does not imply that such a body cannot perfectly well enter into engagements with others in what does not derogate from this contract; for, in regard to foreigners, it becomes a simple being, an individual.

But the body politic or sovereign, deriving its existence only from the sanctity of the contract, can never bind itself, even to others, in anything that derogates from the original act, such as alienation of some portion of itself, or submission to another sovereign. To violate the act by which it exists would be to annihilate itself; and what is nothing produces nothing.

As soon as the multitude is thus united in one body, it is impossible to harm one of the members without attacking the body, still less to harm the body without the members feeling the effects. Thus duty and interest alike oblige the two contracting parties to give mutual assistance; and those same men must seek to combine in this double relationship all the advantages implicit in it.

Now, the sovereign, being formed solely by the individuals who compose it, neither has nor can have any interest contrary to theirs; thus the sovereign power need make no guarantee to its subjects, because it is impossible for the body to wish to harm all its members; and we shall see hereafter that it can harm no one as an individual. The sovereign, for the simple reason that it is so, is always everything that it should be.

But this is not the case regarding the relation of subjects to the sovereign, which, notwithstanding the common interest, could not depend on them to fulfill their engagements, unless there were a way to ensure their fidelity.

Indeed, every individual can, as a man, have a particular will contrary to, or divergent from, the general will which he has as a citizen; his private interest may appear to him quite different from the common interest; his absolute and naturally independent existence may make him envisage what he owes to the common cause as a gratuitous contribution, the loss of which would be less harmful to others than the payment of it would be onerous to him; and, viewing the moral person that constitutes the State as an abstract being because it is not a man, he would be willing to enjoy the rights of a citizen without being willing to fulfill the duties of a subject. The perpetuation of such injustice would bring about the ruin of the body politic.

So that the social pact not be a pointless device, it tacitly includes this engagement, which can alone give force to the others — that whoever refuses to obey the general will shall be constrained to do so by the whole body; which means nothing else than that he shall be forced to be free; for such is the condition which, uniting every citizen to the fatherland, protects him from all personal dependency, a condition that ensures the control and working of the political machine, and alone renders legitimate civil engagements, which, without it, would be absurd, tyrannical, and subject to the most enormous abuses.

Chapter VIII

THE CIVIL STATE

The transition from the state of nature to the civil state produces a very remarkable change in man, by substituting in his behavior justice for instinct, and by imbuing his actions with a moral quality they previously lacked. Only when the voice of duty prevails over physical impulse, and law prevails over appetite, does man, who until then was preoccupied only with himself, understand that he must act according to other principles, and must consult his reason before listening to his inclinations. Although, in this state, he gives up many advantages that he derives from nature, he acquires equally great ones in return; his faculties are used and developed; his ideas are expanded; his feelings are ennobled; his entire soul is raised to such a degree that, if the abuses of this new condition did not often degrade him below that from which he has emerged, he ought to bless continually the wonderful moment that released him from it forever, and transformed him from a stupid, limited animal into an intelligent being and a man.

Let us simplify this whole scheme into terms easy to compare. What man loses because of the social contract is his natural liberty and an unlimited right to anything that tempts him and that he can attain; what he gains is civil liberty and property in all that he possesses. So not to misunderstand these gains, we must clearly distinguish natural liberty, which is limited only by the powers of the individual, from civil liberty, which is limited by the general will; and we must distinguish possession, which is nothing but the result of force or the right of first occupancy, from property, which can be based only on a lawful title.

We might also add to the advantages of the civil state moral freedom, which alone enables man to be truly master of himself; for the impulse of mere appetite is slavery, while obedience to a self-prescribed law is freedom. But I have already said too much on this subject, and the philosophical meaning of the term *freedom* need not concern us here.

Chapter IX

REAL ESTATE

Every member of the community at the moment of its founding gives himself up to it, just as he is, that is, with all his being, his powers, and property. By this act, possession does not change its nature when it changes hands, and become property in those of the sovereign; but, as the powers of the State (*cité*) are incomparably greater than those of an individual, public possession is also, in fact, more secure and more irrevocable, without being more legitimate, at least in respect of foreigners; for the State, with regard to its members, is owner of all their property by the social contract, which, in the State, serves as the basis of all rights; but with regard to other powers, it is owner only by the right of first occupancy which it derives from individuals.

The right of first occupancy, although more real than that of the strongest, becomes a true right only after the establishment of the right of property. Every man has by nature a right to all that he needs; but the positive act which makes him proprietor of certain property excludes him from ownership of other property. His portion having been allotted, he must confine himself to it, and he has no further right to the property of the collectivity. That is why the right of first occupancy, so weak in the state of nature, is respected by all citizens. In this right men respect not so much what belongs to others as what does not belong to themselves.

In order to legalize the right of first occupancy over any real estate whatsoever, the following conditions are necessary: first, the land must not yet be inhabited by any one; secondly, a man must occupy only the area required for his subsistence; thirdly, he must take possession of it, not by ceremonial statements, but by labor and cultivation, the only mark of ownership which, in the absence of legal title, ought to be respected by others.

Indeed, if we accord the right of first occupancy to necessity and labor, why not extend it as far as it can go? Is it impossible to assign limits to this right? Will the mere setting foot on common ground be sufficient to give an immediate claim of ownership? Will the power of driving away other men from it for a moment suffice to deprive them forever of the right of returning to it? How can a man or a people take possession of an immense territory and rob the whole human race of it except by a punishable usurpation, since other men are deprived of the place of residence and the sustenance that nature gives to them in common? When Núñez de Balboa on the seashore took possession of the Pacific Ocean and of all of South America in the name of the crown of Castille, was this sufficient to dispossess all the inhabitants, and exclude from it all the princes in the world? There could be innumerable ceremonies of the same kind; and the Catholic king in his study might, by a single stroke, have claimed possession of the whole world, only eliminating from his empire lands previously occupied by other princes.

We perceive how the lands of individuals, united and contiguous, become public territory, and how the right of sovereignty, extending itself from the subjects to the land they occupy, becomes at once real and personal; which places the possessors in greater dependency, and transforms their own powers into a guarantee of their fidelity — an advantage that ancient monarchs did not understand, for, calling themselves only kings of the Persians or Scythians or Macedonians, they seem to have regarded themselves as rulers of men rather than as masters of countries. Monarchs of today call themselves more cleverly kings of France, Spain, England, etc.; in thus holding the land they are quite sure of holding its inhabitants.

The unusual feature of this alienation is that the community, in receiving the property of individuals, so far from robbing them of it, only assures them lawful possession, and changes usurpation into true right, enjoyment into ownership. Also, the possessors being considered as holders of the public property, and their rights being respected by all members of the

State, as well as defended by all its power against foreigners, they have, as it were, by a transfer advantageous to the public and still more to themselves, acquired all that they have given up — a paradox easily explained by distinguishing between the rights that the sovereign and the proprietor have over the same property, as we shall see hereafter.

It might also happen that men begin to unite before they possess anything, and that afterwards taking over territory sufficient for all, they enjoy it in common, or split it among themselves, either equally or in parts determined by the sovereign. In whatever way this acquisition is made, the right that every individual has over his own property is always subordinate to the right that the community has over all; otherwise there would be no stability in the social union, and no real force in the exercise of sovereignty.

I shall close this chapter and this book with a remark which can serve as a basis for the whole social system; it is that instead of destroying natural equality, the fundamental pact, on the contrary, substitutes a moral and lawful equality for the physical inequality that nature imposed upon men, so that, although unequal in strength or intellect, they all become equal by convention and legal right.*

---

* Under bad governments this equality is only apparent and illusory; it serves only to keep the poor in their misery and the rich in their usurpations. In fact, laws are always useful to those who possess and injurious to those that have nothing; whence it follows that the social state is advantageous to men only so far as they all have something, and none of them has too much.

Book II

Chapter I

THAT SOVEREIGNTY IS INALIENABLE

The first and most important consequence of the principles established above is that the general will alone can direct the forces of the State according to the object of its founding, which is the common good; for if the opposition of private interests has rendered necessary the establishment of societies, it is the concord of these same interests that has rendered it possible. That which is common to these different interests forms the social bond; and unless there were some point in which all interests agree, no society could exist. Now, it is solely with regard to this common interest that the society should be governed.

I say, then, that sovereignty, being nothing but the exercise of the general will, can never be alienated, and that the sovereign power, which is in fact a collective being, can be represented only by itself; power indeed can be transmitted, but not will.

In fact, if it is not impossible that a particular will might agree on some point with the general will, it is at least impossible that this agreement should be lasting and steady; for the particular will naturally tends to certain preferences, and the general will to equality. It is still more impossible to have a guarantee for this agreement, even though it should always exist; it would not be a result of art, but of chance. The sovereign may indeed say: "I want now what a certain man wants, or at least what he says that he wants"; but he cannot say: "What that man wants tomorrow, I shall also want," since it is absurd that the will should take on chains as regards the future, and since it is not incumbent on any will to consent to anything contrary to the welfare of the being that wills. If, then, the people simply promises to obey, it dissolves itself by that act and loses its character as a people; the moment there is a master, there is no longer a sovereign, and forthwith the body politic is destroyed.

This does not imply that the orders of the leaders cannot pass for decisions of the general will, so long as the sovereign, free to oppose them, refrains from doing so. In such a case the consent of the people should be inferred from the universal silence. This will be explained at greater length.

Chapter II

THAT SOVEREIGNTY IS INDIVISIBLE

For the same reason that sovereignty is inalienable it is indivisible; for the will is either general,* or it is not; it is either that of the body of the people, or that of only a part of it. In the first case, this declared will is an act of sovereignty and constitutes law; in the second case, it is only a particular will, or an act of magistracy — it is at most a decree.

But our politicians, being unable to divide sovereignty in its principle, divide it in its object. They divide it into force and will, into legislative power and executive power; into rights of taxation, of justice, and of war; into internal administration and foreign relations — sometimes conflating all these branches, and sometimes separating them. They make the sovereign into a fantastic being, formed of disparate parts; it is as if they created a man from several different bodies, one with eyes, another with arms, another with feet, and nothing else. The Japanese conjurers, it is said, cut up a child before the eyes of the spectators; then, throwing all its limbs into the air, they make the child come down again alive and whole. Such almost are the jugglers' tricks of our politicians; after dismembering the social body, by magic worthy of the circus, they recombine its parts, in any unlikely way.

This error arises from their not having formed clear ideas about the sovereign authority, and from their regarding as elements of this authority what are only emanations from it. Thus, for example, the acts of declaring war and making peace have been regarded as acts of sovereignty, which is not the case, since neither of them is a law, but only an application of the law, a particular act which determines the case of the law, as will be clearly seen when the idea attached to the word *law* is defined.

By following out the other divisions in the same way, it would be found that, whenever sovereignty appears divided, we are mistaken in our thinking; and that the rights which are considered as parts of that sovereignty are

---

* That a will may be general, it is not always necessary that it should be unanimous, but it is necessary that all votes should be counted; any formal exclusion destroys the generality.

all subordinate to it, and always imply supreme wills of which these rights are merely functions.

It would be impossible to describe the obscurity into which this lack of precision has thrown the conclusions of writers on the subject of political rights when they have meditated on the respective rights of kings and peoples, on the principles that they had established. Every one can see, in chapters III and IV of the first book of Grotius, how that learned man and his translator Barbeyrac become entangled and embarrassed in their sophisms, for fear of saying too much or not saying enough according to their views, and so offending the interests that they had to conciliate. Grotius, having taken refuge in France, discontent with his own country, and wishing to pay court to Louis XIII, to whom his book is dedicated, spares no pains to despoil the people of all their rights, and, in the most artful manner, bestow them on kings. This also would clearly have been the inclination of Barbeyrac, who dedicated his translation to the king of England, George I. But unfortunately the expulsion of James II, which he calls an abdication, forced him to be reserved and to equivocate and evade, in order not to make William appear a usurper. If these two writers had adopted true principles, all difficulties would have been removed, and they would have been always consistent; but they would have spoken the truth with regret, and would have paid court only to the people. Truth, however, does not lead to fortune, and the people confer neither embassies, nor professorships, nor pensions.

Chapter III

WHETHER THE GENERAL WILL CAN ERR

It follows from what precedes that the general will is always right and always tends to the public good; but it does not follow that the deliberations of the people always have the same rectitude. Men always desire their own good, but do not always discern it; the people are never corrupted, though often deceived, and it is only then that they seem to will what is evil.

There is often a great deal of difference between the will of all and the general will; the latter regards only the common interest, while the former has regard to private interests, and is merely a sum of particular wills; but take away from these same wills the pluses and minuses which cancel one another,* and the general will remains as the sum of the differences.

* "Every interest," says the Marquis d'Argenson, "has different principles. The accord of two particular interests is formed by opposition to that of a third." He might

If citizens deliberate when adequately informed and without any communication among themselves, the general will would always result from the great number of slight differences, and the resolution would always be good. But when factions, partial associations, are formed to the detriment of the whole society, the will of each of these associations becomes general in relation to its members, and particular with reference to the State; it may then be said that there are no longer as many voters as there are men, but only as many voters as there are associations. The differences become less numerous and yield a less general result. Lastly, when one of these associations becomes so great that it dominates all the others, you no longer have as the result a sum of small differences, but a single difference; there is then no longer a general will, and the opinion which prevails is only a particular opinion.

It is important, then, in order to have a clear declaration of the general will, that there should be no factions in the State, and that every citizen should express only his own opinion.* Such was the unique and sublime institution of the great Lycurgus. But if there are factions, it is necessary to multiply their number and prevent inequality, as Solon, Numa, and Servius did. These are the only proper precautions for ensuring that the general will may always be enlightened, and that the people may not be deceived.

Chapter IV

THE LIMITS OF THE SOVEREIGN POWER

If the State or polity is but a moral person, the life of which consists in the union of its members, and if the most important of its functions is that of self-preservation, it needs a universal and coercive force to move and organize every part in the manner most appropriate for the whole. As nature

---

have added that the accord of all interests is formed by opposition to that of each. Unless there were different interests, the common interest would scarcely be felt and would never meet with any obstacles; everything would go of itself, and politics would cease to be an art.

* "It is true," says Machiavelli, "that some divisions injure the State, while some are beneficial to it; those are injurious to it which are accompanied by cabals and factions; those assist it which are maintained without cabals, without factions. Since, therefore, no founder of a State can provide against enemies in it, he ought at least to provide that there shall be no cabals" (*History of Florence*, Book VII).

gives every man an absolute power over all his limbs, the social pact gives the body politic an absolute power over all its members; and it is this same power which, when controlled by the general will, bears, as I said, the name of sovereignty.

But besides the public person, we have to consider the private persons who comprise it, and whose life and liberty are naturally independent of it. The question, then, is to distinguish clearly between the respective rights of the citizens and of the sovereign,* as well as between the duties which the former have to fulfill in their capacity as subjects and the natural rights which they ought to enjoy in their character as men.

We agree that whatever part of his power, property, and liberty each person alienates by accepting the social compact is only what is useful and important to the community; but we must also agree that the sovereign alone is judge of what is important.

All the services that a citizen can render to the State he owes to it as soon as the sovereign demands them; but the sovereign, for its part, cannot impose on its subjects any burden which is useless to the community; it cannot even wish to do so, for, by the law of reason, just as by the law of nature, nothing is done without a cause.

The engagements which bind us to the social body are obligatory only because they are reciprocal; and their nature is such that in fulfilling them we cannot work for others without also working for ourselves. Why is the general will always right, and why do all invariably desire the prosperity of each, unless it is because there is no one who appropriates to himself this word *each* without also thinking of himself when voting on behalf of all? This proves that equality of rights and the notion of justice that it produces are derived from the preference which each gives to himself, and consequently from man's nature; that the general will, to be truly such, should be so in its object as well as in its essence; that it ought to proceed from all in order to be applicable to all; and that it loses its natural rectitude when it tends to some individual and specific object, because in that case, judging what is unknown to us, we have no true principle of equity to guide us.

Indeed, as soon as a particular fact or right is in question with regard to a point which has not been regulated by an anterior general convention, the matter becomes contentious; it is a proceeding in which the private persons interested are one of the parties and the public the other, but in which I perceive neither the law which must be followed, nor the judge who should

---

* Attentive readers, do not, I beg you, hastily charge me with contradiction here. I could not avoid it in terms owing to the poverty of the language, but wait.

decide. It would be ridiculous in such a case to wish to refer the matter for a formal decision of the general will, which can be nothing but the decision of one of the parties, and which, consequently, is for the other party only a will that is foreign, partial, and inclined on such an occasion to injustice as well as liable to error. Therefore, just as a particular will cannot represent the general will, the general will in turn changes its nature when it has a particular concern, and cannot, as general, decide about either a person or a fact. When the people of Athens, for instance, elected or deposed their leaders, decreed honors to one, imposed penalties on another, and by multitudes of particular decrees exercised indiscriminately all the functions of government, the people no longer had any real general will; they no longer acted as a sovereign power, but as magistrates. This will appear contrary to common ideas, but I must be allowed time to expound my own.

From this we must understand that what generalizes the will is less the number of voices than the common interest that unites them; for, under this system, each person necessarily submits to the conditions which he imposes on others — an admirable union of interest and justice, which gives to the deliberations of the community a spirit of equity that seems to disappear in debates about any private affair, for want of a common interest to unite and identify the guidelines of the judge with that of the concerned party.

By whatever path we return to our founding principle we always arrive at the same conclusion, that is, that the social compact establishes among the citizens such an equality that they all pledge themselves under the same conditions and ought all to enjoy the same rights. Thus, by the nature of the compact, every act of sovereignty, that is, every authentic act of the general will, binds or favors equally all the citizens; so that the sovereign recognizes only the body of the nation, and singles out none of those who compose it.

What, then, constitutes a real act of sovereignty? It is not an agreement between a superior and an inferior, but an agreement of the collective body with each of its members; a lawful agreement, because it has the social contract as its foundation; equitable, because it is common to all; useful, because it can have no other object than the general welfare; and stable, because it has the public force and the supreme power as a guarantee. So long as the subjects submit only to such agreements, they obey no one, other than their own will; and to ask how far the respective rights of the sovereign and citizens extend is to ask up to what point the latter can make engagements among themselves, each with all and all with each.

Thus we see that the sovereign power, wholly absolute, wholly sacred, and wholly inviolable, does not, and cannot, transcend the limits of general agreements, and that every man can fully control what is left to him of his property and liberty by these agreements; so that the sovereign never has a right to burden one subject more than another, because then the matter would become particular and his power would no longer apply.

These distinctions once understood, so untrue is it that in the social contract there is on the part of individuals any real relinquishment, that their situation, as a result of this contract, is in reality preferable to what it was before, and that, instead of an abdication, they have only made an advantageous exchange of an uncertain and precarious mode of existence for a better and more assured one, of natural independence for liberty, of the power to injure others for their own security, and of their strength, which others might overcome, for a right which the social union renders inviolable. Their lives, also, which they have devoted to the State, are continually protected by it; and in exposing their lives for its defense, what do they do but give back what they have received from it? What do they do but what they used to do more frequently and with more risk in the state of nature, when, engaging in inevitable battles, they defended at the peril of their lives their means of preservation? All have to fight for their country in case of need, it is true; but then no one ever has to fight for himself. Do we not gain, moreover, by incurring, for what insures our security, a part of the risks that we would have to incur for ourselves individually, as soon as we were deprived of it?

Chapter V

THE RIGHT OF LIFE AND DEATH

It may be asked how individuals who have no right to dispose of their own lives can transmit to the sovereign this right which they do not possess. The question appears hard to solve only because it is poorly phrased. Every man has a right to risk his own life in order to preserve it. Has it ever been said that one who throws himself out of a window to escape from a fire is guilty of suicide? Has this crime, indeed, ever been imputed to a man who perishes in a storm, although, on embarking, he was not oblivious to the danger?

The social contract has as its end the preservation of the contracting parties. He who desires the end also desires the means, and some risks, even some losses, are inseparable from these means. He who is willing to preserve his life at the expense of others must also give it up for them when necessary. Now, the citizen is not a judge of the peril to which the law requires that he expose himself; and when the prince has said to him: "It is expedient for the State that you should die," he ought to die, since it is only on this condition that he has lived in security up to that time, and since his life is no longer merely a gift of nature, but a conditional gift of the State.

The penalty of death inflicted on criminals may be regarded almost from the same point of view; it is in order not to be the victim of an assassin that a man consents to die if he becomes one. In this contract, far from disposing of his own life, he thinks only of protecting it, and it is not to be supposed that any of the contracting parties contemplates at the time being hanged.

Moreover, every evildoer who attacks social rights becomes by his crimes a rebel and a traitor to his country; by violating its laws he ceases to be a member of it, and even makes war upon it. In that case, the preservation of the State is incompatible with his own — one of the two must perish; and when a guilty man is executed, it is less as a citizen than as an enemy. The proceedings and the judgment are the proofs and the declaration that he has broken the social contract, and consequently that he is no longer a member of the State. Now, as he has acknowledged himself to be such, at least by his residence, he ought to be cut off from it by exile as a violator of the compact, or by death as a public enemy; for such an enemy is not a moral person, he is simply a man; and this is a case in which the right of war is to slay the vanquished.

But, it will be said, the condemnation of a criminal is a particular act. Granted; but this condemnation does not belong to the sovereign; it is a right which that power can confer, though itself unable to exercise it. All my ideas are connected, but I cannot expound them all at once.

Again, the frequency of capital punishments is always a sign of weakness or indolence in the government. There is no man so worthless that he cannot be made good for something. We have a right to kill, even for example's sake, only those who cannot be kept alive without danger.

As regards the right to pardon or to exempt a guilty man from the penalty imposed by the law and inflicted by the judge, it belongs only to a power which is above both the judge and the law, that is to say, the sovereign; still its right in this is not very clear, and the occasions for exercising it are very rare. In a well-governed State there are few punishments, not because many pardons are granted, but because there are few criminals; the multitude of crimes insures impunity when the State is decaying. Under the Roman Republic neither the Senate nor the consuls attempted to grant pardons; not even the people granted any, although they sometimes revoked their own sentences. Frequent pardons proclaim that crimes will soon need them no longer, and every one sees to what that leads. But I feel my heart murmuring and holding back my pen; let us leave these questions to be discussed by the just man who has not erred, and who never needed pardon himself.

Chapter VI

THE LAW

By the social compact we have given existence and life to the body politic; the question now is to endow it with movement and will by legislation. For the original act by which the body is formed and consolidated determines nothing in addition as to what it must do for its own preservation.

What is right and conformable to order is such by the nature of things, and independently of human conventions. All justice comes from God, He alone is the source of it; but if we understood how to receive it direct from so lofty a source, we would need neither government nor laws. Without doubt there is a universal justice emanating from reason alone; but this justice, in order to be accepted among us, should be reciprocal. Regarding things from a human standpoint, the laws of justice are inoperative among men for want of a natural sanction; they only bring good to the wicked and evil to the just when the latter observe them with everyone, and no one observes them in return. Conventions and laws, then, are necessary to couple rights with duties and apply justice to its object. In the state of nature, where everything exists in common, I owe nothing to those to whom I have promised nothing; I recognize as belonging to others only what is useless to me. This is not the case in the civil state, in which all rights are determined by law.

But then, finally, what is a law? So long as men are content to attach to this word only metaphysical ideas, they will continue to debate without being understood; and when they have stated what a law of nature is, they will know no better what a law of the State is.

I have already said that there is no general will with reference to a particular object. In fact, this particular object is either in the State or outside of it. If it is outside the State, a will which is foreign to it is not general in relation to it; and if it is within the State, it forms part of it; then there is formed between the whole and its part a relation which makes of it two separate beings, of which the part is one, and the whole, less this same part, is the other. But the whole less one part is not the whole, and so long as the relation endures, there is no longer any whole, but two unequal parts; whence it follows that the will of the one is no longer general in relation to the other.

But when the whole people decree concerning the whole people, they consider themselves alone; and if a relation is then constituted, it is between the whole object under one point of view and the whole object under another point of view, without any division at all. Then the matter respecting which they decree is general like the will that decrees. It is this act that I call a law.

When I say that the object of the laws is always general, I mean that the law considers subjects collectively, and actions as abstract, never a man as an individual nor a particular action. Thus the law may indeed decree that there shall be privileges, but cannot confer them on any person by name; the law can create several classes of citizens, and even assign the qualifications which shall entitle them to rank in these classes, but it cannot nominate such and such persons to be admitted to them; it can establish a royal government and a hereditary succession, but cannot elect a king or appoint a royal family; in a word, no function which has reference to an individual object appertains to the legislative power.

From this standpoint we see immediately that it is no longer necessary to ask whose office it is to make laws, since they are acts of the general will; nor whether the prince is above the laws, since he is a member of the State; nor whether the law can be unjust, since no one is unjust to himself; nor how we are free and yet subject to the laws, since the laws are only registers of our wills.

We see, further, that since the law combines the universality of the will with the universality of the object, whatever any man prescribes on his own authority is not a law; and whatever the sovereign itself prescribes respecting a particular object is not a law, but a decree, not an act of sovereignty, but of magistracy.

I therefore call any State a republic which is governed by laws, under whatever form of administration it may be; for then only does the public interest predominate and the commonwealth count for something. Every legitimate government is republican;* I will explain hereafter what government is.

Laws are properly only the conditions of civil associations. The people, being subjected to the laws, should be the authors of them; it concerns only the associates to determine the conditions of association. But how will they

---

* I do not mean by this word an aristocracy or democracy only, but in general any government directed by the general will, which is the law. To be legitimate, the government must not be combined with the sovereign power, but must be its minister; then monarchy itself is a republic. This will be made clear in the next book.

be determined? Will it be by a common agreement, by a sudden inspiration? Has the body politic an organ for expressing its will? Who will give it the foresight necessary to frame its acts and publish them at the outset? Or how shall it declare them in the hour of need? How would a blind multitude, which often knows not what it wishes because it rarely knows what is good for it, execute by itself an enterprise so great, so difficult, as a system of legislation? By themselves, the people always desire what is good, but do not always discern it. The general will is always right, but the judgment which guides it is not always enlightened. The general will must be made to see objects as they are, sometimes as they ought to appear; it must be shown the good path that it is seeking, and guarded from the seduction of private interests; it must be made to observe closely times and places, and to balance the attraction of immediate and palpable advantages against the danger of remote and concealed evils. Individuals see the good which they reject; the public desire the good which they do not see. All alike have need of guides. The former must be compelled to conform their wills to their reason; the public must be taught to understand what they want. Then from the public enlightenment results the union of understanding and will in the social body; and from that the close cooperation of the parts, and, lastly, the maximum power of the whole. Hence arises the need of a legislator.

Chapter VII

THE LEGISLATOR

In order to discover the rules of association that are most suitable to nations, a superior intelligence would be necessary who could see all the passions of men without experiencing any of them; who would have no affinity with our nature and yet know it thoroughly; whose happiness would not depend on us, and who would nevertheless be quite willing to interest himself in ours; and, lastly, one who, storing up for himself with the progress of time a far-off glory in the future, could labor in one age and enjoy in another.* Gods would be necessary to give laws to men.

The same argument that Caligula adduced as to fact, Plato put forward with regard to right, in order to give an idea of the civil or royal man whom he is in quest of in his work the *Statesman*. But if it is true that a great prince

---

* A nation becomes famous only when its legislation is beginning to decline. We are ignorant during how many centuries the institutions of Lycurgus conferred happiness on the Spartans before they were known in the rest of Greece.

is a rare man, what will a great legislator be? The first has only to follow the model which the other has to conceive. The latter is the engineer who invents the machine, the former is only the workman who assembles it and turns it on. In the birth of societies, says Montesquieu, it is the leaders of the republics who frame the institutions, and afterwards it is the institutions which mold the leaders of the republics.

He who dares undertake to give institutions to a nation ought to feel himself capable, as it were, of changing human nature; of transforming every individual, who in himself is a complete and independent whole, into part of a greater whole, from which he receives in some manner his life and his being; of altering man's constitution in order to strengthen it; of substituting a social and moral existence for the independent and physical existence which we have all received from nature. In a word, it is necessary to deprive man of his native powers in order to endow him with some which are alien to him, and of which he cannot make use without the aid of other people. The more thoroughly those natural powers are deadened and destroyed, the greater and more durable are the acquired powers, and the more solid and perfect also are the institutions; so that if every citizen is nothing, and can be nothing, except in combination with all the rest, and if the force acquired by the whole be equal or superior to the sum of the natural forces of all the individuals, we may say that legislation is at the highest point of perfection which it can attain.

The legislator is in all respects an extraordinary man in the State. If he ought to be so by his genius, he is not less so by his office. It is neither magistracy nor sovereignty. This office, which constitutes the republic, does not enter into its constitution; it is a special and superior office, having nothing in common with human jurisdiction; for, if he who rules men ought not to control legislation, he who controls legislation ought not to rule men; otherwise his laws, being ministers of his passions, would often serve only to perpetuate his acts of injustice; he would never be able to prevent private interests from corrupting the sacredness of his work.

When Lycurgus gave laws to his country, he began by abdicating his royalty. It was the practice of the majority of the Greek towns to entrust to foreigners the framing of their laws. The modern republics of Italy often imitated this usage; that of Geneva did the same and found it advantageous.* Rome, at her most glorious epoch, saw all the crimes of tyranny

---

* Those who consider Calvin only as a theologian are but little acquainted with the extent of his genius. The preparation of our wise edicts, in which he had a large share, does him as much credit as his *Institutes*. Whatever revolution time may bring about in

spring up in her bosom, and saw herself on the verge of destruction, through uniting in the same hands legislative authority and sovereign power.

Yet the Decemvirs themselves never appropriated the right to pass any law on their sole authority. Nothing that we propose to you, they said to the people, can pass into law without your consent. Romans, be yourselves the authors of the laws which are to secure your happiness.

He who frames laws, then, has, or ought to have, no legislative right, and the people themselves cannot, even if they wished, divest themselves of this incommunicable right, because, according to the fundamental compact, it is only the general will that binds individuals, and we can never be sure that a particular will is conformable to the general will until it has been submitted to the free votes of the people. I have said this already, but it is not useless to repeat it.

Thus we find simultaneously in the work of legislation two things that seem incompatible — an enterprise surpassing human powers, and, to execute it, an authority that is a mere nothing.

Another difficulty deserves attention. Wise men who want to speak to the vulgar in their own language instead of in a popular way will not be understood. Now, there are a thousand kinds of ideas which it is impossible to translate into the language of the people. Views very general and objects very remote are alike beyond its reach; and each individual, approving of no other plan of government than that which promotes his own interests, does not readily perceive the benefits that he is to derive from the continual deprivations which good laws impose. In order that a newly formed nation might approve sound maxims of politics and observe the fundamental rules of state-policy, it would be necessary that the effect should become the cause; that the social spirit, which should be the product of the institution, should preside over the institution itself, and that men should be, prior to the laws, what they ought to become by means of them. Since, then, the legislator cannot employ either force or reasoning, he must have recourse to an authority of a different order, which can compel without violence and persuade without convincing.

It is this which in all ages has constrained the fathers of nations to resort to the intervention of heaven, and to give the gods the credit for their own wisdom, in order that the nations, subjected to the laws of the State as to

---

our religion, so long as love of country and of liberty is not extinct among us, the memory of that great man will not cease to be revered.

those of nature, and recognizing the same power in the creation of man and in that of the State, might obey willingly, and bear submissively the yoke of the public welfare.

The legislator puts into the mouths of the immortals that sublime reason which soars beyond the reach of common men, in order that he may win over by divine authority those whom human prudence could not move.* But it does not belong to every man to make the gods his oracles, nor to be believed when he proclaims himself their interpreter. The great soul of the legislator is the real miracle which must give proof of his mission. Any man can engrave tables of stone, or bribe an oracle, or pretend secret intercourse with some divinity, or train a bird to speak in his ear, or find some other clumsy means to impose himself on the people. He who is acquainted with such means only will perchance be able to assemble a crowd of foolish persons; but he will never found an empire, and his extravagant work will soon perish with him. Empty deceptions form but a transient bond; it is only wisdom that makes it lasting. The Jewish law, which still endures, and that of the child of Ishmael, which for ten centuries has ruled half the world, still bear witness today to the great men who dictated them; and while proud philosophy or blind party spirit sees in them nothing but lucky impostors, the true statesman admires in their systems the great and powerful genius which directs durable institutions.

It is not necessary from all this to conclude with Warburton that politics and religion have among us a common aim, but only that, in the origin of nations, one serves as an instrument of the other.

Chapter VIII

THE PEOPLE

As an architect, before erecting a large edifice, examines and tests the soil in order to see whether it can support the weight, so a wise lawgiver does not begin by drawing up laws that are good in themselves, but considers first whether the people for whom he designs them are fit to maintain them. It is

---

* "It is true," says Machiavelli, "there never was in a nation any promulgator of extraordinary laws who had not recourse to God, because otherwise they would not have been accepted; for there are many advantages recognized by a wise man which are not so self-evident that they can convince others" (*Discourses on Titus Livius,* Book I, chapter II).

on this account that Plato refused to legislate for the Arcadians and Cyrenians, knowing that these two peoples were rich and could not tolerate equality; and it is on this account that good laws and worthless men were to be found in Crete, for Minos had only disciplined a people steeping in vice.

A thousand nations that have flourished on the earth could never have tolerated good laws; and even those that might have done so could have succeeded for only a very short period of their whole duration. The majority of nations, as well as of men, are tractable only in their youth; they become incorrigible as they grow old. When once customs are established and prejudices have taken root, it is a perilous and futile enterprise to try and reform them; for the people cannot even endure that their ills be touched with a view to their removal, like those stupid and cowardly patients who shudder at the sight of a physician.

But just as some illnesses unhinge men's minds and deprive them of all remembrance of the past, so we sometimes find, in the history of States, epochs of violence, in which revolutions produce an influence upon nations such as certain crises produce upon individuals, in which horror of the past takes the place of forgetfulness, and in which the State, inflamed by civil wars, springs forth so to speak from its ashes, and regains the vigor of youth in springing from the arms of death. Such was Sparta in the time of Lycurgus, such was Rome after the Tarquins, and such among us moderns were Holland and Switzerland after the expulsion of their tyrants.

But these events are rare; they are exceptions, the explanation of which is always found in the particular constitution of the excepted State. They could not even happen twice with the same nation; for it may render itself free so long as it is merely barbarous, but can no longer do so when the resources of the State are exhausted. Then commotions may destroy it without revolutions being able to restore it, and as soon as its chains are broken, it falls in pieces and ceases to exist; henceforward it requires a master and not a liberator. Free nations, remember this maxim: Liberty may be acquired but never recovered.

There is for nations as for men a period of maturity, which they must await before they are subjected to laws; but it is not always easy to discern when a people is mature, and if time is rushed, the labor is abortive. One nation is governable from its origin, another is not so at the end of ten centuries. The Russians will never be really governed, because they have been governed too early. Peter had an imitative genius; he had not the true genius that creates and produces anything from nothing. Some of his measures were beneficial, but the majority were ill-timed. He saw that his people were barbarous, but he did not see that they were unripe for government; he wished to civilize them, when it was necessary only to discipline them. He wished to produce at once Germans or Englishmen, when he should have begun by making Russians; he prevented his subjects from ever becoming what they might have been, by persuading them that they were what they were not. It is in this way that a French tutor trains his pupils to shine for a moment in childhood, and then to be for ever a nonentity. The Russian Empire will desire to subjugate Europe, and will itself be subjugated. The Tartars, its subjects or neighbors, will become its masters and ours. This revolution appears to me inevitable. All the kings of Europe are working in concert to accelerate it.

Chapter IX

THE PEOPLE (CONTINUED)

As nature has set limits to the stature of a properly formed man, outside of which it produces only giants and dwarfs; so likewise, with regard to the best constitution of a State, there are limits to its possible size so that it may be neither too large to enable it to be well-governed, nor too small to enable it to maintain itself by itself. There is in every body politic a maximum of force which it cannot exceed, and which is often diminished as the State grows. The more the social bond is extended, the more it is weakened; and, in general, a small State is proportionally stronger than a large one.

A thousand reasons demonstrate the truth of this maxim. In the first place, administration becomes more difficult at great distances, as a weight becomes heavier at the end of a longer lever. It also becomes more burdensome in proportion as its parts are multiplied; for every town has first its own administration, for which the people pay; every district has its administration, still paid for by the people; next, every province, then the superior governments, the satrapies, the vice-royalties, which must be paid for more dearly as we ascend, and always at the cost of the unfortunate people; lastly comes the supreme administration, which overwhelms everything. So many additional burdens perpetually exhaust the subjects; and far from being better governed by all these different orders, they are less well governed than if they had but a single order above them. Meanwhile, hardly any resources remain for cases of emergency; and when it is necessary to have recourse to them the State trembles on the brink of ruin.

Nor is this all; not only has the government less vigor and speed in enforcing observance of the laws, in putting a stop to vexations, in reforming abuses, and in forestalling seditious schemes which may be conducted in distant places; but the people have less affection for their leaders whom they never see, for their country, which is in their eyes like the world, and for their fellow-citizens, most of whom are strangers to them. The same laws cannot be suitable to so many different provinces, which have different customs and different climates, and cannot tolerate the same form of government. Different laws beget only trouble and confusion among the nations which, living under the same leaders and in constant communication, mingle or intermarry with one another, and, when subjected to other customs, never know whether their patrimony is really theirs. Talents are hidden, virtues ignored, vices unpunished, in that multitude of men, unknown to one another, whom the seat of the supreme administration gathers together in one place. The leaders, overwhelmed with business, see nothing themselves; clerks govern the State. In a word, the measures that must be taken to maintain the general authority, which so many officers at a distance wish to evade or impose upon, absorb all governmental attention; no regard for the welfare of the people remains, and scarcely any for their defense in time of need; and thus a body too vast for its constitution sinks and perishes, crushed by its own weight.

On the other hand, the State must secure a certain foundation, that it may possess stability and resist the shocks which it will doubtless experience, as well as sustain the efforts which it will be forced to make in order to maintain itself; for all nations have a kind of centrifugal force, by which they continually act against one another, and tend to aggrandize themselves at the expense of their neighbors, like the vortices of Descartes. Thus the weak are in danger of being quickly swallowed up, and none can preserve itself long except by putting itself in a kind of equilibrium with all, which renders the compression almost equal everywhere.

Hence we see that there are reasons for expansion and reasons for contraction; and it is not the least of a statesman's talents to find the proportion between the two which is most advantageous for the preservation of the State. We may say, in general, that reasons for expansion, being only external and relative, ought to be subordinated to the others, which are internal and absolute. A healthy and strong constitution is the first thing to be sought; and we should rely more on the vigor that springs from a good government than on the resources furnished by a vast territory.

States have, however, been constituted in such a way that the necessity of making conquests entered into their very constitution, and in order to maintain themselves they were forced to enlarge themselves continually. Perhaps they rejoiced in this happy necessity, which nevertheless revealed to them, with the limit of their greatness, the inevitable moment of their fall.

Chapter X

THE PEOPLE (CONTINUED)

A body politic may be measured in two ways, by the extent of its territory, and by the number of its people; and there is between these two modes of measurement an appropriate ratio according to which the State may be given its genuine dimensions. It is the men who constitute the State, and it is the soil that sustains the men; the ratio, then, is that the land should suffice for the maintenance of its inhabitants, and that there should be as many inhabitants as the land can sustain. In this ratio is found the maximum power of a given number of people; for if there is too much land, the care of it is burdensome, the cultivation inadequate, and the output superfluous, and this is the immediate cause of defensive wars. If there is not enough land, the State is at the mercy of its neighbors for the additional crops; and this is the immediate cause of offensive wars. Any nation which has, by its position, only the alternative between commerce and war is weak in itself; it is dependent on its neighbors and on events; it has only a short and precarious existence. It conquers and changes its situation, or it is conquered and reduced to nothing. It can preserve its freedom only by virtue of being small or large.

It is impossible to express numerically a fixed ratio between the extent of land and the number of men that are reciprocally sufficient, on account of the differences that are found in the quality of the soil, in its degree of fertility, in the nature of its products, and in the influence of climate, as well as on account of those which we observe in the constitutions of the inhabitants, of whom some consume little in a fertile country, while others consume much on an unfruitful soil. Further, attention must be paid to the greater or less fecundity of the women, to the conditions of the country, whether more or less favorable to population, and to the numbers which the legislator may hope to draw together by his institutions; so that an opinion should be based not on what is seen, but on what is foreseen, not on the current size of the population but on the size it ought naturally to attain. In short, there are a thousand occasions on which the particular accidents of situation require or permit that more territory than appears necessary should be taken up. Thus men will spread out a good deal in a mountainous country, where the natural productions, that is, woods and pastures, require less labor, where experience teaches that women are more fecund than in the plains, and where with an extensive inclined surface there is only a small horizontal base, which alone should count for vegetation. On the other hand, people may inhabit a smaller space on the seashore, even among rocks and sands that are almost barren, because fishing can, in great measure, supply the deficiency in the productions of the earth, because men ought to be more concentrated in order to repel pirates, and because, further, it is easier to relieve the country, by means of colonies, of the inhabitants with which it is overburdened.

In order to establish a nation, it is necessary to add to these conditions one which cannot supply the place of any other, but without which they are all useless — it is that the people should enjoy abundance and peace; for the time of a State's founding is, like that of constituting soldiers into a regiment, the moment when the body is least capable of resistance and most easy to destroy. Resistance would be easier in a state of absolute disorder than at a moment of fermentation, when each is occupied with his own position and not with the common danger. Should a war, a famine, or a sedition erupt at this critical period, the State is inevitably overthrown.

Many governments, indeed, may be established during such storms, but then it is these very governments that destroy the State. Usurpers always bring about or select tumultuous times for passing, under cover of the public agitation, destructive laws which the people would never adopt when sober-minded. The choice of the moment for the establishment of a government is one of the surest marks for distinguishing the work of the legislator from that of the tyrant.

What people, then, is suited for legislation? One that is already united by some bond of interest, origin, or convention, but has not yet borne the real yoke of the laws; one that has neither customs nor superstitions firmly rooted; one that has no fear of being overwhelmed by a sudden invasion, but that, without entering into the disputes of its neighbors, can single-handed resist either of them, or aid one in repelling the other, that in which every member can be known by all, and in which there is no necessity to impose on a man a greater burden than a man can bear; one that can do without other nations, and without which every other nation can make do,* one that

---

* If of two neighboring nations one could not survive without the other, it would be a very hard situation for the first, and a very dangerous one for the second. Every wise nation in such a case will endeavor very quickly to free the other from this dependence. The republic of Thlascala, enclosed in the empire of Mexico, preferred to do without salt rather than buy it of the Mexicans or even accept it gratuitously. The wise Thlascalans saw a trap hidden beneath this generosity. They kept themselves free; and this small State, enclosed in that great empire, was at last the instrument of its downfall.

is neither rich nor poor and is self-sufficient; lastly, one that combines the stability of an ancient people with the docility of a new one. The work of legislation is made arduous not so much by what must be established as by what must be destroyed; and what makes success so rare is the impossibility of finding a meeting of the simplicity of nature and the needs of society. All these conditions, it is true, are with difficulty combined; hence few well-constituted States are seen.

There is still one country in Europe capable of legislation; it is the island of Corsica. The courage and firmness which that brave nation has exhibited in recovering and defending its freedom would well deserve that some wise man should teach it how to preserve it. I have some presentiment that this small island will one day astonish Europe.

Chapter XI

THE DIFFERENT SYSTEMS OF LEGISLATION

If we ask precisely wherein consists the greatest good of all, which ought to be the aim of every system of legislation, we shall find that it is summed up in two principal objects, *liberty* and *equality* — liberty, because any individual dependence is so much force removed from the body of the State; equality, because liberty cannot survive without it.

I have already said what civil liberty is. With regard to equality, we must not understand by this word that the degrees of power and wealth should be absolutely the same; but that, as to power, it should fall short of all violence, and never be exercised except by virtue of station and of the laws; while, as to wealth, no citizen should be rich enough to be able to buy another, and none poor enough to be forced to sell himself,* which supposes, on the part of the wealthy, moderation in property and influence, and, on the part of ordinary citizens, moderation of avarice and covetousness.

It is said that this equality is an abstract chimera which cannot exist in practice. But if the abuse is inevitable, does it follow that it is unnecessary even to regulate it? It is precisely because the force of circumstances always

* If, then, you wish to give stability to the State, bring the two extremes as near together as possible; tolerate neither rich people nor beggars. These two conditions, naturally inseparable, are equally fatal to the general welfare; from the one class spring tyrants, from the other, the supporters of tyranny; it is always between these that the traffic in public liberty is carried on; the one buys and the other sells.

tends to destroy equality that the force of legislation should always tend to maintain it.

But these general objects of every good institution ought to be modified in each country by the relations which arise both from the local situation and from the character of the inhabitants; and it is with reference to these relations that we must assign to each nation a particular system of institutions, which shall be the best, not perhaps in itself, but for the State for which it is designed. For instance, if the soil is unfruitful and barren, or the country too confined for its inhabitants, turn your attention to arts and manufactures, and exchange their products for the provisions that you require. On the other hand, if you occupy rich plains and fertile slopes, if, in a productive region, you are in need of inhabitants, bestow all your cares on agriculture, which multiplies men, and drive out the arts, which would only end in depopulating the country by gathering together in a few spots the few inhabitants that the land possesses.* If you occupy extensive and convenient coasts, cover the sea with vessels and foster commerce and navigation; you will have a short and brilliant existence. If the sea on your coasts bathes only rocks that are virtually inaccessible, remain fish-eating barbarians; you will lead more peaceful, perhaps better, and certainly happier lives. In a word, besides the maxims common to all, each nation contains within itself some cause that influences it in a particular way, and makes its legislation suitable for it alone. Thus the Hebrews in ancient times, and the Arabs more recently, had religion as their chief object, the Athenians literature, Carthage and Tyre commerce, Rhodes navigation, Sparta war, Rome valor. The author of the *Spirit of the Laws* has shown in a multitude of instances by what arts the legislator directs his institutions towards each of these objects.

What makes the constitution of a State really solid and enduring is the observance of expediency in such a way that natural relations and laws always coincide, the latter only serving, as it were, to secure, support, and rectify the former. But if the legislator, mistaken in his object, takes a principle different from that which springs from the nature of things; if the one tends to servitude, the other to liberty, the one to riches, the other to population, the one to peace, the other to conquests, we shall see the laws imperceptibly weakened and the constitution impaired; and the State will

---

* Any branch of foreign commerce, says the Marquis d'Argenson, diffuses merely a deceptive utility through the kingdom generally; it may enrich a few individuals, even a few towns, but the nation as a whole gains nothing, and the people are none the better for it.

be ceaselessly agitated until it is destroyed or changed, and invincible nature has resumed her sway.

Chapter XII

CLASSIFICATION OF THE LAWS

So that everything may be duly regulated and the best possible form given to the commonwealth, there are various relations to be considered. First, the action of the whole body acting on itself, that is, the relation of the whole to the whole, or of the sovereign to the State; and this relation is composed of that of the intermediate terms, as we shall see hereafter.

The laws governing this relation bear the name of political laws, and are also called fundamental laws, not without some justification if they are wise ones; for, if in every State there is only one good method of regulating it, the people who discovered it ought to adhere to it; but if the established order is bad, why should we regard as fundamental laws that prevent it from being good? Besides, in any case, a nation is always at liberty to change its laws, even the best; for if it likes to injure itself, who has a right to prevent it from doing so?

The second relation is that of the members with one another, or with the body as a whole, and this relation should, in respect of the first, be as small, and, in respect of the second, as great as possible; so that every citizen may be perfectly independent of all the rest, and in absolute dependence on the State. And this is always effectuated by the same means, for it is only the power of the State that secures the freedom of its members. It is from this second relation that civil laws arise.

We may consider a third kind of relation between the individual man and the law, that of punishable disobedience; and this gives rise to the establishment of criminal laws, which at bottom are not so much a particular species of laws as the sanction of all the others.

To these three kinds of laws is added a fourth, the most important of all, which is engraved neither on marble nor on bronze, but in the hearts of the citizens; a law which creates the real constitution of the State, which acquires new strength daily, which, when other laws grow obsolete or pass away, revives them or reinforces them, preserves a people in the spirit of their institutions, and imperceptibly substitutes the force of habit for that of authority. I speak of manners, customs, and above all of opinion — a province unknown to our politicians, but one on which the success of all the rest depends; a province with which the great legislator is occupied in private, while he appears to confine himself to particular regulations, that are merely the sides of the arch, of which customs and morals, slower to develop, ultimately form the immovable keystone.

Of these different types of law, political laws, which constitute the form of government, alone relate to my subject.

Book III

Before speaking of the different forms of government, let us try to determine the precise meaning of that word, which has not yet been explained clearly.

Chapter I

GOVERNMENT IN GENERAL

I warn the reader that this chapter must be read carefully, and that I do not know the art of making myself intelligible to those that will not be attentive.

Every free act has two causes which together produce it; one is moral, that is, the will that determines the act; the other is physical, that is, the power that executes it. When I walk toward an object, first I must want to go toward it; in the second place, my feet must take me to it. Should a paralytic wish to run, or an agile man not wish to do so, both will remain where they are. The body politic has the same driving forces; in it, we discern force and will, the latter under the name of *legislative power*, the former under the name of *executive power*. Nothing is, or ought to be, done in it without them.

We have seen that the legislative power belongs to the people and can belong only to them. On the other hand, it is easy to see from the principles already established, that the executive power cannot belong to the people generally as legislative or sovereign, because that power is used only in particular acts, which are not within the province of the law, nor consequently within that of the sovereign, all the acts of which must be laws.

The public force, then, requires a suitable agent to concentrate it and set it in motion according to the directions of the general will, to serve as a means of communication between the State and the sovereign, to create in some manner in the public person what the union of soul and body creates in a man. This is, in the State, the function of the government, improperly confused with the sovereign of which it is only the minister.

What, then, is the government? An intermediate body established between the subjects and the sovereign for their mutual correspondence, charged with the execution of the laws and with the maintenance of liberty both civil and political.

The members of this body are called magistrates or *kings*, that is, *governors*; and the body as a whole bears the name *Prince*.* Those therefore who claim that the act by which a people submits to its leaders is not a contract are quite right. It is absolutely nothing but a commission, an employment, in which, as simple officers of the soverign, they exercise in its name the power of which it has made them depositaries, and which it can limit, modify, and take back when it pleases. The alienation of such a right, being incompatible with the nature of the social body, is contrary to the object of the association.

I therefore give the name *government* or supreme administration to the legitimate exercise of the executive power, and I give the name of Prince or magistrate to the man or body charged with that administration.

It is in the government that are found the intermediate powers, the relations of which constitute the relation of the whole to the whole, or of the sovereign to the State. This last relation can be represented by that of the extremes of a continuous proportion, of which the proportional mean is the government. The government receives from the sovereign the orders it gives to the people; and so that the State may be in stable equilibrium it is necessary, everything being balanced, that there should be equality between the product or the power of the government taken by itself, and the product or power of the citizens, who are sovereign on the one hand and subjects on the other.

Moreover, we could not alter any of the three terms without at once destroying their proportionality. If the sovereign wishes to govern, or if the magistrate wishes to legislate, or if the subjects refuse to obey, disorder prevails over order, force and will no longer act in concert, and the State being dissolved falls into despotism or anarchy. Lastly, as there is but one proportional mean between each relation, there is only one good government possible in the State; but as a thousand events may change the relations of a people, not only may different governments be good for different peoples, but for the same people at different times.

To try and give an idea of the different relations that may exist between

---

* It is for this reason that at Venice the title of Most Serene Prince is given to the College, even when the Doge does not attend it.

these two extremes, I will take for example the population figures as a relation most easy to express.

Let us suppose that the State is composed of ten thousand citizens. The sovereign can only be considered collectively and as a body; but every private person, in his capacity of subject, is considered an individual; therefore the sovereign is to the subject as ten thousand is to one, that is, each member of the State has as his share only one ten-thousandth part of the sovereign authority, although he is entirely subjected to it.

If the nation consists of a hundred thousand men, the position of the subjects does not change, and each alike is subjected to the whole authority of the laws, while his vote, reduced to one hundred-thousandth, has ten times less influence in their enactment. The subject, then, always remaining one, the ratio of the sovereign to the subject increases in proportion to the number of citizens. From which it follows that the more the State is enlarged, the more liberty is diminished.

When I say that the ratio increases, I mean that it is farther removed from equality. Therefore, the greater the ratio is in the geometrical sense, the less is the ratio in the ordinary sense; in the former sense, the ratio, considered in terms of quantity, is measured by the quotient, and in the other, considered in terms of likeness, it is estimated by the similarity.

Now, the less the particular wills correspond to the general will, that is, customs with laws, the more should the repressive power be increased. The government, then, in order to be good, should be relatively stronger in proportion as the people are more numerous.

On the other hand, since the enlargement of the State gives those entrusted with the public authority more temptations and more opportunities to abuse their power, the more force the government should have to restrain the people, and the more should the sovereign have in its turn to restrain the government. I am not speaking here of absolute force, but of the relative force of the different parts of the State.

It follows from this double relationship that the continuous proportion between the sovereign, the Prince, and the people is not an arbitrary idea, but a necessary consequence of the nature of the body politic. It follows, further, that one of the extremes, that is, the people, as subject, being defined and represented by unity, whenever the doubled ratio increases or diminishes, the single ratio increases or diminishes in like manner, and consequently the middle term is changed. This shows that there is no unique and absolute constitution of government, but that there may be as many governments different in nature as there are States different in size.

If, taking these ideas to their extreme, one argues that, in order to find this mean proportional and form the body of the government, it is, according to me, only necessary to take the square root of the number of people, I would answer that I take that number here only as an example; that the relationships of which I speak are not measured solely by the number of men, but in general by the quantity of action, which results from the combination of a multitude of causes; that, moreover, if for the purpose of expressing myself in fewer words, I borrow for a moment geometrical terms, I am nevertheless aware that geometrical precision does not exist in moral quantities.

The government is on a small scale what the body politic which includes it is on a large scale. It is a moral person endowed with certain faculties, active like the sovereign, passive like the State, and it can be broken down into other similar relations from which arises as a consequence a new proportion, and yet another within this, according to the order if the magistracies, until we come to an indivisible middle term, that is, to a single leader or supreme magistrate, who may be represented, in the middle of this progression, as unity between the series of fractions and that of the whole numbers.

Without getting confused by this multiplication of terms, let us be content to consider the government as a new body in the State, distinct from the people and from the sovereign, and intermediate between the two.

There is this essential difference between those two bodies, that the State exists by itself, while the government exists only through the sovereign. Thus the prevailing will of the Prince is, or ought to be, only the general will, or the law; his force is only the public force concentrated in himself; so soon as he wishes to perform some absolute and independent act, the connection of the whole begins to fall apart. If, lastly, the Prince should happen to have a particular will more active than that of the sovereign, and if, to enforce obedience to this particular will, he should use the public force which is in his hands, in such a manner that there would be so to speak two sovereigns, the one *de jure* and the other *de facto*, the social union would immediately disappear, and the body politic would be dissolved.

Further, in order that the body of the government may have an existence, a real life which distinguishes it from the body of the State; so that all its members may be able to act in concert and fulfill the object for which it is instituted, a particular personality is necessary to it, a feeling common to its members, a force, a will of its own focused on its preservation. This individual existence supposes assemblies, councils, a power of deliberating and resolving, rights, titles, and privileges which belong to the Prince exclusively, and which render the position of the magistrate more honorable in proportion as it is more arduous. The difficulty lies in the method of organizing, within the whole, this subordinate whole, in such a way that it may not weaken the general constitution in strengthening its own; that its particular force, intended for its own preservation, may always be kept distinct from the public force, designed for the preservation of the State; and, in a word, that it may always be ready to sacrifice the government to the people, and not the people to the government.

Moreover, although the artificial body of the government is the work of another artificial body, and has in some respects only a derivative and subordinate existence, that does not prevent it from acting with more or less vigor or celerity, from enjoying, so to speak, more or less robust health. Lastly, without directly departing from the object for which it was instituted, it may deviate from it more or less, according to the manner in which it is constituted.

From all these differences arise the different relations which the government must have with the body of the State, so as to accord with the accidental and particular relations by which the State itself is modified. For often the government that is best in itself will become the most corrupt, unless its relations are changed so as to redress the defects of the body politic to which it belongs.

Chapter II

THE PRINCIPLE WHICH CONSTITUTES THE DIFFERENT FORMS OF GOVERNMENT

To explain the general cause of these differences, I must here distinguish the Prince from the government, as I before distinguished the State from the sovereign.

The body of the magistracy may be composed of a greater or smaller number of members. We said that the ratio of the sovereign to the subjects was so much greater as the people were more numerous; and, by an evident analogy, we can say the same of the government with regard to the magistrates.

Now, the total force of the government, being always that of the State, does not vary; from which it follows that the more it uses this force on its own members, the less remains for acting upon the whole people.

Consequently, the more numerous the magistrates are, the weaker is the government. As this maxim is fundamental, let us endeavor to explain it more clearly.

We can distinguish in the person of the magistrate three essentially different wills; first, the will belonging to the individual, concerned only with his personal advantage; secondly, the common will of the magistrates, concerned solely with the interest of the Prince, and which may be called the corporate will, being general in relation to the government, and particular in relation to the State of which the government forms part; in the third place, the will of the people, or the sovereign will, which is general both in relation to the State considered as the whole, and in relation to the government considered as part of the whole.

In a perfect system of legislation the particular or individual will should be null and void; the corporate will belonging to the government quite subordinate; and consequently the general or sovereign will always dominant, and the sole ruling agency of all the others.

On the other hand, according to the natural order, these different wills become more active to the extent that they are concentrated. Thus the general will is always the weakest, the corporate will has the second rank, and the particular will the first of all; so that in the government each member is, firstly, himself, next a magistrate, and then a citizen — a gradation directly opposed to what the social order requires.

But suppose that the whole government is in the hands of a single man; then the particular will and the corporate will are perfectly united, and consequently the latter is in the highest possible degree of intensity. Now, as it is on the degree of will that the use of force depends, and as the absolute power of the government does not vary, it follows that the most active government is that of a single person.

On the other hand, let us unite the government with the legislative authority; let us make the sovereign the Prince, and all the citizens magistrates; then the corporate will, combined with the general will, will be no more active than the latter, and will leave the particular will in all its force. Thus the government, always with the same absolute force, will be at its minimum of relative force or activity.

These relations are incontestable, and other considerations serve still further to confirm them. We see, for example, that each magistrate is more active in his body than each citizen is in his, and that consequently the particular will has much more influence in the acts of government than in those of the sovereign; for every magistrate is almost always charged with some function of government, whereas each citizen, taken by himself, has no function of sovereignty. Moreover, the larger a State's territory, the more its real force is increased, although it does not increase as a result of its size; but, while the State remains the same, it is useless to increase the number of magistrates, for the government acquires no greater real force, inasmuch as this force is that of the State, the quantity of which is always uniform. Thus the relative force or activity of the government diminishes without its absolute or real force being able to increase.

It is certain, moreover, that the dispatch of business is delayed when more people are responsible for it; that, in laying too much stress on prudence, we leave too little to luck; that opportunities are allowed to pass by, and that owing to excessive deliberation the fruits of deliberation are often lost.

I have just shown that the government is weakened as the number of magistrates increases, and I have before demonstrated that the more numerous the people is, the more ought the repressive force to be increased. From which it follows that the ratio between the magistrates and the government ought to be the inverse of the ratio between the subjects and the sovereign; that is, the more the State expands, the more the government should contract; so that the number of leaders should diminish as a result of an increase in the number of the people.

But I speak here only of the relative force of the government, and not of its rectitude; for, on the other hand, the more numerous the magistracy is, the more the corporate will approaches the general will; whereas, under a single magistrate, this same corporate will is, as I have said, only a particular will. Thus, what is lost on one side can be gained on the other, and the art of the legislator consists in knowing how to determine the point at which the force and will of the government, always in reciprocal proportion, are combined in the ratio most advantageous to the State.

Chapter III

CLASSIFICATION OF GOVERNMENTS

We have seen in the previous chapter why the different kinds or forms of government are characterized by the number of members that comprise them; it remains to be seen in the present chapter how this division is made.

The sovereign may, in the first place, place the responsibility for the government in the whole people, or in the majority of the people, in such a way that there may be more citizens who are magistrates than simple individual citizens. We call this form of government a *democracy*.

Or it may confine the government to a small number, so that there may be more ordinary citizens than magistrates; and this form bears the name of *aristocracy*.

Lastly, it may concentrate the whole government in the hands of a single magistrate from whom all the rest derive their power. This third form is the most common, and is called *monarchy*, or royal government.

We should remark that all these forms, or at least the first two, admit of degrees, and may indeed have a considerable range; for democracy may embrace the whole people, or be limited to a half. Aristocracy, in its own way, may confine itself not to a half of the people but to an even smaller number. Even royalty may undergo some division. Sparta by its constitution always had two kings; and in the Roman Empire there were as many as eight Emperors at the same time without it being possible to say that the Empire was divided. Thus there is a point at which each form of government blends with the next; and we see that, under three forms only, the government may adapt to as many different forms as the State has citizens.

What is more, this same government being in certain respects capable of subdivision into other parts, one administered in one way, another in another, there may result from combinations of these three forms a multitude of mixed forms, each of which can be multiplied by all the simple forms.

For ages there has been much debate about the best form of government, without considering the fact that each of them is the best in certain cases, and the worst in others.

If, in the different States, the number of the supreme magistrates must be in inverse ratio to that of the citizens, it follows that, in general, democratic government is suitable to small States, aristocracy to those of moderate size, and monarchy to large ones. This rule stems directly from the principle. But how is it possible to estimate the multitude of circumstances which may produce exceptions?

Chapter IV

DEMOCRACY

He who makes the law knows better than any one how it should be executed and interpreted. It would seem, then, that there could be no better constitution than one in which the executive power is united with the legislative; but it is that very circumstance which makes a democratic government inadequate in certain respects, because things which ought to be specified are not, and because the Prince and the sovereign, being the same person, only form as it were a government without government.

It is not correct that the person who makes the laws execute them, nor that the body of the people divert its attention from general considerations in order to bestow it on particular objects. Nothing is more dangerous than the influence of private interests on public affairs; and the abuse of the laws by the government is a lesser evil than the corruption of the legislator, which is the infallible result of the pursuit of private interests. For when the State is changed in its substance, all reform becomes impossible. A people that would never abuse the government would likewise never abuse its independence; a people that always governed well would not need to be governed.

Taking the term in its strict sense, there never has existed, and never will exist, any true democracy. It is contrary to the natural order that the majority should govern and that the minority should be governed. It is impossible to imagine the people remaining in perpetual assembly to attend to public affairs, and it is readily apparent that commissions could not be established for that purpose without changing the form of administration.

In fact, I think I can posit as a principle that when the functions of government are shared among several magistrates, the least numerous acquire, sooner or later, the greatest authority, if only on account of the facility with which a smaller number of men can transact business.

How difficult it is, moreover, to combine all the features that this kind of government requires! First, a very small State, in which the people may be readily assembled, and in which every citizen can easily know all the others; secondly, great simplicity of customs and morals, which prevents a multiplicity of issues and thorny debates; next, considerable equality in class and fortune, without which equality in rights and authority could not long survive; lastly, little or no luxury, for luxury is either the result of wealth or makes it necessary; luxury corrupts simultaneously the rich and the poor, the former by ownership, the latter by coveting; it betrays the country to indolence and vanity; it deprives the State of all its citizens in order to enslave them to one to another, and all to opinion.

That is why a famous author posited virtue as the founding principle of a republic, for all these conditions could not survive without virtue; but, by not making the necessary distinctions, this brilliant genius often lacked precision and sometimes clarity, and did not see that the sovereign authority being everywhere the same, the same principle ought to have a role in every well-constituted State, in a greater or lesser degree, it is true, according to the form of government.

Let us add that there is no government so subject to civil wars and internal agitations as the democratic or popular, because there is none which tends so strongly and so constantly to change its form, none which demands more vigilance and courage to be maintained in its own form. It is especially in this constitution that the citizen should arm himself with strength and steadfastness, and say every day of his life from the bottom of his heart what a virtuous Palatine* said in the Diet of Poland: *Malo periculosam libertatem quam quietum servitium.*

If there were a nation of gods, it would be governed democratically. So perfect a government is unsuited to men.

Chapter V

ARISTOCRACY

We have here two very different moral persons, that is, the government and the sovereign; and consequently two general wills, one having reference to all the citizens, the other only to the members of the administration. Thus, although the government can regulate its internal policy as it pleases, it can never speak to the people except in the name of the sovereign, that is, in the name of the people themselves. This must never be forgotten.

The earliest societies were aristocratically governed. The heads of families deliberated among themselves about public affairs. The young men yielded readily to the authority of experience. Hence the names *priests, elders, senate, gerontes*. The Indians of North America are still governed in this way at the present time, and are very well governed.

But in proportion as the inequality due to institutions prevailed over natural inequality, wealth or power† was preferred to age, and aristocracy became elective. Finally, the power transmitted with the father's property to the children, rendering the families patrician, made the government hereditary, and people beheld senators who were only twenty years old.

There are, then, three kinds of aristocracy — natural, elective, and hereditary. The first is suitable only for simple nations; the third is the worst of all governments. The second is the best; it is aristocracy in the true sense.

Other than the advantage of the distinction between the two powers, aristocracy has that of the choice of its members; for in a popular government all the citizens are born magistrates; but this one limits them to a small

---

* The Palatine of Posnania, father of the King of Poland, Duke of Lorraine.

† It is clear that the word *optimates* among the ancients did not mean the best, but the most powerful.

number, and they become magistrates by election only;* a method by which integrity, intelligence, experience, and all other grounds of preferment and public esteem are so many fresh guarantees that men will be wisely governed.

Further, assemblies are more easily convened; issues are better discussed and are dispatched with greater order and diligence; while the credit of the State is better maintained abroad by venerable senators, than by an unknown or base multitude.

In a word, it is the best and most natural order of things that the wisest should govern the multitude, when we are sure that they will govern it for its advantage and not for their own. We should not pointlessly multiply means, nor ask twenty thousand men to do what a hundred chosen men can do still better. But we must note that the corporate interest begins here to steer the public force in a lesser degree according to the rule of the general will, and that another inevitable propensity deprives the laws of a part of the executive power.

With regard to special expediencies, a State must not be so small, nor a people so simple and upright, that the execution of the laws follows immediately upon the public will, as in a good democracy. Nor again must a nation be so large that its leaders, who are dispersed in order to govern it, install themselves as sovereigns, each in his own province, and begin by making themselves independent so as at last to become masters.

But if aristocracy requires fewer virtues than popular government, it also requires others that are peculiarly its own, such as moderation among the rich and contentment among the poor; for a rigorous equality would seem to be out of place in it, and was not even observed in Sparta.

Besides, inasmuch as this form of government includes a certain inequality of fortune, it would be well in general that the administration of public affairs be entrusted to those who are best able to devote their whole time to it, but not, as Aristotle maintains, that the rich should always be preferred. On the contrary, it is important that an opposite choice sometimes teach the people that there are, in men's personal merits, reasons for preference more important than wealth.

---

* It is very important to regulate by law the form of election of magistrates; for, in leaving it to the will of the Prince, it is impossible to avoid falling into hereditary aristocracy, as happened in the republics of Venice and Berne. In consequence, the first has long been a decaying State, but the second is maintained by the extreme wisdom of its Senate; it is a very honorable and a very dangerous exception.

Chapter VI

MONARCHY

We have hitherto considered the Prince as a moral and collective person united by the force of the laws, and as the depositary of the executive power in the State. We now have to consider this power concentrated in the hands of a natural person, of a real man, who alone has a right to use it according to the laws. He is what is called a monarch or a king.

Quite the reverse of the other forms of administration, in which a collective being represents an individual, in this one an individual represents a collective being; so that the moral unity that constitutes it is at the same time a physical unity in which all the powers that the law combines in the other with so much effort are combined naturally.

Thus the will of the people, the will of the Prince, the public force of the State, and the particular force of the government, all obey the same motive power; all the parts of the machine are in the same hand, everything moves toward the same end; there are no opposing movements that counteract one another, and no kind of constitution can be imagined in which more action is produced with less effort. Archimedes, quietly seated on the shore, and launching without difficulty a large vessel, represents to me a skillful monarch, governing from his cabinet his vast States, and, while he appears motionless, setting everything in motion.

But if there is no government that has more vigor, there is none in which the particular will has more sway and more easily governs others. Everything moves toward the same end, it is true; but this end is not the public welfare, and the very power of the administration turns continually to the prejudice of the State.

Kings wish to be absolute, and from afar men shout to them that the best way to become so is to make themselves beloved by their people. This maxim is very fine, and also very true in certain respects; unfortunately it will always be ridiculed in royal circles. Power which springs from the affection of the people is doubtless the greatest, but it is precarious and conditional; princes will never be satisfied with it. The best kings wish to have the power to be wicked if they please, without ceasing to be masters. A political sermonizer will tell them in vain that, the strength of the people being their own, it is their greatest interest that the people flourish, numerous, and formidable; they know very well that that is not true. Their personal interest is, in the first place, that the people should be weak and miserable, and should never be able to resist them. Supposing all the subjects always perfectly submissive, I admit that it would then be the Prince's interest that the people should be powerful, in order that this power, being his own, might render him formidable to his neighbors; but inasmuch as this interest is only secondary and subordinate, and as the two suppositions are incompatible, it is natural that princes should always give preference to the maxim that is most immediately useful to them. It is this that Samuel insisted on to the Hebrews; it is this that Machiavelli clearly demonstrated. While pretending to give lessons to kings, he gave great ones to peoples. The *Prince* of Machiavelli is the book for republicans.*

We have found, by general considerations, that monarchy is suited only to large States; and we shall find this again by examining monarchy itself. The more numerous the public administrative body is, the more does the ratio of the Prince to the subjects diminish and approach equality, so that this ratio is unity or equality itself, in a democracy. This same ratio increases in proportion as the government contracts, and is at its maximum when the government is in the hands of a single person. Then the distance between the Prince and the people is too great, and the State lacks cohesion. In order to unify it, then, intermediate orders, princes, grandees, and nobles are required to fill them. Now, nothing at all of this kind is suitable for a small State, which would be ruined by all these orders.

But if it is difficult for a large State to be well governed, it is much more so for it to be well governed by a single man; and every one knows what happens when the king appoints substitutes.

One essential and inevitable defect, which will always make a monarchical government inferior to a republican one, is that in the latter the public voice hardly ever raises to the highest posts any but enlightened and capable men, who fill them honorably; whereas those who succeed in monarchies are most frequently only petty mischief-makers, petty crooks, petty intriguers, whose petty talents, which enable them to climb to high posts in courts, only serve to show the public their ineptitude as soon as they have attained them. The people are much less mistaken about their choice than the Prince is; and a man of real merit is almost as rare in a royal ministry as a fool at the head of a republican government. Therefore, when by some

* Machiavelli was an honorable man and a good citizen; but, attached to the house of the Medici, he was forced, during the oppression of his country, to conceal his love for liberty. The mere choice of his execrable hero sufficiently manifests his secret intention; and the opposition between the maxims of his book the *Prince* and those of his *Discourses on Titus Livius* and his *History of Florence* shows that this profound politician has had hitherto only superficial or corrupt readers. The court of Rome has strictly prohibited his book; I certainly believe it, for it is that court which he most clearly depicts.

fortunate chance one of these born rulers takes the helm of affairs in a monarchy almost wrecked by such a fine set of ministers, it is quite astonishing what resources he finds, something quite epoch-making.

So that a monarchical State might be well-governed, it would be necessary for its greatness or size to be in proportion to the abilities of the person who governs. It is easier to conquer than to rule. With a sufficient lever, the world can be moved by a finger; but to hold it up the shoulders of Hercules are required. However small a State may be, the Prince is almost always too small for it. When, on the contrary, it happens that the State is too small for its leader, something very rare, it is still badly governed, because the leader, always pursuing his own great designs, forgets the interests of the people, and renders them no less unhappy by the abuse of his abundant abilities, than an inferior leader by his lack of talent. It would be necessary, so to speak, for a kingdom to be enlarged or contracted in every reign, according to the capacity of the Prince; whereas, the talents of a senate have more definite limits, the State may have permanent boundaries, and the administration prosper equally well.

The most obvious disadvantage of the government of a single person is the lack of that continual succession which creates in the two others an uninterrupted chain. One king having died, another is necessary; elections leave dangerous intervals; they are stormy; and unless the citizens are of a disinterestedness, an integrity, something this government hardly encourages, intrigue and corruption sweep in. It would be hard for a man to whom the State has been sold not to sell it in his turn, and indemnify himself out of the helpless for the money which the powerful have extorted from him. Sooner or later everything becomes venal under such an administration, and the peace which is then enjoyed under a king is worse than the disorder of an interregnum.

What has been done to prevent these evils? Crowns have been made hereditary in certain families; and an order of succession has been established which prevents any dispute on the demise of kings; that is to say, the inconvenience of regencies being substituted for that of elections, an appearance of tranquillity has been preferred to a wise administration, and men have preferred to risk having as their leaders children, monsters, and imbeciles, rather than have a dispute about the choice of good kings. They have not considered that in thus exposing themselves to the risk of this alternative, they set themselves up for failure. That was a very sensible answer of Dionysius the younger, to whom his father, in criticizing him for a dishonorable action, said: "Did I set you the example in this?" "Ah!" replied the son, "your father was not king."

All things conspire to deprive of justice and reason a man brought up to govern others. Much trouble is taken, so it is said, to teach young princes the art of reigning; this education does not appear to help them. It would be better to begin by teaching them the art of obeying. The greatest kings whom history has celebrated were not trained to rule; that is a science which men are never less masters of than after excessive study of it, and it is better acquired by obeying than by ruling. *Nam utilissimus idem ac brevissimus bonarum malarumque rerum delectus, cogitare quid aut nolueris sub alio principe, aut volueris.*

A result of this lack of coherence is the instability of royal government, which, being regulated sometimes on one plan, sometimes on another, according to the character of the reigning Prince or that of the persons who reign for him, cannot long pursue a definite aim or a consistent course of conduct, a mutability which always makes the State fluctuate between maxim and maxim, project and project, and which does not exist in other governments, where the Prince is always the same. So we see that, in general, if there is more cunning in a court, there is more wisdom in a senate, and that republics pursue their ends by more steadfast and regular methods; whereas every revolution in a royal ministry produces one in the State, the maxim common to all ministers, and to almost all kings, being to reverse in every respect the acts of their predecessors.

From this same lack of coherence issues the solution of a sophism very familiar to royal politicians; this is not only to compare civil government with domestic government, and the Prince with the father of a family, an error already refuted, but, further, to bestow liberally on this magistrate all the virtues he might need, and always to assume that the Prince is what he ought to be — a supposition on which is based the idea that royal government is clearly preferable to every other, because it is without doubt the strongest, and because it only lacks a corporate will that corresponds to the general will.

But if, according to Plato, a king by nature is so unusual a personage, how many times will nature and fortune conspire to crown him? And if royal education necessarily corrupts those who receive it, what should be expected from a succession of men trained to rule? It is, then, voluntary self-deception to confuse royal government with that of a good king. To see what this government is in itself, we must consider it under inept or wicked princes; for such will come to the throne, or the throne will make them such.

These difficulties have not escaped our authors, but they have not been confused by them. The remedy, they say, is to obey without murmuring; God gives bad kings in His wrath, and we must endure them as chastisements of heaven. Such talk is doubtless edifying, but I am inclined to think it would be more appropriate in a pulpit than in a book on politics. What should we say of a physician who promises miracles, and whose whole art consists in exhorting the sick man to be patient? We know well that when we have a bad government it must be endured; the question is to find a good one.

Chapter VII

MIXED GOVERNMENTS

In truth, there is no simple government. A single leader must have subordinate magistrates; a popular government must have a leader. Thus, in the division of executive power, there is always a gradation from the greater number to the less, with this difference, that sometimes the majority depends on the minority, and sometimes the minority on the majority.

Sometimes there is an equal division, either when the constituent parts are in mutual dependence, as in the government of England; or when the authority of each part is independent, but imperfect, as in Poland. This latter form is bad, because there is no unity in the government, and the State lacks cohesion.

Is a simple or a mixed government the better? A question much debated among political thinkers, and one to which the same answer must be made that I have made before about every form of government.

The simple government is the better in itself, for the reason that it is simple. But when the executive power is not sufficiently dependent on the legislative, that is, when there is a closer rapport between the Prince and the sovereign than between the people and the Prince, this defective relationship must be remedied by dividing the government; for then all its parts have no less authority over the subjects, and their division renders them all together less strong against the sovereign.

The same defect is also guarded against by the establishment of intermediate magistrates, who, leaving the government in its entirety, only serve to balance the two powers and maintain their respective rights. Then the government is not mixed, but moderate.

The opposite defect can be guarded against by similar means, and, when the government is too lax, tribunals may be erected to concentrate it. That is customary in all democracies. In the first case the government is divided in order to weaken it, and in the second in order to strengthen it; for the maximum of strength and also of weakness is found in simple governments, while the mixed forms give a medium strength.

Chapter VIII

THAT ALL FORMS OF GOVERNMENT ARE NOT SUITED FOR EVERY COUNTRY

Liberty, not being a fruit of all climates, is not within the reach of all peoples. The more we consider this principle established by Montesquieu, the more do we perceive its truth; the more it is contested, the greater opportunity is given to establish it by new proofs.

In all the governments of the world, the public person consumes, but produces nothing. From where, then, comes the substance it consumes? From the labor of its members. It is the superfluity of individuals that supplies the necessaries of the public. Hence it follows that the civil State can subsist only so long as men's labor produces more than they need.

Now this excess is not the same in all countries of the world. In several it is considerable, in others moderate, in others nothing, in others a minus quantity. This proportion depends on the fertility due to climate, on the kind of labor which the soil requires, on the nature of its products, on the physical strength of its inhabitants, on the greater or less consumption that is necessary to them, and on several other like proportions of which it is composed.

On the other hand, all governments are not of the same nature; there are some more or less wasteful; and the differences are based on this other principle, that the more the public contributions are distanced from their source, the more burdensome they are. We must not measure this burden by the amount of the taxes, but by the distance they have to travel in order to return to the hands from which they have come. When this circulation is prompt and well-established, it matters not whether little or much is paid; the people are always rich, and the finances are always prosperous. On the other hand, however little the people may contribute, if this little does not revert back to them, they are soon exhausted by constantly giving; the State is never rich and the people are always in beggary.

It follows from this that the more the distance between the people and the government is increased, the more burdensome do the taxes become; therefore, in a democracy the people are least encumbered, in an aristocracy they are more so, and in a monarchy they bear the greatest weight. Monarchy, then, is suited only to wealthy nations; aristocracy, to States moderate both in wealth and size; democracy, to small and poor States.

Indeed, the more we reflect on this, the more we find in this the difference between free and monarchical States. In the first, everything is used for the common good; in the others, public and private resources are reciprocal, and the former are increased by the diminution of the latter; lastly, instead of governing subjects in order to make them happy, despotism renders them miserable in order to govern them.

There are, then, in every climate natural causes by which we can assign the form of government which is adapted to the nature of the climate, and even say what kind of inhabitants the country should have.

Unfruitful and barren places, where the produce is not commensurate with the labor, ought to remain uncultivated and abandoned, or should only be peopled by savages; places where men's toil yields only bare necessities ought to be inhabited by barbarous nations; in them any polity would be an impossibility. Places where the excess of the produce over the labor is moderate are suitable for free nations; those in which abundant and fertile soil yields much produce for little labor are willing to be governed monarchically, in order that the superfluity of the subjects may be consumed by the luxuries of the Prince; for it is better that this excess be absorbed by the government than squandered by private persons. There are exceptions, I know; but these exceptions themselves prove the rule, in that, sooner or later, they produce revolutions which restore things to their natural order.

We should always distinguish general laws from the particular causes that may modify their effects. If all southern lands were covered with republics, and all northern lands with despotic States, it would not be less true that, through the influence of climate, despotism is suitable to warm countries, barbarism to cold countries, and a good polity to intermediate regions. I see, however, that while the principle is accepted, its application may be disputed; it will be said that some cold countries are very fertile, and some southern ones very unfruitful. But this is a difficulty only for those who do not examine the matter in all its aspects. It is necessary, as I have already said, to reckon those connected with labor, resources, consumption, etc.

Let us suppose that the product of two districts equal in area is in the ratio of five to ten. If the inhabitants of the former consume four and those of the latter nine parts, the surplus product of the first will be one-fifth, and that of the second one-tenth. The ratio between these two surpluses being then inversely as that of the produce of each, the district that yields only five will give a surplus double that of the district which produces ten.

But it is not a question of a doubled product, and I do not think that any one dare, in general, place the fertility of cold countries even on an equal par with that of warm countries. Let us, however, assume this equality; let us, if you will, put England on the scale with Sicily, and Poland with Egypt;

more to the south we shall have Africa and India; more to the north we shall have nothing. To achieve equality in product, what are the differences in cultivation? In Sicily it suffices to scratch the soil; in England what toil is needed to till it! But where more exertion is required to yield the same product, the surplus must necessarily be very small.

Consider, besides this, that the same number of men consume much less in warm countries. The climate demands that people be moderate to be healthy; Europeans who want to live as at home all die of dysentery and dyspepsia. "We are," says Chardin, "carnivorous beasts, wolves, in comparison with Asiatics. Some attribute the moderation of the Persians to the fact that their country is scantily cultivated; I believe, on the contrary, that their country is not very abundant in provisions because the inhabitants need very little. If their frugality," he continues, "resulted from the poverty of the country, it would be only the poor who would eat little, whereas it is the people generally; and more or less would be consumed in each province, according to the fertility of the country, whereas the same abstemiousness is found throughout the kingdom. They pride themselves greatly on their mode of living, saying that it is only necessary to look at their complexions, to see how much superior they are to those of Christians. Indeed, the complexions of the Persians are smooth; they have beautiful skin, delicate and clear; while the complexions of their subjects, the Armenians, who live in European fashion, are rough and blotched, and their bodies are coarse and heavy."

The nearer we approach the Equator, the less the people have to live on. They scarcely eat any meat; rice, maize, couscous, millet, cassava, are their ordinary foods. There are in India millions of men whose diet does not cost a half-penny a day. We see even in Europe palpable differences in appetite between northern and southern nations. A Spaniard can live for eight days on a German's dinner. In countries where men are most voracious luxury revolves around appetite; in England it is displayed in a table loaded with meats; in Italy you are regaled with sugar and flowers.

Luxury in dress presents similar differences. In climates where the changes of the seasons are sudden and violent, garments are better and simpler; in those where people dress only for ornament, splendor is more sought after than utility, for clothes themselves are a luxury. In Naples you will see men every day walking to Posilippo with gold-embroidered coats, and no stockings. It is the same with regard to buildings; everything is sacrificed to magnificence when there is nothing to fear from the climate. In Paris and in London people must be warmly and comfortably housed; in

Madrid they have superb drawing-rooms, but no windows that shut, while they sleep in mere closets.

Food is much more substantial and nutritious in warm countries; this is a third difference which cannot fail to influence the second. Why do people eat so many vegetables in Italy? Because they are good, nourishing, and flavorful. In France, where they are fertilized only with water, they are not nourishing and count almost for nothing on the table; they do not, however, occupy less soil, and they cost at least as much labor to cultivate. We know from experience that the wheat of Barbary, inferior in other respects to that of France, yields much more flour, and that the wheat of France yields more than the wheat of the north. From this we may infer that a similar gradation is observable generally, in the same direction, from the Equator to the Pole. Now is it not a clear disadvantage to have in an equal quantity of produce a smaller quantity of nutrition?

To all these different reflections I want to add one that springs from, and reinforces, them; it is that warm countries have less need of inhabitants than cold countries, but would be able to maintain a greater number; hence a double surplus is produced, always to the advantage of despotism. The greater the surface occupied by the same number of inhabitants, the more difficult do rebellions become, because conspiracies cannot be concerted promptly and secretly, and because it is always easy for the government to discover the plans and cut off communications. But the more closely packed a numerous population is, the less power a government has to usurp the sovereignty; the leaders deliberate as securely in their offices as the Prince in his council, and the multitude assemble in the town squares as quickly as the troops in their quarters. The advantage, then, of a tyrannical government lies in this, that it can act from great distances. With the help of its collaborators, its power increases with the distance, like that of levers.* That of the people, on the other hand, acts only when concentrated; it evaporates and disappears as it extends, like the effect of gunpowder scattered on the ground, which takes fire only grain by grain. The least populous countries are thus the best adapted for tyranny; wild beasts reign only in deserts.

* This does not contradict what I said before (Book II, chapter ix) on the inconveniences of large States; for there it was a question of the authority of the government over its members, and here it is a question of its power against its subjects. Its scattered members serve as points of support to it for operating at a distance upon the people, but it has no point of support for acting on its members themselves. Thus, the length of the lever is the cause of its weakness in the one case, and of its strength in the other.

Chapter IX

THE SIGNS OF A GOOD GOVERNMENT

When, then, it is finally asked which is the best government, an insoluble, undeterminable question is posed; or, if you will, it has as many correct solutions as there are possible combinations in the absolute and relative situations of nations.

But if it were asked by what sign it can be known whether a given people is well or badly governed, that would be a different matter, and the question of fact might be determined.

It is, however, not settled, because every one wishes to decide it in his own way. Subjects extol the public tranquillity, citizens the liberty of individuals; the former prefer security of property, the latter, that of persons; the former think that the best government is the most authoritarian, the latter maintain that it is the mildest; one party wants crimes to be punished, the other wants them to be prevented; one party thinks it well to be feared by their neighbors, the other party prefers to be unacquainted with them; one party is satisfied when money circulates, the other party demands that the people have bread. Even if there were agreement on these and other similar points, would we know more? Since moral quantities lack a precise mode of measurement, even if we agreed on the sign, how could we do so about the valuation of it?

For my part, I am always astonished that people fail to recognize so simple a sign, or that they should have the insincerity not to agree about it. What is the object of political association? It is the security and prosperity of its members. And what is the surest sign that they are safe and prosperous? It is their number and population. Do not, then, go and seek elsewhere for this contentious sign. All other things being equal, the government under which, without external aids, without naturalizations, and without colonies, the citizens increase and multiply most, is infallibly the best. That under which a people decreases and decays is the worst. Statisticians, it is now your affair; count, measure, compare.*

* On the same principle must be judged the centuries which deserve preference in respect of the prosperity of the human race. Those in which literature and art were seen to flourish have been too much admired, without the secret object of their cultivation being penetrated, without their fatal consequences being considered: *Idque apud imperitos humanitas vocabatur, quum pars servitutis esset.* Shall we never detect in the maxims of books the gross self-interest which makes the authors speak? No, whatever they may say, when, notwithstanding its brilliancy, a country is being depopulated, it is untrue that all

Chapter X

THE ABUSE OF GOVERNMENT AND ITS TENDENCY TO DEGENERATE

As the private will acts incessantly against the general will, so the government makes a continual effort against the sovereignty. The more this effort is increased, the more the constitution is altered; and as there is no other corporate will which, by resisting that of the Prince, creates a balance with it, sooner or later the Prince oppresses the sovereign and violates the social treaty. Therein is the inherent and inevitable vice which, right from the birth of the body politic, tends ineluctably to destroy it, just as old age and death ultimately destroy the human body.

There are two general ways by which a government degenerates, that is, when it contracts, or when the State is dissolved.

The government contracts when it passes from the majority to the minority, that is, from democracy to aristocracy, and from aristocracy to royalty. That is its natural tendency.* If it retrograded from the minority to the majority, it might be said to weaken; but this inverse progress is impossible.

---

goes well, and it is not enough that a poet should have an income of 100,000 livres for his epoch to be the best of all. The apparent repose and tranquillity of the chief men must be regarded less than the welfare of nations as a whole, and especially that of the most populous States. Hail lays waste a few cantons, but it rarely causes scarcity. Riots and civil wars greatly startle the chief men; but they do not produce the real misfortunes of nations, which may even be abated, while it is being disputed who shall tyrannize over them. It is from their permanent condition that their real prosperity or calamities spring; when all is left crushed under the yoke, it is then that everything perishes; it is then that the chief men, destroying them at their leisure, *ubi solitudinem faciunt, pacem appellant.* When the broils of the great agitated the kingdom of France, and the coadjutor of Paris carried a poniard in his pocket to the *Parlement,* that did not prevent the French nation from living happily and harmoniously in free and honorable ease. Greece of old flourished in the midst of the most cruel wars; blood flowed there in streams, and the whole country was covered with men. It seemed, said Machiavelli, that amid murders, proscriptions, and civil wars, our republic became more powerful; the virtues of its citizens, their manners, their independence, were more effectual in strengthening it than all its dissensions had been in weakening it. A little agitation gives energy to men's minds, and what makes the race truly prosperous is not so much peace as liberty.

* The slow formation and the progress of Venice in her lagoons present a notable example of this succession; it is indeed astonishing that, after more than twelve hundred

In reality, the government never changes its form except when its depleted energy leaves it too weak to preserve itself; and if it becomes still more weakened as it expands, its strength will be annihilated, and it will be unable to survive. We must therefore concentrate the energy as it dwindles; otherwise the State that it sustains will fall into ruin.

The dissolution of the State may occur in two ways.

Firstly, when the Prince no longer administers the State in accordance with the laws; and, secondly, when he usurps the sovereign power. Then a remarkable change takes place — the State, and not the government, con-

---

years, the Venetians seem to be still only in the second stage, which began with the *Serrar di Consiglio* in 1198. As for the ancient Doges, with whom they are reproached, whatever the *Squittinio della libertà veneta* may say, it is proved that they were not their sovereigns.

People will not fail to bring forward as an objection to my views the Roman Republic, which followed, it will be said, a course quite contrary, passing from monarchy to aristocracy, and from aristocracy to democracy. I am very far from regarding it in this way.

The first institution of Romulus was a mixed government, which speedily degenerated into despotism. From peculiar causes the State perished before its time, as we see a newborn babe die before attaining manhood. The expulsion of the Tarquins was the real epoch of the birth of the Republic. But it did not at first assume a regular form, because, through not abolishing the patrician order, only a half of the work was done. For, in this way, the hereditary aristocracy, which is the worst of legitimate administrations, remaining in conflict with the democracy, the form of the government, always uncertain and fluctuating, was fixed, as Machiavelli has shown, only on the institution of the tribunes; not till then was there a real government and a true democracy. Indeed, the people then were not only sovereign, but also magistrates and judges; the Senate was only a subordinate tribunal for moderating and concentrating the government; and the consuls themselves, although patricians, although chief magistrates, although generals with absolute authority in war, were in Rome only the presidents of the people.

From that time, moreover, the government seemed to follow its natural inclination, and tend strongly to aristocracy. The patriciate abolishing itself as it were, the aristocracy was no longer in the body of patricians as it is at Venice and Genoa, but in the body of the Senate, composed of patricians and plebeians, and also in the body of tribunes when they began to usurp an active power; for words make no difference in things, and when a nation has chiefs to govern for them, whatever name those chiefs bear, they always form an aristocracy.

From the abuses of aristocracy sprang the civil wars and the triumvirate. Sylla, Julius Cæsar, Augustus, became in fact real monarchs; and at length, under the despotism of Tiberius, the State was broken up. Roman history, then, does not belie my principle, but confirms it.

tracts; I mean that the State dissolves, and that another is formed within it, which is comprised only of the members of the government, and which is for the rest of the people nothing more than their master and their tyrant. So that as soon as the government usurps the sovereignty, the social compact is broken, and all the ordinary citizens, rightfully regaining their natural liberty, are forced, but not morally bound, to obey.

The same thing occurs also when the members of the government usurp individually the power that they ought to exercise only collectively, which is no less a violation of the laws, and creates still greater disorder. Then there are, so to speak, as many Princes as magistrates; and the State, not less divided than the government, perishes or changes its form.

When the State is broken up, the violation of the government, whatever it may be, takes the common name of *anarchy.* To be clear, democracy degenerates into *ochlocracy,* aristocracy into *oligarchy*; I should add that royalty degenerates into *tyranny*; but this last word is equivocal and requires explanation.

In the vulgar sense a tyrant is a king who governs with violence and without regard to justice and the laws. In the strict sense, a tyrant is an individual who arrogates to himself the royal authority without having a right to it. It is in this sense that the Greeks understood the word tyrant; they bestowed it equally on good and bad Princes whose authority was not legitimate.* Thus *tyrant* and *usurper* are two perfectly synonymous words.

To give different names to different things, I call the usurper of royal authority a *tyrant*, and the usurper of sovereign power a *despot*. The tyrant is he who, contrary to the laws, takes it upon himself to govern according to the laws; the despot is he who sets himself above those very laws. Thus the tyrant cannot be a despot, but the despot is always a tyrant.

Chapter XI

THE DISSOLUTION OF THE BODY POLITIC

Such is the natural and inevitable tendency of the best constituted governments. If Sparta and Rome perished, what State can hope to endure forever? If we wish to form an enduring constitution, let us, then, not dream of

---

* *Omnes enim et habentur et dicuntur tyranni, qui potestate utuntur perpetua in ea civitate quae libertate usa est.* (Corn. Nep., *in Miltiad.*, cap. viii) It is true that Aristotle (*Mor. Nicom.*, Book VIII, cap. x) distinguishes the tyrant from the king, by the circumstance that the former governs for his own benefit, and the latter only for the benefit of his

making it eternal. To succeed we must not attempt the impossible, nor flatter ourselves that we can bestow on the work of men a permanence that human things cannot attain.

The body politic, as well as the human body, begins to die from its birth, and contains in itself the causes of its own destruction. But both may have a more or less robust constitution, that can preserve them for a long while. The constitution of man is the work of nature; that of the State is the work of art. It is not men's prerogative to prolong their lives; it is their prerogative to prolong the life of the State as long as possible, by giving it the best constitution possible. The best constituted will come to an end, but later than another, unless some unforeseen accident brings about its premature destruction.

The principle of political life is in the sovereign authority. The legislative power is the heart of the State; the executive power is its brain, giving movement to all the parts. The brain might be paralyzed and yet the individual can still live. A man might be an imbecile but still live; but as soon as the heart stops, the animal dies.

It is not by laws that the State survives, but by the legislative power. The law of yesterday is not binding today; but tacit consent is presumed from silence, and the sovereign is supposed to confirm continually the laws it does not abrogate when able to do so. Whatever it once declared that it wills, it wills so always, unless the declaration is revoked.

Why, then, do people show so much respect for ancient laws? That is exactly the reason. We are right to believe that it is the very excellence of ancient laws that has enabled them to survive so long; if the sovereign had not recognized them as salutary, it would have revoked them a thousand times. That is why, far from being weakened, the laws are ever acquiring fresh vigor in every well constituted State; the prejudice in favor of antiquity makes them more revered every day; while, wherever laws are weakened as they grow old, this fact proves that there is no longer any legislative power, and that the State no longer lives.

---

subjects; but besides the fact that, in general, all the Greek authors have taken the word *tyrant* in a different sense, as appears especially from Xenophon's *Hiero*, it would follow from Aristotle's distinction that, since the beginning of the world, not a single king has yet existed.

Chapter XII

HOW THE SOVEREIGN AUTHORITY IS MAINTAINED

The sovereign, having no other force than the legislative power, acts only through the laws; and the laws being nothing but authentic acts of the general will, the sovereign can act only when the people are assembled. A convention of the people! People will say: What a fantasy! It is a fantasy today; but it was not so two thousand years ago. Have men changed their nature?

The limits of the possible in moral things are less narrow than we think; it is our weaknesses, our vices, our prejudices, that shrink them. Sordid souls do not believe in great men; vile slaves smile mockingly at the word *liberty*.

From what has been done let us consider what can be done. I shall not speak of the ancient republics of Greece; but the Roman Republic was, it seems to me, a great State, and the city of Rome a great city. The last census in Rome showed that there were 400,000 citizens bearing arms, and the last census of the Empire showed more than 4,000,000 citizens, without including subjects, foreigners, women, children, and slaves.

What a difficulty, we might suppose, there would be in assembling frequently the enormous population of the capital and its environs. Yet few weeks passed without the Roman people being assembled, even several times. Not only did they exercise the rights of sovereignty, but a part of the rights of government. They discussed certain issues and adjudicated certain problems, and in the public assembly the whole people were almost as often magistrates as citizens.

By going back to the early times of nations, we would find that the majority of the ancient governments, even monarchical ones, like those of the Macedonians and the Franks, had similar councils. Be that as it may, this single incontestable fact answers all objections; inference from the actual to the possible appears to me sound.

Chapter XIII

HOW THE SOVEREIGN AUTHORITY IS MAINTAINED (CONTINUED)

It is not sufficient for the assembled people to have, at one point in time, determined the constitution of the State by giving their sanction to a body of laws; it is not sufficient for them to have established a permanent government, or to have once and for all provided for the election of magistrates. Besides the extraordinary assemblies which unforeseen events may require, it is necessary to have regular and periodic ones that nothing can cancel or postpone; so that, on the appointed day, the people are rightfully convened by the law, without any formal call.

But, except for these assemblies which are lawful by their date alone, every assembly of the people not convoked by magistrates appointed for that duty and not corresponding to the prescribed forms, must be seen as illegitimate and all that is done in it as invalid, because even the order to assemble must emanate from the law.

As for the more or less frequent meetings of the lawful assemblies, they depend on so many considerations that no precise rules can be formulated about them. But we can say in general that the more strength a government has, the more frequently should the sovereign meet in public.

This, I shall be told, may be good for a lone city; but what is to be done when the State comprises many cities? Will the sovereign authority be divided? Or must it be concentrated in a single city and render subject all the others?

My answer is that neither alternative is good. In the first place, the sovereign authority is simple and undivided, and we cannot divide it without destroying it. In the second place, a city, no more than a nation, can be lawfully subject to another, because the essence of the body politic consists in the union of obedience and liberty, and these words, *subject* and *sovereign,* are correlatives, the notion underlying them being expressed in the one word citizen.

My answer, furthermore, is that it is always bad to merge several towns into a single State, and, in desiring to create such a union, we must not flatter ourselves that we can avoid the usual problems. The defects of large States cannot be used as an objection against a man who only desires small ones. But how can small States be endowed with sufficient force to resist large ones? Just as Greek towns used to resist the great King, and as more recently Holland and Switzerland resisted the House of Austria.

If, however, the State cannot be reduced to proper limits, one option still remains; it is not to allow any capital, but to make the government sit alternately in each town, and also to assemble in them one by one the people of the country.

Populate the territory uniformly, extend the same rights everywhere, spread everywhere abundance and life; this is how the State will become simultaneously the strongest and the best governed that may be possible. Remember that the walls of the towns are constructed solely of the wreckage of farm houses. For every palace that I see built in the capital, I seem to see a whole rural district laid in ruins.

Chapter XIV

HOW THE SOVEREIGN AUTHORITY IS MAINTAINED (CONTINUED)

As soon as the people are lawfully assembled as a sovereign body, the whole jurisdiction of the government ceases, the executive power is suspended, and the person of the lowliest citizen is as sacred and inviolable as that of the first magistrate, because where the represented are, there is no longer any representative. Most of the tumult that arose in Rome in the *comitia* stemmed from ignorance or neglect of this rule. The consuls were then only presidents of the people and the tribunes simple orators;* the Senate had no power at all.

These intervals of suspension, in which the Prince recognizes or ought to recognize the presence of a live superior, have always been dreaded by him; and these assemblies of the people, which are the shield of the body politic and the curb of the government, have in all ages terrified leaders; hence such men are never wanting in solicitude, objections, obstacles, and promises, in an attempt to make the citizens disgusted with the assemblies. When citizens are avaricious, cowardly, pusillanimous, and more desirous of calm than of freedom, they do not long hold out against the strenuous efforts of the government; and thus, as the resisting force constantly increases, the sovereign authority finally disappears, and most of the States fall and perish before their time.

But between the sovereign authority and an arbitrary government there sometimes emerges an intermediate power of which I must speak.

Chapter XV

DEPUTIES OR REPRESENTATIVES

As soon as public service ceases to be the principle concern of citizens, and they prefer helping with their wallets rather than with their persons, the State is already on the brink of ruin. Must they march to battle? They pay troops and stay at home. Is it necessary to go to the council? They appoint deputies and stay at home. Because of indolence and wealth, they ulti-

---

* Almost in the sense given to this term in the Parliament of England. The resemblance between their offices would have set the consuls and tribunes in conflict, even if all jurisdiction had been suspended.

mately create soldiers who enslave their country and create representatives who sell it.

It is the bustle of commerce and of the arts, it is the greedy pursuit of profit, it is indolence and love of comforts, that transform public service into money. People sacrifice a portion of their profit in order to increase it when they like. Give money and soon you will have chains. That word *finance* is a slave's word; it is unknown among citizens. In a state that is really free, the citizens do everything with their hands and nothing with money; far from paying to avoid their duties, they would pay to perform them themselves. Far from me ordinary ideas; I believe that hard labor is less contrary to liberty than taxation is.

The better constituted a State is, the more public affairs outweigh private ones in the minds of the citizens. There is, indeed, a much smaller number of private affairs, because the amount of general prosperity makes each individual more prosperous, and less remains to be sought by individual exertions. In a well governed city-state every one hastens to the assemblies; under a bad government no one budges to attend them, because no one takes an interest in the proceedings; they know in advance that the general will will not prevail, because private concerns have become all-absorbing. Good laws pave the way for better ones; bad laws lead to worse ones. As soon as any one says about the affairs of the State, "Why should I care?" the State is gone.

The decline of patriotism, the active pursuit of private interests, the vast size of States, conquests, and the violations of government led to the idea of deputies or representatives of the people in the national assemblies. It is this which in certain countries they dare to call the Third Estate. Thus the private interest of two orders is placed in the first and second rank, the public interest only in the third.

Sovereignty cannot be represented for the same reason that it cannot be alienated; it consists essentially in the general will, and the will cannot be represented; it is itself or it is something else; there is no middle ground. The deputies of the people, then, are not and cannot be its representatives; they are only its agents and can conclude nothing definitively. Every law which the people in person have not ratified is invalid; it is not a law. The English nation thinks that it is free, but is greatly mistaken, for it is so only during the election of members of Parliament; as soon as they are elected, it is enslaved and counts for nothing. The use it makes of the brief moments of freedom renders the loss of liberty well-deserved.

The idea of representatives is modern; it comes to us from feudal government, that absurd and iniquitous government, under which mankind is degraded and the name of man dishonored. In the republics, and even in the monarchies, of antiquity, the people never had representatives; they did not know the word. It is noteworthy that in Rome, where the tribunes were so sacred, it was not even imagined that they could usurp the functions of the people, and in the midst of so great a multitude, they never attempted to pass on their own authority a single plebiscite. We can imagine, however, the confusion the crowd sometimes caused from what occurred in the time of the Gracchi, when some citizens shouted their votes from the housetops.

Where right and liberty mean everything, inconveniences are nothing. In that wise nation everything was estimated at its true value; it allowed the lictors to do what the tribunes had not dared to do, and was not afraid that the lictors would want to represent it.

To explain, however, in what manner the tribunes sometimes represented it, it suffices to understand how the government represents the sovereign. The laws being nothing but the declaration of the general will, it is clear that in their legislative capacity the people cannot be represented; but they can and should be represented in the executive power, which is only force applied to law. This shows that very few nations would, upon careful examination, be found to have laws. Be that as it may, it is certain that the tribunes, having no share in the executive power, could never represent the Roman people by right of their office, but only by encroaching on the rights of the Senate.

Among the Greeks, whatever the people had to do, they did themselves; they were constantly assembled in the public space. They lived in a mild climate and they were not avaricious; slaves performed the manual labor; the people's great preoccupation was liberty. Without those same advantages, how can people preserve those same rights? Your more rigorous climates give you more wants;* for six months in a year the public place is deserted, and your hoarse voices cannot be heard in the open air. You care more for profit than for liberty, and you fear slavery far less than you do poverty.

What! is liberty secured only through slavery? Perhaps; extremes meet. Everything which is not according to nature has its drawbacks, and civil society more than all the rest. There are circumstances so unfortunate that people can preserve their freedom only at the expense of that of others, and the citizen cannot be completely free except when the slave is enslaved to

---

* To adopt in cold countries the effeminacy and luxuriousness of Orientals is to be willing to assume their chains, and to submit to them even more necessarily than they do.

the utmost. Such was the situation in Sparta. As for you, modern nations, you have no slaves, but you are slaves; you pay for their freedom with your own. In vain you boast of this preference; I consider it more cowardice than humanity.

I do not mean by all this that slaves are necessary and that the right of slavery is lawful, since I have proved the contrary; I only mention the reasons why modern nations who believe themselves free have representatives, and why ancient nations had none. Be that as it may, as soon as a nation appoints representatives, it is no longer free; it no longer exists.

After very careful consideration I do not see that it is possible henceforward for the sovereign to preserve among us the exercise of its rights unless the State is very small. But if it is very small, will it not be subjugated? No; I shall show hereafter* how the external power of a great nation can be combined with benign government and the good order of a small State.

Chapter XVI

THAT THE INSTITUTION OF THE GOVERNMENT IS NOT A CONTRACT

The legislative power, having been, at one point in time, well established, the question is to set up also the executive power; for the latter, which operates only by specific acts, not sharing the essence of the other, is naturally distinct from it. If it were possible for the sovereign, considered as such, to wield executive power, law and fact would be so intermixed that it would no longer be clear what is law and what is not; and the body politic, thus deformed, would soon become prey to the violence against which it was instituted.

The citizens being all equal according to the social contract, all can prescribe what all ought to do, while no one has a right to demand that another do what he is unwilling to do himself. Now, it is precisely this right, indispensable to make the body politic live and move, that the sovereign gives to the Prince when establishing the government.

Some people have claimed that this founding act is a contract between the people and the leaders they choose — a contract by which it is stipulated between the two parties on what conditions one binds itself to rule, the other

---

* It is this which I had intended to do in the sequel to this work, when, in treating of external relations, I came to confederations — a wholly new subject, the principles of which have yet to be established.

to obey. It will be agreed, I am sure, that this is a strange method of contracting. But let us see whether such a position is tenable.

First, the supreme authority can no more be modified than alienated; to limit it is to destroy it. It is absurd and contradictory that the sovereign should acknowledge a superior; to bind itself to obey a master is to regress to primitive freedom.

Further, it is clear that this contract of the people with such or such persons is a particular act; from where it follows that the contract cannot be a law or an act of sovereignty, and that consequently it is illegitimate.

Moreover, we see that the contracting parties themselves would be under the law of nature alone, and without any security for the performance of their reciprocal responsibilities, which is in every way adverse to the civil state. He who disposes of power being always capable of using it, we might as well give the name contract to the act of a man who says to another: "I give you all my property, on condition that you restore to me what you please."

There is but one contract in the State — that of association; and this of itself excludes any other. No public contract can be conceived which would not be a violation of the first.

Chapter XVII

THE INSTITUTION OF THE GOVERNMENT

Under what general concept, then, should we view the act by which the government is founded? I shall note first that this act is complex, or composed of two others, that is, the establishment of the law and the execution of the law.

By the first, the sovereign determines that there shall be a governing body established in such or such a form; and it is clear that this act is a law.

By the second, the people appoint the leaders who will be entrusted with the government when established. Now, these appointments, being a particular act, are not a second law, but only a consequence of the first, and a function of the government.

The difficulty is to understand how there can be an act of government before the government exists, and how the people, who are only sovereign or subjects, can, in certain circumstances, become the Prince or the magistrates.

Here, however, we discover one of those astonishing properties of the body politic, by which it reconciles operations apparently contradictory; for this is made possible by a sudden conversion of sovereignty into democracy in such a manner that, without any perceptible change, and merely by a new relationship of all to all, the citizens, having become magistrates, move from general acts to particular acts, and from the law to the execution of it.

This change of relation is not a subtlety of theory with no real application; it occurs every day in the Parliament of England, in which the Lower House on certain occasions transforms itself into Grand Committee in order to discuss business better, and thus becomes a simple commission instead of the sovereign court that it was the moment before. In this way it afterwards reports to itself, as the House of Commons, what it has just decided in Grand Committee.

Such is the advantage peculiar to a democratic government, that it can be established in fact by a simple act of the general will; and after this, the provisional government remains in power, should that be the form adopted, or establishes in the name of the sovereign the government prescribed by the law; and thus everything is according to rule. It is impossible to found the government in any other way that is legitimate without renouncing the principles heretofore established.

Chapter XVIII

MEANS OF PREVENTING USURPATIONS OF THE GOVERNMENT

From these explanations it follows, in confirmation of chapter XVI, that the act which institutes the government is not a contract, but a law; that the depositaries of the executive power are not the masters of the people, but its officers; that the people can appoint them and dismiss them at pleasure; that for them it is not a question of contracting, but of obeying; and that in undertaking the functions that the State imposes on them, they simply fulfill their duty as citizens, without having in any way a right to argue about the conditions.

When, therefore, it happens that the people institute a hereditary government, whether monarchical in a family or aristocratic in one class of citizens, it is not an engagement that they make, but a provisional form that they give to the administration, until they decide to organize it differently.

It is true that such changes are always dangerous, and that the established government must never be touched except when it becomes incompatible with the public good; but this circumspection is a political truth, not a rule of law; and the State is no more bound to give the civil authority to its leaders than the military authority to its generals.

Moreover, it is true that in such a case all the formalities requisite to distinguish a regular and lawful act from seditious tumult, and the will of a whole people from the clamors of a faction, cannot be too carefully observed. It is especially in this case that only such concessions should be made as cannot in strict justice be refused; and from this obligation also the Prince derives a great advantage in preserving his power in spite of the people, without their being able to say that he has usurped the power; for while appearing to exercise nothing but his rights, he may very easily increase them, and, under the pretext of maintaining public order, obstruct the assemblies designed to reestablish good order; so that he takes advantage of a silence that he prevents from being broken, or of irregularities that he instigates, so as to interpret in his own favor the approbation of those silenced by fear and punish those who dare to speak. It is in this way that the Decemvirs, having at first been elected for one year, and then kept in office for another year, attempted to retain their power in perpetuity by no longer permitting the *comitia* to assemble; and it is by this easy method that all the governments in the world, when once invested with the public force, usurp sooner or later the sovereign authority.

The periodic assemblies of which I have spoken before are designed to prevent or postpone this damage, especially when they need no formal convocation; for then the Prince cannot interfere with them, without openly proclaiming himself a violator of the laws and an enemy of the State.

These assemblies, which have as their object the maintenance of the social treaty, must always be opened with two propositions, which no one should eliminate, and which should pass separately by vote.

The first: "Whether it pleases the sovereign to maintain the present form of government."

The second: "Whether it pleases the people to leave the administration to those at present entrusted with it."

I presuppose here what I believe that I have proved, that there is in the State no fundamental law which cannot be revoked, not even the social compact; for if all the citizens assembled to break this compact by a solemn agreement, no one can doubt that it would be quite legitimately broken. Grotius even thinks that each man can renounce the State of which he is a member, and regain his natural freedom and his property by leaving the country.* Now it would be absurd if all the citizens combined would be unable to do what each of them can do separately.

* It must be clearly understood that no one should leave in order to evade his duty and relieve himself from serving his country at a moment when it needs him. Flight in that case would be criminal and punishable; it would no longer be retirement, but desertion.

Book IV

Chapter I

THAT THE GENERAL WILL IS INDESTRUCTIBLE

As long as a certain number of men consider themselves to be a single body, they have but one will, which relates to the common security and to the general welfare. In such a case all the forces of the State are vigorous and simple, and its principles are clear and luminous; it has no confused and conflicting interests; the common good is everywhere plainly clear and only good sense is required to perceive it. Peace, union, and equality are foes to political subtleties. Upright and guileless men are hard to deceive because of their candor; temptations and subtle tricks do not impress them; they are not even cunning enough to be dupes. When, in the happiest nation in the world, we see troops of peasants deciding the affairs of the State under an oak and always acting wisely, can we refrain from scorning the refinements of other nations, who make themselves illustrious and wretched with so much art and mystery?

A State thus governed needs very few laws; and in so far as it becomes necessary to promulgate new ones, this necessity is universally recognized. The first man to propose them only gives expression to what all have previously felt, and neither factions nor eloquence will be needed to pass into law what every one has already resolved to do, so soon as he is sure that the rest will act as he does.

What misleads theorists is that, seeing only States that are ill-constituted from their beginning, they are struck by the impossibility of maintaining good organization in those States; they laugh to think of all the follies to which a cunning knave, a smooth talker, can persuade the people of Paris or London. They know not that Cromwell would have been put in irons by the people of Berne, and the Duke of Beaufort imprisoned by the Genevans.

But when the social bond begins to fail and the State is weakened, when private interests begin to make themselves felt and small factions to exercise influence on the State, the common interest is harmed and finds opponents; unanimity no longer reigns in the voting; the general will is no longer the will of all; opposition and debates arise, and the best advice is not accepted without disputes.

Finally, when the State, on the verge of ruin, no longer subsists except in a meaningless and illusory form, when the social bond is broken in all hearts, when the basest interest shelters itself impudently under the sacred name of the public welfare, the general will becomes mute; all, under the sway of ulterior motives, no more express their opinions as citizens than if the State had never existed; and, under the name of laws, they deceptively pass unjust decrees that have only private interest as their aim.

Does it follow from this that the general will is destroyed or corrupted? No; it is always constant, unalterable, and pure; but it is subordinated to others which get the better of it. Each, detaching his own interest from the common interest, sees clearly that he cannot completely separate from it; but his share in the harm done to the State appears small to him in comparison with the exclusive advantage that he aims at getting for himself. With this exception, he desires the general welfare for his own interests quite as strongly as any other. Even in selling his vote for money, he does not extinguish in himself the general will, but eludes it. The fault that he commits is to change the nature of the question, and to answer something different from what he was asked; so that, instead of saying by a vote: "It is beneficial to the State," he says: "It is beneficial to a certain man or a certain party that such or such a motion should pass." Thus the law of public order in assemblies is not so much to maintain in them the general will as to ensure that it shall always be consulted and always respond.

I might at this point make many reflections on the simple right of voting in every act of sovereignty — a right which nothing can take away from the citizens — and on the right of speaking, proposing, dividing, and discussing, which the government is always very careful to leave to its members only; but this important matter would require a separate treatise, and I cannot say everything in this one.

Chapter II

VOTING

We see from the previous chapter that the manner in which public affairs are managed may give a sufficiently trustworthy indication of the character and health of the body politic. The more that harmony reigns in the assemblies, that is, the more the voting approaches unanimity, the more also is the general will predominant; but long debates, dissensions, and tumult announce the ascendancy of private interests and the decline of the State.

This is not as clear when two or more orders enter into its constitution, as, in Rome, the patricians and plebeians, whose quarrels often disturbed the *comitia*, even in the greatest days of the Republic; but this exception is more apparent than real, for, at that time, by a vice inherent in the body politic, there were, so to speak, two States in one; what is not true of the two together is true of each separately. And, indeed, even in the stormiest times, the plebiscites of the people, when the Senate did not interfere with them, always passed peaceably and by a large majority of votes; the citizens having but one interest, the people had but one will.

At the other extremity of the circle unanimity returns; that is, when the citizens, fallen into slavery, have no longer either liberty or will. Then fear and flattery change votes into acclamations; men no longer deliberate, but adore or curse. Such was the disgraceful mode of speaking in the Senate under the Emperors. Sometimes it was done with ridiculous precautions. Tacitus observes that under Otho the senators, in pounding Vitellius with curses, sought to make at the same time a frightful tumult, so that, if he happened to become master, he would not know what each of them had said.

From these different reflections are deduced the principles by which we should regulate the method of counting votes and of comparing opinions, depending on whether the general will is more or less easy to ascertain and the State more or less deteriorating.

There is but one law which by its nature requires unanimous consent, that is, the social compact; for civil association is the most voluntary act in the world; every man being born free and master of himself, no one can, under any pretext whatsoever, enslave him without his assent. To conclude that the son of a slave is born a slave is to conclude that he is not born a man.

If, then, at the time of the social compact, there are opponents of it, their opposition does not invalidate the contract, but only prevents them from being included in it; they are intruders among citizens. When the State is established, consent lies in residence; to dwell in the territory is to submit to the sovereignty.*

Excepting this original contract, the vote of the majority always binds all

---

* This must always be understood to relate to a free State; for otherwise family, property, want of an asylum, necessity, or violence, may detain an inhabitant in a country against his will; and then his residence alone no longer supposes his consent to the contract or to the violation of it.

the rest, this being a result of the contract itself. But it will be asked how a man can be free and yet forced to conform to wills that are not his own. How are opponents free and yet subject to laws they have not consented to?

I reply that the question is wrongly put. The citizen consents to all the laws, even to those passed in spite of him, and even to those that punish him when he dares to violate any of them. The unvarying will of all the members of the State is the general will; it is through the general will that they are citizens and free.* When a law is proposed in the assembly of the people, what is asked of them is not exactly whether they approve the proposition or reject it, but whether it conforms or not to the general will, which is their own; each one in casting his vote expresses his opinion thereupon; and from the counting of the votes is obtained the declaration of the general will. When, therefore, an opinion opposed to my own prevails, that simply shows that I was mistaken, and that what I considered to be the general will was not so. Had my private opinion prevailed, I would have done something other than I wished; and in that case I would not have been free.

This supposes, it is true, that all the features of the general will are still in the majority; when they cease to be so, whatever side we take, there is no longer any liberty.

In showing before how particular wills were substituted for general wills in public deliberations, I have sufficiently indicated the useful means for preventing this abuse; I will speak of it again hereafter. With regard to the proportional number of votes for declaring this will, I have also laid down the principles according to which it may be determined. The difference of a single vote destroys unanimity; but between unanimity and equality there are many unequal divisions, at each of which this number can be fixed according to the condition and requirements of the body politic.

Two general principles may serve to regulate these proportions: the one, that the more important and weighty the deliberations, the nearer should the dominant opinion approach unanimity; the other, that the greater the dispatch required in the matter under discussion, the more should we restrict the prescribed difference in the division of opinions; in deliberations which must be decided immediately, the majority of a single vote should suffice. The first of these principles appears more suitable to laws, the second to

* At Genoa we read in front of the prisons and on the fetters of the galley slaves the word, *Libertas*. This employment of the device is becoming and just. In reality, it is only the malefactors in all States who prevent the citizen from being free. In a country where all such people are in the galleys the most perfect liberty will be enjoyed.

affairs under discussion. Be that as it may, it is by their combination that we can set the best proportions for determining the decision of a majority.

Chapter III

ELECTIONS

With regard to the elections of the Prince and the magistrates, which are, as I have said, complex acts, there are two modes of procedure: choice and lot. Both have been used in different republics, and a very complicated mixture of the two is seen even now in the election of the Doge of Venice.

"Election by lot," says Montesquieu, "belongs to the nature of democracy." I agree, but how is it so? "The lot," he continues, "is a mode of election that demeans no one; it gives every citizen a reasonable hope of serving his country." But those are not reasons.

If we are mindful that the election of leaders is a function of government and not of sovereignty, we shall see why the method of election by lot is more in the nature of democracy, in which the administration is so much the better when its acts are less multiplied.

In every true democracy, the magistracy is not a boon but an onerous charge, which cannot fairly be imposed on one individual rather than on another. The law alone can impose this burden on the person upon whom the lot falls. For then, the conditions being equal for all, and the choice not being dependent on any human will, there is no particular application to alter the universality of the law.

In an aristocracy the Prince chooses the Prince, the government is maintained by itself, and voting is rightly established.

The example of the election of the Doge of Venice, far from destroying this distinction, confirms it; this mixed form is suitable in a mixed government. For it is an error to take the government of Venice for a true aristocracy. If the people have no share in the government, the nobles themselves are numerous. A multitude of poor *Barnabotes* never come near any magistracy, and have for their nobility only the empty title of Excellency and the right to attend the Great Council. This Great Council being as numerous as our General Council in Geneva, its illustrious members have no more privileges than our simple citizens (*citoyens*). It is certain that, setting aside the extreme disparity of the two Republics, the burgesses (*la bourgeoisie*) of Geneva exactly correspond to the Venetian order of patricians; our natives (*natifs*) and residents (*habitants*) represent the citizens and people of

Venice; our peasants (*paysans*) represent the subjects of the mainland; in short, in whatever way we consider this Republic apart from its size, its government is no more aristocratic than ours. The whole difference is that, having no leader for life, we do not have the same need for election by lot.

Elections by lot would have few drawbacks in a true democracy, in which, all being equal in morals and ability as well as in ideas and fortune, the choice would become of little consequence. But I have already said that there is no true democracy.

When choice and lot are combined, the first should be used to fill the posts that require special talents, such as military appointments; the other is suitable for those in which good sense, justice, and integrity are sufficient, such as judicial offices, because, in a well-constituted State, these qualities are common to all the citizens.

Neither lot nor voting has any place in a monarchical government. The monarch being by right sole Prince and sole magistrate, the choice of his lieutenants belongs to him alone. When the Abbé de Saint-Pierre proposed to multiply the councils of the King of France and to elect the members of them by ballot, he did not see that he was proposing to change the very form of government.

It remains for me to speak of the method for recording and collecting votes in the assembly of the people; but perhaps the history of the Roman policy in that respect will explain more clearly all the principles that I might be able to establish. It is not unworthy of a judicious reader to see in some detail how public and private affairs were dealt with in a council of 200,000 men.

Chapter IV

THE ROMAN COMITIA

We have no very trustworthy records of the early times of Rome; there is even great probability that most of the things which have been handed down are fables,* and, in general, the most instructive part of the annals of nations, which is the history of their institution, is the most defective. Experience every day teaches us from what causes spring the revolutions of

* The name of *Rome,* which is alleged to be derived from *Romulus,* is Greek and means *force*; the name of *Numa* is also Greek and means *law.* What likelihood is there that the first two kings of that city should have borne at the outset names so clearly related to what they did?

empires; but, as nations are no longer in process of founding, we have scarcely anything but conjectures to explain how they were formed.

The customs that we see at least testify that these customs had a beginning. Of the traditions that go back to these origins, those which the greatest authorities countenance, and which the strongest reasons confirm, should be accepted as the surest. These are the principles I have tried to follow in inquiring how the freest and most powerful nation in the world exercised its supreme power.

After the foundation of Rome, the growing republic, that is, the army of the founder, composed of Albans, Sabines, and foreigners, was divided into three classes, which, from this division, took the name of *tribes*. Each of these tribes was subdivided into ten *curiæ*, and each *curia* into *decuriæ*, at the head of which were placed *curiones* and *decuriones*.

Besides this, a body of one hundred horsemen or knights, called a *centuria*, was drawn from each tribe, whence we see that these divisions, not very necessary in a town, were at first only military. But it seems that an instinct for greatness induced the little town of Rome from the first to adopt a policy suitable to the capital of the world.

From this first division a drawback soon resulted; the tribe of the Albans* and that of the Sabines† remaining always in the same condition, while that of the foreigners‡ increased continually through perpetual accessions, the last soon outnumbered the two others. The remedy which Servius found for this dangerous situation was to change the mode of division, and for the division by races, which he abolished, to substitute another drawn from the districts of the city occupied by each tribe. Instead of three tribes he made four, each of which occupied one of the hills of Rome and bore its name. Thus, in remedying the existing inequality, he also prevented it for the future; and in order that this might be a division, not only of localities, but of men, he prohibited the inhabitants of one quarter from moving into another, which prevented the races from being mingled.

He also doubled the three old *centuriæ* of cavalry and added twelve others to them, but still under the old names — a simple and judicious means by which he created a distinction between the corps of knights and that of the people, without making the latter object.

To these four urban tribes Servius added fifteen others, called rural tribes, because they were comprised of inhabitants of the country, divided

* Ramnenses.
† Tatientes.
‡ Luceres.

into so many cantons. Afterwards many new ones were formed; and the Roman people were ultimately divided into thirty-five tribes, a number that remained the same until the end of the Republic.

This distinction between the urban and the rural tribes had a noteworthy result, because there is no other example of it, and because Rome owed to it both the preservation of her mores and the growth of her empire. It might be supposed that the urban tribes soon arrogated to themselves power and honors, and were ready to disparage the rural tribes. It was quite the reverse. We know the taste of the old Romans for the country life. This taste they inherited from their wise founder, who united with liberty rural and military endeavors, and relegated, so to speak, to the towns arts, trades, intrigue, wealth, and slavery.

Thus, since every eminent man in Rome lived in the fields and tilled the soil, it was expected that supporters of the Republic lived in the country. This condition, being that of the worthiest patricians, was honored by everyone; the simple and laborious life of villagers was preferred to the lax and indolent life of the burgesses of Rome; and many who would have been only wretched proletarians in the city became, as laborers in the fields, respected citizens. It is not without reason, said Varro, that our magnanimous ancestors created in the village the nursery of those hardy and valiant men who defended them in time of war and sustained them in time of peace. Pliny says without hesitation that the rural tribes were honored because of the men who composed them, while the worthless whom they wanted to disgrace were transferred as a mark of ignominy into the urban tribes. The Sabine Appius Claudius, having come to settle in Rome, was there showered with honors and enrolled in a rural tribe, which afterwards took the name of his family. Lastly, all the freedmen entered the urban tribes, never the rural; and during the whole of the Republic there is not a single example of any of these freedmen attaining a magistracy, although they had become citizens.

This policy was excellent, but was pushed so far that finally a change, and certainly an abuse, in government resulted from it.

First, the censors, after having long arrogated the right of transferring citizens arbitrarily from one tribe to another, allowed the majority to be enrolled in whichever they pleased. This permission was certainly in no way useful and took away one of the great resources of the censorship. Further, since the great and powerful all enrolled themselves in the rural tribes, while the freedmen who had become citizens remained with the populace in the urban ones, the tribes in general had no longer any district or territory, but all were so intermingled that it was impossible to distinguish the members of each except by the official registers; so that the idea of the word *tribe* passed from the real to the personal, or rather became almost an illusion.

Moreover, it came about that the urban tribes, being close at hand, were often the most powerful in the *comitia*, and sold the State to those who stooped to buy the votes of the mob of which they were composed.

With regard to the *curiæ*, the founder having set up ten in each tribe, the whole Roman people, at that time enclosed in the walls of the city, consisted of thirty *curiæ*, each of which had its temples, its gods, its officers, its priests, and its festivals called *compitalia*, resembling the *paganalia* that the rural tribes had afterwards.

In the new division of Servius, the number thirty being incapable of equal distribution into four tribes, he was unwilling to touch them; and the *curiæ*, being independent of the tribes, became another division of the inhabitants of Rome. But there was no question of *curiæ* either in the rural tribes or in the people composing them, because the tribes having become a purely civil institution, and another mode of levying troops having been introduced, the military divisions of Romulus were found superfluous. Thus, although every citizen was enrolled in a tribe, it was far from being the case that each was enrolled in a *curia*.

Servius made yet a third division, which had no relation to the two preceding, but became by its consequences the most important of all. He divided the whole Roman people into six classes, which he distinguished, not by the place of residence, nor by the men, but by property; so that the first classes were filled with rich men, the last with poor men, and the intermediate ones with those who enjoyed a moderate fortune. These six classes were subdivided into one hundred and ninety-three other bodies called *centuriæ*, and these bodies were so distributed that the first class alone comprised more than a half, and the last comprised only one. It thus happened that the class least numerous in men had most *centuriæ*, and that the last entire class was counted as only one subdivision, although it alone contained more than a half of the inhabitants of Rome.

So that the people did not discern the consequences of this last form, Servius affected to give it a military appearance. He introduced in the second class two *centuriæ* of armorers, and two of makers of instruments of war in the fourth; in each class, except the last, he distinguished the young and the old, that is to say, those who were obliged to bear arms, and those who were exempted by law on account of age — a distinction that, more than that of property, gave rise to the necessity of frequently repeating the *census* or enumeration; finally, he required the assembly to be held in the *Campus Martius*, and all who were qualified for service by age to gather there with their arms.

The reason why he did not follow in the last class this same division into seniors and juniors is that the honor of bearing arms for their country was not granted to the populace; it was necessary to own homes to obtain the right of defending them; and out of those innumerable troops of beggars with which the armies of kings nowadays glitter, there is not one who would have been driven out with scorn from a Roman cohort, when soldiers were defenders of liberty.

Yet again, there was in the last class a distinction between the *proletarii* and those who were called *capite censi*. The former, not altogether destitute, at least supplied citizens to the State, sometimes even soldiers, when there was need. As for those who had nothing at all and could only be counted by heads, they were regarded as altogether unimportant, and Marius was the first who condescended to enroll them.

Without concluding here whether this third enumeration was good or bad in itself, I think I can state that nothing but the simple manners of early Romans — their disinterestedness, their taste for agriculture, their contempt for commerce and for the ardent pursuit of profit — could have made it possible. In what modern nation would rapacious greed, restlessness of spirit, intrigue, continual changes of residence, and the perpetual revolutions of fortune have allowed such an institution to endure for twenty years without the whole State being subverted? It is, indeed, necessary to observe carefully that morality and the censorship, more powerful than this institution, corrected its imperfections in Rome, and that many a rich man was relegated to the class of the poor for making too much display of his wealth.

From all this we may easily understand why mention is scarcely ever made of more than five classes, although there were really six. The sixth, which furnished neither soldiers to the army, nor voters to the *Campus Martius** and which was almost useless in the Republic, rarely counted as anything.

Such were the different divisions of the Roman people. Let us see now what effect they produced in the assemblies. These assemblies, lawfully convened, were called *comitia*; they were usually held in the *Forum* of Rome or in the *Campus Martius*, and were distinguished as *comitia curiata*,

---

* I say, "to the *Campus Martius*," because it was there that the *comitia centuriata* assembled; in the two other forms the people assembled in the *Forum* or elsewhere; and then the *capite censi* had as much influence and authority as the chief citizens.

comitia centuriata, and *comitia tributa,* in accordance with the one of the three forms by which they were regulated. The *comitia curiata* were founded by Romulus, the *comitia centuriata* by Servius, and the *comitia tributa* by the tribunes of the people. No law received sanction, no magistrate was elected, except in the *comitia;* and since there was no citizen who was not enrolled in a *curia,* in a *centuria,* or in a tribe, it follows that no citizen was excluded from the right of voting, and that the Roman people were truly sovereign *de jure* and *de facto.*

In order for the *comitia* to be lawfully assembled, and for what was done in them to have the force of law, three conditions were necessary: the first, that the body or magistrate which convoked them should be invested with the necessary authority for that purpose; the second, that the assembly should be held on one of the days permitted by law; the third, that the auguries should be favorable.

The reason for the first regulation need not be explained; the second is a matter of organization; thus it was not permitted to hold the *comitia* on feast days and market days, when the country people, coming to Rome on business, had no leisure to pass the day in the assembly. By the third, the Senate kept in check a proud and turbulent people, and tempered the ardor of seditious tribunes; but the latter found more than one means of freeing themselves from this constraint.

Laws and the election of leaders were not the only issues submitted for the decision of the *comitia;* the Roman people having usurped the most important functions of government, the fate of Europe may be said to have been determined in their assemblies. This variety of issues produced the different forms these assemblies took according to the matters that had to be decided.

To judge these different forms, it is sufficient to compare them. Romulus, in instituting the *curiæ,* desired to restrain the Senate by means of the people, and the people by means of the Senate, while ruling equally over all. He therefore gave the people by this form all the authority of numbers in order to balance that of power and wealth, which he left to the patricians. But, according to the spirit of a monarchy, he gave still more weight to the patricians through the influence of their plebeian dependents in securing a plurality of votes. This admirable institution of patrons and dependents was a masterpiece of policy and humanity, without which the patrician order, so opposed to the spirit of a republic, could not have survived. Rome alone had the honor of giving to the world such a fine institution, from which there never resulted any abuse, and which notwithstanding has never been copied.

Since the form of the assembly of the *curiæ* survived under the kings down to Servius, and since the reign of the last Tarquin is not considered legitimate, the royal laws were on this account generally distinguished by the name of *leges curiatæ*.

Under the Republic the assembly of the *curiæ*, always limited to the four urban tribes, and containing only the Roman populace, could not correspond either with the Senate, which was at the head of the patricians, or with the tribunes, who, although plebeians, were at the head of the middle-class citizens. It therefore fell into disrepute; and its degradation was such that its thirty assembled lictors did what the *comitia curiata* ought to have done.

The *comitia centuriata* was so favorable to the aristocracy that we do not at first see why the Senate did not always prevail in the *comitia* which bore that name, and by which the consuls, censors, and other curule magistrates were elected. Indeed, of the one hundred and ninety-three *centuriæ* which made up the six classes of the whole Roman people, the first class comprising ninety-eight, and the votes being counted only by *centuriæ*, this first class alone outnumbered in votes all the others. When all these *centuriæ* were in agreement, the recording of votes was not even completed; what the minority had decided passed for a decision of the multitude; and we may say that in the *comitia centuriata* affairs were regulated rather by the majority of coins (*écus*) than of votes.

But this excessive power was moderated in two ways: first, the tribunes usually, and a great number of plebeians always, being in the class of the rich, counteracted the influence of the patricians in this first class. The second means consisted in this, that instead of making the *centuriæ* vote according to their order, which would have permitted the first class always to begin, one of them* was drawn by lot and proceeded alone to the election; after which all the *centuriæ*, being summoned on another day according to their rank, repeated the election and usually confirmed it. Thus the power of example was taken away from rank to be given to lot, according to the principle of democracy.

From this practice resulted yet another advantage; the citizens from the country had time, between the two elections, to gather information about the merits of the candidate provisionally chosen, and so record their votes with knowledge of the case. But, under pretense of dispatch, this practice was abolished and the two elections took place on the same day.

The *comitia tributa* were properly the council of the Roman people. They were convoked only by the tribunes; in them the tribunes were elected

---

* This *centuria*, thus chosen by lot, was called *prærogativa*, because its suffrage was demanded first; hence came the word *prerogative*.

and passed their plebiscites. Not only had the Senate no status in them — it had not even a right to attend; and, being compelled to obey laws on which they could not vote, the senators were, in this respect, less free than the lowliest citizens. This injustice was altogether impolitic, and alone sufficed to invalidate the decrees of a body to which all the citizens were not admitted. If all the patricians had taken part in these *comitia* according to the rights they had as citizens, having become in that case simple individuals, they would have scarcely influenced a form in which votes were counted by the head, and in which the lowliest proletarian had as much power as the leader of the Senate.

We see, then, that besides the order resulting from these different divisions for the collection of the votes of so great a people, these divisions were not reduced to forms immaterial in themselves, but that each had results corresponding to the purposes for which it was chosen.

Without entering upon this in greater detail, it follows from the preceding explanations that the *comitia tributa* were more favorable to popular government, and the *comitia centuriata* to aristocracy. With regard to the *comitia curiata*, in which the Roman populace alone formed the majority, as they served only to favor tyranny and evil designs, they deserved to fall into discredit, the seditious themselves refraining from a means which would too plainly reveal their projects. It is certain that the full majesty of the Roman people was found only in the *comitia centuriata*, which were alone complete, seeing that the rural tribes were absent from the *comitia curiata* and the Senate and the patricians from the *comitia tributa*.

The mode of collecting the votes among the early Romans was as simple as their customs, although still less simple than in Sparta. Each cast his vote with a loud voice, and a recording officer duly registered it; a majority of votes in each tribe determined the suffrage of the tribe; a majority of votes among the tribes determined the suffrage of the people; and so with the *curiæ* and *centuriæ*. This was a good practice so long as integrity prevailed among the citizens and every one was ashamed to cast his vote publicly for an unjust measure or an unworthy man; but when the people were corrupted and votes were bought, votes were cast in secret in order to defy purchasers and give crooks an opportunity of not being traitors.

I know that Cicero criticizes this change and attributes to it in part the fall of the Republic. But although I feel the weight which Cicero's authority ought to have in this matter, I cannot accept his opinion; on the contrary, I think that through not making sufficient changes of this kind, the downfall of the State was hastened. As the regimen of healthy persons is unfit for the ill, so we should not desire to govern a corrupt people by the laws that suit a good nation. Nothing supports this maxim better than the duration of the republic of Venice, only the shadow of which now exists, solely because its laws are suitable to none but worthless men.

Tablets, therefore, were distributed to the citizens by means of which each could vote without his decision being known; new formalities were also established for the collection of tablets, the counting of votes, the comparison of numbers, etc.; but this did not prevent suspicions as to the fidelity of the officers* charged with these duties. At length edicts were framed, the multitude of which proves their uselessness.

Towards the closing years, they were often compelled to resort to extraordinary measures to correct the defects of the laws. Sometimes miracles were feigned; but this method, which might impress the people, did not impress those who governed them. Sometimes an assembly was hastily summoned before the candidates had had time to canvass. Sometimes a whole sitting was consumed in talking when it was clear that the people having been won over were ready to pass a bad resolution. But ultimately ambition eluded everything; and it seems incredible that in the midst of so many abuses, this great nation, thanks to its ancient institutions, did not cease to elect magistrates, to pass laws, to judge issues, and to dispatch public and private affairs with almost as much facility as the Senate itself could have done.

Chapter V

THE TRIBUNESHIP

When an exact relation cannot be established among the constituent parts of the State, or when indestructible causes are incessantly changing their relations, a special magistracy is instituted, which is not incorporated with the others, but which restores each part to its true relation, forming a connection or middle term either between the Prince and the people, or between the Prince and the sovereign, or if necessary between both at once.

This body, which I shall call the *tribuneship*, is the guardian of the laws and of the legislative power. It sometimes serves to protect the sovereign against the government, as the tribunes of the people did in Rome; sometimes to uphold the government against the people, as the Council of Ten now does in Venice; and sometimes to maintain an equilibrium among all parts, as the ephors did in Sparta.

---

* *Custodes, diribitores, rogatores, suffragiorum.*

The tribuneship is not a constituent part of the State, and should have no share in the legislative or in the executive power; but it is in this itself that its own power is greatest; for, while unable to do anything, it can prevent everything. It is more sacred and more venerated, as defender of the laws, than the Prince who executes them and the sovereign that enacts them. This was very clearly seen in Rome, when those proud patricians, who always scorned the people, were forced to bow before a simple officer of the people, who had neither auspices nor jurisdiction.

The tribuneship, wisely moderated, is the strongest support of a good constitution; but if its power is ever even a little in excess, it overthrows everything. Weakness is not natural to it; and provided it has some power, it is never less than it should be.

It degenerates into tyranny when it usurps the executive power, of which it is only the moderator, and when it wishes to make laws it should only defend. The enormous power of the ephors, which was without danger as long as Sparta preserved her morality, accelerated the incipient corruption. The blood of Agis, slain by these tyrants, was avenged by his successor; but the crime and the punishment of the ephors alike hastened the fall of the republic, and, after Cleomenes, Sparta mattered no longer. Rome, too, perished in the same way; and the excessive power of the tribunes, usurped by degrees, served, with the help of laws framed on behalf of liberty, as a shield for the emperors who destroyed liberty. As for the Council of Ten in Venice, it is a tribunal of blood, horrible both for the patricians and for the people; and, far from nobly defending the laws, since their degradation, it does nothing but strike secret blows that men dare not notice.

The tribuneship, like the government, is weakened by the increase of its members. When the tribunes of the Roman people, at first two in number and afterwards five, wished to double this number, the Senate allowed them to do so, being quite sure of controlling some by means of others, which did not fail to happen.

The best means for preventing the usurpations of such a formidable body, a means of which no government has hitherto availed itself, would be, not to make this body permanent, but to set intervals during which it should remain suspended. These intervals, which should not be long enough to give abuses time to grow, can be determined by law in such a way that they can be easily shortened in case of need by means of extraordinary commissions.

This method appears to me problem free, because, as I have said, the tribuneship, forming no part of the constitution, can be eliminated without harm; and it strikes me as efficacious, because a newly established magistrate does not start with the power that his predecessor had, but with the one the law gives him.

Chapter VI

DICTATORSHIP

The inflexibility of the laws, which prevents them from adapting to events, can in certain cases make them pernicious, and thereby cause the ruin of the State in a time of crisis. The order and delay of procedure require a space of time which circumstances sometimes do not allow. A thousand cases may arise which the legislator has not foreseen, and to perceive that everything cannot be foreseen is a very necessary kind of foresight.

It is therefore not a good idea to establish political institutions so rigidly as to take away the power to suspend their consequences. Even Sparta allowed her laws to sleep.

But only the greatest dangers can outweigh that of changing the public order, and the sacred power of the laws should never be interfered with except when the survival of the country is at stake. In these rare and obvious cases, the public security is provided for by a special act, which entrusts its care to the most worthy man. This commission can be conferred in two ways, according to the nature of the danger.

If an increase in the activity of the government suffices to remedy this evil, we may concentrate it in one or two of its members; in that case it is not the authority of the laws that is changed but only the manner of their administration. But if the danger is such that the formal process of law is an obstacle to our security, a supreme leader is named, who may silence all the laws and suspend for a moment the sovereign authority. In such a case the general will is not in doubt, and it is clear that the primary intention of the people is that the State should not perish. In this way the suspension of the legislative power does not involve its abolition; the magistrate who silences it can make it speak; he dominates it without having power to represent it; he can do everything but make laws.

The first method was used by the Roman Senate when it asked the consuls, by a consecrated formula, to provide for the safety of the Republic. The second was adopted when one of the two consuls appointed a dictator,* something of which Alba had furnished the precedent to Rome.

---

* This nomination was made by night and in secret as if they were ashamed to set a man above the laws.

At the beginning of the Republic they very often had recourse to dictatorship, because the State had not yet a sufficiently firm foundation to be able to maintain itself by the vigor of its constitution alone.

Public morality making superfluous many precautions that might have been necessary at another time, there was no fear either that a dictator would abuse his authority or that he would attempt to keep it beyond his term. On the contrary, it seemed that so great a power must be a burden to the person invested with it, such haste did he make to divest himself of it, as if to take the place of laws were an office too arduous and too dangerous.

Therefore it is the danger, not of its being abused, but of its degradation, that makes me blame the indiscreet use of this supreme magistracy in early times; for while it was freely used at elections, at dedications, and in purely formal matters, there was reason to fear that it would become less formidable in case of need, and that the people would grow accustomed to regard as an empty title that which was only used in empty ceremonies.

Toward the close of the Republic, the Romans, having become more circumspect, used the dictatorship sparingly with as little reason as they had formerly been prodigal with it. It was easy to see that their fear was ill-founded; that the weakness of the capital then constituted its security against the magistrates whom it had within it; that a dictator could, in certain cases, defend the public liberty without ever being able to assail it; and that the chains of Rome would not be forged in Rome itself, but in her armies. The slight resistance which Marius made against Sylla, and Pompey against Cæsar, showed clearly what might be looked for from the authority within against the force without.

This error caused them to commit great mistakes; such, for example, was that of not appointing a dictator in the Catiline affair; for as it was only a question of the interior of the city, or at most of some province of Italy, a dictator, with the unlimited authority that the laws gave him, would have easily broken up the conspiracy, which was suppressed only by a combination of fortunate accidents which human prudence could not have foreseen.

Instead of that, the Senate was content to entrust all its power to the consuls; whence it happened that Cicero, in order to act effectively, was constrained to exceed his authority in a material point, and that, although a first rush of enthusiasm caused his conduct to be approved, he was afterwards justly called to account for the blood of citizens shed contrary to the laws, a reproach which could not have been brought against a dictator. But the consul's eloquence won over everybody; and he himself, although a Roman, preferred his own glory to his country's good, and sought not the most certain and legitimate means of saving the State but rather the way to garner all the honor for this affair.* Therefore he was justly honored as the liberator of Rome and justly punished as a violator of the laws. However brilliant his return to power may have been, it was certainly a pardon.

Moreover, in whatever way this important commission may be conferred, it is important to determine its duration for a very short term which can never be prolonged. In the crises which cause it to be established, the State is soon destroyed or saved; and, the urgent need having passed away, the dictatorship becomes tyrannical or useless. In Rome the dictators held office for six months only, and the majority abdicated before the end of this term. Had the term been longer, they would perhaps have been tempted to prolong it still further, as the Decemvirs did their term of one year. The dictator only had time to provide for the necessity which had led to his election; he had no time to think of other projects.

Chapter VII

THE CENSORSHIP

Just as the declaration of the general will is made by the law, the declaration of public opinion is made by the censorship. Public opinion is a kind of law of which the censor is minister, and which he only applies to particular cases in the manner of the Prince.

The censorial tribunal, then, far from being the arbiter of the opinion of the people, only declares it, and so soon as it departs from this position, its decisions are fruitless and ineffectual.

It is useless to distinguish the character of a nation from the objects of its esteem, for all these things depend of the same principle and are necessarily intermixed. In all the nations of the world it is not nature but opinion which decides the choice of their pleasures. Reform men's opinions and their mores will be purified by themselves. People always like what is becoming or what they judge to be so; but it is in this judgment that they make mistakes; the question, then, is to guide their judgment. He who judges of mores judges of honor; and he who judges of honor takes his law from opinion.

The opinions of a nation spring from its constitution. Although the law does not regulate morality, it is legislation that gives it birth, and when legislation becomes impaired, morality degenerates; but then the judgment of the censors will not do what the power of the laws has failed to do.

---

* He could not be satisfied about this in proposing a dictator; he dared not nominate himself, and could not feel sure that his colleague would nominate him.

It follows from this that the censorship may be useful to preserve morality, never to restore it. Institute censors while the laws are vigorous; so soon as they have lost their power all is over. Nothing that is lawful has any force when the laws cease to have any.

The censorship supports morality by preventing opinions from being corrupted, by preserving their integrity through wise applications, sometimes even by defining them when they are still uncertain. The use of seconds in duels, carried to a mad extreme in the kingdom of France, was abolished by these simple words in an edict of the king: "As for those who have the cowardice to appoint seconds." This judgment, anticipating that of the public, immediately decided it. But when the same edicts wanted to declare that it was also cowardice to fight a duel, which is very true, but contrary to common opinion, the public ridiculed this decision, on which its judgment was already formed.

I have said elsewhere* that as public opinion is not subject to constraint, there should be no vestige of this in the tribunal established to represent it. We cannot admire too much the art with which this force, wholly lost among the moderns, was set in operation among the Romans and still better among the Lacedæmonians.

A man of bad character having brought forward a good measure in the Council of Sparta, the ephors, without paying attention to him, caused the same measure to be proposed by a virtuous citizen. What an honor for the one, what shame for the other, without praise or blame being given to either! Certain drunkards from Samos† defiled the tribunal of the ephors; on the morrow a public edict granted permission to the Samians to be filthy. A real punishment would have been less severe than such impunity. When Sparta pronounced what was or was not honorable, Greece did not appeal those decisions.

Chapter VIII

CIVIL RELIGION

Men had at first no kings except the gods and no government but a theocracy. They reasoned like Caligula, and at that time they reasoned rightly. A long period is needed to change men's feelings and ideas in order that

---

* I merely indicate in this chapter what I have treated at greater length in the *Letter to M. d'Alembert.*

† They were from another island, which the delicacy of our language forbids us to name on this occasion.

they may resolve to take a fellow man as a master and flatter themselves that all will be well.

From the single fact that God was placed at the head of every political society, it followed that there were as many gods as nations. Two nations foreign to each other, and almost always hostile, could not for long acknowledge the same master; two armies engaged in battle with each other could not obey the same leader. Thus from national divisions resulted polytheism, and, from this, theological and civil intolerance, which are by nature the same, as will be shown hereafter.

The fancy of the Greeks that they recognized their own gods among barbarous nations arose from their regarding themselves as the natural sovereigns of those nations. But in our days that is a very ridiculous kind of erudition which turns on the identity of the gods of different nations, as if Moloch, Saturn, and Chronos could be the same god! As if the Baal of the Phœnicians, the Zeus of the Greeks, and the Jupiter of the Latins could be the same! As if there could be anything in common among imaginary beings bearing different names!

But if it is asked why under paganism, when every State had its cult and its gods, there were no wars of religion, I answer that it was for the same reason that each State, having its own form of worship as well as its own government, did not distinguish its gods from its laws. Political warfare was also theological; the regions of the gods were, so to speak, fixed by the limits of the nations. The god of one people had no right over other peoples. The gods of the pagans were not jealous gods; they shared among themselves the empire of the world; even Moses and the Hebrew nation sometimes countenanced this idea by speaking of the god of Israel. It is true that they regarded as nought the gods of the Canaanites, proscribed nations, devoted to destruction, whose country they were to occupy; but see how they spoke of the divinities of the neighboring nations whom they were forbidden to attack: "The possession of what belongs to Chamos your god," said Jephthah to the Ammonites, "is it not lawfully your due? By the same title we possess the lands which our conquering god has acquired."* In this, it seems to me, there was a well-recognized parity between the rights of Chamos and those of the god of Israel.

But when the Jews, subjected to the kings of Babylon, and afterwards to the kings of Syria, obstinately refused to acknowledge any other god but

---

* *"Nonne ea quae possidet Chamos deus tuus tibi jure debentur?"* (Judges xi: 24). Such is the text of the Vulgate. Père de Carrières has translated it thus: "Do you not believe that you have a right to possess what belongs to Chamos your god?" I am ignorant

their own, this refusal, seen as a rebellion against the conqueror, drew upon them the persecutions which we read of in their history, and of which no other instance appears before Christianity.*

Every religion, then, being exclusively attached to the laws of the State which prescribed it, there was no other way of converting a people than to conquer it, and no other missionaries than conquerors; and the obligation to change their form of worship being the law imposed on the vanquished, it was necessary to begin by conquering before speaking of conversions. Far from men fighting for the gods, it was, as in Homer, the gods who fought for men; each demanded victory from his own god and paid for it with new altars. The Romans, before attacking a place, summoned its gods to abandon it; and when they left to the Tarentines their exasperated gods, it was because they then regarded these gods as subjected to their own and forced to pay them homage. They left the vanquished their gods as they left them their laws. A crown for the Capitoline Jupiter was often the only tribute that they imposed.

At last, the Romans having extended their religion and their laws with their empire, and having themselves often adopted those of the vanquished, the nations of this vast empire, since the right of citizenship was granted to all, found little by little that they had multitudes of gods and religions, almost the same everywhere; and this is why paganism was at length known in the world as one and the same religion.

It was in these circumstances that Jesus came to establish on earth a spiritual kingdom, which, separating the theological system from the political system, destroyed the unity of the State, and created the intestine divisions which have never ceased to arouse Christian nations. Now this new idea of a kingdom in the other world having never been able to enter the minds of the pagans, they always regarded Christians as actual rebels, who, under cover of a hypocritical submission, only sought an opportunity to make themselves independent and supreme, and to usurp by cunning the authority which, in their weakness, they pretended to respect. This was the cause of persecutions.

---

of the force of the Hebrew text, but I see that in the Vulgate Jephthah positively acknowledges the right of the god Chamos, and that the French translator weakens this acknowledgment by an "according to you" which is not in the Latin.

* There is the strongest evidence that the war of the Phocæans, called a sacred war, was not a war of religion. Its object was to punish sacrilege, and not to subdue unbelievers.

What the pagans had feared came to pass. Then everything changed; the humble Christians altered their tone, and soon this supposed kingdom of the other world became, under a visible leader, the most violent despotism in this world.

As, however, there have always been a Prince and civil laws, a perpetual conflict of jurisdiction has resulted from this double power, which has rendered any good polity impossible in Christian States; and no one has ever succeeded in understanding whether he was bound to obey the ruler or the priest.

Many nations, however, even in Europe or on its outskirts, wished to preserve or to reestablish the old system, but without success; the spirit of Christianity prevailed over everything. The sacred cult always retained or regained its independence of the sovereign, and without any necessary connection with the body of the State. Muhammad had very sound views; he thoroughly unified his political system; and so long as his form of government survived under his successors, the caliphs, the government was quite unified and in that respect good. But the Arabs having become flourishing, learned, cultivated, lax, and cowardly, were subjugated by the barbarians, and then the division between the two powers began again. Although it may be less apparent among the Muhammadans than among the Christians, the division nevertheless exists, especially in the sect of Ali; and there are States, such as Persia, in which it is still seen.

Among us, the kings of England have established themselves as heads of the church, and the Tsars have done the same; but by means of this title they have made themselves its ministers rather than its rulers; they have acquired not so much the right to change it as the power to maintain it; they are not its legislators but only its princes. Wherever the clergy form a corporation,* they are masters and legislators in their own country. There are, then, two powers, two sovereigns, in England and in Russia, just as elsewhere.

Of all Christian authors, the philosopher Hobbes is the only one who has clearly seen the evil and its remedy, and who has dared to propose to unite

---

* It must, indeed, be remarked that it is not so much the formal assemblies, like those in France, that bind the clergy into one body, as the communion of churches. Communion and excommunication are the social pact of the clergy, a pact by means of which they will always be the masters of nations and kings. All priests who are of the same communion are fellow citizens, though they are as far asunder as the poles. This invention is a masterpiece of policy. There was nothing similar among pagan priests; therefore they never formed a body of clergy.

the two heads of the eagle and to restore political unity, without which no State or government will ever be well constituted. But he ought to have seen that the domineering spirit of Christianity was incompatible with his system, and that the interest of the priest would always be stronger than that of the State. It is not so much what is horrible and false in his political theory as what is just and true that has rendered it odious.*

I believe that by developing historical facts from this point of view, the opposite opinions of Bayle and Warburton might easily be refuted. The former of these maintains that no religion is useful to the body politic; the latter, on the other hand, asserts that Christianity is its strongest support. To the first it might be proved that no State was ever founded without religion serving as its basis, and to the second, that the Christian law is more injurious than useful to a firm constitution of the State. In order to succeed in making myself understood, I need only give a little more precision to the exceedingly vague ideas about religion in its relation to my subject.

Religion, considered with reference to society, which is either general or particular, may also be divided into two kinds, that is, the religion of the man and that of the citizen. The first, without temples, without altars, without rites, limited to the purely internal worship of the supreme God and to the eternal duties of morality, is the pure and simple religion of the Gospel, the true theism, and what may be called the natural divine law. The other, inscribed in a single country, gives to it its gods, its peculiar and tutelary patrons. It has its dogmas, its rites, its external religion prescribed by the laws; outside the single nation which observes it, everything is for it infidel, foreign, and barbarous; it extends the duties and rights of men only as far as its altars. Such were all the religions of early peoples, to which may be given the name of divine law, civil or positive.

There is a third and more extravagant kind of religion, which, giving to men two sets of laws, two leaders, two fatherlands, imposes on them contradictory duties, and prevents them from being simultaneously devout men and citizens. Such is the religion of the Lamas, such is that of the Japanese, such is Roman Christianity. This may be called the religion of the priest. There results from it a kind of mixed and unsocial law which has no name.

Considered politically, these three kinds of religion all have their

* See, among others, in a letter from Grotius to his brother of the 11th April, 1643, what that learned man approves and what he blames in the book *De Cive*. It is true that, inclined to indulgence, he appears to pardon the author for the good for the sake of the evil, but everyone is not so merciful.

defects. The third is so evidently bad that it would be a waste of time to stop and prove this. Whatever destroys social unity is good for nothing; all institutions which put a man in contradiction with himself are worthless.

The second is good so far as it combines divine worship with love for the laws, and, by making their fatherland the object of citizens' adoration, teaches them that to serve the State is to serve the guardian deity. It is a kind of theocracy, in which there ought to be no pontiff but the Prince, no other priests than the magistrates. Then to die for one's country is to achieve martyrdom, to violate the laws is to be impious, and to subject a guilty man to public execration is to subject him to the wrath of the gods: *Sacer esto*.

But it is bad in so far as being based on error and falsehood, it deceives men, renders them credulous and superstitious, and obscures the true worship of the Deity with superficial rituals. It is bad, again, when, becoming exclusive and tyrannical, it makes a nation sanguinary and intolerant, so that it thirsts after nothing but murder and massacre, and believes that it is performing a holy action in killing whosoever does not acknowledge its gods. This puts such a people in a natural state of war with all others, which is very harmful to its own security.

There remains, then, the religion of man or Christianity, not that of today, but that of the Gospel, which is quite different. By this holy, sublime, and pure religion, men, children of the same God, all recognize one another as brethren, and the social bond which unites them is not dissolved even at death.

But this religion, having no particular relation with the body politic, leaves to the laws only the force that they derive from themselves, without adding to them any other; and thereby one of the great bonds of the particular society remains ineffective. What is more, far from attaching the hearts of citizens to the State, it detaches them from it as it does from all earthly things. I know of nothing more contrary to the social spirit.

We are told that a nation of true Christians would form the most perfect society conceivable. In this supposition I see only one great difficulty — that a society of true Christians would be no longer a society of men.

I say even that this supposed society, with all its perfection, would be neither the strongest nor the most durable; by virtue of its perfection it would lack cohesion; its perfection, indeed, would be its destroying vice.

Each man would perform his duty; the people would be obedient to the laws, the leaders would be just and moderate, and the magistrates upright and incorruptible; the soldiers would scorn death; there would be neither vanity nor luxury. All this is very good; but let us look further.

Christianity is an entirely spiritual religion, concerned solely with heavenly things; the Christian's country is not of this world. He does his duty, it is true; but he does it with a profound indifference as to the good or ill success of his efforts. Provided that he has nothing to reproach himself with, it matters little to him whether all goes well or ill down here. If the State is flourishing, he scarcely dares to enjoy the public felicity; he fears to take a pride in the glory of his country. If the State declines, he blesses the hand of God which lies heavy on his people.

In order that the society might be peaceable and harmony maintained, it would be necessary for all citizens without exception to be equally good Christians; but if unfortunately there happens to be in it a single ambitious man, a single hypocrite, a Catiline or a Cromwell, for example, such a man will certainly get the better of his pious compatriots. Christian charity does not encourage men to think ill of their neighbors. As soon as a man has found by cunning the art of dominating them and securing for himself part of the public authority, he is invested with dignity; God wills that he be respected. Soon he exercises dominion; God wills that he be obeyed. Does the depositary of this power abuse it? This is the rod with which God punishes His children. They would have scruples about driving out the usurper; it would be necessary to disturb the public peace, to use violence, to shed blood; all this ill accords with the meekness of the Christian, and, after all, does it matter whether they are free or enslaved in this vale of woes? The essential thing is to reach paradise, and resignation is but one means the more toward that.

What if foreign war comes on? The citizens march to battle without anxiety; none of them think of flight. They do their duty, but without an ardent desire for victory; they know better how to die than to conquer. What matters it whether they are the victors or the vanquished? Does not Providence know better than they what is needful for them? Conceive what an advantage a bold, impetuous, enthusiastic enemy can derive from this stoical indifference! Set against them those noble peoples who are consumed with a burning love of glory and of country. Suppose your Christian republic confronted with Sparta or Rome; the pious Christians will be beaten, crushed, destroyed, before they have time to collect themselves, or they will owe their survival only to the contempt which the enemy may conceive for them. To my mind that was a noble oath of the soldiers of Fabius; they did not swear to die or to conquer, they swore to return as conquerors, and kept their oath. Never would Christians have done such a thing; they would have believed that they were tempting God.

But I am mistaken in speaking of a Christian republic; each of these two words excludes the other. Christianity preaches only servitude and dependence. Its spirit is too favorable to tyranny for the latter not to profit by it always. True Christians are made to be slaves; they know it and are hardly aroused by it. This short life has too little value in their eyes.

Christian troops are excellent, we are told. I deny it; let them show me any that are such. For my part, I know of no Christian troops. The crusades will be cited. Without disputing the valor of the crusaders, I shall observe that, far from being Christians, they were soldiers of the priest, citizens of the Church; they fought for their spiritual country, which the Church had somehow rendered temporal. Property regarded, this brings us back to paganism; as the Gospel does not establish a national religion, any sacred war is impossible among Christians.

Under the pagan emperors Christian soldiers were brave; all Christian authors affirm it, and I believe it. There was a rivalry of honor against the pagan troops. As soon as the emperors became Christians, this rivalry no longer subsisted; and when the cross had driven out the eagle, all the Roman valor disappeared.

But, setting aside political considerations, let us return to the subject of rights and determine principles on this important point. The right which the social pact gives to the sovereign over its subjects does not, as I have said, go beyond the limits of public utility.* Subjects, then, owe no account of their opinions to the sovereign except so far as those opinions are of importance to the community. Now it is very important for the State that every citizen should have a religion which may make him delight in his duties; but the dogmas of this religion concern neither the State nor its members, except so far as they affect morality and the duties which he who professes it is bound to perform toward others. Each may have, in addition, such opinions as he pleases, without its being the business of the sovereign to know them; for, as he has no jurisdiction in the other world, the destiny of his subjects in the life to come, whatever it may be, is not his affair, provided they are good citizens in this life.

There is, therefore, a purely civil profession of faith, the articles of which it is the duty of the sovereign to determine, not exactly as dogmas of religion, but as sentiments of sociability, without which it is impossible to

* "In the commonwealth," says the Marquis d'Argenson, "each is perfectly free in what does not injure others." That is the unalterable limit; it cannot be more accurately placed. I could not deny myself the pleasure of sometimes quoting this manuscript, although it is not known to the public, in order to do honor to the memory of an illustrious and honorable man, who preserved even in office the heart of a true citizen, and just and sound opinions about the government of his country.

be a good citizen or a faithful subject.* Without having power to compel any one to believe them, the sovereign may banish from the State whoever does not believe them; it may banish him not as impious, but as unsociable, as incapable of sincerely loving the law, justice and of sacrificing, if need be, his life to his duty. But if any one, after publicly acknowledging these dogmas, behaves like an unbeliever in them, he should be punished with death; he has committed the greatest of crimes, he has lied before the laws.

The dogmas of civil religion ought to be simple, few in number, stated with precision, and without explanations or commentaries. The existence of the Deity, powerful, wise, beneficent, prescient, and bountiful, the life to come, the happiness of the just, the punishment of the wicked, the sanctity of the social contract and of the laws; these are the positive dogmas. As for the negative dogmas, I limit them to one only, that is, intolerance; it belongs to the creeds which we have excluded.

Those who distinguish civil intolerance from theological intolerance are, in my opinion, mistaken. These two kinds of intolerance are inseparable. It is impossible to live at peace with people whom we believe to be damned; to love them would be to hate God who punishes them. It is absolutely necessary to convert them or to punish them. Wherever theological intolerance is allowed, it cannot but have some effect in civil life;† and as soon as it has any, the sovereign is no longer sovereign even in secular affairs; from that time the priests are the real masters; the kings are only their officers.

Now that there is, and can be, no longer any exclusive national religion, we should tolerate all those which tolerate others, as long as their dogmas have nothing contrary to the duties of a citizen. But whosoever dares to say: "Outside the Church no salvation," ought to be driven from the State, unless the State be the Church and the Prince be the pontiff. Such a dogma belongs only in a theocratic government; in any other it is pernicious. The reason for which Henry IV is said to have embraced the Roman Catholic religion ought to have made any honorable man renounce it, and especially any prince who knew how to reason.

---

* Cæsar, in pleading for Catiline, tried to establish the dogma of the mortality of the soul; Cato and Cicero, to confute him, did not waste time in philosophizing; they were content to show that Cæsar spoke as a bad citizen and put forward a doctrine pernicious to the State. Indeed, it was that which the Roman Senate had to decide, and not a theological question.

† Marriage, for example, being a civil contract, has civil consequences, without which it is even impossible for society to subsist. Let us, then, suppose that a clergy

Chapter IX

CONCLUSION

After laying down the principles of political right and attempting to found the State on this basis, it still remains for us to strengthen it in its foreign relations; which would include the law of nations, commerce, the right of war and conquests, public law, alliances, negotiations, treaties, etc. But all this constitutes a new subject too vast for my limited scope. I ought always to have confined myself to a narrower sphere.

---

should succeed in arrogating to itself the sole right to perform this act, a right which it must necessarily usurp in every intolerant religion; then, is it not clear that in taking the opportunity to strengthen the Church's authority, it will render ineffectual that of the Prince, which will no longer have any subjects except those which the clergy are pleased to give it? Having the opinion of marrying or not marrying people, according as they hold or do not hold such or such a doctrine, according as they admit or reject such or such a formulary, according as they are more or less devoted to it, is it not clear that by behaving prudently and keeping firm, the Church alone will dispose of inheritances, offices, citizens, and the State itself, which cannot subsist when only composed of bastards? But, it will be said, men will appeal as against abuses; they will summon, issue decrees, and seize on the temporalities. What a pity! The clergy, however little they may have, I do not say of courage, but of good sense, will let this be done and go their way; they will quietly permit appealing, adjourning, decreeing, seizing, and will end by remaining masters. It is not, it seems to me, a great sacrifice to abandon a part, when one is sure of getting possession of the whole.

Rethinking
The First and Second Discourses
and
The Social Contract

Rousseau, Cultural Critic

GITA MAY

Enlightenment aesthetics generally stressed the social usefulness of the arts. The *philosophes,* unlike the seventeenth-century *moralistes,* were not disabused, world-weary observers of human foibles with no hope for the future betterment of society. They were passionately dedicated to improving social and political conditions, and even though their program was far from monolithic, it rested on a shared belief that the writer and artist should not be content merely to create entertaining, decorative works aimed at pleasing the rich and powerful.

Such seventeenth-century *moralistes* as La Rochefoucauld and La Bruyère had been conservative misanthropes who harbored a rather dim and pessimistic view of human nature. Their pithy maxims and observations sought to unmask the hidden, selfish motivations that drive even our apparently most virtuous acts. Self-interest, according to them, is at the core of human behavior and behind our most seemingly altruistic, charitable, and philanthropic endeavors lurks the irrepressible (if subconscious) need for self-aggrandizement. The Augustinian notion that, without the saving grace of faith, humanity is mired in evil and sin informs the ethics of the *moralistes*. This bleak and rather desolate theological and psychological landscape, however, is redeemed and ennobled by writers who succeeded in distillating their darkest thoughts in patiently honed, brilliantly provocative aphorisms. Classical art represents a triumph of beauty and orderliness of form over the chaotic, dark impulses of the human heart. This perfection and economy of style is evident in La Rochefoucauld's maxims, in Poussin's compositions, and in the architectural symmetry of Versailles. Art strove mightily to compensate for the irremediable frailties inherent in our sinful nature by exalting and glorifying the cultural achievements possible in an absolute monarchy, incarnated by the Sun King, Louis XIV.

The *philosophes,* on the other hand, held fast to the notion that art has a positive, indeed aggressively political role to play in society. And no one was more passionately dedicated to the notion of art as a force capable of liberating the most creative human energies and impulses, even in a corrupt society, as the France of Louis XV and Louis XVI was viewed by the *philosophes,* than Denis Diderot, the Encyclopedist and for many years Jean-Jacques Rousseau's best friend. In his plays, novels, and art criticism Diderot advocated a bold renewal and regeneration of all the art forms, and one of his major goals was to formulate a new relationship between culture and society, as well as between the creative individual and society. All his life, he approached the artist's creative process and procedures and the interrelation between art and society with the liveliest interest and with a keen personal sense of sympathetic, enthusiastic involvement.

Whereas Rousseau perceived a profound and fatal cleavage between art and moral values, Diderot tirelessly sought to reconcile the respective exigencies of the aesthetically pleasing and the socially useful. He did not look on the arts as above or separate from life, and from the outset he acknowledged the essential roles of passion and enthusiasm in the creative process and of subjective sensibility in aesthetic appreciation and pleasure. The sublime, in particular, had great appeal for him, and it reinforced his rejection of neoclassicism in favor of a new aesthetic stressing the overpowering rather than pleasing emotions and experiences.

The Paris to which Rousseau came in August of 1742 was the capital not only of France, but of the Western world. The thirty-year-old Rousseau was then an obscure Genevan who had sought to escape the restrictive environment of his native city and his own troubled family through a series of wanderings and unsuccessful and unsatisfying attempts at various jobs, including working as an apprentice to an engraver, doing a stint as a valet, being a music teacher, serving as a secretary in a land survey office, and tutoring the children of a rich merchant in Lyons. As an exciting center of intellectual and cultural activity, Paris was a magnet for young men like Diderot and Rousseau, who came from the French provinces and even beyond to test their mettle and seek fame.

By the time Rousseau decided to conquer the French capital, he had already experienced many trials and torments as a youth left to his own devices. As a semi-orphan (his mother died shortly after his birth) abandoned by an emotionally unstable father, he had had to face injustice and indifference on the part of adults in charge of his care. Although he would later become a harsh critic of city life, as a young man he saw the French capital as the only place that could satisfy his dream of self-fulfillment.

In his early wanderings Rousseau had briefly visited Paris in 1732. His first impressions of the city turned out to be deeply disappointing. In his own mind and fertile imagination he had pictured it as a beautiful, orderly city, even more imposing in its appearance than Turin, which had greatly impressed him with its splendid urban architecture, broad streets and avenues, and great mansions. What struck him upon his arrival in Paris was the stark contrast between the rich and powerful and the poor and disenfranchised. There was the Paris of elegant mansions, sophisticated salons, and a refined, pleasure-loving society. Brilliant, witty conversation and gallantry prevailed in the salons. On the other hand, ordinary people lived in crowded, squalid tenements in narrow, unpaved streets and alleys. What struck him, above all else, was the sordid poverty and filth in which they were forced to live.

Rousseau, who wholly identified with the common people, never overcame this initial negative impression:

> As I entered through the Faubourg Saint-Marceau, I saw nothing but dirty, stinking little streets, ugly black houses, a general air of squalor and poverty, beggars, cart pushers, clothes menders, hawkers of herbdrinks and of old hats. All this so affected me at the outset that all the real magnificence I have since seen in Paris has not overcome this first impression, and I have always retained a secret aversion for living in the capital. I can state that all the time I subsequently resided there was employed toward seeking means that would enable me to live elsewhere.[1]

The publication of Rousseau's *Discourse on the Sciences and Arts* in 1751 determined the course of his whole life and career. The years spent in Paris had only confirmed him in his belief that urban civilization was irremediably corrupt and beyond redemption. His strictures against the French capital may have had something to do with his own personal disappointments. He had arrived in Paris in the summer of 1742 with high hopes, fifteen louis in his pocket, as well as his comedy *Narcisse* and a new scheme for musical notation from which he expected fame and fortune. But nothing came of these ambitious projects. Instead, he had to live in squalid lodgings and resort to expedient means in order to survive. But this was also the time he met and befriended Denis Diderot, a struggling young writer hailing from Langres.

They were both of the same age, both were sons of artisans, both were poor, both had been drawn to Paris for similar reasons, and both had a great number of interests in common, such as a passion for knowledge, music, chess, a rebellion against the establishment, and a need for recognition. Diderot, however, had already begun to gain a reputation, to make friends in the world of letters, and to establish himself with publishers as a translator of English works, notably his copiously annotated version of the English philosopher Shaftesbury's *Inquiry concerning Merit and Virtue*. More importantly, in 1746 he had been contracted as co-editor, with the mathematician Jean le Rond d'Alembert, to bring out a French translation of the commercially successful Ephraim Chambers' *Cyclopedia*. This ambitious enterprise rapidly turned into an original work eventually amounting to seventeen folio volumes of text and an additional twelve of plates, and its publication was a stormy one because of its official condemnation, both by state and Church.

In early October of 1749 an event took place that propelled Rousseau out of his obscurity. On July 24 of that year Diderot had been imprisoned in the medieval fortress of Vincennes, a few miles east of Paris, for the publication of his *Letter on the Blind*, a work deemed dangerous to religion and morals. When Diderot, who had been in solitary confinement for a month, was granted the privilege of receiving visitors, Rousseau hastened to see him. Because of lack of money, he had to make the journey on foot from central Paris, a good six-mile walk each way.

The summer of 1749 had been unusually hot, and the heat wave continued well into autumn. Knowing that he would tend to rush impetuously in order to see his imprisoned friend as soon as possible, Rousseau put in his pocket a well-known literary periodical, the *Mercure de France*, so that he would have something to read during the stops he would impose upon himself on the way. Directing his steps eastward, he left behind him the city, its imposing structures and teeming streets, and soon reached the more countrified suburbs. As both the heat and fatigue overtook him, he sat down underneath an oak tree and pulled out of his pocket the *Mercure de France*. Perusing the periodical in order to force himself to take a much-needed rest he came across the announcement of a 1750 literary prize essay contest offered by the academy of Dijon, one of the many provincial academies gracing the cultural landscape of Old Regime France.

The question proposed by the academy of Dijon was not a startling one, for it invited contestants to participate in a longtime debate: "Has the Revival of the Sciences and Arts Contributed to Improving Morality?" The stakes were high, for the whole notion of progress was in question. The *philosophes*, including Diderot himself, were passionately committed to the idea that Enlightenment meant that advancement in both the sciences and arts would also necessarily have a direct and positive impact on human moral betterment.

As Rousseau sat beneath his oak tree, recovering from the heat and fatigue, he pondered the question proposed by the academy of Dijon, and a stunning, overpowering vision came to him: "The moment I read this I beheld another universe and I became another man."[2] In his mind's eye he perceived a profound split between progress in the arts and sciences on the one hand and the more problematic and complex question of ethics on the other. This was a moment of extraordinary inspiration and insight in Rousseau's intellectual and moral life. He intuitively sensed that his answer to the academy of Dijon question would have to be a resounding NO to the smug and arrogant belief that progress in the sciences and arts automatically also meant progress in the realm of human morality. In a state of feverish excitement he immediately scribbled in pencil the ideas that came to him in a rush, and these would constitute the most eloquent section of the *Discourse on the Sciences and Arts,* the so-called Prosopopoeia to Fabricius.[3] A Prosopopoeia is a rhetorical device consisting in addressing an absent, dead, or imaginary figure, in this case, Fabricius, the Roman general and statesman, reputed for his civic virtue:

> O Fabricius! What would your noble soul have if, unhappily for you, called back to life, you had seen the pompous visage of Rome, the city saved by your valor and on which your name bestowed more glory than all her conquests? "My Gods!" you would have said, "what has become of the thatched roofs and rustic hearths where moderation and virtue once dwelled? What fatal splendor has displaced Roman simplicity?

When Rousseau eloquently invoked the ghost of the civic-minded Fabricius returning in order to contemplate sadly the fate of his city which by now had become the capital of a dissolute, pleasure-seeking empire, he was of course clearly referring to Paris. The French capital was, according to Rousseau, the very embodiment of the fundamental weaknesses of contemporary society, notably its obsession with materialistic gains and gratifications and its moral cynicism. Even more importantly, Rousseau's major thesis was that the sciences and arts not only remained passively subservient to the most oppressive forces in society but also actively contributed to their perpetuation.

Rousseau was still in a state of great agitation "close to delirium" when he reached the Vincennes prison. Diderot, for his part, had been deeply affected by his imprisonment and solitary confinement, so contrary to his own gregarious nature. He immediately noticed his friend's state of excitement. Rousseau responded by reading the Prosopopoeia to Fabricius he had excitedly penciled under the oak tree. Diderot not only urged Rousseau to vie for the prize, he also exhorted him to pursue this negative, controversial view, for he perceived it as a provocative paradox that would give his friend a better chance at winning the prize against the majority of the contestants, who would in all probability subscribe to the overly optimistic notion that there is a necessary correlation between progress in the arts and sciences and morality.[4]

Little did Diderot fathom the intensity, depth, and sincerity of Rousseau's negative response to the Academy of Dijon proposal, and its consequences. Rousseau's *Discourse on the Sciences and Arts* constituted far more than a paradox, an intellectual or ideological game play in which the *philosophes* liked to indulge. The eloquent and belligerently negative stance he took in the *Discourse on the Sciences and Arts* represented an existential posture, a deeply personal, moral lifetime commitment that would soon alienate Rousseau from the *philosophes,* including his friend Diderot. With his tendency at rhetorical hyperbole, in his *Confessions* Rousseau ascribes to what he views as Diderot's undue influence not only much of the responsibility for the negative response to the Dijon Academy proposal, but also indirectly for the many misfortunes that befell him after what he melodramatically characterizes as "this moment of frenzy." Yet, at the same time, he proclaims that it was the extraordinary vision he experienced under the oak tree that ultimately not only inspired him to write the Prosopopoeia to Fabricius but also emotionally and morally sustained him for the following several tumultuous years:

> All my petty passions were stifled by an overwhelming enthusiasm for truth, liberty, and virtue, and what is most astonishing is that this state of excitement was sustained in my heart for more than four or five years as intensely perhaps as has ever been entertained in the heart of any human being.[5]

Rousseau's writings on literature and the arts make clear that his aesthetics were inseparable from his ethical and political ideas. Although music, fiction, poetry, and the theater are intimately intertwined in almost all his work, for Rousseau the development of the arts, the progressive refinement in manners, mores, and standards of beauty, and the impressive advances and achievements in architecture, theater, opera, literature, and painting had not been matched by political, social, and moral progress and only testified to an ever-widening rift between culture and morality.

Rousseau's 1758 *Letter to d'Alembert on the Theatre* has come to occupy an increasingly central place in his oeuvre. It is indeed of crucial importance, for no other writing by him so intimately and consistently interweaves his politics and his aesthetics, or so powerfully underscores the problematic role the arts play in society. Allan Bloom, the translator of the

Letter to d'Alembert on the Theatre and the *Emile,* who achieved controversial celebrity with his book on *The Closing of the American Mind,* speaks of it as an unjustly neglected work.[6]

If Rousseau so sharply focused on the theater, it was not so much, as has so frequently been stated, to protect the virtue of his Genevan compatriots against the corrupting influence of Voltaire and the Encyclopedists as to show how our instinctive sociability (the pleasure we derive from dealing with our fellow human beings) becomes denatured in a corrupt society. Neither does he seek to emulate Pascal in a wholesale denunciation of any form of diversion. Far from it. Rather he seeks to transform the very notion of theatricality in order to bring it into greater conformity with our natural impulses as well as with his idea of a new political order.

The sophistication and codification of the French theater only demonstrated its hopeless artificiality and irrelevance. Rousseau's ferocious onslaught on the contemporary French theater, on its hallowed traditions and repertoire, and on what he views as the dubious morality of the profession of the actor and especially the actress, rests on the belief that it is irremediably artificial and outdated. *The Lettre to d'Alembert on the Theatre* constitutes a passionate plea for a total renewal of public spectacles in favor of a new kind of participatory theatricality involving all citizens in one way or another: in informal balls where young people of marriageable age can meet, in healthy outdoor activities such as athletic games and competitions, or in patriotic events celebrating the great civic virtues that are the bedrock of a true republic.[7]

Rousseau boldly challenged the commonly held and cherished notion that great scientific and artistic accomplishments necessarily contribute to the betterment of the human condition. This meant that he would have to stand alone against the *philosophes,* and especially against his friend Diderot. One cannot but wonder why Diderot did not immediately recognize the *Discourse on the Sciences and Arts* as a clear and flagrant repudiation of everything the *Encyclopédie* stood for. Indeed he did everything in his power to promote the success of the *Discourse.* Perhaps it was because he was a loyal, generous, and steadfast friend eager to see Rousseau's essay win the prize, but perhaps also because he not only admired Rousseau's rhetorical virtuosity, but also subconsciously acknowledged that the darker, more ominous message of the *Discourse* deserved to be taken seriously.

For Diderot had his own doubts about the role of culture in modern society. His endorsement of Greuze's overtly didactic compositions, his harsh strictures against such contemporary practitioners of the slyly erotic and titillating art of Boucher and Fragonard, and his creation of a new dramatic genre reflecting the concerns of middle-class people and their family problems are proof that his preoccupations are not as far removed as one would like to think from Rousseau's stance. Furthermore, the lesson that the cynical and ne'er-do-well Rameau's Nephew proclaims he finds in Molière's plays is a compendium of ways in which to indulge one's favorite vices with impunity: "When I read *The Miser,* I say to myself, 'Be as miserly as you like, but don't talk like the miser.' When I read Tartuffe, I say 'Be a hypocrite if you choose, but don't talk like one. Keep any useful vices, but don't acquire the tone and air which would make you ridiculous.' "[8] The lesson is clear: In a society with a devalued morality every individual becomes an actor — that is, one well-versed in the art of wearing a mask and in the ruses of deception. Similarly, Diderot was as capable as Rousseau of railing against the nefarious effect of superfluity and luxury on the moral fiber of a society, as is evidenced in his *Satire against Luxury in the Style of Persius.*[9] Like Rousseau, Diderot denounces the loss of all moral values as a result of an economy based upon personal enrichment and general ostentatiousness.

In his *Discourse on the Sciences and Arts* Rousseau deliberately set out to contrast the simple, frugal ways of Sparta with the high culture of Athens as a strong warning that as a nation grows rich and powerful and as its prosperity increases, it may come to give in to a fatal craving for luxury, urbanity, and refined manners and pleasures. This narcissistic preoccupation with pleasure, politeness, elegance, and good taste will be fatally inimical to morality and to the survival of such basic, simple, and essential virtues as truthfulness, sincerity, loyalty, courage, humanity, and love of duty and of freedom. Furthermore, instead of contributing to the happiness and well-being of people, the advancement of the sciences and arts has all too often fostered unrealistic aspirations and ambitions, thereby creating frustrated misfits: "How much better it would have been if all those who could not go far in a career in letters had been turned away at the entrance and steered toward arts useful to society. A person who will never be more than a bad poet or a third-rate geometer might have become an excellent cloth maker."

We like to believe that culture represents our highest and noblest aspirations. Rousseau, for his part, was convinced that its role is far more problematic. All too often it serves as the complicitous handmaiden of the establishment and contributes to the perpetuation of the *status quo.* Despite their rhetorical hyperbole Rousseau's stern admonitions are particularly relevant in our own self-indulgent, cynical postmodern age, for they pointedly remind us that culture profoundly affects the fate of a nation by either fostering or discouraging those virtues that are at the core of its political survival.

NOTES

1. Rousseau, *Confessions,* Book 4 in *Oeuvres complètes de Rousseau* (Paris: Bibliothèque de la Pléïade, Gallimard, 1964), I, 159 (my translation).

2. Rousseau, *Confessions,* Book 8, 351.

3. In his *Confessions,* Book 8, 351, Rousseau states that he wrote the Prosopopoeia to Fabricius "in pencil under an oak tree."

4. Rousseau, *Confessions,* Book 8.

5. Rousseau, *Confessions,* Book 8.

6. *Letter to M. d'Alembert on the Theatre,* tr. Allan Bloom (Glencoe, Illinois: The Free Press of Glencoe, 1960), xviii.

7. Whether the grandiose *Fêtes de la Révolution* answered Rousseau's wish for popular, patriotic but generally simple and informal events is not certain. Cf. Emmet Kennedy, *A Cultural History of the French Revolution* (New Haven: Yale University Press, 1989) and Mona Ozouf, *Festivals and the French Revolution,* tr. Alain Sheridan (Cambridge, Mass.: Harvard University Press, 1988). Also cf. Gita May, "Rousseau's *Lettre à d'Alembert sur les spectacles* and Revolutionary Aesthetics," Actes du *Colloque de Montréal sur Rousseau et la Révolution,* ed. J. Roy (Ottawa: Association nord-américaine des études sur Jean-Jacques Rousseau, 1991), 199–207.

8. Diderot, *Rameau's Nephew and Other Works,* tr. J. Barzun and R. H. Bowen (Garden City, N.Y.: Doubleday, 1956), 50.

9. Diderot, *Salon de 1767,* in *Salons III; Ruines et paysages,* ed. E. M. Bukdahl, M. Delon, A. Lorenceau (Paris: Hermann, 1995), 549–57.

Rousseau on Society and the Individual

ROBERT N. BELLAH

Jean-Jacques Rousseau was one of the strangest, and one of the most intelligent, men of the eighteenth century — of any century. He said himself that he was a man of paradoxes, and several of his most important works begin, famously, with paradoxes. *The Social Contract:* "Man was born free and everywhere he is in chains." *Emile:* "Everything is good as it leaves the hands of the Author of things; everything degenerates in the hands of man." And *The Reveries of a Solitary Walker:* "So now I am alone in the world, with no brother, neighbor or friend, nor any company left me but my own. The most sociable and loving of men has with one accord been cast out by all the rest." The third paradox concerns Jean-Jacques alone; the other two concern the whole of humanity.

The paradox on which I wish to focus in this chapter is as follows: no one has argued more strongly than Rousseau that human nature is fundamentally individualistic, yet no one has more clearly seen what humans owe to society. According to him society is what makes us fully human and society is what debases us below our natural state. Rousseau has a story to tell which explains how all this came to be; it is a very complex story, so complex that scholars continue to disagree about how to interpret it. Yet it is a story which is still very much part of the self-understanding of the modern world. We have much to learn from it, not only about Rousseau, but about ourselves, who are, more than we are aware, still under his influence. I want to tell that story briefly by examining the arguments of the Second *Discourse* and *The Social Contract*, considering in passing the First *Discourse* and several other of his writings. Then I want to test whether these arguments are true, scientifically and morally. I hope only to lead readers into conversation with Rousseau's great texts themselves; I cannot replace Rousseau's answers nor foresee the answers that his future readers will give.

Many have noted that Rousseau was born and raised a Protestant in Calvin's city, Geneva. His Deism distanced him from the Protestant and Catholic churches alike, but his sympathies[1] and perhaps the inner structure of his thought had a Protestant cast. Charles Taylor has argued that Rousseau's contrast between that which is good from the hands of God and the evil men have made of it brought an Augustinian, even a hyper-Augustinian, strand into eighteenth-century thought,[2] and we should remember that Augustine was the church father who had the greatest influence on Protestantism. Rousseau's pessimism about human progress in history was surely one of the reasons for his alienation from the literary and philosophical circles of his day. Those thinkers who were determined to erase the infamy of Christian superstition were not happy to see its shadow reappearing in one of their own.

It is commonly held that Rousseau, along with many eighteenth-century thinkers, believed that human nature is basically good, that he rejected the idea of original sin, and Rousseau himself said as much. But on closer inspection Rousseau's view of human nature is perhaps closer to that of orthodox Christianity, especially Protestantism, than is usually recognized. Adam and Eve in the Garden of Eden were not evil — they hadn't sinned. From the hand of God they were, like all of creation, good. It was their own action, their own sin, that brought about the Fall and distorted all subsequent human nature, so in this sense sin is not original. Human nature for Rousseau is good only in the state of nature, before the beginning of society. It was the human creation of society, with all its attendant vices, that began the fatal process of human distortion and degeneration. Further, just as Christians can be saved from their sinful state through belief in Jesus Christ and membership in the Church which is his body on earth, so human beings for Rousseau may regain something like their natural freedom if they enter the social contract and gain civil freedom, or if they as individuals attain moral freedom. But these forms of salvation for Rousseau, in spite of his Pelagianism, are more difficult to attain and rarer than those offered by Christianity; his view of human history is marked by a more than Augustinian gloom.[3]

There is one further parallel between Christian teaching and that of Rousseau which will lead me into the central concern of this essay. Adam's fall was not viewed as wholly a disaster. Without it there would have been no salvation history of the human race, no need for the redeemer, Jesus Christ. The human condition in the Garden of Eden has been referred to as "dreaming innocence," an existence so simplified as to be hardly human. Viewing Paradise in this way, the fall has been seen as fortunate, a *felix culpa,* for it is only through it that we became fully human, though in need of salvation. For Rousseau man in the state of nature is solitary, without language or culture, satisfied with meeting only his simplest biological needs, in short, little different from non-human animals. But entering society brings dramatic changes. In Chapter 8 of Book I of *The Social Contract*, Rousseau puts it succinctly:

> The transition from the state of nature to the civil state produces a very remarkable change in man, by substituting in his behavior justice for instinct, and by imbuing his actions with a moral quality they previously lacked. Only when the voice of duty prevails over physical impulse, and law prevails over appetite, does man, who until then was preoccupied only with himself, understand that he must act according to other principles, and must consult his reason before listening to his inclinations. Although, in this state, he gives up many advantages that he derives from nature, he acquires equally great ones in return; his faculties are used and developed; his ideas are expanded; his feelings are ennobled; his entire soul is raised to such a degree that, if the abuses of this new condition did not often degrade him below that from which he emerged, he ought to bless continually the wonderful moment that released him from it forever, and transformed him from a stupid, limited animal into an intelligent being and a man.

A happy fall indeed.

Although he sometimes, as in the above quotation, describes the shift from the state of nature to the civil state as occurring in a single jump, at other times, especially in the Second *Discourse,* he describes the transition as more gradual, with several intermediary stages. Jean Starobinski, a leading French specialist on Rousseau, has described these stages in some detail and it is useful to follow his discussion in order to understand better the role of society in Rousseau's conception of social evolution.[4] It is true that Rousseau insisted that his views on the original state of nature "are not to be taken as historical truths, but merely as hypothetical and conditional reasonings." Nonetheless, his account of the several stages of the transition between the state of nature and the formation of civil society is circumstantial, including references to existing peoples representing various stages, and some of it could still be defended today as having a degree of historical accuracy. In these respects Rousseau's account is more than the "just so" story which the accounts of Hobbes and Locke, for example, so clearly are.

In the state of nature itself humans are solitary, without speech or culture, have only the briefest of contacts with each other, and do not even know that they will die; they are, in effect, without self-consciousness. Mating consists of only passing encounters, and even children, though briefly suckled by their mother (Rousseau blithely informs us that children among primitives grow up much more quickly than among us), "no sooner gained strength to run about in quest of food than they separated even from her." Eventually mother and child came not even to recognize each other. These utterly unsociable creatures are governed, says Rousseau, by two principles prior to reason: "one of them interests us deeply in our own preservation and welfare, the other inspires us with a natural aversion to seeing any other being, but especially any being like ourselves, suffer or perish." The first principle, self-preservation, Rousseau shares with Hobbes and Locke, but he does not draw a Hobbesian conclusion from it. Precisely because humans are solitary, the quest for self-preservation involves no necessary hostility toward others nor even any competition with them. The second principle, quite absent in Hobbes but essential to Rousseau, he calls pity, and defines as a sentiment, not a rule of reason. It is the feeling of pity which will hinder "even a robust savage from plundering a feeble child, or an infirm old man" unless in the direst need himself. And although pity does not rise to the level of the golden rule, it results in a "maxim of natural goodness a great deal less perfect, but perhaps more useful, *Do good to yourself with as little prejudice as you can to others*" (Rousseau's emphasis). We will have to consider below whether pity as Rousseau defines it, is, after all, compatible with the radically non-social nature he is trying to describe.

However hypothetical this starting point may be, the succeeding stages begin to be empirically recognizable. But why should there be any succeeding stages — why not an everlasting contentment with the "natural" state? Rousseau gives two kinds of reasons, internal and external. Starting first with the internal reasons, there are two things about human nature even in its earliest stage which makes it different from that of other animals. Whereas animals operate solely according to the laws of mechanics and are strictly governed by instinct (here Rousseau follows Descartes), humans have the "spiritual" capacity for "willing, or rather choosing," and "the consciousness of this power." In other words humans are free; they have the "quality of a free agent." But there is another quality equally if not more important than freedom that distinguishes man from beast, *perfectibility*, "a faculty which, as circumstances offer, successively unfolds all the other faculties, and resides among us not only in the species, but in the individuals that compose it." Yet neither of these internal potentialities, freedom and perfectibility, though they make possible developments not open to other animals, necessitate such developments. It is, rather, the external reasons, "accidents" Rousseau calls them, which pressure men to take the first steps toward what will prove a fatal course:

> After having showed that *perfectibility,* the social virtues, and the other faculties, which natural man had received as potentialities, could never be developed of themselves, that they needed the fortuitous concurrence of several foreign causes, which might never arise, and without which he must have eternally remained in his primitive condition, I must proceed to consider and bring together the different accidents which may have perfected the human understanding while debasing the species, and made man wicked by making him sociable, and from so remote a time bring man at last and the world to the point at which we now see them. (Rousseau's emphasis)

One of these accidents, perhaps the most important (and one often invoked today by scholars who think about social evolution) was population increase. What was easy when men were few became more difficult when they multiplied. It was need that motivated ingenuity, leading to the invention of hooks and lines, bows and arrows, and it was need that led men, solitary by nature, to begin to associate, although the association was transitory, lasting only as long as the need was felt. It was also need that instigated the first use of language in the hitherto silent species. "The first language of man," said Rousseau, "was the cry of nature," imploring "assistance in great danger, or relief in great sufferings."[5] These earliest forms of association, based only on moments of temporary mutual need, as in a common hunt, "scarcely required a more refined language than that of crows and monkeys." This is what Starobinski calls the first stage, "one in which pressed by need [men] begin to associate themselves for a common effort: occasional collaboration, where anarchic hordes without permanence are constituted."[6]

Once technological advances began, they led to others at an increasing rate resulting in a "first revolution," from which emerged what Starobinski calls the "patriarchal age." This stage he identifies with life in the Paleolithic, though it is the first of the stages to be represented by still living peoples.[7] Huts and villages were constructed, family life began, language reached a degree of subtlety similar to our own, but private property was still minimal, the land being used in common for hunting and gathering. Rousseau's description of this age is both idyllic and ominous:

> They now began to assemble round a great tree: singing and dancing, the genuine offspring of love and leisure, became the amusement or rather

the occupation of the men and women, free from care, thus gathered together. Everyone began to notice the rest, and wished to be noticed himself; and public esteem acquired a value. He who sang or danced best; the handsomest, the strongest, the most dexterous, or the most eloquent, came to be the most respected: this was the first step toward inequality, and at the same time toward vice.

In this stage some differences between the strong and the weak, the skilled and the less skilled, the beautiful and the less beautiful, began to appear, and, though ideas of justice and morality began to emerge, retribution for wrongs was left to the action of those aggrieved, there being no law. Nonetheless this was a happy state, what Starobinski calls a golden age.[8] Rousseau describes it as follows:

> [Though] natural compassion had already suffered some alteration, this period of the development of human faculties, holding a just mean between the indolence of the primitive state and the petulant activity of egoism [*amour propre*], must have been the happiest and most durable epoch. The more we reflect on this state, the more convinced we shall be, that it was the least subject of any to revolutions, the best for man, and that nothing could have drawn him out of it but some fatal accident, which, for the common good, would never have happened. The example of savages, most of whom have been found in this condition, seems to confirm that mankind was formed ever to remain in it, that this condition is the real youth of the world, and that all ulterior improvements have been so many steps, in appearance towards the perfection of individuals, but in fact towards the decrepitness of the species.

Before turning to the "great revolution" which would end this golden age, the age Rousseau's description of which has led people to attribute to him the idea of the "noble savage," a term he did not use, we must look at another key but problematic distinction in his account, that between "*amour de soi*" and "*amour propre*." Careful translators distinguish them by translating the first as "love of self" and the second as "self-love." Unfortunately Lester Crocker, whose translation of the Second *Discourse* is used in this volume, is inconsistent in his translation of these terms, which in normal French do indeed mean the same thing, so Rousseau's distinction cannot be followed in his translation. According to Rousseau's analysis in note O of the Second *Discourse,* the love of self (*amour de soi*) in the true state of nature is a natural passion little different from the animal instinct of self-preservation. In particular, it involves no comparisons with others, for in his solitary state "man seldom consider[s] his fellows in any other light than he would animals of another species." This primitive love of self, then, involves no consciousness of others as comparable to one's self, and, conversely, no consciousness of self as comparable to others. It is selfish only in an innocent sense, since it lacks any desire to elevate the self at the expense of others. Self-love (*amour-propre*), on the other hand, is based fundamentally on invidious comparisons with others and so gives rise to all the vices of pride, envy, resentment, and spite. As we have seen, self-love is present already in the golden age, but its consequences will grow steadily worse in succeeding historical periods.

Turning then to the great revolution, let us consider how Rousseau describes it and to what causes he attributes it:

> [F]rom the moment it appeared an advantage for one man to possess enough provisions for two, equality vanished; property was introduced; labor became necessary; and boundless forests became smiling fields, which had to be watered with human sweat, and in which slavery and misery were soon seen to sprout out and grow with the harvests.
>
> Metallurgy and agriculture were the two arts whose invention produced this great revolution. . . [I]t is iron and corn, which have civilized men, and ruined mankind.

Starobinski identifies this change with the Neolithic revolution as currently understood, although we know that agriculture considerably predated metallurgy, particularly the iron metallurgy that Rousseau had in mind. Nonetheless, Rousseau, who began the Second Part of the Second *Discourse* by finding the first man who enclosed a piece of ground to be the cause of crimes, wars, murders, misfortunes, and horrors, was probably right in seeing agriculture as the origin of private property in land and the exploitation of agricultural surplus (Starobinski notes that though he does not use the terms Rousseau accurately describes the transition from a subsistence economy to a production economy)[9] as the most fundamental cause of human inequality. Such an insight was not new: "Subjection enters the house with the plough" is a saying attributed to the Prophet Muhammad.[10] And recent scholars have shown that agrarian societies had greater inequality than any other societies before or since.[11]

The problem that soon arose under the new agricultural regime was that even those who prospered and who had extensive property could claim no right to it, for the very idea of law and right did not yet exist. Even though one had, as Locke had argued, a just claim to the soil to which one had added one's labor, there was no reason for others to respect such a claim. Thus, says Rousseau:

> There arose between the title of the strongest and that of the first oc-
> cupier a perpetual conflict, which always ended in battle and bloodshed.
> The new state of society became the most horrible state of war.

At this point Rousseau, though rejecting the Hobbesian view of human nature and the original condition of men, comes to agree with Hobbes that a war of all against all indeed lies in the human past (and always potentially in the present as well). Even in the golden age of hunters and gatherers there had been a difference between the strong and the weak and the begin-ning of invidious self-love (*amour-propre*), but the new situation gave rise to the distinction between rich and poor and invidious self-love grew exponentially.

In this situation of calamity, according to Rousseau, "[t]he rich in par-ticular must have soon perceived how much they suffered by a perpetual war, of which they alone supported all the expense, and in which, though all risked life, they alone risked any property." For Rousseau, the claim to legitimacy of ownership by the rich, even when based on the right of first possession, was without foundation as long as many who had no property "suffered grievously for want of what [the rich] had too much of." Without justification for his wealth or forces sufficient to defend himself against all comers "the rich man . . . at last conceived the deepest project that ever entered the human mind: this was to employ in his favor the very forces that attacked him, to make allies of his enemies, to inspire them with other maxims, and make them adopt other institutions as favorable to his preten-sions, as the law of nature was unfavorable to them." Thus was born the social contract and the civil society based on it. In the words of the rich, Rousseau defines the essence of the new order: "[I]nstead of turning our forces against ourselves, let us collect them into a sovereign power, which may govern us by wise laws, may protect and defend all the members of the association, repel common enemies, and maintain a perpetual concord and harmony among us." Thus emerged the first state.

For Rousseau, it is clear that the new order, establishing justice and right in name but not in fact, was a trick the rich played on the poor:

> Such was, or must have been the origin of society and of law, which gave
> new fetters to the weak and new power to the rich; irretrievably de-
> stroyed natural liberty, fixed for ever the laws of property and inequality;

changed an artful usurpation into an irrevocable right; and for the benefit of a few ambitious individuals, subjected the rest of mankind to perpetual labor, servitude and misery.

It is not necessary to follow the argument in the remaining pages of the Second *Discourse,* describing as they do in depressing detail how civil society degenerates gradually into sheer tyranny and the relation between rich and poor turns into the relation between master and slave. Given that the social contract guarantees life and property, however unequally, it might appear that Rousseau is describing a Hobbesian contract between ruler and subject in which the latter gives up his freedom in exchange for his life. But such is not the case. Rousseau refutes the idea that the social contract is based on acquiescence to the rule of the stronger. However deluded the poor and the weak are when they are persuaded to enter the social contract, they do so believing that what they give up in the way of freedom of action will be returned to them by the rule of law, to which all, rich and poor, ruler and ruled, are to be subject. There is even the first appearance of the idea of the general will that will be central to the argument of *The Social Contract:* "The multitude having, in regard to their social relations, *concentrated, all their wills in one,* all the articles, in regard to which this will expresses itself, become so many fundamental laws, which oblige without exception all the members of the State" (my emphasis). Here Rousseau touches on the matter of right, which will be central in the later book, as opposed to fact which largely occupies him here.

Before turning to *The Social Contract,* which in comparison to the historical narrative, however hypothetical, of the Second *Discourse,* would seem to be an abstract, logical, even mathematical argument, we might assess briefly the empirical validity of the story so far. As I have implied, the story of the transition from the hunting and gathering societies of the Paleolithic, to the agricultural societies of the Neolithic, to the formation of the early state, though not reliable in detail, is not radically different from the story we would tell today. Rousseau's account of social evolution was the first of many, and not the least accurate, that have been told subsequently. But what of Rousseau's starting point, the original state of nature, on which he staked so much?

Why Rousseau believed that man in the state of nature was solitary is not easy to answer. One can point to his own life: he lost his mother shortly after his birth and his father left him at the age of ten. Subsequently his movements were frequent and his attachments few and mostly fleeting. One can perhaps see a source in his Protestant background where the individual is seen as ultimately alone in the presence of God. Most obviously, in the tradition of modern political philosophy by which he was greatly influenced even when he argued against it, man was seen as originally solitary: in Hobbes's famous phrase human life in the "naturall condition of mankind" was "solitary, poore, nasty, brutish, and short."[12]

Whatever the sources of Rousseau's idea, the empirical basis for it, unlike that for much of his subsequent account, is entirely lacking. Not only are the chimpanzees, with whom we are most closely related, and with whom we share a common ancestor four or five million years ago, as well as the other great apes, social, but so are all the primates, whose origin is at least forty million years ago. That is a long way back to go to find a solitary ancestor and such an ancestor would hardly qualify as a man, even in Rousseau's stripped down version of the state of nature. As far as the genus *Homo* is concerned, of which we have evidence for several million years, again everything points to the fact that all the species of the genus were social. Of course Rousseau did not have the advantage of paleontology to help him reconstruct the early history of man, but there is a glaring error in his argument where he seems almost willfully to overlook an obvious fact. This mistake is his attempt to minimize the length of time it takes for a child to become independent. The long dependency of human childhood not only necessitates the continuing relation of mother and child, but some degree of cross gender cooperation in its care and feeding. Some recognition of kinship and local group relations appears to have existed among all humans and among most of our close primate relatives.

Finally, one must doubt whether the solitary animals that Rousseau describes could have had the sentiment of pity that he attributes to them. Pity as he describes it, a concern for the sufferings of others, would seem to imply just the degree of identification with another that Rousseau wants to deny was yet possible. For putting oneself in the place of the other entails just that capacity to see oneself as the other sees one, which would also generate the comparative self-consciousness that Rousseau called self-love (*amour-propre*). Only a social animal can have pity of the sort Rousseau describes and the other side of the generous love of another which he calls pity is always the possibility of the self-consciousness that is a form of self-love.[13]

It is, then, safe to say that human beings are social by nature and that society is not an artificial creation at a late stage of social evolution. What difference does this make to how we think about Rousseau's ideas? We will have to return to this subject later, but we can say that the extreme tension that Rousseau finds between the human desire for liberty and the obligations that any kind of society requires may be less "natural" than he assumes. The understanding of human beings as social by nature would seem to mitigate the pessimism of his account, though it would still require us to explain tensions between individual and society where they actually exist. But when Rousseau says that "[t]he subjecting of man to law is a problem in politics which I liken to that of the squaring of the circle in geometry,"[14] he assumes a creature more recalcitrant to the demands of society than humans in fact are.

Nonetheless, to the extent that Rousseau believed that human beings are deeply asocial, the theoretical problem of how society is possible is acute, and in *The Social Contract* required all his genius to explain. Here he does not entirely ignore the historical conditions leading up to the social contract as explained in the Second *Discourse*, but he concentrates on what could possibly make it legitimate in the eyes of intransigently individualistic humans. He states the "fundamental problem" of which the social contract is the solution as follows:

> To find a form of association that may defend and protect with the whole force of the community the person and property of every associate, and by means of which each, joining together with all, may nevertheless obey only himself, and remain as free as before. (Book 1 , ch. 6)

He spells out the solution as follows:

> [The contract to form such an association implies] the total alienation to the whole community of each associate with all his rights; for, in the first place, since each gives himself up entirely, the situation is equal for all; and, the conditions being equal for all, no one has any interest in making them burdensome to others. . .
>
> In short, each giving himself to all, gives himself to no one; and since there is no associate over whom we do not acquire the same rights which we concede to him over ourselves, we gain the equivalent of all that we lose, and more power to preserve what we have.
>
> If, then, we set aside whatever does not belong to the essence of the social contract, we shall find that we can reduce it to the following terms: "Each of us puts in common his person and all his power under the supreme direction of the general will; and in return each member becomes an indivisible part of the whole." (Book 1, ch. 6)

Here we have a series of assertions that must seem bewildering, especially to Americans. On the one hand there is an intense desire to maintain one's liberty, even "to remain as free as before," that is, in the totally asocial state of nature. On the other hand there seems to be an extreme abdication of just that freedom, in that one alienates one's self, one's property, and all one's rights to the community. In part Rousseau seems to be getting ahead of himself here, for it can be only hypothetical rights that are being alienated. In the state of nature there are no rights; rights derive exclusively from the social contract. Even though Rousseau reassures us quickly that we will get everything back, we aren't so sure. Especially important for him, by giving ourselves to all, we give ourselves to nobody. Living in a still quasi-feudal society where personal dependence on others was everywhere (including in his own life), Rousseau believed dependence on the community to be far preferable. But personal dependence is not so central an issue for us. What about "total alienation to the whole community"? For freedom-loving Americans that is hard to take. From being a radical individualist, Rousseau seems to have turned into a radical communitarian in the strong sense that makes Americans nervous.

If we are nervous already then we will be really upset by Rousseau's next move: "So that the social pact not be a pointless device, it tacitly includes this engagement, which can alone give force to the others — that whoever refuses to obey the general will shall be constrained to do so by the whole body; which means nothing else than that he shall be *forced to be free*." (Book 1, ch. 7, my emphasis. Consult the whole passage.)

We have noted Rousseau's penchant for paradox. We should remember that a paradox is not a contradiction. Something important may be going on in this strange expression, "forced to be free." Some critics have found that something indeed important is going on: the invention of totalitarianism, the state forcing the individual to be "free" in some preordained way that is in fact the total violation of freedom. Given the whole context of Rousseau's work and the argument of *The Social Contract,* the idea of a totalitarian Rousseau is hard to understand except as the result of the overheated sensitivities about totalitarianism in the mid-twentieth century. At one level all he is saying is that it is law that makes us free (for in the state of nature there is no law and, once we are no longer isolated, no freedom) and that law is only law when it is enforced. We will be forced to be law-abiding, for only thus can we be free. But he is probably saying more than that.

What more is going on begins to be apparent in the opening paragraph of Book 2:

The first and most important consequence of the principles established above is that the general will alone can direct the forces of the State according to the object of its founding, which is the common good; for if the opposition of private interests has rendered necessary the establishment of societies, it is the concord of these same interests that has rendered it possible. That which is common to these different interests forms the social bond; and unless there were some point in which all interests agree, no society could exist. Now, it is solely with regard to this common interest that the society should be governed. (Book 2, ch. 1)

Although we Americans are familiar with the phrase "common good," we have difficulty understanding it as meaning anything other than the sum of private goods. But that is just what Rousseau says the common good is not:

There is often a great deal of difference between the will of all and the general will; the latter regards only the common interest, while the former has regard to private interests, and is merely a sum of particular wills. (Book 2, ch. 3)

The distinction between the will of all and the general will is critical.[15] It is one of the most important distinctions between Rousseau's position, which we might characterize as civic republicanism, and that of Locke, which we might characterize as classical liberalism. The liberal view is expressed by Mandeville in the idea that the pursuit of private vice will result in public good, or Adam Smith's notion of the "invisible hand" of the market which guarantees that the individual pursuit of self-interest will result in an increase in wealth in the society as a whole. The Lockean strand in the Anglo-American tradition is so powerful that we suspect Rousseau of a totalitarian willingness to sacrifice the individual good to the common good if he means by the latter anything other than the sum of private goods.

The difference between the liberal and the civic republican positions is sometimes expressed by a contrast between negative liberty and positive liberty. Negative liberty protects individuals from the abrogation of their rights by the state. Positive liberty requires the active participation of citizens in their own government. Pushed to the extreme, the emphasis on positive liberty can be seen as totalitarian: individuals are "forced to be free." But Rousseau's position does not fit easily into this dichotomy, for he is as adamant as any liberal in defense of the rights of individuals, that is, of negative liberty. He holds that the idea that "government is allowed to sacrifice an innocent man for the safety of the multitude" is "one of the most execrable that tyranny ever invented." In fact "if a single citizen perished who could have been saved; if a single one were wrongly held in prison; and if a single suit were lost due to evident injustice" then "the civil state is dissolved."[16] Even the ACLU could hardly go further than that. So Rousseau's insistence that the general will is not the same as the will of all has nothing to do with any willingness to trample on individual rights.

Perhaps we can begin to understand the elusive idea of the general will if we ask ourselves what we mean when we use the term so common in contemporary political discourse, "special interests." We mean that some individuals or groups — very rich persons, corporations, labor unions, etc. — are putting their own interests ahead of the general interest. But again what is the general interest? Do we really mean, as the cynics would say, that we object to the special interests of others and would prefer that our own special interests be honored instead? That would hardly seem to capture the passion that the denunciation of special interests arouses in the citizenry. But can we imagine that the general interest is merely the additive sum of everyone's special interest? Could it be, for example, that if every one of us preferred to ride in our own individual automobile and spend no tax money on public transportation that would be in the general interest? James Stockinger, one of the wisest commentators on Rousseau that I know, puts it well when he writes:

> The central theoretical point is that the general will is the result of an ongoing disposition on the part of each citizen or member of a community to ask himself or herself "What is best for all of us?," rather than the Lockean question, "What's in it for me?"[17]

If Rousseau believed, as he did, that the civil state is dissolved if a single individual is unjustly treated, he *also* believed that if the citizens never think of the general interest, what is best for all of us, but only of what's in it for me, then there too the civil state is dissolved. And, since the civil state is the only protector of our liberty once society has developed, without it we are subject to sheer tyranny. Thus, finally to return to the meaning of the paradox "forced to be free," if it doesn't mean the violation of our individual rights, as it clearly doesn't, it does mean that if we want to retain our freedom we will have to think of the common good, for if we don't, then our freedom will be lost. That is a theme which is central to the entire political thought of Alexis de Tocqueville.

While it is important to get clear on what Rousseau means by the social contract and the general will on which it is based, we must still ask where this rather abstract idea fits into his understanding of the social history of mankind. In one sense it is a purely theoretical construction which can be used as a measure by which to judge all past and present societies. Since

Rousseau's description of the social contract as a measure is sternly uncompromising, it is evident that virtually all existing societies are illegitimate and that what we have instead of a civil state is a more or less disguised return to the state of nature in which the rich and strong tyrannize over the poor and weak. That is pretty much what Rousseau did think. Although he was very moderate in his advice as to practical political action, his ideas were indeed revolutionary and would have revolutionary consequences.

Even so, Rousseau's idea of the social contract in its pure form was not entirely a theoretical construct. He thought it had actually existed in human history and he described the conditions that made it possible. His usual examples were Sparta (which seems to have been his type-case), republican Rome, and (in theory if not in fact) his home city of Geneva. It is obvious that these are all city states, and he makes it clear that a republic based on a genuine social contract could not exist in any other kind of society. He often contrasted the relatively small and rigorous republican cities with the great luxurious cities that were capitals of empires: Sparta with Athens, republican Rome with imperial Rome, Geneva with Paris. In every case the civil freedom of the republic was lost in the inevitable tyranny befitting an imperial city.[18]

But although size is critical, it is not the only precondition of a true republic. The single most important precondition is the quality of the people:

> As an architect, before erecting a large edifice, examines and tests the soil in order to see whether it can support the weight, so a wise lawgiver does not begin by drawing up laws that are good in themselves, but considers first whether the people for whom he designs them are fit to maintain them. (Book 2, ch. 8)

The quality of the people is indicated by their mores,[19] that is, their manners and morals, their customs. For Rousseau, as for Tocqueville after him (there were classical precedents as well), the mores are more important than the laws, for without suitable mores the laws will not function. So what kind of mores are requisite for a true republic? On this issue Rousseau is both specific and narrow. The proper mores will exist only among a people at a late stage of patriarchal society, his golden age. For him it is essential that the society be young. "The majority of nations, as well as of men, are tractable only in their youth; they become incorrigible as they grow old" (Book 2, ch. 8). As he explains in detail in the First *Discourse,* old societies, that is, ones advanced in the arts and sciences and in the luxury that attends them, will be so permeated by vicious mores that they will never endure the rigors of a true republic; they are incapable of freedom. What is critical about youth, whether in an individual or in a society, is the capacity to become virtuous, something that Rousseau does not discuss extensively in our texts but which he does discuss at length in *Emile*.[20] On occasion, civil wars and revolutions can allow a people to regain the vigor of youth. "Such was Sparta in the time of Lycurgus, such was Rome after the Tarquins, and such among us moderns were Holland and Switzerland after the expulsion of their tyrants." But once the opportunity is past, it cannot be regained: "Liberty may be acquired but never recovered." (Book 2, ch. 8).

But even the healthy mores that go with youth or youth regained are not enough. There is another factor, rare, indispensable: the presence of a legislator. The reader should peruse chapter 7 of Book 2 of *The Social Contract,* entitled "The Legislator," although that is only one of the places where Rousseau discusses the issue. Here it is enough to say that the legislator must be an extraordinary person, perhaps even someone we could call charismatic, personally disinterested and concerned only with the good of the new state. And we should remember that even the best of legislators would be helpless unless the people for whom he is legislating has mores that can be molded into good laws. The necessary coincidence of such an extraordinary leader and a society at just the right stage of development would appear to be so rare as scarcely to exist. That is what Rousseau believed; he was no optimist.

But there is one more qualification that brings us to an issue we have not directly discussed so far in this chapter: religion. Even the wisest and most charismatic of legislators will not convince a people by reason alone. Only the sanction of the gods will make the new republic possible: "The legislator puts into the mouths of the immortals that sublime reason which soars beyond the reach of common men, in order that he may win over by divine authority those whom human prudence could not move" (Book 2, ch. 7). In a footnote to this passage Rousseau cites Machiavelli, but he could also have cited Spinoza. For all of them the primary model of the legislator is Moses who was able to impose his God-given laws on a people such that it has survived for millennia. The achievement of most legislators has been more transient. Among Rousseau's prime examples, as we would suspect, were Lycurgus, for Sparta, Numa, for Rome, and, interestingly enough, Calvin, for Geneva.[21]

But it is not only at the inception of a new republic that the gods must be invoked: a civil society requires a civil religion. The chapter "On Civil Religion" near the end of *The Social Contract* has been considered horrifying by some and we will have to consider why. The content of Rousseau's civil religion is far from horrifying. It would seem to be moderation itself:

The dogmas of the civil religion ought to be simple, few in number, stated with precision, and without explanation or commentaries. The existence of the Deity, powerful, wise, beneficent, prescient, and bountiful, the life to come, the happiness of the just, the punishment of the wicked, the sanctity of the social contract and of the laws; these are the positive dogmas. As for the negative dogmas, I limit them to one only, that is, intolerance. (Book 4, ch. 8)

Not only are the positive dogmas of the civil religion few and so general that all the existing religions, at least those of Rousseau's day, could affirm them, but Rousseau explicitly stated that citizens could hold whatever other religious beliefs they chose without the knowledge or interference of the state, so long as they did not violate these few. The founders of the American republic, being good deists, that is more or less on the same page as Rousseau in their religious beliefs, were fairly explicit in thinking that just this set of beliefs was essential if the new republic was to survive. That is why I took from Rousseau the term "civil religion" in my 1967 essay "Civil Religion in America."[22]

So what is so horrifying? It is the following illiberal conclusion:

Without having power to compel any one to believe [these dogmas], the sovereign may banish from the state whoever does not believe them; it may banish him not as impious, but as unsociable, as incapable of sincerely loving law and justice and of sacrificing, if need be, his life to his duty. But if any one, after publicly acknowledging these dogmas, behaves like an unbeliever in them, he should be punished with death; he has committed the greatest of crimes, he has lied before the laws.[23] (Book 4, ch. 8)

Rousseau would enforce tolerance by being intolerant of intolerance. That is shocking to us today as we have learned that to tolerate intolerance is the price of our liberty. But the societies of Rousseau's day had not learned the first lesson of tolerance. He was himself the victim of intolerance — it was for his views of religion that he was persecuted, and both in Catholic France and in Protestant Switzerland. Even in America, where the founders of our republic believed that the dogmas of Rousseau's civil religion were a prerequisite for a free society, but without Rousseau's draconian provisions for enforcing them, tolerance of deviant religious views was limited, if not in law, then in public opinion. Thomas Paine discovered how unpopular a self-proclaimed atheist could be on these shores, in spite of his many services to the republic.

It is important to remember that the idea that shared religious belief is a prerequisite for social coherence long predated Rousseau and has survived long after him, though in various forms. Tocqueville said of religion in America that it was "the first of their political institutions." For Durkheim religion was the expression of social solidarity. It would take us too far afield to explore the ramifications of this idea, which at face value would seem to be in complete contradiction to our American belief in the separation of church and state and the idea that religion is essentially private. To understand why Rousseau held a belief that seems so alien to us, we must see that he, along with many others, doubted whether religion and morality, and morality and politics, can really be separated. If republican politics depend on republican mores, and if republican mores depend on republican religion, then republican politics depend on republican religion. It is for this reason that Tocqueville, speaking of the Americans, said "they have a democratic and a republican religion," and he included American Catholics as well as Protestants.

Remember that Rousseau had no interest in enforcing religious beliefs and practices as such. In the passage outlining his draconian enforcement he says he would banish unbelievers "not as impious, but as unsociable, as incapable of sincerely loving law and justice." In short, Rousseau, and in this view the founders of the American republic resembled him, was trying to balance two potentially contradictory intentions: they felt that they needed to found society in religious belief, but they wanted that belief to be minimal and tolerant. Neither Rousseau's minimalist civil religion nor that of the American founders seems vigorous enough to sustain the task assigned them. Rousseau apparently sensed that, for he relied on more than deist dogmas to create the solidarity necessary in his true republic.

In several places he speaks of the civic celebrations that are essential to the life of a republic, but nowhere more clearly than in his *Letter to M. d'Alembert on the Theatre*. He contrasts the passivity of the audience in a darkened theater, seduced by unseemly and privatized emotions,[24] with the open air celebrations of republican peoples. In particular he describes the festivals of the Genevans which he knew from his own experience:

> [O]ne must have been there with the Genevans to understand with what ardor they devote themselves to [the festivities]. They are unrecognizable; they are no longer that steady people which never deviates from its economic rules; they are no longer those slow reasoners who weigh everything, including joking, in the scale of judgment. The people are lively, gay, and tender; their hearts are then in their eyes as they are

always on their lips; they seek to communicate their joy and their pleasures. They invite, they importune, and coerce the new arrivals and dispute over them. All the societies constitute but one, all become common to all. It is a matter of indifference at which table one sits.[25]

Here it is as if the general will becomes visible; that which people share overcomes that which separates them. It is hard not to see in Rousseau's description a precursor of Durkheim's idea of "collective effervescence," the ritual occasions in which society becomes visible to itself as he put it in *Elementary Forms of the Religious Life*.

One must remember, too, that the late eighteenth century saw a critical moment in the development of modern nationalism. Rousseau was not without a role in that development. The content of civic festivities is patriotism. He describes what followed a joyous dance of his father's military company after the completion of their exercises:

The dance was suspended, now there were only embraces, laughs, healths, and caresses. There resulted from all this a general emotion that I could not describe but which, in universal gaiety, is quite naturally felt in the midst of all that is dear to us. My father, embracing me, was seized with trembling which I think I still feel and share. "Jean-Jacques," he said to me, "love your country. Do you see these good Genevans? They are all friends, they are all brothers; joy and concord reign in their midst. You are a Genevan."[26]

Rousseau put on the title page of *The Social Contract* and certain of his other works, "J. J. Rousseau, Citizen of Geneva." Perhaps it was the Geneva of his dreams of which he was a citizen, for he never lived there again after running away at the age of fifteen. And *Emile* and *The Social Contract* were publicly burned by the Genevan authorities shortly after their publication. Today the great *Pléiade* edition of the complete works of Rousseau is underwritten in part by the City of Geneva, at last proud of one of its most illustrious sons. But the paradox of the solitary walker as citizen of Geneva remains one of the most poignant in a life of paradox.

Perhaps we can say that Rousseau avoided nothing, that he lived in his person the conflicts of emerging modernity. He experienced great joy and great suffering, but he did not share in any triumphant confidence about human progress. If the conflict between the individual and society is less deeply embedded in human nature than he thought, it is nonetheless one of the great tensions of modernity. No one saw more clearly than he, in spite of his deep devotion to individual freedom, that the new self-assertion of the individual in the modern age[27] was fraught with danger. To continue the passage with which I began this chapter:

> What man loses because of the social contract is his natural liberty and an unlimited right to anything that tempts him and that he can attain; what he gains is civil liberty and property in all that he possesses. So not to misunderstand these gains, we must clearly distinguish natural liberty, which is limited only by the powers of the individual, from civil liberty, which is limited by the general will; and we must distinguish possession, which is nothing but the result of force or the right of first occupancy, from property, which can be based only on a lawful title.
>
> We might also add to the advantages of the civil state moral freedom, which alone enables man to be truly master of himself; for the impulse of mere appetite is slavery, while obedience to a self-prescribed law is freedom. (Book 1, ch. 8)

For those who believe that all we need to understand about society is that it is composed of competing individuals, each with his consumer preferences, Rousseau's insistence on the tension between individual and society becomes invisible, because, as Margaret Thatcher put it, "society does not exist." But if the will of all replaces the general will, Rousseau would argue, any hope of civil freedom will evaporate and the "soft despotism" that Tocqueville, in this respect his disciple, predicted, will be upon us. It is hard to overestimate Rousseau's deep and continuing influence. Kant, Hegel, Tocqueville, Durkheim, and a host of others owe him vital elements in their thought. Yet for Americans today and for people all over the world who are influenced by American culture, he is a difficult thinker. Rebellious against authority, yet enraptured by Genevan festivities, Rousseau reminds us that society is both the problem and the answer. We will forget him only at our peril.

NOTES

1. "Experience teaches that of all the Christian sects, Protestantism, as the wisest and gentlest, is also the most peaceful and social. It is the only one in which the laws can maintain their dominion and the leaders their authority." J.-J. Rousseau, *The Geneva Manuscript,* in *On the Social Contract,* ed. Roger D. Masters (New York: St. Martin's Press, 1978), 201.

2. Charles Taylor, *Sources of the Self* (Cambridge, Mass.: Harvard University Press, 1989), 356.

3. In spite of his gloomy view of human progress, Rousseau remained

personally happy, or so he claimed in his last work, *The Reveries of the Solitary Walker,* trans. Charles E. Butterworth (New York: Harper and Row, 1967).

4. Jean Starobinski, "Introduction" to *Discours sur l'Origine et les fondements de l'inégalité,* in Jean-Jacques Rousseau, *Oeuvres Complètes* (Paris: *Bibliothèque de la Pléïade,* 1964), Vol. 3, xlii–lxxi.

5. In *Essay on the Origin of Languages* Rousseau writes that among men in Northern climes "[t]he first words among them were not *love me [aimez-moi]* but *help me [aidez-moi]*." See Jean-Jacques Rousseau and Johann Gottfried Herder, *On the Origin of Language,* trans. John H. Moran (Chicago: University of Chicago Press, 1966), 47.

6. Starobinski, "Introduction," lxii.

7. Starobinski, "Introduction," lxii.

8. Starobinski, "Introduction," lxii.

9. Starobinski, "Introduction," lxiii.

10. Cited by Ernest Gellner in *Plough, Sword and Book* (Chicago: University of Chicago Press, 1988), 10.

11. Gerhard Lenski, *Power and Privilege; a Theory of Social Stratification* (New York: McGraw-Hill, 1966).

12. Thomas Hobbes, *Leviathan* [1651], Pt. I, ch. 13.

13. I don't want to say that "pity" or what today we might more likely call "empathy" necessarily implies invidious comparison, only that the possibility is always present. Indeed "pity" has been criticized as a way of "looking down" on another: "Oh you poor thing, you're so much worse off than I am."

14. *Considerations on the government of Poland,* in Jean-Jacques Rousseau, *Political Writings,* translated and edited by Frederick Watson (Madison, University of Wisconsin Press, 1986), 161–162.

15. Rousseau's distinction between the general will and the will of all is expressed by Durkheim in his frequently reiterated assertion that society is more than the sum of its parts. Indeed the strongly objective meaning of society in Durkheim owes more than a little to Rousseau. See "Rousseau's *Social Contract*" in Emile Durkheim, *Montesquieu and Rousseau: Forerunners of Sociology* (Ann Arbor: University of Michigan Press, 1960.) On Durkheim's view of society see Robert N. Bellah, Introduction to *Emile Durkheim on Morality and Society* (Chicago: University of Chicago Press, 1973).

16. In *Discourse on Political Economy* in Jean-Jacques Rousseau, *On the Social Contract,* ed. Roger D. Masters (New York: St. Martin's Press, 1978), 220.

17. James Stockinger, "Locke and Rousseau: Human Nature, Human Citizenship, and Human Work," unpublished Ph.D. dissertation, Department of Sociology, University of California, Berkeley, 1990, 226.

18. Rousseau was not immune to empirical evidence. He had held that Sparta, unlike Athens, had no theater until a scholar pointed out to him that the ruins of a theater had been discovered there. (See J.-J. Rousseau, *Politics and the Arts: Letter to M. d'Alembert on the Theatre,* trans. Allan Bloom (Glencoe, Ill.: Free Press, 1960), 152, note 64. Rousseau accepted the correction. One would wonder what he would say to the fact that democracy survived far longer in Athens than in any Greek city. Perhaps he would say it was not real democracy.

19. French *moeurs*. Allan Bloom hesitates to translate this term by "mores," its Latin root, but prefers the rather awkward "morals [manners]." (See *Letter to d'Alembert,* 149, note 3.) Mores, however, has become standard in translations of the same French word in Tocqueville and is a familiar term in social science.

20. Jean Jacques Rousseau, *Emile or On Education,* Allan Bloom tr. (New York: Basic Books, 1979).

21. He writes, "Those who consider Calvin only as a theologian are but little acquainted with the extent of his genius." (*The Social Contract,* Book 2, ch. 8)

22. Robert N. Bellah, "Civil Religion in America," *Daedalus,* 96 (1), 1967, 1–21. Reprinted in Bellah, *Beyond Belief: Essays on Religion in a Post-Traditional World* (Berkeley: University of California Press, 1991 [1970]), 168–189.

23. It would be helpful to compare Rousseau's position on the punishment of unbelievers in the civil dogmas with the punishments proposed in Book 10 of Plato's *Laws,* 907d to the end of the book. Although Plato's treatment of civil theology in the *Laws* is clearly a model for Rousseau, the differences are as significant as the similarities.

24. It is worth remembering that Rousseau, so passionately opposed to the establishment of a theater in republican Geneva, was himself a passionate theatergoer and the composer of a successful opera, *Le Devin du Village (The Village Soothsayer).* He was also the author of one of the most widely read (and sentimental) novels of the eighteenth century, *Julie, ou La Nouvelle Héloïse.* Another paradox?

25. Rousseau, *Letter to d'Alembert,* 127.

26. Rousseau, *Letter to d'Alembert,* 135.

27. Hans Blumenberg, *The Legitimacy of the Modern Age* (Cambridge, Mass.: MIT Press, 1983 [1966]).

Rousseau and the Self without Property

DAVID BROMWICH

"The first man," writes Rousseau in a phrase like a thunderclap, "who after enclosing a piece of ground, took it into his head to say, *This is mine,* and found people simple enough to believe him, was the real founder of civil society." Rousseau does not much care for this man. Still, the claim to personal property was original, if only in the sense in which the Fall was original. It earns its place therefore at the start of the "conjectural history" of human nature that occupies much of the *Discourse on Inequality*. The history takes us broadly speaking from nature to culture — from a creature of two primary instincts, self-preservation and sympathy, to one in whom a third instinct, self-improvement, has taken control and changed the shape of all experience. A world originally of separate beings, not bound together as a herd, "free, healthy, honest and happy, as much as their nature would admit," was altered "from the moment one man began to stand in need of another's assistance." In the very idea of convenience, Rousseau sees the germ of an economy of privilege: "from the moment it appeared an advantage for one man to possess enough provisions for two, equality vanished." The enjoyment of privilege brings in its turn a love of luxury, a ceaseless clamor for distinction and honors, vastly expanded trade for goods that only enhance distinction, and, to complete the cycle, the creation of still more refined and artificial "needs." Meanwhile, the man who says *This is mine* is on the way to forgetting what it could mean to say *This is me.*

Rousseau believed that there was an intimate relation between inequality and a wrong understanding of the self. The pervasive modern error, he thinks, is to identify the self with its socialized qualities — distinctions, honors, reputation, official character — in short its properties, in the widest sense of the word. A modern man or woman is to be understood in terms of *amour-propre,* or sociable self-love; what he or she has lost is *amour de soi-même,* or care for the true self. These words are not so directly employed in the *Discourses* as they are in other works, but their centrality is implicit throughout. Rousseau comes to the marrow of his purpose when he says, in part two of the Second *Discourse,* that with the rise of artificial society "It became to the interest of men to appear what they really were not." How it came to pass that *to be* and *to appear* are different things is explained in an important note:

> We must not confuse selfishness (*amour-propre*) with self-love (*amour de soi-même*); they are two very distinct passions both in their nature and their effects. Self-love is a natural sentiment, which inclines every animal to look to his own preservation, and which, guided in man by reason and qualified by pity, is productive of humanity and virtue. Selfishness is but a relative and factitious sentiment, engendered in society, which inclines every individual to set a greater value upon himself than upon any other man.

This distinction is vital to Rousseau's task as a breaker of illusions. It also serves to connect his ethics with a reading of human psychology.

Amour-propre, he explains, is "a sentiment arising from comparisons," from our thought of the way other people appear and the way our own demeanor probably strikes them. On the other hand, *amour de soi-même* comes from "every man in particular considering himself as the only spectator who observes him, as the only being in the universe which takes any interest in him, as the only judge of his own merit." So the self has its own history. I move from a nature in which I am myself the only spectator of my thoughts, feelings, and actions, to a social and cultural stage on which the imagined gaze and known interests of a crowd of others come into my mind and shape every possible thought, feeling, and action. Morality, which begins as an inquest into native feeling, ends as a protocol of assent; and as the approval of others perfects my self-approval, conformity at last takes the place of conscience. Human action thereby becomes a spectacle in the precise sense that I conceive of my choices as occurring under the scrutiny of others. The *Discourse on the Sciences and Arts* suggests an unstated corollary. The theater, and the other arts in their different ways, by their status as "fine" or "polite," vindicate our attachment to spectacle. They abstract *amour-propre* into a received idea of taste, and support a conventional morality with all the possible intricacy of manners.

The hypothesis of a "state of nature" had been used before, by Hobbes, Locke, and others to show how their vision of politics answered to an essential fact about human nature. Rousseau says memorably against these state-of-nature theorists that for all the machinery they deploy to recover the origins of morality "not one of them has got there." Their portraits of natural man have been drawn from modern citizens, with all the modern appetites, refinements, and corruptions. If we truly imagine natural man as a self-sustaining being, we shall see that his life is far from "nasty, brutish, and short," though it is indeed solitary. Nor can such a primitive being truly be judged wicked. He does not know evil for the same reason that he does not know good. So far, it is a superb polemic; but, having arrived at this point, the reader may have a question to put to Rousseau. Why should we treat *any* conjectural history as more than a fanciful exercise? Rousseau wants his account to replace the earlier accounts of natural man because such stories are used for more than entertainment. It is necessary to reflect on "the constitution of natural man" in order to arrive at a just estimate of our present state — and this, even though the earlier state "if it ever did, does not now, and in all probability never will exist." To know what we may become, we have to judge ourselves against what we are by nature. We must try to know what man was like before society captured him.

Though Rousseau's idea of the state of nature is a fiction, it is not meant to be an altogether attractive one. He points out that the "sublime maxim of rational justice, *Do to others as you would have others do to you,*" must have been unknown to natural man. The principle of reciprocity had not yet entered his idea of conduct, any more than consciousness of others had entered his idea of himself. Another notable good is missing from his state. Furnished with the habits that we now possess, we can hardly imagine not desiring to sustain a pleasure — Rousseau admits this propensity, and does not see it as a source of corruption — but before society comes on the scene, nothing good can be relied on to happen twice. Improvement only follows in channels worn by the arts of memory, but those arts no more belong to nature than the other arts and sciences. "The art perished with the inventor; there was neither education nor improvement; generations succeeded generations to no benefit; and as all constantly set out from the same point, whole centuries rolled on in the rudeness and barbarity of the first age; the race was grown old, and man was a child." No modern citizen could rationally desire to live in such a state. Yet Rousseau does not rest his argument here. We are lost if we fail to consider the ways in which our progress has also been a catastrophe.

The latter part of the story Rousseau largely trusts us to fill in for ourselves, and some of the work has already been done in the First *Discourse*. His criticism there was mainly directed against the flatterers of the rich and powerful — those who, in their striving for honors and preferment, debase the very arts and sciences they are supposed to exalt. It is impossible to read his observations on this subject without feeling that his indictment fits the "culture industry" of the modern commercial democracies. Whatever one makes of Rousseau as an observer of the eighteenth century, he is an extraordinarily accurate prophet of the twenty-first. The vein of horror, mockery, and distrust that is so notable a feature of the *Discourses* feels like a natural response to the mesh of therapeutics, pharmacology, miscellaneous information and mass entertainment that now sets the cultural tone in America, and that is coming to define what the world agrees to call civilization. Indeed, the current uses of the words *culture* and *technology* closely follow the implications of Rousseau's *arts* and *sciences*. Let us, then, pursue the comparative estimate of natural man and social man, which the two *Discourses* together suggest. What do we find when we look at the life our culture and technology have made for us?

"The savage," observes Rousseau, "lives within himself, whereas social man, constantly outside himself, knows only how to live in the opinion of others." One would expect an apologist for culture eventually to argue that living outside oneself is a good thing. This has become a conventional academic sentiment, over the past two decades, but with a simplicity of optimism that would have startled even Rousseau. The contemporary theorists of society and the arts known as "postmodern" have sided with social man to the furthest reach of artifice. Experience, they say, can never be individually known; it comes to us "mediated" by its reflections in culture and technology. We have crossed the line whether we like it or not, and stand together now as creatures utterly outside ourselves, spectators watching the other spectators watching an image of something somebody once called "myself." Suppose that they are right. The analysis certainly puts us in possession of a clue to the texture of American life. The aim of the contemporary media, one may judge by experience, is not only to place us but to keep us outside ourselves by showing that the correct inner response is already there — predigested, programmed, and requiring nothing but a tacit consent which we express through cooperation and reiteration. The canned laughter of TV sitcoms is an example of this process and a metaphor for what it wants to accomplish everywhere. The response of the audience is built into the product itself. In other settings too, the responsive signals of the ideal spectator are in your eye and ear as you watch and listen, though with variations suitable to the different media. In the typical format of rock or rap video, for example, the built-in response is danced and sung by spectators within the performance, the clapping, nodding, approving minions of the lead singer or group. The habits of such spectatorship bear an inverse relation to the duties of citizenship. If the right way to allow people to acquire a moral self is to leave them time to think, and show them the value of having time for thinking, the popular arts of our day go far to discourage this. The result aimed at by the productions of culture and technology is to clinch a sensational effect or to gratify a familiar need. They rivet attention in a way calculated to blot out and tranquilize thought.

How would one describe the popular culture of America to the sort of witness — a sensitive and unfamiliar observer — whom Rousseau admonishes us always to employ against ourselves? From talk shows to live police hunts captured with a hand-held camera, to Internet search engines and their advertising inserts, to the standard sadistic fare of the video arcades, to the seasonal blockbuster action thrillers with a line of dialogue per bullet, to the routine use of the cell phone by citizens while driving a Sport Utility Vehicle or walking the dog — in all its varied aspects, our culture is plainly ingenious, efficient, exciting, hypnotic, brutal, sedative, and ultimately stupefying. These traits taken together, of course, would be nothing new to Rousseau. What has been added in our time is the ambition of culture and of technology to fill every crevice and outpost of human experience. Culture has been sapped of the power to reflect on itself, and released from the duty to reform itself. The maxim of a cynical and profiteering aestheticism, "We don't make the culture, we only reflect it," has become the slogan of every hustler in need of a literate excuse.

Yet the sensational effects are on the surface. The deeper malady lies in what the culture teaches implicitly by its examples: that we human beings are endlessly malleable and adaptive creatures, and that our nature is to want to crowd our lives with moments of choice among various possible and optional goods, all of them tempting, none of them intrinsically more valuable than the others. The lifework of the citizen as pictured in our culture is: to produce what people consume. The end of life is to become a fulfilled consumer. The market, with its evangelizing techniques and rhetoric — the very word *market* has taken on an aura that is religious — now penetrates our daily lives as never before. In all sectors of the mass media and the personal media, the boundary between content and advertisement has been effaced, so that children far into adolescence find the distinction incomprehensible. The norm that is inculcated by the morale of the popular arts and sciences is hyperactive listlessness, in the service of an ideal that a modern philosopher, Slavoj Zizek, has aptly described as *interpassivity*. To look at the society of the spectacle in the light of natural man is to want to ask again what has gone wrong.

Oddly, at this point a consolation is suggested by Rousseau. He suspects that we are creatures of culture far more shallowly than we are taught — far less completely than culture itself would have us be. Most people, even in America today, still live a large portion of their lives outside the routines of culture. For we do have a distinct life of thinking, feeling, and acting, a life that is partly the creation of nature and necessity. The monstrous fiction that culture altogether defines us is refuted not only by our authentic experience of stray passions and instincts, such as love, sex, sympathy, and self-preservation, but also by occasional deeper experiences of those rare works of art which are not only or mainly the productions of a shared culture of the arts and sciences. Such a work has the power to break through the complacent satisfaction that is nurtured by even the most exquisite productions of conventional culture. Rousseau would seem to have acknowledged as much in various reserve clauses that appear in his replies to the critics of the *Discourse on the Sciences and Arts* and in the *Discourse on Inequality* itself. One of his recurrent suggestions is that the arts and sciences are compelled to act as a cure for diseases of which they themselves are the leading cause.

The *Social Contract* has in view another kind of cure: a moral education achieved through a practice of politics without end. Here the opposition of the natural and the social self, the tension between *amour de soi-même* and *amour-propre,* the mutual repulsion of a conscience that takes no account of others and a gregariousness that feeds on vanity — these contraries are at last surmounted by being writ large as the separation between the public and the private good. The people of a free and rational republic are sure to find that acting for long-term prudence and the public good is a tangible expression of a genuine care for the self. The result, as Rousseau presents it, is a moral system that naturally extends the sublime morality of *Do to others as you would have others do to you*. Citizens are asked to judge for others as they would judge for themselves if none had a proper self, and a moral law that evades the scrutiny of individuals is made to cover society as a whole. In this way, the problem is not so much solved as restated. But with an immense advantage: a more than personal agency is now in place to unmask the false and disclose the true self. We know how to interpret the result because we are looking at the false and the true self of society. No personal *amour-propre* can obstruct the judgment where the vanity of all has been conquered by all.

A lot of people for a long time have thought such speculations worse than fanciful. Rousseau consistently taught that imitation is a treachery against ourselves, yet a generation of French politicians, the Jacobins of the 1790s, contended for the honor of being the most perfect of his imitators. It has been said of them, with truth, that they committed their acts of terror with less compunction as his disciples, since his writings assured them that whatever they did was done on behalf of all humanity. (This pattern of influence is traced in fascinating detail in Carol Blum's study *Rousseau and the Republic of Virtue.*) The most eloquent arraignment of Rousseau as a sponsor of revolutionary terror came from Edmund Burke in his *Letter to a Member of the National Assembly.* "The professor of vanity" is Burke's nickname for the author of the *Social Contract* and the *Confessions;* to the question which of the fanatics of 1791 most resembles Rousseau, he answers with grim irony "in truth they all resemble him." It is curious to see Burke single out, as Rousseau's great moral fault, vanity — vanity of all things, in the defender of *amour de soi-même,* who counted himself the sworn enemy of people existing in the opinion of others. Yet Burke's insight is genuine and it is deep. There is something not only selfish but contagiously selfish about the man who claims to stand utterly alone with his conscience. He of all others is likeliest to draw the heedless emulation of souls eager for the intoxicant of new feelings. Whereas, Burke implies, a more docile and circumspect person is restrained from such influences by the force of custom, by inertia and acquiescence, virtues that are the opposite of romantic.

And yet, Rousseau's own politics in practice were moderate. When reading his most spartan and utopian passages, one must not forget that he shared with his century a peculiar taste for schemes of perfectibility. This is an epochal trait, not to be compared with anything more recent, except, perhaps, the taste for science fiction. Both genres offer allegorical equipment for living, ways of enchanting us into an understanding of the world. Neither can be pronounced innocent of desiring to effect real changes in society, but both rely implicitly on an audience well versed in the uses of metaphor. When Rousseau, in the *Social Contract,* says that frequent pardons signify that great crimes soon will go unpunished — but then adds that his heart whispers and restrains his pen — he does not mean that literally he cannot write another word or draw a logical inference on the punishment of death. Rather, he has found a way to suggest without saying: "Great crimes are wicked; and we should not be afraid of inflicting death on the wicked; but I am fallible, and so are you, reader; remember this when you talk of giving the state the power to kill." The doctrine of the general will cannot be excused as a metaphor, but the fairest conclusion may be that of T. H. Green, the great nineteenth-century theorist of obligation, who thought the phrase mainly significant as an appeal to the "common good" in settings where "obedience to it is a means to an end desirable in itself or absolutely." In this sense, the general will is a name for a residual sentiment of unconscious approval that all states require. It was, added Green, an error for Rousseau to have confounded the sentiment with the power of the people to give approval in the form of a vote.

Rousseau is vulnerable on many grounds. But the argument that carries through all his books is an extreme statement of a principle and it yields a perpetual challenge. The argument denies that the improvement of society is the improvement of humanity. It asks us to consider whether the prestige enjoyed by the idea of "progress" may not be philosophically absurd — a way of talking with apparent meaning but without sense, which flatters the self-esteem of persons who have lost the power of judging good and bad or right and wrong. They have been taught by society to think that whatever comes to us wrapped as progress cannot be bad or wrong. Yet no greater deception, Rousseau believes, has ever been practiced by human nature against itself than the belief that by a fortunate necessity we are socialized into virtue. The notion that morality is at bottom a social good that tallies with the achievement of good works, worldly esteem, and prosperity — this heresy of Protestantism, which the seventeenth century knew by the name of Arminianism, had left its tracks all over the new creed of progress and it went against the deepest of Rousseau's convictions, namely that true virtue is of the heart and not to be known by worldly deeds. He has been widely, indeed epidemically, misunderstood as therefore saying that human beings are essentially good. At the earliest moment described in his conjectural history, he supposed that they were neither good nor evil. They were self-sufficient and episodically attentive to others. But in this world, as we know this world, Rousseau no more believed that people are essentially good than his near contemporary Jonathan Edwards did. He seems to have felt that individuals have a nature, a character, as inveterate as their manner of pausing to listen or show concern. This nature is a given fact. It is also a new fact — it brings something into the world. Conventional morality will never realize that this new fact is unassimilable. There is something that is yourself that is not anyone's property, not even your own, but this is a truth society cannot bear to know.

How did Rousseau arrive at his truth? The First *Discourse* was really a prelude: a circumstantial attack on fashion, including the fashion of progress, and a cursory view of the frenzy for distinction that is another name for the desire to resemble a herd of indistinguishable others. As he advanced to the Second *Discourse* and later works, Rousseau's inquest into the sickness of imitative conduct drove him gradually deeper, until he was left to grapple with a metaphor that seems to govern the field of social relations. His iconoclasm is directed finally against the idea that the self is identical with its properties, the things it is attached to and the things it owns. To regard property as a part of nature is to confuse the costume with the body and substance of things. Property, propriety, with the realm of the *propria* and *amour-propre* that they sanction, all this undergrowth of the arts and sciences can ramify so densely, so indecently in the name of decency that most people are convinced most of the time that the claim that is thus made rightly supersedes every other imperative. We come to believe that a second nature is our only nature after all.

Some way into his enterprise, Rousseau saw that property, when placed at the head of our moral knowledge of others, has the same corrupting effect that culture has when allowed to shape our self-imaginings. An important clue lies in his *Letter to d'Alembert*. This great pamphlet argues that even the finest work of art confronts a division between the truth of its subject matter and the treatment that will hold the audience. When asked to choose between a theatrical lie and an untheatrical truth, even the greatest artist will often choose the lie. Or rather, the economy of art will make the choice almost without the intervention of the artist. In the case in question, the character of Alceste in Molière's comedy *The Misanthrope,* Rousseau invites us to notice how the traits of a cold and unworldly arrogance, which belong to a true misanthrope, are allowed insensibly to pass out of focus. It could hardly be otherwise in the theater, where such a portrayal would be tedious. Instead, the character is rendered laughable by his commonplace love of flattery and a helpless desire to conciliate those he adores, qualities that of course have nothing to do with misanthropy. Thus the unsociable man is exposed as an adept in secret of all the sociable vices. The story appeals to the sense of ridicule that is part of our *amour-propre,* but the result is a sacrifice of truth to theatrical plausibility. What happens in *The Misanthrope* will be found to occur, says Rousseau, only more penetrably in the lesser productions of culture. They want to hold us in our seats, and they give us an appetite for unreality.

Rousseau, then, writes steadily against art and science, against culture and technology, and against a convenience that society prizes for the sake of its own advancement. At the same time he defends a self that is inward, a self that does not exist merely in the opinion of others. His perception, and it was never in the history of human feelings an obvious one, is that society cannot do anything to assist this principle or germ of the self. It can only allow it to exist. We are compelled to respect the self by virtue of its existence as such, not for any attribute or quality or property. It is natural for us to use society as a medium for ordinary commerce between persons, which disposes for the individual's inspection an array of collaborative thoughts and feelings, ways of knowing people and ways of joining them in common projects. So long as society confines itself to this function of merely exhibiting the possible combinations, it remains nothing but a useful extension of the world in which the earliest human creatures, who Rousseau believes may have been arboreal, occasionally linked with each other from tree to tree.

But the error of the social self is to suppose that the complication, elaboration, and fortification of the group in its character as a group would be the end desired by a single being reasonably reflecting on its own welfare. We know on the contrary that people in the mass take on a character more base and presumptuous — above all, more refined in the excuses they make for their own perpetuation — than the most ingeniously perverse and self-justifying individual. Beneath the forms of caring that are native to the social self, which say, and believe when they hear themselves say, that they care for the good of the individual, can be glimpsed an active jealousy of the inward self that will stop at nothing. What the attitude suggests is prudent guidance; what it means is the opposite of love. Here our *amour-propre* is an outward expression, in the great book of manners which all obey more than we know we obey, of a wish for collective stability as an end, a wish that never really is identical with the desire of a single separate man or woman. So long as the wishful social body retains expressive dominance, and stays sure of its good intentions, there is no enormity of delusion or crime of which it is not capable.

We have a bad reason, besides dullness, for accepting the moral claim of *amour-propre.* There is an innocence about the inward self which we are apt to judge warily because it looks so like indifference. Yet the person who consults *amour de soi-même* is limited in the wrongs that he or she is likely to commit. This limitation has partly to do with the eccentric manner in which motives work their way toward conduct for the unconnected individual. It is also a fact, seldom brought into such discussions, that individuals commonly show a surprising readiness to forgive, when assurance can be had that important others are not watching. This is a profound though unprincipled and capricious form of charity, unknown to society at large. But sooner or later people merge into one group and another, beyond their own conscious wish for such an identity, thanks to the sheer convenience of custom and the enchantment of imitation. We come to feel a craving for distinction when we learn what other people want. "Born originals, how comes it to pass that we die copies?" asked Edward Young in his *Conjectures on Original Composition,* a work published four years after the *Discourse on Inequality.* We do become copies, to a greater degree than any of us anticipates — the social side of our nature both urges and rewards it.

Rousseau's task, at this late stage of development, is not so much to persuade as to warn. To the extent that you agree with society, and believe there is nothing that is yourself that is not someone's property, to that extent you cut off your original contribution to human hopes and fears. You treat yourself as one more dispensable proof of the satisfactoriness of the available options.

Common-sense detractors of Rousseau have always replied that it is only by collaboration that any enlightened change ever comes to pass. This is true in a conspicuous and pragmatic sense, and it is not denied by Rousseau. But though such reforms may be a necessary condition for, they do not add up to the actual extensions of, the kind of human imagining Rousseau's admirers generally have in view when honoring him. To deepen our knowledge of the kind of creature we are, it is not enough to expose ourselves to occasional disagreements among agreeable persons. We require, even when we cannot fully comprehend, the influx of a moral energy that may come suddenly and seem to shake the ground beneath us. There is (Rousseau would have us believe) such a thing as moral originality. The consequences of his suggestion themselves have made a change in the self-imagining of human beings. The writings of Shelley and Tolstoy for example were sustained attempts to follow Rousseau's beginning. This is true not least in works like *The Mask of Anarchy* and *The Death of Ivan Ilych*, which show the triumph of the social will over an intuition of personal freedom. The same idea of moral originality must have been vivid to John Stuart Mill in *On Liberty,* where the teachings of Rousseau are mentioned as acts of courage which their earliest readers could not but resist, but by which the moral world has been incalculably enlarged.

What kind of courage does such originality bring? We hear its ground note in the opening of Rousseau's *Confessions:* "I have resolved on an enterprise which has no precedent, and which, once complete, will have no imitator. My purpose is to display to my kind a portrait in every way true to nature, and the man I shall portray will be myself." Rousseau could not have meant to say that nobody after him would write an autobiography. In announcing that his enterprise was without precedent and would be without imitators, he was saying that there were memories, tones and colors from experience, which by their nature seemed to be uniquely his. Not in spite of that fact, but because of it, his story would have exemplary value. Could the same be true of the story of any of us? Rousseau implies that it could: potentially, any of us. It is not written in the book of usable hours that we shall die copies. The paradox remains that Rousseau, who distrusts writing as he distrusts any technology, should have elected to convey his teachings and his memories into the world through writing. But of all mediums writing offers the densest fabric by which the weave of a particular character may be known. Perhaps by its very nature, it can come to be a defense against the delusions of egotism, just as the social contract is a defense against the delusions of sociability.

From the way in which the idea of true self-love is made to emerge in the *Discourses,* a reader might fairly guess a circumstance that is confirmed in Rousseau's final work, another kind of memoir, the *Reveries of the Solitary Walker.* He followed a strict personal code in which the requirements of sincerity and accuracy were blended. He thought it permissible to embellish a tale that shades the truth, so long as the lie harms no one and is told for the sake of wit or fancy. On the other hand, according to his code, it is forbidden to tell the slightest falsehood that could stain the character of another person; and it is compulsory (where relevant) to recount any circumstantial truth that could reflect discredit upon oneself. Here again we meet Rousseau's emphasis on the good of exposure and its connection with a self-knowledge freed from artifice. The inward self relates to the full amplitude of experience, and so its intimate knowledge matters more, in the sense that it deserves more attention, than fidelity to the course and catalogue of things-that-have-happened. Together the *Confessions* and *Reveries* represent the *faiblesse,* the unexceptional weakness or frailty, the susceptibility to mundane faults of the person from whom the philosophy proceeds. It seems possible that Rousseau intended these works to remind us of the very mixed human materials from which any philosophy is worked up from experience to theory.

His view of the personal accent of all experience cannot be reduced to a difference between subjective and objective reports, any more than his definition of *amour de soi-même* can be reduced to a preference for spontaneous over responsible feelings. I submit myself to the tribunal of other human beings or fellow citizens in the same stroke by which I subject myself to a judgment of my own. The two processes will have become the same when all are persuaded to shed the vanity that leads them to favor themselves. This is where the arts take on their immense power to charm and corrupt, since they encourage us to confuse vanity with the dramatic allure of "consistency." And this is where the moral imagination must assume the place of authority vacated by art. Most lives, once looked at close, are wretchedly inconsistent, but a love of pattern and probability blinds us to this discovery until we forget that it is a truth about ourselves.

Rousseau's understanding of ethics, aesthetics, and psychology all point to a charitable and not a self-serving conclusion. A good book is one in which the reader is not invited to acquit the author. A good society is one in which a citizen will not be unfairly punished for the choice to reveal a truth about himself. It was necessary for autobiography to be invented at the same time as the social contract in order for each to justify the other.

Rousseau, Robespierre, Burke, Jefferson, and the French Revolution

CONOR CRUISE O'BRIEN

From the beginning of the second phase of the French Revolution — the manic phase beginning with the deposition of the King by the Paris mob on the 10th August 1792 — Revolutionary France saw Rousseau and Burke as polar opposites representing good and evil, respectively.

For the French Revolutionaries, Rousseau was the great mentor and exemplar. His *Social Contract* was "the beacon of legislators." Rousseau had of course been loved and admired by all sorts of French people — including Louis XVI and Marie Antoinette — in pre-revolutionary France. But that was the sentimental, idealistic Rousseau of *La Nouvelle Héloïse,* of *The Reveries of a Solitary Walker,* of *Emile,* and especially *The Profession of Faith of a Savoyard Vicar.*

That was what we might call the "nice cop" Rousseau. The cult of the "tough cop" Rousseau, and *The Social Contract,* came in with the second phase of the French Revolution following the deposition of the King and the rise of the Jacobins and in particular of Maximilien Robespierre for whom *The Social Contract* was both the object of a cult and the guarantee of his own personal political holiness and absolute power for a time, as the arch-priest of the cult. Rousseau was also, in a curious way, the guarantee of Robespierre's *impartiality,* as a being above normal politics, spokesman for a mysterious and awe-inspiring entity: the General Will. In his address to the French of the eighty-three Departments in the summer of 1792 — about the summit period of his personal authority — Robespierre came forward confidently in the persona of spokesman for the General Will, addressing the Jacobins whom he now totally dominated:

"For us, we are not of any party, we serve no faction, you know it, brothers and friends, our will is the General Will."

"Our will is the General Will." Once accepted as spokesman for the General Will, itself an absolute, Robespierre was able to wield absolute power, even at a time when he held no office.

He was seen as the "guide" or "legislator" who makes his appearance in chapters 6 and 7 of Book 2 of *The Social Contract.* The function of the guide or legislator is to direct the General Will, "to show it how to see objects as they are, sometimes as they ought to be."

In 1793–1794, to be designated by Robespierre, with no evidence at all, as opposed to the General Will, was invariably the prelude to the fatal prosecution of the individual concerned, to a trial with the result known in advance, and then to speedy execution.

The cult of the General Will flourished, in a way, even after the fall of Robespierre. The Thermidorians, having killed Robespierre, declared that he had falsified Rousseau and that they themselves were the true heirs to Rousseau. On 14 September 1794 the Thermidorian-dominated Convention ordered that Rousseau's remains be brought from his original burial place on the Isle of Poplars in Ermenonville and placed in the Pantheon in Paris with appropriate ceremony. Gordon MacNeil describes the central place of *The Social Contract* in the ceremonies: "*The Social Contract,* the 'beacon of legislators' was carried on a velvet cushion, and a statue of its author in a cask pulled by twelve horses."

In substance, the ceremonies were less like an apotheosis than like an exorcism. There was no heir to Robespierre. The Thermidorians had killed Robespierre and declared that he had falsified Rousseau, of whom they themselves were the true heirs. But they could not agree among themselves about what *The Social Contract* meant, still less were they able to execute people in its name. The Revolution was fading, soon to be replaced by the Empire. And there the cult of Rousseau suddenly stopped. It vanished for the long period during which Napoleon Bonaparte held supreme power.

Napoleon Bonaparte had a definite personal reason for dismantling the cult of Rousseau. Rousseau had glorified General Paoli who had fought for Corsican independence. Indeed Rousseau had glorified him in a characteristic passage, asserting absolutism in the name of freedom. In Rousseau's fragment of a constitution for Corsica, he represents his hero General Paoli as landing on an island and addressing his people in the following words, provided for him by Rousseau, and redolent of Rousseau's politics:

"Corsicans be silent: I am going to speak in the name of all. . . . Let those who will not consent, depart, and let those who consent raise their hands."

For Napoleon this was not only pernicious nonsense but also dangerous because it challenged his personal right to be Emperor of the French. If Paoli had succeeded, as Rousseau wished, Napoleon could not have become Emperor of the French because he would not have been French at all, but a citizen of an insignificant independent Corsica. So throughout the long period of Napoleon's dominance, in the Consulate followed by the Empire, Rousseau was in total eclipse.

After the end of the Napoleonic period and the restoration of the Monarchy, the cult of Rousseau resumed in France, and still flourishes. But it has been mainly a literary cult, without direct political application. There may have been an exception. It seems to me that Marx's combination of a cult of freedom with intimations of absolutism may well derive ultimately from Rousseau and specifically from *The Social Contract.* But so far as I know, Marx never explicitly acknowledged any such debt, and in the absence of evidence, speculation cannot be usefully pursued.

The second phase of the French Revolution, from August 1792 on, saw the virtual deification of Robespierre, as the infallible interpreter of Rousseau's General Will. The same period saw the diabolization of Edmund Burke in the France of the second phase of the Revolution. To the parliamentary revolutionaries of the first phase (1789 to 1792) Burke had been merely irritating as predicting their own failure, with absolute accuracy. But to the revolutionaries of the second phase — 1792 to 1794 — and principally to Robespierre — Burke's insights were dangerous. Burke was dangerous, first of all, because he had predicted their own emergence and diagnosed their characters. In *Letter to a Member of the National Assembly,* published in January 1791, Burke had predicted the failure of the "moderates" who then dominated the Assembly and the advent to power of a fiercer and more ruthless revolutionary strain. He begins by showing the infirmity of the moderates and goes on to depict the character of the men who are about to replace them. He depicts the moderates as working together with the extremists in a common cause but hoping to dominate them "on the credit of the sobriety with which they show themselves disposed to carry on what may seem most plausible in the mischievous projects they pursue in common." From that piece of analysis, Burke proceeds immediately to his clinching prediction:

"But these men naturally are despised by those who have heads to know, and hearts that are able to go through, the necessary demands of bold wicked enterprises. They are naturally classed below the latter description, and will only be used by them as inferior instruments. They will be only the Fairfaxes of your Cromwells."

Burke here predicts in January 1791 the transit of power within the Revolution, which would come about in the second half of 1792. And it was this transit, of course, that led directly to what Burke also foresaw: the execution/assassination of the king of France. Burke predicted that in that same *Letter to a Member of the National Assembly,* in which he predicted the emergence of those who would carry it out:

"Nothing that I can say, or that you can say, will hasten them [the hard-line revolutionaries] by a single hour, in the execution of a design which they have long since entertained. In spite of their solemn declarations, their soothing addresses and the multiple oaths they have taken and forced others to take, they will assassinate the king when his name will no longer be necessary to their designs, but not a moment sooner."

Burke's profound understanding of the workings of the French Revolution, attained very early on, is nowhere more evident than in his prediction, contained in his *Reflections on the Revolution in France* that the Revolution would necessarily end in military dictatorship:

> It is known that armies have hitherto yielded a very precarious and uncertain obedience to any senate, or popular authority; and they will least of all yield it to an assembly which is to have only a continuance of two years. The officers must totally lose the characteristic disposition of military men, if they see with perfect submission and due admiration, the dominion of pleaders; especially when they find, that they have a new court to pay to an endless succession of those pleaders, whose military policy, and the genius of whose command (if they should have any) must be as uncertain as their duration is transient. In the weakness of one kind of authority, and in the fluctuation of all, the officers of an army will remain for some time mutinous and full of faction, until some popular general, who understands the art of conciliating the soldiery, and who possesses the true spirit of command, shall draw the eyes of all men upon himself. Armies will obey him on his personal account. There is no other way of securing military obedience in this state of things. But the moment in which that event shall happen, the person who really commands the army is your master; the master (that is little) of your king, the master of your assembly, the master of your whole republic.

The seizure of power by Napoleon Bonaparte — the event predicted in this remarkable passage — occurred on 18 Brumaire (9 November 1799), four years after the death of the predictor.

According to a writer in the *London Review of Books* (February 1989) "Burke has always been ignored in France." Quite untrue, both in the past and in the present. Burke's *Reflections on the Revolution in France* was translated into French in the month after its English publication. The French edition sold two thousand copies in its first two days and was immediately at the center of a fierce controversy. This was during the "constitutional" initial phase of the French Revolution, a phase for which Burke rightly saw no future. Nor was Burke exactly ignored during the Terror when mere possession of his book was enough to send its possessor to the guillotine. Nor in the next century did Michelet ignore Burke when he called *Reflections* "that infamous book" and loudly and inaccurately denounced its author.

By the time, however, when the readers of the *London Review of Books* were learning how the French had "always ignored" Burke, the school of French historiography now in the ascendant was already paying respectful attention to him. The attitudes of that school — far more critical of the French Revolution than any of its predecessors — are reflected in the great *Critical Dictionary of the French Revolution,* edited by François Furet and Mona Ozouf, and published in Paris in 1988 (an English edition followed in 1989). *The Critical Dictionary* contains a respectful entry on Burke by Gérard Gengembre. Burke is the only English speaker to be included among the seventeen thinkers in the section "Historians and Commentators." The only other non-Francophones to figure in the list are four Germans: Fichte, Hegel, Kant, and Marx. Gengembre's essay concludes: "Study of this penetrating foreigner's scrutiny of France remains profitable for anyone who would understand what was truly at stake in a Revolution from which the whole modern French political tradition ultimately derives." The "penetrating foreigner" bit is better in the original French: "ce regard étranger, d'une clairvoyance pénétrante." Pity that English-speaking readers should miss that keyword "clairvoyance."

Thomas Jefferson, Burke's contemporary, became the French Revolution's warmest admirer in America right at the beginning of the Revolution, and so remained throughout the Terror. He was one of the first Americans to obtain a copy of Burke's *Reflections,* immediately after its publication in America. Before that he had — like most Americans — reacted favorably to what he knew of Burke, because Burke had been the leading figure in the parliamentary minority in Britain which had opposed the coercion of America. But when Jefferson read *Reflections,* and found Burke implacably opposed to the French Revolution, he decided that Burke's opposition to the coercion of America must have been corruptly motivated. Jefferson wrote to a sympathetic English correspondent on 11 May 1791:

"The Revolution of France does not astonish me as much as the Revolution of Mr. Burke. I wish I could believe the latter proceeded from as pure motives as the former. But what demonstration could scarcely have established before, less than the hints of Dr. Priestley [Dr. Joseph Priestley, leading English radical, and a friendly correspondent of Jefferson] and Mr. Paine establish firmly now [sic]. How mortifying that this evidence of the rottenness of his mind must oblige us now to ascribe to wicked motives those actions of his life which wore the mask of virtue and patriotism."

Jefferson's sputtering indignation at *Reflections* was no doubt quite sincere. But it also served a political purpose. Most Americans, from 1789 to 1795, were highly sympathetic to the French Revolution which they tended to see as resembling their own Revolution and somehow complementary to it. But enthusiasm for the French Revolution was not evenly distributed throughout America. In the North, dominant commercial interests, considering that the fast expanding trade with Britain was vital to America's future, were suspicious of enthusiasm for the French Revolution, seeing that enthusiasm as having the potential to carry America into a war with Britain which would be ruinous to American prosperity. The economically backward and debt-ridden Southern states had no such reasons to hold back. American enthusiasm for the French Revolution was seen by Jefferson as a major asset for the South — and Jefferson's Virginia in particular — in the burgeoning struggle for dominance within the new Republic. Jefferson saw this clearly and cleverly exploited enthusiasm for the French Revolution as a weapon against John Adams — his main potential rival for the succession to the Presidency. Jefferson drew attention to similarities between Burke's *Reflections* and certain writings of John Adams. The controversy was damaging to Adams and politically profitable to Jefferson. And it paved the way not only for Jefferson's own presidency but for three Virginian presidencies, of two terms each.

Jefferson never, so far as I know, explicitly acknowledged a debt to Rousseau. To do so would have been politically compromising, since most Americans were more religious than most Europeans and most religious people classified Rousseau — not quite accurately — along with Voltaire as undermining all forms of religion. Jefferson, throughout his life, remained suspect to Americans with strong religious convictions. Toward the end of his life, after the British had burned down the center of Washington and destroyed the nucleus of the Library of Congress, Jefferson offered to sell his own splendid collection of books to Congress to make up for the loss. Religious people in Congress warned against accepting the gift because Jefferson's library contained the works of Voltaire and Rousseau. Congress, nonetheless, bought the collection. But Jefferson would not have been surprised at the objection. Rousseau, like Voltaire, was a compromising ally, politically speaking. Jefferson, always keenly alert, in his long march to the presidency, to considerations of political advantage and disadvantage, must have been well aware that to acknowledge a debt to Rousseau would have been politically damaging. So such a debt was never acknowledged but we are not to understand from that, that the debt was not there.

The debt appears in Jefferson's relation to the concept of "civil religion," a phrase which appears to have been coined by Rousseau.

The Jefferson of the early 1790s, the champion of the French Revolution, was an ardent believer in, and prophet of, civil religion in the sense adumbrated by Rousseau. That is, he sought to animate an apparently secular and political idea — that of liberty — by breathing into it the kind of emotions and dispositions with which religion had been invested in the Ages of Faith. Of this religion Thomas Jefferson was more than a prophet, he was a pope. As author of the Declaration of Independence he possessed the *Magisterium* of liberty. He could define heresy and excommunicate heretics. To fail to acknowledge (for example) that the French Revolution constituted an integral part of the holy cause of liberty along with the American Revolution constituted heresy, and the heretic had to be driven from public life.

The words "heresy" and "holy cause" appear repeatedly in Jefferson's correspondence between 1789 and 1794 and occasionally even later. And they are always there to link the American Revolution with the French one and to sanctify the linkage.

Yet Jefferson's most profoundly revealing implicit acknowledgement of a debt to Rousseau comes from a period — early 1798 — when the Revolution was already in retreat before the rise of Napoleon, and Jefferson's own faith in the Revolution was already well on the wane. His correspondence from this period shows that he no longer wanted America to be directly dominated, or even strongly influenced, by the French Revolution. But he still wishes that the French Revolutionaries should succeed in occupying and dominating Britain — an event which appeared to many quite probable in the last years of the eighteenth century. The conquest of Britain by revolutionary France would be a victory, in Jefferson's opinion, for the principles of the American Revolution. "Nothing can establish firmly the republican principles of *our government* (my italics) but establishment of them in England. France will be the apostle for this."

"The apostle. . ." The idea of Revolutionary France as having a quasi-divine mission had dominated Jefferson's vision of international politics in the period 1789–94 at the height of his mystical enthusiasm for the French Revolution. By the late 1790s that faith had disappeared in relation to French influence over America. But Jefferson could still see conquest by the French as a kind of redemption for a more benighted Britain. To a correspondent, Peregrine Fitzhugh, who had apparently expressed some qualms about Jefferson's enthusiasm for the subjugation of England by revolutionary France, Jefferson wrote on 23 February 1798:

> The ensuing month will probably be the most eventful ever yet seen in Modern Europe. It may probably be the season preferred for the projected invasion of England. It is indeed a game of chances. The sea which divides the combatants gives to fortune as well as to valor its share of influence on the enterprise. But all the chances are not on one-side. The subjugation of England would indeed be a general calamity. But happily it is impossible. Should it end in her being only republicanized, I know not on what principle a true republican of our country could lament it, whether he considers it as extending the blessings of a purer government to other portions of mankind, or strengthening the cause of liberty in our own country by the influence of that example. I do not indeed wish to see any nation have a form of government forced on them; but if it is to be done, I should rejoice at its being a freer one.

They may not be "subjugated," but if the government "forced" on them is "a freer one," Jefferson would rejoice. The concept that people might be "forced to be free" originated with Rousseau, in *The Social Contract* (Book 1, chapter 7, last paragraph). Jefferson never acknowledged any intellectual or moral debt to Rousseau but the debt is evident in this peremptory paradox. "Forced to be free" is a truly revolutionary concept, common to the French Revolution, and to its twentieth-century heir, the Russian Revolution.

Rousseau, Burke, Robespierre, Jefferson: this quartet of late eighteenth-century movers and shakers has challenged my imagination for many years. Such relations as existed among the four men were uneven and partly equivocal. By 1778, when Rousseau died, Burke had been a Member of the British Parliament for thirteen years and had attracted a great deal of attention, mainly as the strongest parliamentarian opponent of the American war. Rousseau would have at least heard of him. But Rousseau's direct political interests — never more than fleeting — appear to have been confined to continental Europe. When Rousseau visited Britain in 1766 — just after Burke's election to Parliament — he was in close touch with James Boswell and David Hume, both of whom knew Burke well. Burke seems to have discussed Rousseau's visit with them. But if they discussed Burke with Rousseau, the discussion seems to have left no trace. In any case Rousseau soon quarreled with both of them — as he did with almost all of his acquaintances throughout his life — and he cut short his unhappy visit to Britain.

Burke, on the other hand, took quite a keen interest in Rousseau. Burke wrote "sharply critical" reviews of Rousseau's *Letter to d'Alembert* in the *Annual Register* for 1759 and of *Emile* for the same publication in 1762. When Rousseau became a posthumous hero of the French Revolutionaries — from 1789 to the end of the Revolution — Burke's animosity against him increased and hardened in tone. To an unknown acquaintance Burke wrote in January 1790 about the literary heroes of the French Revolutionaries of that time: "Such masters, such scholars. Who ever dreamt of Voltaire and Rousseau as legislators? The first has the merit of writing agreeably; and nobody has ever united blasphemy and obscenity so happily together. The other was not a little deranged in his intellects, to my almost certain knowledge. But he saw things in bold and uncommon lights, and he was very eloquent."

Just one year later, in January 1791, Burke returned to the subject of Rousseau with a vengeance, in *Letter to a Member of the National Assembly* [of revolutionary France]. Rousseau was a topical subject when Burke was writing. On 22 December, less than a month before Burke's *Letter* was written, the National Assembly had decreed that "there shall be erected to the author of *Emile* and *Du Contrat Social* a statue bearing the inscription: LA NATION FRANCAISE LIBRE A J.J. ROUSSEAU," Burke writes:

The Assembly recommends to its youth a study of the bold experimenters in morality. Everybody knows that there is a great dispute amongst their leaders, which of them is the best resemblance to Rousseau. In truth, they all resemble him. His blood they transfuse into their minds and into their manners. Him they study; him they meditate; him they turn over in all the time they can spare from the laborious mischief of the day, or the debauches of the night. Rousseau is their canon of holy writ; in his life he is their canon of *Polycletus;* he is their standard figure of perfection. To this man and this writer, as a pattern to authors and to Frenchmen, the foundries of Paris are now running for statues, with the kettles of their poor and the bells of their churches. If an author had written like a great genius on geometry, though his practical and speculative morals were vicious in the extreme, it might appear that in voting the statue, they honoured only the geometrician. But Rousseau is a moralist, or he is nothing. It is impossible, therefore, putting the circumstances together, to mistake their design in choosing the author, with whom they have begun to recommend a course of studies.

Their great problem is to find a substitute for all the principles which hitherto have been employed to regulate the human will and action. They find dispositions in the mind, of such force and quality, as may fit men, far better than the old morality, for the purposes of such a state as theirs; and may go much further in supporting their power, and destroying their enemies. They have therefore chosen a selfish, flattering, seductive, ostentatious vice, in the place of plain duty. True humility, the basis of the Christian system, is the low, but deep and firm foundation of all real virtue. But this, as very painful in the practice, and little imposing in the appearance, they have totally discarded. Their object is to merge all natural and all social sentiment in inordinate vanity. In a small degree, and conversant in little things, vanity is of little moment. When full grown, it is the worst of vices, and the occasional mimic of them all. It makes the whole man false. It leaves nothing sincere or trust-worthy about him. His best qualities are poisoned and perverted by it, and operate exactly as the worst. When your lords had many writers as immoral as the object of their statue (such as Voltaire and others) they chose Rousseau; because in him that peculiar vice which they wished to erect into a ruling virtue, was by far the most conspicuous.

We have had the great professor and founder of *the philosophy of vanity* in England. As I had good opportunities of knowing his proceedings almost from day to day, he left no doubt in my mind, that he entertained no principle either to influence his heart, or to guide his understanding, but *vanity*. With this vice he was possessed to a degree little short of madness. It is from the same deranged eccentric vanity, that this, the insane *Socrates* of the National Assembly, was impelled to publish a mad Confession of his mad faults, and to attempt a new sort of glory, from bringing hardily to light the obscure and vulgar vices which we know may sometimes be blended with eminent talents. He has not observed on the nature of vanity, who does not know that it is omnivorous; that it has no choice in its food; that it is fond to talk even of its own faults and vices, as what will excite surprise and draw attention, and what will pass at worst for openness and candor. It was this abuse and perversion, which vanity makes even of hypocrisy, which has driven Rousseau to record a life not so much as chequered, or spotted here and there, with virtues, or even distinguished by a single good action. It is such a life he chooses to offer to the attention of mankind. It is such a life, that with a wild defiance, he flings in the face of his Creator, whom he acknowledges only to brave. Your Assembly, knowing how much more powerful example is found than precept, has chosen this man (by his own account without a single virtue) for a model. To him they erect their first statue. From him they commence their series of honours and distinctions.

It is that new-invented virtue which your masters canonize, that led their moral hero constantly to exhaust the stores of his powerful rhetoric in the expression of universal benevolence; whilst his heart was incapable of harbouring one spark of common parental affection. Benevolence to the whole species, and want of feeling for every individual with whom the professors come in contact, form the character of the new philosophy. Setting up for an unsocial independence, this their hero of vanity refuses the just price of common labour, as well as the tribute which opulence owes to genius, and which, when paid, honours the giver and the receiver; and then he pleads his beggary as an excuse for his crimes. He melts with tenderness for those only who touch him by the remotest relation, and then, without one natural pang, casts away, as a sort of offal and excrement, the spawn of his disgustful amours, and sends his children to the hospital of foundlings. The *bear loves, licks, and forms her young; but bears are not philosophers* (my italics).

According to his own account in his *Confessions,* Rousseau had sent off all his five children by Thérèse Levasseur to the foundling asylum as soon as possible. If we accept Rousseau's own account, Burke's last comment above appears well merited.

Of Robespierre's own connections with the other three eighteenth-century figures under consideration here, only the connection with Rousseau and especially with *The Social Contract* is well attested. Robespierre's rise and his ascendancy of 1793–94 were based on being accepted as the authentic interpreter of the otherwise enigmatic *Social Contract*. Robespierre was no ordinary political leader but the high priest of a dominant cult. High priest and also supreme judge. He alone would determine who was obedient to the General Will and who was refractory to it. Those judged refractory went to the guillotine as soon as Robespierre made known his verdict. All this authority was based on Robespierre's acceptance as Rousseau's living voice.

For our other two subjects — so far as I can find — Robespierre never made known a personal verdict. Nevertheless we know what he thought about Burke. The mere possession of Burke's *Reflections on the Revolution in France* became a capital offense under the Terror, and that could not have been done without the sanction of the all-powerful Robespierre.

Concerning the remaining member of our quartet, Robespierre's opinions, so far as I know, have left no trace. He must have known, I think, of Jefferson's oft expressed admiration of the French Revolution which did not cease with Robespierre's advent to power or during Robespierre's dictatorship. But, assuming that Robespierre did know of Jefferson's admiration for the French Revolution, Robespierre could not have been greatly impressed by that. Robespierre felt that the French Revolution belonged to the French alone. He was correspondingly suspicious of foreign sympathizers with the French Revolution, most of whom, he thought, were probably spies. Many of the victims of the Terror, under Robespierre, were foreign residents, strong sympathizers with the French Revolution. One of these was Anacharsis Cloots. Cloots, of Prussian origin, became a naturalized Frenchman and almost ecstatic in his enthusiasm for the French Revolution. He even wrote a long letter to Edmund Burke in which he invited Burke to come to France and enlist in the cause of the Revolution. *"Leave your island, my dear Burke, come to France!"* Burke, of course, did not reply, but Cloots was duly guillotined, under Robespierre, by the Revolution he had so enthusiastically embraced.

A similar case was that of Tom Paine who also became a naturalized Frenchman and also wrote to Burke extolling the French Revolution. Paine was imprisoned under the Terror and was probably only saved from execution as a result of Robespierre's own fall and execution in Thermidor 1794.

Jefferson did eventually condemn what he called "the atrocities of Robespierre." But that was in 1795 and Robespierre was not only dead but anathema to the new masters of the French Revolution. Throughout the period of the ascendancy of Robespierre, Jefferson continued to approve the Revolution in general terms and did not acknowledge that Robespierre had committed any atrocities. In January 1793 — the month of the execution of Louis XVI — Jefferson wrote a letter to his protégé William Short, in which he acknowledged virtually no limit to the slaughter that might legitimately be perpetrated by the French Revolutionaries: "The liberty of the whole earth was dependent on the issue of the contest, and was ever such a prize won with so little innocent blood? My own affections have been deeply wounded by some of the martyrs to this cause, but rather than it should have failed, I would have seen half the earth desolated. Were there but an Adam and Eve left in every country, and left free, it would be better than it is now."

That was the paroxysm of Jefferson's enthusiasm for the French Revolution. But he continued to support the Revolution throughout the Terror and did not condemn it until well after Robespierre's fall and death. Two centuries later Pope Pius XII went through a similar evolution after the fall and death of Adolf Hitler.

In conclusion I should like to consider the reason for Rousseau's astonishing popularity in France, both in his own time and in the nineteenth and twentieth centuries.

The origin of that popularity may be precisely dated. It began in 1749 when the academy of Dijon offered a prize for an essay on the effect of the progress of civilization on morals. Rousseau decided to compete for the prize. His idea of how to treat the subject seems originally to have been an orthodox one: progress beneficial to morals. But Diderot — then still his friend — showed Rousseau a better idea. Why not enlist the power of paradox and describe the superiority of the savage state? Rousseau took the hint, deployed his paradox and won the prize.

Henceforward, paradox was among the principal weapons of his formidable controversial armory. Another great resource was his grasp of the power latent in confident, fulminating assertion, unsupported either by argument or common sense. The most notable example of all this was the famous sentence:

"Man was born free and everywhere is found enslaved and in chains."

It is obvious, that man was never "born free." A baby is dependent for years after its birth and, if not taken care of, will die in infancy. Everybody of course knew that then, just as well as everybody knows it now. Yet the French of the late eighteenth century obviously were delighted with the idea of "born free and everywhere enslaved." Why should this be?

General de Gaulle, who had a profound understanding of the psychic processes underlying modern French history, dated the maturing of the processes which were to lead to the French Revolution from 15 January 1757, the date on which the French were beaten by the Prussians in the battle of Rossbach. There is no doubt that this was a traumatic event for the French people. France had been the predominant power in continental Europe for more than a hundred years. The Monarchy needed the prestige of military success. Defeat by a power classified as minor — Prussia — undermined the monarchy. Then there was the fact that France's ally in the Seven Years War was Catholic Austria. The Catholic Church, seen as blessing the Austrian alliance, became increasingly discredited by the discredit of the alliance itself. Both Church and Monarchy were largely discredited after Rossbach, and the discredit of each of the partners also told upon the other.

But even before the revolutionary process set in in earnest (after 1757) both Church and Monarchy were losing authority during the long, frivolous and inglorious reign of Louis XIII. The Catholic Church, the social and moral pillar of the Monarchy, was already tottering under the assaults of the *philosophes* well before 1750. The Church was undermined in its moral authority. But also, by the second half of the century, the authority of those who had undermined the Church's authority was itself being undermined. Few believed what the Church taught any more, but even those who did not believe were growing dissatisfied with the confident cerebrality and the cold mockeries of the victorious *philosophes*.

In short there was what would later be called "a gap in the market." Rousseau had an unerring eye and ear for such a gap and confidently moved in to fill it. He did so in 1761 with *La Nouvelle Héloïse*. What he offered was a vague religious emotionalism and rhetoric, disconnected from all intellectual dogma, and also from inconvenient restrictions on practice. You could feel good without actually having to endure restrictions on practice. This worked like a charm: French people loved Rousseau then as they have never loved any of the other *philosophes*. And — with the comparatively brief apparent exception of the Napoleonic years — the French have loved him ever since. His admirers generally cite Rousseau's *style* as the reason for their admiration. But Rousseau's style is no more than the very efficient medium for the conveyance of a perennially seductive message: how to know you are good without having to give anything away.

Rousseau's place in France now appears perennially secure. He simply comes with the language. But Rousseau also holds an influential place within the English-speaking world through the vogue for the "politically correct" and "multiculturalism" now dominant in certain faculties of several major American universities. These work in Rousseau's manner: through strong, repeated, unargued assertion: "Hey ho, hey ho, Western culture's got to go" chanted the students. No matter that the students in question have no other culture than the culture of the English language, the only language that they know, or have any intention of knowing. They are in fact monocultural multiculturalists; intellectual monsters, incapable of doing anything except exercising a kind of power through agreed nonsense, and feeling good while doing so.

All that is very much in the spirit of Rousseau. I believe that Rousseau has been, and still remains a noxious force within Western culture. He is noxious because of a fundamental lack of seriousness. He does not think or argue. He talks for effect and teaches others to do the same. Unfortunately there are some in every generation who are seduced either by his message or — more probably — by the example of his successes. The malignant magic of the grand charlatan is liable to be with us for a long time.

Rethinking the Western Tradition